A WALL
IS JUST
A WALL

REIKO
HILLYER

A WALL IS JUST A WALL

The Permeability of the Prison in the Twentieth-Century United States

DUKE UNIVERSITY PRESS DURHAM AND LONDON 2024

Printed in the United States of America on acid-free paper ∞
Project Editor: Lisa Lawley
Designed by Matthew Tauch
Typeset in Garamond by Westchester Publishing Services

Library of Congress Cataloging-in-Publication Data
Names: Hillyer, Reiko, [date] author.
Title: A wall is just a wall : the permeability of the prison in the
twentieth-century United States / Reiko Hillyer.
Description: Durham : Duke University Press, 2024. | Includes
bibliographical references and index.
Identifiers: LCCN 2023036597 (print)
LCCN 2023036598 (ebook)
ISBN 9781478030133 (paperback)
ISBN 9781478025870 (hardcover)
ISBN 9781478025887 (ebook)
Subjects: LCSH: Louisiana State Penitentiary. | Prison administration—
United States. | Prisoners—United States—Social conditions. | Prisoners—
Civil rights—United States. | Prisoners—Family relationships—United
States. | Conjugal visits—United States. | Clemency—United States. |
BISAC: SOCIAL SCIENCE / Penology | SOCIAL SCIENCE / Sociology /
General
Classification: LCC HV9469 .H55 2024 (print) | LCC HV9469 (ebook) |
DDC 365/.973—dc23/eng/20231114
LC record available at https://lccn.loc.gov/2023036597
LC ebook record available at https://lccn.loc.gov/2023036598

Cover art: Jesse Krimes, *Apokaluptein:16389067:II*, Eastern State
Penitentiary, 2015. Digital image transfer, acrylic paint, prison
sheets, wood, drywall, spackle. Courtesy of the artist.

To Benjamin James Hall, 1974–2020

CONTENTS

ACKNOWLEDGMENTS

As I write this, I am preparing to teach a history course at the Columbia River Correctional Institution in Portland, Oregon, as part of the Inside-Out Prison Exchange Program. The course will bring free undergraduate students and incarcerated students together to study in the same class. Though I have taught this course for a decade, this is the first time I am teaching the class since COVID-19 restrictions shut it down in March 2020. The interruption of the class was not only devastating but revealed—as the pandemic did with so many of our institutions and habits—the selectiveness of COVID-19's reach and the selectiveness of our compassion. The incarcerated students were particularly vulnerable to the virus, and the vernacular created around the pandemic manifested assumptions about human disposability that were constructed in real time. Terms like *lockdown*, *social distance*, *risk*, and *public safety* echoed the lexicon of incarceration and exile and redrew boundaries regarding whose safety mattered and who was deemed fit for premature death. In an ideological sleight of hand, the most vulnerable among us were cast as the most dangerous. My first expression of appreciation goes to those students at Columbia River in 2020 who struggled to stay engaged in our course while struggling to stay alive. They remind me of the stakes of this project.

My experience teaching the Inside-Out course, which insists on breaking down the barriers that divide the incarcerated and the free, provided the genesis for this book. In 2023 the class will conclude with a theater piece devised by the students and, thanks to a seed grant from the Whiting Foundation that was followed by a Creative Heights grant from the Oregon Community Foundation, we will be adapting this piece for the professional stage. The guiding question for this project has been, How can we make the prison more porous? As such, I offer this round of thanks to all who have helped make the Columbia River Correctional Institution more porous and introduced me to the transformative possibilities of cracking open the doors. These include all of my Inside-Out students since 2012; you have opened my heart and changed the course of my life. I am particularly grateful to the corrections administrators who have supported our work: Brandie Fazal, James Hanley, Elizabeth LaCarney, and the administration and staff at Lewis & Clark College who labor to make Inside-Out possible: Jerusha Detweiler-Bedell, Scott Feikert, Judy Finch, Alexis Rehrmann, and Bruce Suttmeier, as well as my colleagues in the History Department. One of the greatest gifts that has recently emerged from teaching Inside-Out at Lewis & Clark has been the talent and collaboration of Rebecca Lingafelter, who has taught my students that we carry history in our bodies and can use our bodies to tell stories. Her generosity, creativity, and trust are treasures I cherish. I was first introduced to the expansive promises of making art in a history class by Emily Squires, who made me believe that everyone is an artist. Both Emily and Rebecca have stretched my creative scope beyond the methodologies normally available to the historian. While writing about history is a creative act, understanding the past and how it shapes the present requires more tools than my primary discipline can provide. I am grateful to Emily and Rebecca for helping me integrate my artistic and scholarly selves. Finally, I throw a rose and bow to Lori Pompa for the vision and commitment it required to found Inside-Out twenty-five years ago.

I have conversed and corresponded with a number of people—friends, comrades, colleagues, and activists, some of whom are currently or were formerly incarcerated—whose insights, life experiences, and scholarship have informed and deepened this book. These include Hilda Aronson, Rachel Barkow, Sophie Cull, Sterling Cunio, Clifford Hampton, Michelle Jones, Aliza Kaplan, Markus Kondkar, Anoop Mirpuri, Bidish Sarma, Emerson Simmons, and Kempis "Ghani" Songster. Criminal justice scholar, *Angolite* journalist, and activist Burk Foster was incredibly generous in sharing his archives, time, humor, and passion with me. Andrew Hundley and Kerry Myers of the Louisiana Parole Project led me to documents, research assistants, and hope. Marianne Fischer-Giorlando, affectionately known as "Dr. G." by those incarcerated at the Louisiana State Penitentiary at Angola, welcomed me into her home, treated me to ice cream, invited my questions, and shared obscure material about the penitentiary; her expertise in its history is unmatched. I am grateful to know Calvin Duncan and honored to call him my friend. His struggle to prove his innocence while incarcerated at Angola, his brilliant and tireless work as a jailhouse lawyer, and his journey to Lewis & Clark Law School have served as an inspiration, but, more specifically, his intimate knowledge of Louisiana law was instrumental to me as I endeavored to track the demise of clemency in a state where it had been so routine.

I could not have told this story without having had the opportunity to interview key people. I am so grateful to Arnie King for his time, and I honor his struggle and his triumph. I thank Ed Mead for sharing his perspective and experience and thank Daniel Berger for putting us in contact. I appreciated the wisdom that Norris Henderson shared in our conversation; since being released from prison, he continues social justice work that he had begun on the inside, embodying the principle that those who are closest to the problem are closest to the solution. My greatest thanks go to Wilbert Rideau, whose candor, intellect, and resilience enriched every conversation. He read drafts of my chapters, kept me honest, and breathed life and urgency into my work. The records that he and his fellow prison journalists have left through their research and writing at the *Angolite* constitute an astounding archive of the true history of our prison system.

Because much of this manuscript was completed during the peak of COVID-19, I relied tremendously on research assistants, without whom the book would not have been possible. For their doggedness, I thank Jan Hillegas, Raegan Johnson, K. Howell Keiser, Kirsten Lee, Ashley Steenson, and Cara Tippett. Charlotte Rosen is simply a badass; her own scholarship is brilliant and important, and the research she conducted for me on furloughs launched my argument. I extend especially warm thanks to research assistant Kelsey Jenkins; I was so honored to be invited to her wedding in Louisiana, and the conversations I had there with people with experience on both sides of Angola's gates echoed in my ears as I wrote this book. Thank you to the Lewis & Clark students who expertly conducted research essential to this project: Claire Duncan, Lucy Hamil, Grey Sutor, and Maya Winshell. It was truly sweet to collaborate with you. I am grateful to librarian E. J. Carter at the Aubrey R. Watzek Library at Lewis & Clark for all of the times he found obscure reports and corrections journals for me. I also relied on the extra footwork of archivists around the country, such as those at the California State Archives, the Louisiana State University Library in Baton Rouge, the State Library of Massachusetts, and, in particular, Shaun Stalzer at the Mississippi State Archives. For material support, I am deeply indebted to the American Philosophical Society, the National Endowment for the Humanities, and the Vital Projects Fund working through the Proteus Fund.

My support system within academia and beyond has bolstered my self-discipline and self-care in equal measure. I thank my dear colleagues in the History Department at Lewis & Clark College: Andy Bernstein, David Campion, Nancy Gallman, Susan Glosser, Ben Westervelt, and especially Mo Healy for much-needed girl-time on the Hosford Middle School benches. I could not have sustained my momentum had it not been for Dawn Odell; I am so grateful for her companionship and conviviality on our precious writing retreats and for giving me permission to embrace all of it. Amy Baskin is the glue that holds me together. She has the strength of duct tape and the grace of *kintsugi*. I appreciate the others beyond my campus who read and critiqued my work, including Seth Cotlar, Radhika Natarjan, and Padraig Riley. I am forever sustained and grounded by my friendships with Monica Gisolfi and Jeffrey Trask, and to them I say *Itada-kimasu*. I also hold gratitude for Marla Pallin, Tamara Metz, and Heather Watkins, members of my chosen family, for their consistent companion-ship and support. Thank you to the devoted and loving caregivers, Linda Angst, Crystal Malgren, and Gardner Dunavant, for comprising the vil-lage that it takes to raise our youngest child.

Of the many people who have laid eyes on this manuscript and lent their wisdom to its improvement, there are those who deserve special mention. From my first conversation with Elizabeth Ault at Duke Uni-versity Press, I was taken with her belief in my book and the rigor of her questions. With the indispensable and patient help of Benjamin Kos-sack, Elizabeth's continued support has fostered my progress. I cannot say enough about Nancy Grey Osterud, so I will say too little: I could not have done this without her. Though it will make her blush, I look to Micol Sigel as a role model, and her imprint is all over this book. In the course of the many conversations during hikes up El Tepozteco over the past decade, Micol introduced me to the Inside-Out Prison Exchange Program and, later, talked me through many aspects of my project. She has nour-ished my work as a colleague, comrade, and friend in more ways than she knows. Micol also introduced me to Garret Felber, whose ethics, mind, and heart are a gift to me and to many others. That his feedback sharpened my argument—*dayenu*, as we say; "that would have been enough." But Garrett's work, from the Liberation Literacy initiative to the Study and Struggle project to the historic Making and Unmaking Mass Incarceration

Conference, breaks down walls wherever he goes. Eden Wurmfeld, my lifelong friend, is once again helping to raise me. Her interest in Inside-Out as a cinematic subject has provided a new path for the next chapters of my professional and personal development; that she is willing to give so much of her time and talent and that we are finally able to collaborate after over forty years of friendship fills my heart. David Menschel has nurtured this project in innumerable ways, and his faith in its value lent urgency to my efforts. In the course of reading chapter after chapter, David's comments helped me refine my central questions and, more important, helped me develop confidence in my voice. One of his many brilliant political insights is the centrality of narrative to politics. I hope that this book can contribute to changing the narrative. I was sustained by my sister Linda Hillyer throughout this process. During our precious visits, we travel to conversational lands of capitalism, disability, art, Buddhism, and childhood as we explore our pasts and our presents together. Unexpectedly, Linda's own life experience yielded treasures such as interview subjects and obscure prison newspapers.

Though my stepdaughter Zulema is living the Bushwick life and my mother is halfway around the world, I feel their presence and their support for my work. I am so proud of Zulema's accomplishments and the ease and grace with which she has made the transition to adulthood. My dear brother Jonathan's curiosity reminds me of the audience that I am writing for, and I thank him for his interest and his love. My father, Raphael Hillyer, likely entered a prison only once: as the violist of a string quartet engaged to play a chamber music concert for incarcerated people. While he told this story with some titillation, the episode was consistent with his belief in the power of music to transcend social boundaries. As I write this, I have just celebrated his yahrzeit, which I spent listening to his recording of the Bach cello suites. His playing sang the ineffable union of pain and beauty, and I thank him for reminding me that they are conjoined.

My daughter Ryo, six and a half at the time of this writing, regularly schools me in the construction of ideology with her searing questions. She makes me a better person and she makes my heart grow three sizes. Ryo, the miracle is you. Thank you, Elliott, whose work in transnational and borderlands history has influenced me beyond measure. Elliott has introduced me to the constructedness of boundaries, the possibilities of a radical imagination, the varieties of political activism, and the importance of balancing work, play, justice, and love. As the unicorn who can legitimately multitask, he probably scratches his head about my need for deep focus. I am all the more grateful for his gift of space when I needed it, and for his gift of adventure when I didn't know I needed it.

Finally, I dedicate this book to Ben Hall. You may have felt like you were not worthy enough for this world, but it turns out the world wasn't worthy of you. Rest in peace, my friend.

Introduction

And, if I know any thing at all
it's that a wall is just a wall
and nothing more at all.
It can be broken down.
—**ASSATA SHAKUR**, *Assata: An Autobiography*, 1987

We begin, as always, seated in a circle. Blue denim, chinos, blue denim, sweatpants, blue denim, white canvas, blue denim, flowered skirt. We alternate, the incarcerated and the free. The room is chirping and crowing with what people in the free world call small talk. For the incarcerated students, these exchanges are the jewels of all too rare, yet simple, human communication. After the classmates have had a chance to greet each other, I say, "Let's close our eyes." The room settles, and all that can be heard is the hum of the fluorescent lights. Suddenly, the classroom door opens. "Med line!" a correctional officer shouts, and we remember where we are. When the officer leaves and the room stills once again, I say, "Please go around the circle and just say one word to describe how we are feeling at this moment. Joel, will you start?" "Tired." "Excited." "Happy." "Anxious." "Overwhelmed." "Grateful." The voices swirl around the room like burning sage. Classroom 4 in the Columbia River Correctional Institution has been anointed.[1]

As I begin to pass blank sheets of white paper and Sharpie markers around the circle, I explain the first activity. "We are going to get into pairs. One inside [incarcerated] student, one outside [free] student. You'll move your chairs to face each other, and each of you will have two minutes to complete a blind contour drawing of your partner. What's a blind contour drawing? You draw for two minutes but you cannot lift your pen or look down at your page." The students giggle and guffaw, making self-deprecating comments about their drawing skills, but they are game. I set the timer and they begin, eyes locked on each others' faces. Earnest focus is occasionally punctured by chuckles. When the two minutes are up and the students look down at their handiwork, the room roars with laughter.[2]

I ask the students how it felt to engage in the exercise. "It was really intense and intimate to be looking so closely at someone's face for that long," says one student. Another comments, "I really wanted to do justice to my partner's face, and I felt bad that my drawing looked so ridiculous!"

I remind the students that today's class is going to be devoted to discussing Bryan Stevenson's *Just Mercy: A Story of Justice and Redemption*. Stevenson is the founder of the Equal Justice Initiative, a legal practice committed to defending the most desperate: children, the poor, the wrongly convicted, those condemned to death. The book recounts his own experiences as an attorney, explores the lives of his clients, and probes the inequity of the criminal justice system.[3] I ask the students why I might have tasked them with making blind contour drawings of each other to open this particular class. Trey, an inside student, perceives an analogue: "Stevenson's grandma tells him that he can't understand most of the important things from a distance. She said, 'You have to get close.' I think that exercise made us get close." For Gabriel, an outside student, the activity resonates in a different way:

> You told us we couldn't look down to see if we were portraying our partner accurately. We only had two minutes and couldn't correct the image or go back and edit. This is like what happened with Charlie in the book and the way we treat juveniles in the criminal justice system. The prosecutor or judge makes a decision, and doesn't care if it accurately conveys the real person in front of them. And if they make a mistake, they aren't willing to go back and correct it. If the perpetrator changes or grows, the judge doesn't go back and update the picture. I feel like the convicted people in *Just Mercy* are treated like a bunch of blind contour drawings.

During the remainder of the class, we discuss *Just Mercy*, and we conclude with a writing exercise. I remind the students, "Bryan Stevenson likes to say that each of us is more than the worst thing we have ever done. He emphasizes this point by asking us to question our treatment of juveniles in particular, who, if they face long sentences, are treated as if they are frozen at fourteen and have no potential to change." I ask them to respond to the prompt: "How have you changed since you were fourteen years old? What would people fail to see about you if they froze you at fourteen?"

Since 2012, I have taught a college history class at Columbia River Correctional Institution (CRCI) in Portland, Oregon, as part of the Inside-Out Prison Exchange Program. This program, founded at Temple University by Lori Pompa, trains instructors in a particular pedagogy: all classes are integrated with an equal number of undergraduates and incarcerated students who learn together as peers and equals. Undergraduate students in the course Crime and Punishment in US History are from Lewis & Clark College, where I am an associate professor, and the incarcerated students are confined at CRCI, a minimum-security men's facility that houses both people serving shorter sentences and those at the end of very long sentences.[4] In the words of Inside-Out instructors Simone Weil Davis and Barbara Sherr Roswell, the program offers "an alternative model of community-engaged learning unfettered by paternalistic notions of 'charity' or 'service'" that, influenced by the work of Paolo Freire and Myles Horton, is rooted in "reciprocity, dialogue, and collaboration."[5]

There is no other class I teach in which all students are so fully *present*. The stakes and the rewards of the encounter between undergraduates at a liberal arts college and incarcerated people are high precisely because such an encounter is so rare.[6] Since the prison has been constructed, both rhetorically and physically, as impermeable, it is nearly impossible for those without loved ones in prison to imagine interacting with those who live inside. Even telling people about the program sometimes elicits responses such as, "Is it safe?" or "Why are you teaching college to a bunch of murderers?" The program insists on challenging those preconceptions by penetrating the walls; normalizing human interaction across the walls; and, through exchange, collaboration, and mutual learning, dismantling the barriers that prevent us from seeing each other as neighbors.

Year after year, when participants are asked to reflect on the class, incarcerated students comment that our classroom is an emancipatory space. In the class they are allowed to use their minds, express their thoughts, expand their knowledge and skills, and earn college credit. Even more significantly, their experiences as incarcerated people are cherished as valuable wisdom alongside and against the scholarship we read.[7] While the undergraduate students might be more accustomed to abstract analysis, the incarcerated students carry the truths of own lives. Engaged in mutual knowledge production and braiding personal experience with historical scholarship, we create an imaginative, generative, and communal and community-building space.[8] Because the outside students represent the broader public from which the incarcerated students have been cast out, their attention, their listening, and their acceptance temporarily ameliorate a sense of exile. "Look into my eyes so you can see that I am flesh and bones," explains Tony Vick, an Inside-Out participant serving two life sentences at Riverbend Maximum Security Prison in Tennessee. "After you see me and I see you, we can no longer pretend that the other does not exist . . . eyes to eyes."[9] One CRCI student recalled, "There was nowhere else I'd rather be . . . as I learned and listened to my classmates I felt so alive. . . . This class shown me I'm important, that I matter!" For a student named Henry, at the tail end of a twenty-two-year sentence, the integration of incarcerated and free students was a chance to imagine otherwise, to create an alternative social world, a collective insurgency of affection, eyes to eyes:

> It is a strange thing to come into a prison to learn together and build a community where it is so discouraged to do so. In many ways we create our own world as we steal time in a space where many might imagine such a magical experience could never transpire. While we are longing to exit this space, you all desire to beat the door down to get back inside. Our intentionality creates a world that did not exist before which demonstrates that it is possible to do so, to build the world as it *could* be together. . . . It is this deliberate and creative practice in the world that will chip away at the foundations of the prison. . . . We must build something that is similar to what we've done with each other in this class.[10]

As a historian, I came to wonder if the walls had always been so impenetrable. When researching a 1968 prison strike at the Virginia State Penitentiary, I noticed that incarcerated musicians were able to leave the penitentiary to give concerts and several prisoners were granted furloughs to participate in high school chess tournaments well into the 1970s.[11] Going back even further, Norfolk Prison in Massachusetts was founded in 1927 as a "model prison community" whose stated mission was to keep incarcerated people engaged with, rather than removed from, the outside world.[12] While Malcolm X was incarcerated at Norfolk from 1948 to 1952, he participated in the Norfolk Prison Debating Society and debated university teams. The Wallkill Correctional Facility in New York State was constructed in 1932 in a college campus style with no walls or fence; when eight prisoners escaped one year later, the *New York Times* declared, "Wallkill Prison without Walls a Success; Only Eight Break Trust in an Air of Freedom."[13] Tyrone Werts, a cofounder of Inside-Out who was incarcerated in Pennsylvania for thirty-six years, has said, "The walls aren't just here to keep us in. They are there to keep you out."[14] Was this always so? Was it possible that our contemporary practice of exile is a departure from a longer tradition of permeable prisons? What reasons did people have for tolerating or encouraging interactions between those who were incarcerated and those outside? What does this practice and its demise tell us about the function of the prison in society? If prisons had remained porous, would we still have locked up 2.5 million people behind their walls?

* * *

Prison walls have not always been impermeable, and permeability has been both a vehicle for social control and a way for prisoners to resist it. During one month in 1968, dozens of men incarcerated at Louisiana State Penitentiary, the notorious prison known as Angola (after the former plantation grounds it occupies), were allowed to leave temporarily for various purposes. Under supervision and rigorously screened, members of Angola's Bridge Club traveled to play in bridge tournaments; imprisoned participants in Alcoholics Anonymous and Narcotics Anonymous spoke at schools, churches, and business associations throughout the state; a country and western band composed of six incarcerated men, the Westernaires, played as many as three concerts a week at nursing homes, hospitals, and high schools.[15] That same year, a beloved television cowboy known as Buckskin Bill who earned fame for his children's show *Storyland* invited the Westernaires to star in their own weekly television show, *Good Morning, Angola Style*. Angola's Jaycees—a chapter of the national leadership training and civic organization—traveled nearly two hundred miles to Monroe, Louisiana, to attend a two-day state Jaycee convention, where their branch won a standing ovation at the opening banquet. Some of these men, like many of those at Angola, had been convicted of murder, kidnapping, or armed robbery.[16]

The journeys of these "traveling ambassadors" were documented and celebrated in a feature story in the *Angolite*, the prison magazine produced by men incarcerated at the Louisiana State Penitentiary. Significantly, this article was reprinted in a local free-world newspaper, the *Rayne Acadian-Tribune*, demonstrating the public's attention to the sojourners.[17] The anonymous author used his "Viewpoint" column in the *Angolite* to assert that these trips were crucial to informing the public that a "convict" was not a "brute dressed in a striped suit and restrained by a ball and chain." Mobility served a larger purpose than temporary escape or even personal expression. Logging thousands of miles, Angola's ambassadors would "carry the truth to the public," the reporter declared. Though corrections officials often explained that the privilege of leaving the prison under these sanctioned conditions served the purpose of rehabilitation, incarcerated travelers perceived their exposure to the public as opportunities to rehabilitate the crude stereotypes held by those who called themselves law-abiding citizens. They hoped to prove "a simple lesson—the convict, despite his faults and failings, is not an ogre. He is little different from the rest of the people who populate these United States. And the sooner all folks come to realize that the majority of convicts present no threat to them or their way of life, the sooner will the walls come tumbling down."[18]

Angolites, despite being confined at a facility long known as "America's worst prison," appreciated the opportunity to fashion constructive social identities in public.[19] As a prison journalist noted, the warden, C. Murray Henderson (who with his wife accompanied the Jaycees on their trip to Monroe), "does not subscribe to the theory of isolation for offenders. His position is that a man in whom confidence and trust are placed is a man willing to accept responsibility, and that's what prison is about."[20] Henderson pointed out that prisoners do not have a political lobby, and that the resulting public ignorance obstructed an understanding of prisoners' potential to return to society. Thus, he worked to "bring realities of prison and prisoners to the public . . . gambling on their conscience and basic sense of decency."[21] The risk was not that prisoners might escape or commit crimes but that they might be rejected by the public. Incarcerated people engaged in countless daily maneuvers to attain the privilege of gaining access to the traveling circuit and, once outside, used the opportunity to impress members of the public so that they could gain future allies in their petitions to gain early release.[22]

Beyond Angola, Americans of African descent were still fighting to be free. In 1968 Louisiana schools were not yet fully desegregated, Black protestors were boycotting businesses that refused to serve Black customers, white Louisianans took advantage of racist real estate practices and were fleeing to the suburbs to avoid the democratization of urban public spaces, the Deacons of Defense had begun arming themselves to protect civil rights activists from routine acts of vigilante violence and police terror, and federal courts had recently ordered state officials to eliminate barriers to Black voter registration.[23] The inmate clubs at Angola were all segregated, and Walter Watson of the Human Relations Club was the only Black prisoner allowed on the June 1968 tour. The traveling ambassadors were making their circuits just two months after the assassination of Martin Luther King Jr., whose murder was interpreted by white conservatives as a comeuppance that sealed the equivalence of civil disobedience with violent crime: "[King's] brand of 'non-violence'—provocative and contemptuous of law—begets violence just as violence undisguised does," wrote a journalist for the *Shreveport Journal*.[24] Into the schools, churches, and rotary clubs of this turbulent state, Angola's incarcerated ambassadors arrived as unlikely messengers.

According to an incarcerated journalist, the time was right for Warden Henderson's vision: alongside calls for "law and order," national alarm about youth rebellion, drug use, and crime momentarily—and perhaps counterintuitively—created a "public demand" to hear from incarcerated people. "Fearing the worst," this prisoner inferred, "the idea of getting convicts to talk to society's youth about the error of their ways and the pain and horrors awaiting them if they did not change their direction was appealing to parents, teachers, ministers and local law enforcement authorities, who hoped that perhaps the kids would be more willing to listen to a convict than to time-worn lectures from figures of authority."[25] Incarcerated people, whatever their transgressions, possessed insight and even the authority to give advice. Such advice might reinforce traditional hierarchies and emphasize personal responsibility, but it came from the mouths of people whose incarceration qualified them as dispensers of wisdom born of personal experience. Teenagers might listen to their stories of transformation more than they would their own parents. The fundamental assumption that undergirded these encounters was that people can change.

Traveling outside the walls of the Louisiana State Penitentiary was part of a broader logic that assumed and accepted that almost everyone imprisoned at Angola would eventually get out. Until the late 1970s, even those with life sentences were routinely released after ten years and six months via a commutation from the governor as long as they kept a good prison record.[26] Thus, prisoners' withdrawal from free society was understood to be temporary, and their visits outside nourished the connective tissue that would help secure their eventual reintegration into the body politic. By interacting with the public, incarcerated people could develop a sense of dignity beyond the reductive labels imposed by the criminal justice system. And, by contributing to society through music, lectures, or charity work, they could counter the public's preconceived ideas about convicts. The traveling ambassadors refused stigma and social disfranchisement by claiming a positive identity beyond the site of the prison and by developing a track record of accomplishments that would earn them early release.[27]

Norris Henderson, who began serving his life sentence at Angola for second-degree murder in 1977, recalls being allowed to leave the prison so frequently as a member of the Jaycees, the Lifers' Club, and the prison football team that he took traveling as "a given."[28] But by the late 1980s these travels had nearly disappeared. Law-and-order district attorney Harry Connick Sr. ominously warned the Louisiana public in 1979, "The truth is few convicted criminals are sent to the penitentiary" and "of those criminals who are sent to Angola, virtually none ever serves his full sentence."[29] Disgusted by a suite of practices designed "to reduce the terms of prisoners sent to jail," Connick railed against furloughs, work release, pardon, and commutation—some of which had been Louisiana tradition for the better part of the century and were fervently supported by corrections administrators.[30] New legislation prohibited the granting of furloughs to those convicted of violent crimes, drug crimes, or habitual offenses, eliminating nearly all the men at Angola from eligibility. After a prisoner working in the governor's mansion killed his girlfriend while out on furlough in 1988, Governor Buddy Roemer suspended furloughs indefinitely.[31]

One of the organizations hit hardest by new restrictions on travel was the Angola Jaycees, which had conducted robust external programs on juvenile delinquency, drug addiction, and crime prevention. Fundraising activities that brought incarcerated people outside the prison were also banned, such as the Cop-Con Walk, in which teams of police officers and Angola inmates walked across the state of Louisiana to raise money for the Cystic Fibrosis Foundation. The corrections secretary, as well as current and former wardens, had all supported these programs and lamented their restriction.[32] Outside organizations that had relied upon inmate speakers decried the change. As Ned Hicks, the president of American Prison Ministry, commented, "I feel it's detrimental to the public interest because it denies the public the ability to hear what's happening with their tax dollars straight from the inmate's mouth. . . . The only way the public is going to be made aware of the inmate world is through personal contact."[33]

For the prisoners who had been allowed to leave Angola temporarily, the end of these trips eliminated an essential route to self-definition. There were concrete future benefits to making contacts with people on the outside, and being trusted was a transformative feeling.[34] Furloughs provided a salve for "perhaps most unrecognized pains of imprisonment . . . the overwhelming sense of personal insignificance that goes with being a prisoner." Without these opportunities, an incarcerated person could hope for no relief from the daily reminder, "in a thousand different ways, that he is nothing and incapable of being anything different."[35] This plaint was repeated across the next two generations and echoed by thousands of souls, including those in my Inside-Out class.

New legislation also curtailed what was called the 10/6 rule, the practice by which the governor would release those with life sentences after ten years and six months with the approval of the warden. Louisiana was not an outlier in practicing early release. In 1913 the federal system defined a life sentence as fifteen years. For much of the twentieth century, a life sentence rarely meant a lifetime of confinement anywhere in the nation. As political scientist Marie Gottschalk notes, "The years that prisoners spent in Louisiana's infamous Angola prison were oftentimes brutal and dehumanizing, but they nearly always had an end date."[36] The change to this decades-long practice was so sudden that incarcerated people recognized it as a revolution. Most painfully, prisoners were now frozen in time at the moment of their offense, not just frozen in space. Now, none of their good deeds, personal transformation, compliance, vocational training, or even hospice service would ever provide them with a second chance. Herbert Williams, who by the year 2000 had served thirty-four years of a life sentence, explained the changes he had seen this way: "It was bad back then, but still you went home sooner or later."[37] Even prison administrators recognized what politicians refused to admit: true life sentences were as novel as they were unconscionable. At the funeral of a man named Earl, who passed away in 1980 at Angola after serving thirty-three years, Warden Hilton Butler opined, "He didn't deserve to die like he did. You know, forgotten and alone." While acknowledging that "nobody liked Earl," he concluded, "No man deserves that. . . . He was a trusty with an excellent record. A man just ain't supposed to die like that in prison."[38]

In 1970, just 143 people were serving life without parole sentences in Louisiana. By 2021, the lifer population had grown to 4,400.[39] While the increasing separation of the prison from free society has redrawn the prison boundary, incarcerated people are also restrained by a tightened temporal boundary that fastens them in their past. Nonetheless, prisoners change just as the prison has changed around them. They continue to grow, hope, work, and serve one another, demonstrating that they are not the same people they were when they committed their original crimes. Darren James, who has served thirty years since being incarcerated at age nineteen, has been involved in the Islamic community and Alcoholics Anonymous, but is most proud of the work he has done in the prison hospice, a feature of prison that has developed in response to its aging population. As James notes, "We human beings, we make mistakes, you know, I'm not my worstest mistake. I am not that person."[40] Daryl Waters also presses beyond the confines of his original conviction: "All we regard is a thug on the street twenty-four, twenty five years ago, so we're angry at that person, not realizing that that person doesn't exist for at least twenty years."[41] These men refuse to be turned to stone. They also know that the laws that keep them locked up are not written in stone. In 1968, at the height of Jim Crow, people had a greater chance of leaving a brutal Louisiana prison, either temporarily or by early release, than they would fifty years later. For those incarcerated during those fifty years, the ground had shifted dramatically. We now understand that mass incarceration is relatively new. What is even newer is mass disappearance.[42]

* * *

Historians of US prisons have only begun to analyze the changing relationship of prisons to the outside world. Prisons are not static institutions that have simply multiplied. Their conditions have changed, and these transformations have reflected and shaped shifting notions of prisoners' relationship to free society. *A Wall Is Just a Wall: The Permeability of the Prison in Twentieth-Century United States* explores the thickening and hardening of prison walls in the post–World War II period and demonstrates that US prisons were relatively permeable until the 1990s. Throughout the twentieth century, even the harshest prison systems in the United States were rather porous; incarcerated people were regularly released from prison for Christmas holidays, to visit sick relatives, to play concerts, and to participate in professional boxing matches. Such freedoms, always conditional, were granted as mechanisms of state control. Mississippi, whose penal practices were infamous for their brutality, was the first state to provide conjugal visits to prisoners, and its governors led the nation in the number of commutations and pardons they issued, even at the height of Jim Crow. This book examines the invention and decline of these and other practices that crossed prison boundaries. At a time when prisons are located mainly in rural areas and designed for the purpose of achieving higher degrees of confinement and social isolation, it is important to recognize that their separation from free society was not always as absolute as it is today. In order to understand the nature, assumptions, and consequences of mass incarceration, we must grapple with the increasingly permanent exclusion of prisoners from society as both cause and consequence of punitive policies that are relatively recent.[43]

Each part of *A Wall Is Just a Wall* centers on a particular policy and practice that connected people inside prisons to those outside: gubernatorial clemency and pardons; conjugal and family visits; and temporary furloughs. The rise and fall of these ways of crossing the barriers between the prison and the free world have rarely been studied by historians of mass incarceration. This book demonstrates that the impermeability of the prison is neither natural nor inevitable but rather a recent, uneven, and contested phenomenon. I do not aim to unearth a "golden age" of prisons but to show that their current isolation and invisibility is neither necessary nor inevitable. *A Wall Is Just a Wall* explores the carceral state, going beyond public policies made outside the prison walls and illuminating prisoners' lived experiences as they suffered, critiqued, survived, and resisted penal practices designed to bring about what scholars and activists have called their social death.[44]

The book is organized in three parts of three chapters each. Part I, "The Boundaries of Mercy," focuses on the practices of gubernatorial clemency, particularly in the US South. In this region, the practice has been both paternalistic and capricious, simultaneously upholding the hierarchies of white supremacy and offering a back door to freedom. Historians of the South have observed that most governors were generous in granting clemency well into the twentieth century and have shown that clemency practices during the era of Jim Crow reinforced hierarchies of race and labor relations. By demanding deference and relying upon sovereign discretion, clemency can be interpreted as fortifying state power over vulnerable citizens.[45] While legal scholars have agreed that clemency has atrophied in recent decades nationwide, a history of the practice across the twentieth century is needed to fully appreciate the significance of its decline for incarcerated people.[46]

The demise of clemency has contributed to a dramatic increase in the number of people serving life without the possibility of parole, which must be seen as the historical aberration that it is.[47] Previously, life sentences were regularly tempered with mercy, by either a governor or a parole board; the rejection of mercy was a new instrument of social death. For most of the twentieth century the life sentence was the cornerstone of an indeterminate sentencing paradigm that could contain both paternalistic notions of sovereign discretion and modern penal principles of rehabilitation. Until the 1970s, a "life" sentence, which in practice ranged between ten and twenty years, provided the offender with an opportunity for review and thus a plausible expectation of release for good conduct. The decline of discretion reflects a radically new outlook: that it is reasonable to confine a person until death. As Christopher Seeds puts it, "Just as the life with parole sentence was at the crux of the transformation in US punishment at the end of the nineteenth century, the life without parole, or LWOP, sentence stands among the most prominent penal developments of the late twentieth century."[48] These developments are entwined with the nation's history of slavery and Jim Crow. Under Jim Crow, because white supremacy ordered the whole society, imprisonment was not the only means of enforcing it. In the embers of Jim Crow, the decline of mercy turned the prison into a new vehicle of exclusion by means of perpetual confinement.

The first three chapters of *A Wall Is Just a Wall* examine the regularity and then the demise of gubernatorial clemency in the South with a close investigation of Louisiana and Mississippi. In the South, clemency has a peculiar relationship to the rise of carceral practices because governors who frequently granted clemency were conservative champions of white supremacy and law and order. Simultaneously, as an apparent relic of Old South noblesse and an expression of the rehabilitative ideal commonly associated with prisons outside the South, clemency is a prism that forces us to question neat categories of "liberal" and "conservative" stances toward carceral policy. Further, it troubles our understanding of a punitive backlash as it took shape in the South as governors there continued to exercise their clemency power at rates far beyond what is typical today, even after tough-on-crime policies became common sense. Southern governors' disinclination to grant clemency began in the wake of the civil rights movement. Until then, the architecture of Jim Crow was enough to keep former prisoners in check. When the structures that guaranteed white control over Black lives were dismantled, prison became a site of more rigid containment and permanent exile. The paternalism and force characteristic of Jim Crow allowed for the exercise of mercy; the New Jim Crow rendered prisoners beyond redemption.[49]

In part II, "Strange Bedfellows," I trace the implementation and decline of programs that allowed spouses and other family members to visit prisoners for as long as seventy-two hours in a homelike setting, relatively free from supervision. According to Sylvia E. Harvey, this practice "revolutionized the way families maintained ties through the confines of imprisonment."[50] By the 1990s, seventeen states allowed some form of conjugal visitation, but by 2015, private, extended visits had disappeared in all but three. Conjugal visits were instituted for reasons both humanitarian and cynical; their termination hardened the carceral boundary and deprived incarcerated people of essential emotional sustenance. Drawing upon prison newspapers that articulate the complex meanings of the privilege of conjugal visits, primary sources from the field of penology and corrections, as well as court cases in which incarcerated plaintiffs argue that such visits are a basic right, "Strange Bedfellows" explores the reasons for their rise and fall.

The history of conjugal visits can tell us a great deal about changing notions of rehabilitation, risk, and sexuality in relation to the hardening of the carceral state.[51] As with clemency, debates about conjugal visits reveal unexpected allegiances and strange bedfellows that scramble any pat political categories. Supporters of the practice included prison reformers, correctional officers, and Christian evangelicals, which reminds us that those who shape penal policy are varied, and a measure that might be seen as backward in one context might be heralded as benevolent in another. These visits were allowed in states as different as California and Mississippi for reasons that both affirmed the basic dignity of prisoners and saw them as continued objects of social control. Finally, this web of advocates and its success in instituting conjugal visits from the late 1960s through the 1980s disrupts our conventional chronology of the rise of law-and-order politics. Just as "crime in the streets" became the mantra of mass incarceration, prisons across the nation began experimenting with visitation policies that are difficult to imagine being accepted today.

Despite the outpouring of literature on prisoners' movements and prison conditions, historians have neglected to examine conjugal visits.[52] Visitation is a crucial topic for analysis if we are to grasp the lived experience of incarceration and prisoners' struggles to maintain their family ties. In advocating for conjugal visits, prisoners challenged their social death by insisting upon their emotional, sexual, and social needs and on their connections with the outside world. Using a variety of arguments, they asserted their rights to intimacy and pleasure and their membership in a community beyond prison walls. This struggle, which required organizing prisoners with their families on the outside, was an effort to attain visibility and claim belonging.

Part III, "Weekend Passes," explores furloughs, which allowed prisoners—including those convicted of murder and sentenced to life without parole—to leave the prison for hours or even days at a time. In the Jim Crow South, furloughs first took the form of "Christmas leaves"; hundreds of prisoners were released over the holidays so that they could go home for ten days. Variations on this practice eventually became a cornerstone of what was called "community corrections," the postwar philosophy that those convicted of crime were best treated and supervised outside a prison setting in order to optimize their reintegration into the community. Furloughs were commonplace and relatively uncontroversial in all fifty states from the late 1960s until 1988, when the moral panic fomented by the Willie Horton scandal cast Massachusetts's furlough policy into doubt and sent Governor Michael Dukakis's presidential campaign into a tailspin. As a result of this infamous case, in which Horton, a Black man, committed violent crimes while out on furlough, prison furloughs became a proxy for national debates about crime and punishment. In the heyday of community corrections, the public was regarded as responsible for reintegrating former prisoners into society, but now politicians and the media represented the public as perpetual potential victims who required constant protection from the threat of violence. Although prisoners, their families, and correctional administrators mobilized to protect furloughs, the backlash strangled discretionary release of any kind. In Massachusetts and across the nation, the demise of furloughs signaled the erosion of the rehabilitative promise, the repudiation of correctional experts, the abandonment of discretion, and changing calculations of risk. Part III ends by tracking the demise of clemency in Massachusetts following the Horton scandal and brings the reader back to the themes of mercy and redemption that open the book.

The close examination of clemency, conjugal visits, and furloughs reveals unexpected allegiances that transgress the default categories of liberal and conservative. For example, conjugal visits at the Mississippi State Penitentiary began in the early twentieth century as an incentive to extract more labor from Black people who supposedly were incapable of moral rehabilitation, but by the 1960s they were seen as a progressive and humane way of keeping families intact until prisoners were released and could rejoin their loved ones. California looked to Mississippi as a model when it initiated its own conjugal visit program in 1968. Governor Ronald Reagan, who traced the roots of the putative rise in crime to the moral breakdown of American society, supported conjugal visits as a means of preventing homosexual acts among incarcerated men. As political scientist Naomi Murakawa has shown, those who have influenced correctional policy are not monolithic, nor can the prison boom be explained solely as a victory of the Republican Party's law-and-order platform over the Democratic Party's support of civil rights. What to do with those who have transgressed society's mores is an age-old question, and the variety and contingency of the answers remind us of the conflicting and contradictory motives that can guide criminal justice policy.[53]

Along with shuffling default political categories, *A Wall Is Just a Wall* disaggregates various actors and groups that are too often lumped together or overlooked entirely. As geographer Ruth Wilson Gilmore reminds us, "the state" includes a contradictory and dynamic set of institutions, each of which faces challenges to its legitimacy.[54] While scholars such as historian Daniel Chard and sociologist Joshua Page have begun to unearth a social and political history of prison guards, few have examined corrections professionals as a distinct set of actors.[55] In the case of furloughs, for example, corrections administrators and social scientists, along with governors of both parties, supported the practice, but they found themselves at odds with those in law enforcement. As clemency became politicized and governors were increasingly reluctant to grant it, prison wardens vocally defended discretionary release of prisoners who, on the basis of their firsthand knowledge, presented no threat. The decline of both furloughs and clemency indicates that shrinking faith in official discretion was accompanied by a tendency to dismiss the expertise of corrections professionals, who, because they were engaged with incarcerated people on a daily basis, had concrete reasons for advocating policies that politicians rejected for motives of their own.

By tracking debates about prison practices, *A Wall Is Just a Wall* reframes standard chronological accounts of the development of mass incarceration. The first wave of scholarship identified what it called the punitive turn as a conservative backlash against the gains made by civil rights activists. A more recent body of work has emphasized the complicity of liberals in the expansion of the carceral state and has connected debates over criminal legal policy to broader questions about welfare and poverty.[56] This book reveals threads that do not conform to this historical trajectory and traces new connections among them. Because the fear of prison unrest converged with increased attention to prisoners' rights, prison officials experimented with practices that facilitated movement across prison walls at the same time as law-and-order rhetoric and policy became a new political consensus. Since conjugal visits and furloughs could serve as mechanisms of control, they were popularized at the very moment when racialized fearmongering about crime in the streets inspired intensified policing and harsher sentencing. At this contradictory juncture, social scientists, politicians, journalists, and corrections administrators advocated more interchange between the prison and the free world, fashioning a common sense that seems radical today. The crisis produced by prison overcrowding also disrupts neat periodization. During the 1980s, a decade usually associated with the "prison boom," Mississippi and other states did not respond to overcrowding by expanding their prison systems but turned to mass clemencies as a vehicle to reduce their prison populations.[57] This moment reminds us of the varying ways that clemency can be used—even in moments of heightened fears of crime—to address the crisis of incarceration.[58]

By the 1990s, however, thanks to the moral panics fomented by politicians, the insinuation of victim impact statements into the sentencing process, and the belief that habitual criminals were gaining rights at the expense of law-abiding citizens, prisoners began to lose hard-won channels to the outside world and their customary expectation of eventual release. Tropes of "revolving door prisons" and "country club prisons" drew upon the antiwelfare rhetoric of the time, helping to undergird a movement that critics call penal harm, which justified not only longer sentences but harsher conditions.[59] Just as the antiwelfare movement suggested a zero-sum understanding of government spending so that whatever benefits the racialized poor received were imagined at coming at the expense of employed taxpayers, the penal harm movement endorsed the termination of conjugal visits and furloughs as indulgent luxuries, the putative "pink Cadillacs" of prison life. For incarcerated people, increasing isolation from the outside was an interpersonal and emotional form of deprivation, and they and their loved ones protested its imposition. The penal harm movement, which among other changes shut down flows into and out of prison, allows us to comprehend the shift from a social welfare state to a punitive state in experiential as well as rhetorical terms.[60] Further, linking the austerity of prison life to the austerity of services in the free world reinforces Ruth Wilson Gilmore and Craig Gilmore's claim that mass incarceration is a key, "perhaps *the* key, political attack on the political ground created in the New Deal and Civil Rights era."[61] Conservative radio broadcaster Paul Harvey offered a road map of this offensive when in 1980 he said, "Many are willing to go to jail because life behind bars is more comfortable than what they're accustomed to outside. . . . Inmates in Angola play sports, get furloughs home, enjoy TV, or sit around and smoke pot. . . . When the slum kid is fed, clothed, and comforted more in jail than out, confinement is not the deterrent it used to be."[62]

As this book bridges the registers of policy and personal experience, so too does it move across multiple scales and beyond the physical institution of the prison. I examine the prison as part of a larger carceral geography in three main ways: I look at regional connections and networks of prison practices across states; I track spatial flows of people into and out of prison, as well as the increasing spatial constriction of incarcerated people as these flows were cut off; and I consider how prison became such an extreme state of exile at one end of what theorists call the carceral continuum.[63]

Most detailed studies of prison systems in the United States necessarily focus on an individual state, as the majority of criminal justice legislation occurs on the state level.[64] But what went on in one state had repercussions for the others; states looked to each other for both models and omens, and a national network of wardens and penologists codified and traded ideas. This multistate study, ranging from Louisiana and Mississippi to California and Massachusetts, attends to regional specificity and local conditions while challenging our assumptions about such differences. The analysis of the plantation prison as an extension of slavery and Jim Crow is so entrenched that we are scarcely able to perceive that rehabilitative and progressive possibilities might have emerged there as well, even if they were articulated in a different dialect. Moreover, mid-twentieth-century penologists and lawmakers outside the South closely studied southern prisons, pruning their paternalistic practices and grafting them onto what they regarded as modern penological science. If we adopt sociologist Liam Kennedy's contention that notions of rehabilitation are malleable and can fit into different styles of penal governance, we can perceive how penal rhetoric and practice migrate, operate, and mutate in various contexts.[65] While looking at several states allows the reader to perceive a circuitry of penal practices, it also reveals the multiple meanings of those practices. Thus, this study examines the variations of those practices across space, as well as over time.

Just as penal harm introduced a zero-sum idea of prisoners' dignity and victims' rights, a zero-sum idea of risk has animated the afterlife of incarceration, extending carceral tentacles into everyday life beyond prison. The prison is more than just a building. The militarization of the landscape; the fluidity of practices of surveillance and control; the predatory and punitive infrastructure of bail, fines, and fees; and the collateral consequences that follow formerly incarcerated people outside the gates— all demonstrate that the prison is a locus in a broader web of carcerality that extends beyond its walls.[66] Black activists have long articulated that the ghetto and the prison existed on a continuum of carceral coercion and surveillance. As the political prisoner, radical bookstore owner, jailhouse lawyer, and Black Puerto Rican anarchist Martin Sostre argues, "As long as you are oppressed by the State and the State is in control this [society] is a minimum security prison. Inside [the prison] is maximum security."[67] But prison is still, and always has been, a distinct place set apart both in imagination and in fact. Even as carceral practices have extended beyond the prison, politicians have pledged allegiance to the discursive and material hardening of boundaries around the prison as the only line of defense between safety and danger. Despite the metastasis of carcerality into free spaces over the past fifty years, policymakers have articulated their stake in both rhetorically and physically separating the world of the free and that of the captive.

Looking at the hardening of prison's boundaries offers new vantage points for appreciating the varied role of the state and for considering the work that the prison does to manifest and serve the state's purpose. As Ruth Wilson Gilmore has asserted, as the state lost legitimacy to enact Keynesian projects—that is, state-funded infrastructure programs and social services to stimulate economic growth—it morphed from a social welfare state to a domestic warfare state.[68] *A Wall Is Just a Wall* looks at the different ways that the state exerts power in different times and places and parses how the shift from welfare to warfare was articulated and experienced in prison settings. Jackie Wang asks rhetorically whether it is possible that once the government abrogated its obligations to social welfare, "the only remaining entitlement—the entitlement that has come to give the state as an entity its coherence—is the entitlement of *security*."[69] The state-as-protector justified new obstacles to release as preemptive moves toward the holy grail of zero risk, merging algorithmic forms of governance with hysterical fear.[70]

In this sense, Willie Horton and his ghosts must be understood as representing something new. Useful here is Ruth Wilson Gilmore and Craig

Gilmore's idea that the state's management of race is not static any more than ideas about race are static: "The state's management of racial categories is analogous to the management of highways or ports or telecommunication: racist ideological and material practices are infrastructure that needs to be updated, upgraded, and modernized periodically: That is what is meant by racialization."[71] Once a sovereign's repudiation of his discretionary power was cast as fairness and the political race to the bottom cemented additional layers to prison walls, a new logic was born: Those branded as criminals will always be dangerous.[72] According to Jonathan Simon, the resulting fear of violent crime forms "the emotional core, the sense of grievance" that fuels the reordering of government priorities.[73] As Gilmore and Gilmore put it, "As in any protection racket the protector requires the threat from which we need protection. . . . If they didn't exist, they would have to be invented."[74] Those convicted of crimes now suffer perpetual exclusion, figured as a breed apart, fixed in an identity outside of society's moral circle.[75]

Thus, an exploration of changing penal practices and the evolution of the "protection racket" not only sheds light on theories of the state but illuminates the contingency of ideas about risk, public safety, and redeemability. In the early nineteenth century, rural prisons in northern states were ostensibly created to insulate criminals from the corrupting influence of society in order to reform them, but by the late twentieth century, the intention was to protect society from dangerous criminals on the loose. Penal practices that were common throughout much of the twentieth century suggest that, far from being an objective, measurable trait that inheres in an individual person or category of people, risk has been fluid, contested, and provisional. Governors in the Jim Crow South, empowered by the laws and customs of white supremacy, saw no risk to their safety when they employed people convicted of murder to work as domestic servants in the governor's mansion; corrections officials saw little risk to the public when they advocated in the 1970s that prisoners serving sentences for violent crimes be allowed to go home on weekends to see their families; governors were not hamstrung by anxiety about risk when they routinely released people convicted of first-degree murder who had served only ten years in prison.

Shifting notions of what constitutes risk dovetail with increasing skepticism about redeemability and rehabilitation. If most prisoners are figured as always posing a risk to the public regardless of their time spent or growth in prison, then prisoners are immutably beyond rehabilitation and redemption. The increasingly permanent exile of prisoners is connected to Jonathan Simon's observation that recent decades have seen the correctional subject more tightly tethered to his crime. This shift is documented in the changing eligibility standards for furloughs in Arizona: in 1988, for the first time, furlough eligibility was based on the class and nature of the original offense rather than one's institutional record.[76] The rigid logics of risk management not only chain prisoners to their past but, like a kind of postmodern phrenology, purport to determine the future.[77] According to Richard Berk, who researches predictive policing and teaches criminology at the University of Pennsylvania, developments in algorithmic policing and data science make it possible to "calculate the likelihood that someone will engage in criminal activity before they are born."[78] The deployment of predictive data reifies racially discriminatory patterns of law enforcement and lends a scientific veneer to preemptively retributive justice. Examining the decline of clemency, conjugal visits, and furloughs offers us a way to understand this transformation and historicizes this new common sense.

The continued relevance of prison as a distinct place resonates in the now conventional wisdom that the tide of law and order was accompanied by a shift in penological goals from rehabilitation to containment, which has been documented by a number of scholars of criminology and social science.[79] While the decline of the rehabilitative ideal has been taken for granted, *A Wall Is Just a Wall* examines what this decline meant in a qualitative sense for incarcerated people. Containment and warehousing are not only principles of punishment or powerful spatial metaphors; first and last, they are embodied experiences. The public's faith in prison's efficacy relies not on the institution's capacity to rehabilitate but on its ability to keep criminals behind thick walls. To the extent that a prison remains a site to fix a body in space and inflict pain, prison walls matter very much to those who reside within them. Scholars have exposed the dehumanizing material conditions of supermax and solitary confinement, but we need to historicize this increasing isolation and examine its consequences, along a spectrum of mobility and privileges, for incarcerated people.[80] To more fully understand how prisoners experienced the shift to containment, we must examine both the lived experience of those inside the container and the changing constitution of its walls.[81]

For their part, incarcerated people have resisted the tightened constraints on their lives. When clemencies dried up and furloughs ended, prisoners experienced devastating losses. Despite the fact that their original crimes have become permanent brands, incarcerated people struggle to place themselves in history, both by testifying to their own transformation and by tracking the law's transformation over time. Having complied with the customary conditions of their confinement in order to make meaning as well as earn privileges and mercy, incarcerated people developed a collective consciousness of their just deserts and critiqued the prison against its own claims and the politicians who seemed to be playing games with their lives. They adapted to and resisted the new probability of dying in prison in ways that challenged laws and allowed them to write new stories about themselves.[82] Whatever the leakage of incarceration into freedom, the ideological and literal sequestration of incarcerated people has constituted a significant shift in policy and lived experience.

Most studies of mass incarceration attribute the expansion of the carceral state to increasingly punitive sentencing but stop short at the prison door and do not fully engage the experience of prisoners as they witnessed their fates and their immediate conditions and possibilities for freedom change during their own lifetimes. This book takes seriously the lived experience and consciousness of prisoners who used all of the levers at their disposal to survive and challenge their confinement. While many prisoners denounced furloughs and conjugal visits as bribes, others begrudgingly accepted such reforms as a strategic step or relished them as a means of immediate improvement in the conditions of their lives. Practices such as granting clemency, conjugal visits, and furloughs were the objects of collective mobilization by prisoners and claimed as an entitlement. By agitating for such possibilities, incarcerated people revealed their strategies for survival as well as both individual and collective betterment. At the same time, because the practices in question were framed by prisoners' keepers as privileges rather than rights they could be taken away, exposing the ultimate power of the prison. Looking at the rise and fall of practices that held out the promise of belonging to a world beyond the prison, all of which dissipated during prisoners' lifetimes, helps us to understand their exile from the perspective of captivity and loss. I track how changes in penal rhetoric and strategies of governance shaped the lives of prisoners, paying attention to carrots as well as sticks.

Finally, because recent studies have been conducted at the peak of mass incarceration, scholars and activists have warned that making prison kinder only legitimates it, and have demonstrated that past reforms have only led to a strengthening of the carceral state.[83] Yet this hindsight has underestimated the contingencies and possibilities of the past. Given the growth of the carceral state, it is tempting to regard those advocating for reforms such as furloughs and conjugal visits as disingenuous, cynical, or hopelessly naive. But the assumptions that undergirded these practices reveal a moment when the permeability of the prison was interpreted as a stage in its dissolution. These assumptions—the belief that incarceration was almost always temporary, the idea that most people who were incarcerated should have ways to sustain their relationships with loved ones as well as the public, the trust that even those convicted of violent crimes could and should move about unescorted outside prison, and the faith that people who broke the law need not be perpetually ostracized for their crime and instead should be shown mercy—were as normative then as they are anathema now. If challenging hegemonic institutions such as the prison requires a fundamental change in consciousness, we must time-travel to those moments when today's assumptions were not common sense. According to Ruth Wilson Gilmore, "the ways people think about the world, and understand themselves in it, define in large part what they do to endure or change the world."[84] I share Jonathan Simon's view: "To go forward, we must look back. Along with tens of thousands of individuals, mass incarceration has also swept away a landscape of criminological ideas and projects that, as of the late 1970s, was a thriving field of intense intellectual competition." Looking back at these ideas and practices can allow us to "enter a kind of literary Pompeii in which the authors have been captured in positions of struggle relevant to the fault lines of the moment, oblivious to the lava flow about to overtake them."[85] The fundamental idea that public safety could be best ensured by making the prison more permeable is one of those pillars of thought buried under the lava flow. Recent writing follows the extension of the carceral state into so-called free territory, but the historic permeability of the prison holds possibilities for freedom as well. Most fundamentally, we must reckon with the reality that people—even those who have committed horrible acts of violence—change over time. There are people currently incarcerated who remember when this was common sense.

Just as the institution of slavery determined the social organization of slave society by tethering both enslaved and free people to its logic, the prison is both a discrete space and one that is constitutive of a broader social order. In her description of the gradual decay of slavery in Maryland, historian Barbara J. Fields reminds her readers that even the "hemorrhage of the slave population did not signal the end of slavery as an overriding fact of life for the people—especially the black people—of Maryland." She adds, "Perhaps slavery might be likened in this to a radioactive object: constantly emitting radiation, nonetheless, radioactive. Or perhaps to a strong dye that, even as it faded, tinted freedom in somber shades."[86]

This book explores what it may have felt like for prisoners to experience the somber shades of freedom. From the vantage point of captivity in prison, the world outside remained a North Star. However mythical, clouded, or disappointing, freedom was not impossible to reach throughout most of the twentieth century. The taste of freedom offered by furloughs and conjugal visits and the promise of clemency shaped prisoners' sense of self, their understandings of the ethics of the criminal justice system, their relationship to the outside world, and how they spent their time while inside. The foreclosure of these possibilities was devastating.

Thus, creating possibilities to collapse the boundaries between inside and outside is a practice of refusing the ideological and material boundaries that produce disposable and punishable categories of people. The practice of encounter between inside and outside cuts through media sensationalism, political posturing, fearmongering, and panic. Through "getting close" we embody the possibility that things could be otherwise. As political philosopher Lisa Guenther has said of building bridges between inside and outside prison, "This is what abolition looks like . . . the creation of new ways of thinking, seeing, feeling, speaking, and experiencing a world that is shared in common with all other human . . . beings. So, coming together is a small act of resistance at the scene of the 'crime' itself."[87] Henry, the incarcerated student whom we met earlier, recognized the possibility of creating a collective that would resuscitate prisoners from social death and practice an otherwise that could transcend the finite nature of the class:

> Our time together has not truly come to an end, this world we've created is in no way transitory. We carry it beyond the threshold of these doors. Inside we go on to mentor others as we carry your faces and words in our hearts remembering that you treated us as human beings; you go on to continue building the world around you in how you interact, love, vote, and speak to power. We will always have the context we shared together; no one can take that from us and no one can stop us from recreating what is possible to create with others.[88]

Radical change must be ushered and experienced in steps that are imaginable in order to change people's views of what is possible. By providing wedges that literally open the prison doors, we can overcome the panic with which we have been infected and make the unthinkable thinkable. Eye to eye, we can mend the social fabric. We must confront the fact that prison walls were *made*. And, in the words of Frederick Douglass, "What man can make, man can unmake."[89]

PART I. THE BOUNDARIES OF MERCY

Clemency, Jim Crow, and Mass Incarceration

1 Clemency in the Age of Jim Crow

Mercy and White Supremacy

In January 2012, just as he was leaving office, Republican governor Haley Barbour of Mississippi granted clemency to over two hundred people who had committed felonies. More than two dozen of them had been convicted of murder or manslaughter. Despite the fact that nearly 90 percent of those clemencies were for people who had already served their prison terms, his move so outraged Mississippians across the political spectrum that his previously ascendant political career flagged, and lawmakers and members of the general public began to call for a constitutional amendment to curtail the governor's power to issue executive clemency.[1] Among those released from prison were a man convicted of killing his estranged wife and another who had killed a man during a robbery. Both prisoners had been assigned to work in the governor's mansion as "trusties." Barbour, whom one journalist described as "a beefy southerner who kept a confederate flag autographed by Jefferson Davis in his office," defended his action to the press, saying that it was "Mississippi tradition" to release mansion trusties.[2] When called to task by an irate public, Barbour explained, "Historically governors have granted pardons to the trusties that work in the mansion. . . . Servants in the mansion for decades, I'm sure more than a century, have been convicts." In reference to one person serving a sentence for murder whose sentence he had commuted, Barbour asserted, "This man did commit an awful, awful crime, but the way this system is worked, if you get in there and work hard enough, take on enough responsibility, if you earn it, you get a second chance."[3]

What is this "Mississippi tradition," and what can it tell us about the contours of mercy, discretion, and redemption in the one of the most punitive states in the country? For most of the twentieth century, the vigorous use of gubernatorial clemency was a vital and uncontroversial aspect of the criminal justice system in the American South.[4] Whether to check overly harsh sentences, manage the prison population, provide labor for employers, or convey compassion, southern governors curbed and legitimated the retributive potential of the criminal justice system with mercy. Rather than demonstrating weakness, a governor reaffirmed his executive authority through the regular exercise of his clemency prerogative. Normatively speaking, a Jim Crow governor strengthened his legitimacy through noblesse, rewarded those who were docile, and selectively included the incarcerated among those he was duty bound to protect. Just as enslavers had flexed their power by attempting to replace an enslaved person's kinship network with the "fictive kinship" to the master, so too could a governor enhance his power by granting grace: an act of clemency communicated, "You owe your life to me."[5]

Historians of southern justice have observed that most governors regularly granted clemencies well into the twentieth century.[6] Amy Louise Wood, for example, has demonstrated that "the prolynching firebrand and unapologetic Negrophobe" governor of South Carolina, Coleman Blease (1911–15), extended executive clemency to at least 1,740 prisoners, Black and white, during his four-year tenure, in effect releasing nearly 90 percent of the state's entire prison population.[7] Martha A. Meyers has correlated clemency rates in Jim Crow Georgia with the price of cotton, demonstrating that the need for labor, particularly of Black men, tracked with the likelihood of release.[8] These and other scholars have shown that clemency practices during the era of Jim Crow scaffolded hierarchies of race and labor; by demanding supplication and relying on sovereign discretion, clemency buttressed state power over vulnerable citizens and secured the architecture of Jim Crow.[9]

This section of the book examines the regular practice of gubernatorial clemency in the American South through a close investigation of Mississippi and Louisiana. In the South, clemency has a peculiar relationship to carceral practices because southern governors who liberally used their clemency power were often avowed zealots of white supremacy. In the Jim Crow South, gubernatorial mercy was the velvet glove of racism. Weaving Old South paternalism with the rehabilitative ideal commonly associated with prisons outside the region, clemency challenges neat political categories as they pertain to criminal justice policy.[10] Scholars have demonstrated that by the late 1960s, southern politicians successfully relied on seemingly race-neutral calls for law and order as a "Southern strategy" to win voters both within and outside the South in the wake of the civil rights movement.[11] Yet this narrative obscures the gubernatorial clemency that persisted in the southern penal system throughout most of the twentieth century.[12] Even as Jim Crow began to crumble, governors continued to exercise mercy as evidence of their patriarchal benevolence and as an alibi for labor extraction. Remarkably, with much more regularity than they would today, southern governors rewarded both Black and white prisoners who adhered to prescribed codes of racial deference and etiquette.[13]

Nearly all explanations of the clemency power point out that it has ancient roots and is recognized all over the world.[14] In the United States, while clemency procedures differ from state to state and personal discretion is intrinsic to gubernatorial clemency, states generally adopted the principle outlined by Alexander Hamilton in *Federalist 74* advocating executive clemency on the federal level as a means to address peculiar circumstances not accounted for by the rules of law: "Humanity and good policy conspire to dictate, that the benign prerogative of pardoning should be as little as possible fettered or embarrassed."[15] Throughout US history, presidents and governors have exercised this prerogative to promote national unity after periods of unrest or insurrection, to mitigate the impact of laws of which they disapproved, to reward individuals for exceptional deeds, and—at times, more notoriously—to pander to their supporters.[16] As Carolyn Strange has shown, critics of clemency in the early republic argued that vesting so much authority in the governor was undemocratic, but throughout the early twentieth century, gubernatorial discretion survived vigorous assaults from those concerned about coddling criminals and those who anticipated corruption.[17] While clemency may appear to be an exercise of unfettered personal power, insulated from judicial review, legal scholars claim that it should be considered a power that is exercised on behalf of the public.[18] According to pardon attorney Margaret Colgate Love, "The framers of the Constitution believed that pardon should be considered a public act of office rather than a private act of grace."[19] Far from being capricious, executives who used it were fulfilling their constitutional duty to check a fallible legal system. Over 120 years after Hamilton's statement on federal clemency, a member of the Colorado Board of Pardons agreed, suggesting in 1911, "For one abuse of the pardon power there are a thousand abuses of the convicting power."[20]

The majority of states vest their governors with the power to grant clemency, and this power is almost entirely unreviewable by the courts.

According to legal scholar Elizabeth Rapaport, "'Clemency, like 'mercy,' characterizes a judgment or action when a person with the power to exact punishment . . . declines to exact all or some of what he or she is entitled to exact. No wrongdoer . . . has a right to such lenity."[21] Before the advent of parole, clemency was the most commonly used mechanism for correcting and mitigating sentences.[22] Some states have pardon boards that make recommendations to the governor, but in most cases the governor is free to exercise discretion. Governors use their clemency powers for a wide range of reasons: to correct miscarriages of justice, to provide labor for employers, and to wield the benevolence expected of their office. In the South, where a culture of personalism and discretion prevailed over abstract notions of bureaucratic fairness, a governor's robust use of clemency made sense: to Wood, a governor's "paternalistic benevolence shored up his power by reinforcing the lower classes' bonds of obedience and deference to him by making it seem as if the law was merciful when it was, in fact, quite draconian."[23]

Mississippi and Louisiana provide useful case studies because both states had vigorous clemency practices throughout the period when their criminal legal systems were explicitly rooted in Jim Crow. By now it is widely known that incarceration in the states of the former Confederacy was a modern invention, concocted to ensnare, disfranchise, and contain freedpeople and exploit them as cheap labor. Parchman Farm, the Mississippi State Penitentiary, was at the center of this process. Opened in 1904 under the administration of Governor James Vardaman on twenty thousand acres in the Mississippi delta, it was designed to end the practice of leasing convicts to private businesses. As historian David Oshinsky and others have shown, for most of the twentieth century, Parchman operated as a "gulag" of the state, justified by the ideology that violence and backbreaking labor were the necessary retribution for alleged criminal behavior.[24] Louisiana State Penitentiary, known as Angola, had even clearer roots in the system of plantation slavery and peonage. Located fifty miles north of Baton Rouge on a parcel of land larger than Manhattan, Angola sits on a site that the state purchased in 1901, consolidating several adjacent cotton and sugarcane plantations; the largest was named Angola, purportedly after the homelands of enslaved Africans. The prison is hemmed in by the Mississippi River on three sides and the rugged Tunica Hills and their deep gorges on the other. The Angola prison farm, whose main purpose was not rehabilitation but profit through exploiting prisoners' labor, "brought the practices of plantation slavery well into the twentieth century."[25] When Black Panther Party member Albert Woodfox arrived at Angola in 1965, he later recalled, "The legacy of slavery was everywhere. It was in the ground under our feet and in the air we breathed, wherever we looked." The most brutal work assignment, cutting sugar cane, was reserved mainly for Black prisoners. According to Woodfox, "There were old-timers at Angola who made good money breaking prisoners' bones so men could get out of work."[26] As recently as 1979, prisoners who toiled in the fields were referred to as "hands," reminiscent of how white landowners referred to those whom they enslaved.[27] As of 2020, Angola housed over fifty-three hundred prisoners, 75 percent of whom were African American.[28]

Despite their ferocious, racist violence, these plantation prisons were in many ways more permeable than most prisons are today. Parchman has been described as a prison without walls; operating more like an antebellum plantation than a supermax prison, its perimeter was guarded by armed inmates, and there were few escapes.[29] Yet at both Parchman and Angola, inmates were regularly released for various purposes: to go home during the Christmas holidays, to play concerts elsewhere in the state, to attend to ill family members, or to participate in professional athletic events.[30] In 1953 Angola's inmate orchestra, the Cavaliers, even provided the entertainment for a high school prom.[31] While an official parole system did not formally exist in Louisiana until the 1920s and in Mississippi until 1944, most prisoners, even those with life sentences, did not serve more than eight to ten years.[32] Parchman and Angola were brutal but porous, perhaps because they were a metonym of the broader regime of Jim Crow in which the lived experience of even so-called free Black southerners resembled that of inmates on parole. If the line between freedom and incarceration was blurred by Jim Crow, then the physical boundary between inside and outside the prison was also not impregnable—but only at the discretion of the white authorities who ruled both.

This chapter and the two chapters that follow track the regularity and demise of gubernatorial clemency with a focus on Mississippi and Louisiana, where clemencies were routine for most of the twentieth century. In Mississippi clemency was underwritten by the ideology of paternalism. Governors regularly released prisoners who demonstrated subservience, performed labor for white people, or served under their own supervision in the governor's mansion. This form of leniency was unquestioned as mortar for the social hierarchy. In Louisiana, the clemency was more systematized due to the practice of the so-called 10/6 rule, the customary commutation of a person's life sentence after ten years and six months behind bars. The assumption that a well-behaved prisoner would receive clemency was so entrenched as to be considered a contractual arrangement. Chapter 2 follows southern clemency practice from the 1960s through the 1980s, as white conservatives equated political activism with crime and began to curtail the tradition of clemency, revolutionizing prisoners' expectations of release. Despite fearmongering rhetoric, however, southern governors continued to free mansion trusties who embodied white supremacist norms of deference and to advocate mass clemencies as a way of alleviating prison overcrowding. Chapter 3 traces the decline of clemency in late twentieth century. As clemency became politicized and tough-on-crime legislation foreclosed possibilities for their release, prisoners mobilized to agitate for clemency and restore a collective memory of clemency as an entitlement. In doing so they drew on the language of redemption while casting their continued incarceration as a betrayal. The final section of chapter 3 returns to the case of Haley Barbour and explains what his clemencies tell us about the conditions of mercy.

THE "MISSISSIPPI TRADITION"

According to the Mississippi Constitution of 1890, the governor has absolute powers of clemency, and considering clemency petitions has long been a routine part of the governor's job. This is the same constitution that introduced voting restrictions that effectively disfranchised African American men. Mississippi governor A. J. McLaurin (1896–1900), reflecting on his power to pardon, stated that "pardoning is the authority vested in the individual who believes that people are good and deserve a second chance."[33] In the early twentieth century, before a formal parole system was established in 1944, gubernatorial clemency was the only mechanism for relief from a long prison sentence. Mississippi governors had several forms of clemency at their disposal: a "definite suspension," a short-term leave from prison—for a holiday, funeral, or other family business—that in other states might be called a furlough; an "indefinite suspension," which released a prisoner indefinitely but included the possibility of revocation for any reason at any time; and a pardon, which attached no conditions and erased a prisoner's conviction.

The entire clemency process involved a ritual of prisoners' supplication and the intercession of respectable white patrons. But many languished in prison. Rather than allowing this disparity to lead to cronyism, Mississippi governors regularly visited the "forgotten men" who had "no people or friends to make appeals for them."[34] In the 1930s, Governor Mike Conner (1932–36) frequently traveled to Parchman to interview incarcerated people and hear testimonies from spouses and community members in his "mercy court," an occasion that could result in the release of numerous prisoners.[35] Conner's successors continued the tradition. On his monthly visits to Parchman, Governor Paul B. Johnson Sr. (1940–43) listened "with sympathy as old and young, white and black, men and women, related the history of crimes inspired by hot tempers, jealousy, revenge, and self-defense, while several insisted they were convicted on circumstantial evidence and deserved their freedom." Some of these unfortunates, whom Johnson deemed "human driftwood," dropped to their knees in front of him to plead for relief. One journalist described Governor Johnson's visit to Parchman in a manner that recalls Abraham Lincoln greeting former slaves as he walked through defeated Richmond, Virginia, in 1865: "[Johnson's] easily distinguishable black hat acting like a magnet to draw prisoners from all over the farm who heard quickly via grapevine that the chief executive 'has come to let some of us out.'"[36]

Some Mississippians objected to governors' relative leniency in granting clemency because prisoners who were pardoned were not under continuing supervision. When "twenty killers [were] freed by Governor White" in 1909, the editor of the *Delta Democrat-Times* wondered aloud whether "the governors of Mississippi make blood streaked hands seem more honorable than vile."[37] Parole, the supervised and conditional release of prisoners, was the hallmark of the ideology of rehabilitation, which saw treatment tailored to the individual offender as the most efficient crime control strategy and the most humane alternative to retribution. Parole systems were established outside the South in the early twentieth century. In Mississippi, as elsewhere, advocates eventually turned to parole, contending that "it is impossible to rebuild men in 'dirty, medieval jails,'" and seeking to "prevent liberated prisoners from returning to crime and to make useful citizens out of them."[38] Mississippi's parole law established a three-member board and made prisoners eligible for parole after serving one-third of their sentences, excluding those who had three felony convictions.[39]

Prisoners recognized the value of parole, both for its real material benefits and for signaling that they might be regarded as human beings. However harrowing life might have been outside Parchman's boundaries, it was still more like freedom. The editor of Parchman's prison newspaper, *Inside World*, took an optimistic view of the program: "In accord with the progressive ideas of our modern era, Mississippi . . . has at its disposal the means to parole any inmate that it feels will be a good parole risk. . . . ANY, inmate of Parchman has at least SOME, hope of eventual release from this institution. . . . No man is considered an incorrigible or hopeless criminal. . . . Mississippi has proven beyond a doubt that any man sentenced to prison may be returned safely to society."[40]

To the extent that clemency rates fell in the early twentieth century, it was because parole became its substitute. But in Mississippi, as elsewhere, the tradition of gubernatorial clemency continued after the establishment of parole in 1944. Throughout most of the twentieth century it was a regular practice for Mississippi governors to exercise their clemency powers, whether to grant an inmate convicted of murder a six-month leave "on the basis of extenuating circumstances which includes humanitarian purposes and an extreme hardship situation," as in the case of prisoner Nevada Atterberry as late as 1975, or to release an inmate convicted of murder after eight years, because, in the words of Governor William Waller, "justice has been served."[41] Governors might grant suspensions quite liberally, as in the case of prisoner Sid Bretheren, sentenced to life for the rape of a twelve-year-old girl. Even after having been punished in prison six times for violating prison rules such as beating another prisoner with a hoe and crushing his jaw, Brethren had since "made a good record" and was granted eight ten-day holiday suspensions and returned promptly from each.[42] Even Governor James P. Coleman (1956–60), who repeatedly said that he would hesitate to use his clemency power, granted more than 160 indefinite suspensions when he left office in 1960. After his defeat, he said that his greatest accomplishment was preserving segregation in public schools.[43] Even a segregationist was more lenient about clemency than more moderate governors would be generations later.

No issue better embodies the relationships among paternalism, Jim Crow, and clemency than the custom of governors releasing those prisoners employed at the governor's mansion. While governors used prisoners' labor at their mansions throughout the United States, the practice has been more common in the states of the former Confederacy.[44] In Mississippi this practice sat at the intersection of white supremacy, convict labor, and fiscal conservatism; the use of prisoners as servants at the mansion was officially sanctioned by the Mississippi Legislature in 1912 as a means of reducing expenses for the governor's family. Customarily, only people of

African descent who had been convicted of murder or manslaughter were selected. Governors and correctional officials explained that people who committed violent crimes usually did so out of passion, and thus were not chronically dangerous. Moreover, given their life sentences, they had the greatest incentive to prove themselves worthy of mercy. And mercy they received. For most of the twentieth century, governors granted clemency to those who served in the governor's mansion. This gesture must be seen in the context of the racist paternalism in which, according to historian Sarah Haley, elite white southerners generally managed "black subordinates through benevolence" and in light of the fact that the regime of Jim Crow was enough to terrorize former prisoners into submission in a "free world" that was less than free for those of African descent.[45]

The origin story of this tradition in Mississippi was that of prison trusty Henry Trott. Under the administration of Governor Earl L. Brewer (1912–16), Trott, who was serving a life sentence for murder, was employed as a yardman and chauffeur and as a bodyguard to the governor's daughter.[46] Historians of the mansion explain that little Claudia Brewer, having "developed a fond attachment for her protector," slipped a note under her father's dinner plate one evening. The note read, "Please set Henry free." At the end of Brewer's term, the governor asked his daughter to present Trott and Emmett Fields, another trusty who had been convicted of murder, with official documents. As historians of the mansion described the scene, "Unable to read the document, Henry did not comprehend its importance until the younger man said, 'Henry, don't you know what it is? Little Missy done set us free!'"[47] According to one reporter, "Overjoyed, they thanked him with tears streaming down their faces."[48] This figure of the Black prisoner shedding tears of gratitude after long, devoted service to the white family and household reveals the legacy of the "faithful slave" image and the potential of clemency—especially of Black prisoners engaged in coerced domestic labor—to "transform mastery into generosity."[49]

This practice, which continued for decades, was romanticized and mythologized by the press. In 1927, the *Jackson Daily News* reported that the "negro convicts" employed as trusties in Governor Henry L. Whitfield's (1921–24) mansion stood in all-night vigil and then "dropped on their knees in fervent prayer . . . croon[ing] weird and mournful melodies" at his deathbed.[50] By 1946 the tradition of pardoning mansion servants was considered so "long established" that Fielding L. Wright (1946–52), on assuming office after the death of Governor Thomas L. Bailey (1944–46), granted clemency to all the mansion trusties who had been convicted of murder and served his predecessor.[51] At the end of his first full term in 1952, Governor Wright released all thirteen of his incarcerated mansion staff. In 1956, Governor Hugh L. White (1952–56) issued full pardons to all of the Black men who had been providing domestic services at the mansion; seven of them had been convicted of murder, and one of manslaughter. The *Clarion-Ledger* explained in boilerplate language that "upon expiration of a governor's term in office, custom is that the governor issues full pardons to all who serve him faithfully and who have conducted themselves within the proper bounds of society."[52] A prisoner named Sylvester Wright, convicted of murder, was aware of the norm when he requested clemency from Governor Coleman after serving ten years of a life sentence: "I was assigned to the Governor's mansion as a servant, and in keeping with the custom of such cases, I am respectfully petitioning for a pardon."[53]

While those who approved of this practice claimed that "distinguished visitors to the executive mansion . . . unfailingly commended the dignified and graceful manner in which the inmates performed their duties," by the early 1960s critics of convict labor contended that the use of prisoners in this manner at the Kentucky governor's mansion was "undignified, outmoded, and should be stopped." The trusties, who were paid eight cents per day, should be "replaced with good union members," and the mansion could ill-afford to have untrained staff who might pilfer from the governor's cupboard. It was better to hire "the kind of staff befitting the state's Mansion and Kentucky's reputation for gracious hospitality."[54] This criticism was rooted in concern about competition from cheap labor rather than fear of danger or early release. The American Federation of Labor and Congress of Industrial Organizations' *Labor News* argued that the practice was "as undignified as slavery" and "has no place in this state in 1962," but it did not suggest that employing violent criminals posed any physical risk.[55]

"PLEASE LET HIM OUT OF THE PEN": CLEMENCY PETITIONS AND MERCY'S MIXED BLESSINGS

Haley Barbour had his history right when he claimed that governors automatically released those who worked in the mansion at the end of the governor's term and that liberal use of clemency had long been the norm in the state. Prisoners who did not serve in the mansion had to petition the governor for clemency with letters of support and recommendations from the parole board. As the nucleus of a process both bureaucratic and personal, successful petitions for clemency reveal whom a governor considered fit for mercy, as well as the strategies and protocols of community members seeking the governor's favor. In examining samples of these petition files, a few patterns stand out. On some occasions pleas for clemency challenged the guilt of the prisoner or the validity of the conviction, but most argued that the inmate would be more useful outside prison than inside. Black prisoners were as likely to receive clemency consideration as white prisoners. White patrons suggested that, although Black petitioners were naturally impulsive and violent, they could be made tractable under proper guardianship and supervision. These pleas bespeak a web of social relations in which reputable white citizens acted as patrons to mostly African American convicts and offer a glimpse of white Mississippians' ideologies about criminal behavior, racial etiquette, and justice.

Clemency appeals were usually legitimated, if not spearheaded, by respectable white people in the community who attested to the prisoner's character.[56] Potential employers, prison superintendents, judges, and even prosecuting attorneys wrote governors to persuade them of the prisoner's work ethic and trustworthiness. One district attorney who successfully prosecuted a white man for manslaughter in 1960 wrote to Governor Ross Barnett (1960–64) nineteen months later, "Naturally, I don't apologize for participation in the trial; I was simply doing my duty. But in my considered opinion, I believe he deserves your careful consideration."[57] This practice of vouching for inmates often rested on personal contact with the governor and on personal, usually hierarchical, relations with the inmate. A relative of Governor Barnett wrote that he had "a big favor to ask of you" regarding "my dear ole cook I've had for 38 years. . . . Her son Robert Lewis just steals so badly until they just keep him in the pen all the time. . . . His mother is 67 years of age and needs him. . . . Please let Lewis out of the pen and come home and work for her, see?" He noted that "she is deaf and mostly dumb" and "is sick a lot and lives alone," adding, "I want you to know I will appreciate this too, and you give him a good talk, and maybe he won't ever steal again."[58]

On the one hand, some petitioners excused crimes committed by Black people because they assumed that Black people were inherently predisposed to criminality. Though it may seem counterintuitive, the alleged immutability of a Black person's tendency toward criminal behavior could justify leniency. A 1947 letter advocating for a Black prisoner named Sam implied that his violent behavior just couldn't be helped: "My recollection is that Sam negrolike lost his control and killed the woman."[59] But on the other hand, white people petitioning on behalf of Black inmates assured the governor that the candidates for clemency adhered to social norms and understood their proper place, emphasizing the prisoner's willingness to work, loyalty, and submissiveness. J. C. Bassett, who was the sheriff at the time of the 1945 conviction of Ben Arledge, wrote on Arledge's behalf, "I have known this old Negro for a long time, and know for a fact that he is a hard working man, and a good farm negro."[60] Eddie Campbell, writing in 1954 to urge Governor Coleman to release L. C. Blackwell, who had served seven years of an eighteen-year sentence for manslaughter, avowed that "Blackwell . . . was considered a good Negro up until he shot his mother-in-law." Twenty-two people, including sheriffs and merchants, expressed support for Blackwell's petition.[61] Inmate Jim Allen was "known here as a good negro, in other words he would work and attend to his own business."[62] Both Blackwell and Allen were "good negroes": Blackwell's violent act was not threatening because it was not directed at white people; Allen was "good" because did not engage in politically questionable collective activities but minded "his own business."

Some successful clemency cases suggest that crimes against Black people were not considered serious. Jim Allen, sentenced to life for murder, had killed a Black person entering his house, thinking that his home was being invaded. Court clerk J. C. Jourdan wrote, "I have never felt that negroes should be governed by exactly the same laws that other people are governed with, and I feel that Jim has been sufficiently punished for the crime and would appreciate it if you would grant him a suspension."[63] Allen was released on parole after serving eleven years. In the case of Parker Allen, an African American man convicted of killing a "negro woman" in 1937, Governor White issued an indefinite suspension after Allen served a mere two years because, according to the white people in the community, the woman whom he killed had been "a common whore," a "common street walker," and a "notorious character." A prominent white attorney asserted that Allen was "a frugal negro who owned his own home and seventy acres of fairly good land" and was now in danger of losing his home and his family due to his incarceration. "This, of course, has nothing to do with a meritorious application for clemency," the lawyer conceded, but "the people here in Hernando who were familiar with the woman he killed feel that it was good riddance. She was a common harlot and a trouble maker."[64] Although most Black lives didn't matter, some mattered more—or less—than others.

White people serving as sponsors who promised to employ inmates after their release were likely self-serving. Because parole laws required that an inmate have a job lined up at the time of release, some Mississippians smelled a racket, arguing that influential people sponsored inmates in order to secure their labor.[65] A member of the Mississippi State Parole Board decried planters who "get men out on parole just for the length of time it took to make a crop."[66] Requests for releases reveal such calculations. A landowner wrote in 1962, "I would be glad to employ" inmate Wilson Carter "at once . . . especially as his wife has been one of my sharecroppers ever since he was sent to the penitentiary."[67] The president of a stationary company was more direct: "We badly need someone to live on my farm and work at the everyday chores, and help [our] nurse who is caring for our invalid mother. . . . After interviewing this parolee, Mr. Harpole [the superintendent] recommended this colored man for our purposes."[68] Another wrote to Governor White "about three Negros [sic] I mentioned to you in conversation. . . . These Negros are needed here in Farm work, and I believe they have learned a lesson."[69] A Jackson banker wrote to Governor Coleman's assistant on behalf of Mrs. J. H. Tripp, who, as a result of bad health, needed a servant: "She has learned that one Bertha Parker . . . who was convicted of manslaughter . . . would make a good cook and maid." Mrs. Tripp went to Parchman to speak to Parker, and received Superintendent Harpole's blessing. "The man she killed was a colored man named Redman, and there were certain elements which could have amounted to self-defense in connection with the killing."[70] There was nothing final about a court's decision; far from throwing away the key, Mississippi governors regularly responded to such personal pleas by opening the gates.

Despite white people's assumptions about Black criminality, their demand for Black labor under their control and their confidence in Black subservience seemed to outweigh their fear of future danger. White people believed that under the proper supervision, Black people would behave. K. S. Archer, a city clerk, pleaded with Governor Wright to release a "simple minded negro" named Lawyer Price from Parchman after Price had served several years for frightening white women when he was drunk: "This Moronic negro has more than paid for that drunken spree," he noted. "We will be glad to have him under our watchcare and believe that he can be made a law abiding member of the community."[71] Black

Mississippians convicted of murder were routinely released into the hands of white employers. In the case of Sam Bland, the white person requesting Bland's labor pleaded, "Mr. Moore is a large land owner in this county and needs labor very badly, we don't think you would make a mistake to let Mr. Moore *have this negro*."[72] Walter and Lena Sillers asked an official at Parchman to identify a woman to serve as a cook in their household. In turn, the prison official contacted the governor to request a six-month suspension for a woman named Rosalie James who had been convicted of murder: "Lena has no cook, can not get one and is not well and I feel that this woman is deserving of consideration, also that she will make them an excellent servant."[73] Significantly, none of those who were looking for servants and farmworkers raised the possibility that people serving time for violent crimes might be violent in the future.

While it was commonplace for clemency requests for Black prisoners to be laced with racism and expectations of subordination, some petitioners recognized flaws in the criminal justice system and even portrayed clemency as a corrective to prejudiced white juries. For example, Lewis Aldridge, a Black man convicted of murder in 1937, was granted an indefinite suspension two years later. The white man who endorsed his release wrote, "Their verdict showed that there was doubt in their minds, but Aldridge was just another negro and no doubt the jury felt that if he was not guilty of this crime, that he was guilty of another crime."[74] Cliff Adams was convicted and sentenced to life, but his brother later confessed to the crime. His advocate wrote to the governor, "You know that a different rule applies in the trial of negroes who are charged with crime, as the presumption of innocence is never indulged in their favor, but on the contrary they are required to prove their innocence."[75] The plea from another attorney vouching for Adams smacks of paternalism: "The little Ole negro, nor his people have any money. . . . Here's hoping that your excellency will grant this Ole negro his freedom."[76] A former employer vouching for Alfred Lee Small conceded that "white jury prejudice is very bad at the present time" and remarked that "with the negro feeling like it is, especially in this section [that] white juries don't find negroes not guilty of almost anything." Though the petitioner blamed the crime on whiskey, he insisted that he had "never known [Small] to be disorderly or drunk or out of place." Startlingly, the petitioner suggested an equivalence between this Black convict and free white men: "I feel the negro is unjustly punished because I don't think he did any more than you or I would have done under the circumstances."[77] Paternalism could simultaneously excuse criminal behavior, reiterate racist hierarchies, *and* serve as an interruption of a racist criminal justice system.

For former prisoners, the benefits of release were tempered by a nerve-racking existential limbo; according to the terms of an indefinite suspension, the governor could revoke it at any time. A shift in the terms of release could cause tremendous trepidation. Rosalie James, serving as a cook for the Sillers family, was suddenly required to report to the welfare office more frequently. The welfare officer reported, "I tried to convince Rosalie that it did not make any difference but somehow she felt that it did, and that she might any time be picked up and returned to Parchman."[78] Members of the parole board recognized the tenuousness of indefinite suspension and its potential use as a tool of coercion. Under a suspended sentence, an opportunistic employer could "'jackpot' a number of convicts by getting them suspended sentences and hold over their heads the threat of return to prison for the duration of their working for him, or for the duration of their lives for that matter."[79] Those with suspended sentences understood that they were under surveillance indefinitely.

On the other hand, continued interactions with the criminal justice system and penal officials' evaluation processes could serve as an opportunity to convince the state that a formerly incarcerated person could be trusted to obey social norms. Here the coercive choreography of Jim Crow intersected with what penologists considered "rehabilitation." Though scholars have demonstrated that the rehabilitative ideal that justified northern penal regimes did not extend to the disproportionately Black prisoners in the South, arguments for clemency frequently traded in the currency of rehabilitation and reform. As the social worker in the case of Rosalie James observed, "Supervision is usually thought of as a means of rehabilitation of the individual. If that philosophy is applied to this case, we would say that Rosalie has been rehabilitated and that further supervision would serve only to keep her in touch with the governor's office."[80]

In a number of cases, advocates made pleas for clemency on the basis of the poverty or ill-health of the prisoner's family. A pastor, writing to the governor to vouch for J. T. Alsobrook, declared that Alsobrook's recent baptism had restored a "bright spirit of life" and an interest in the welfare of his "*ten* little brothers and sisters."[81] A lawyer advocating for a young man convicted of burglary pleaded that the prisoner's father badly needed his labor and that "this boy has a wife and small child that have no means of support other than living with her folks, and I understand that if he could be released from the penitentiary it could possibly save his marriage."[82] In sum, the conditions of clemency illuminate the paternalistic character of gubernatorial mercy as well as the parameters of acceptable behavior for convicts. Clemency and brutality could go hand in hand. Humanitarian intervention by governors in the Jim Crow South, notes Amy Louise Wood, was "inextricably bound to Jim Crow norms."[83]

CLEMENCY AS CONTRACT IN LOUISIANA

While Parchman has often been called one of the worst prisons in America, Louisiana is currently the world's prison capital. The state incarcerates people at a higher rate and for longer periods than any other state. In 2017 there were 11,238 people serving life and "virtual life" sentences of fifty years or more in Louisiana's prisons, and these inmates made up one-third of the overall prison population.[84] But this was not always the case. From 1926 to 1972, people sentenced to life in prison were routinely released after ten and a half years through a clemency process, and during that period, Louisiana's governors released over 95 percent of the state's lifers.[85]

Henry L. Fuqua (1924–26), the general manager of Angola from 1916 until he was elected governor in 1924, illustrates the genealogy of this policy. The son of a Confederate infantry commander, he initiated the practice of using inmates as guards to cut costs. Fuqua believed that clemency was central to the criminal justice system. It was not a matter of sentiment or largesse, but akin to a "bilateral contract, with the State on one side naming the conditions, and the prisoner on the other side living up to the conditions, and at the prescribed time asking that the State make good on its part of the contract." Fuqua did not perceive those convicted of crimes as irredeemable. He argued that although a prisoner "may have blood on his hands, . . . even he is not cut off from this ray of hope, for the law holds open the door and invites him, not simply by implication, but by specific mention . . . and affixes the time at which he may ask for another chance in life. To close that door against his hopes is to nullify the great principle written in the law and make the future for him black indeed."[86] When Fuqua visited Angola during his campaign for governor, prisoners reportedly greeted him as "Marse [i.e., Master] Henry," which suggests that paternalism would bring leniency and elicit the racial deference he expected in return.[87] Editors of the prison magazine, the *Angolite*, reported that "many convicts cried when they received news of [Fuqua's] death."[88]

Following Fuqua, according to criminal justice scholar Burk Foster, the 10/6 rule was an uncontroversial "fact of the working system. The warden approved, the pardon board agreed, the governor signed, the convict was released."[89] For decades, both statute and case law established clemency after ten years and six months as a general expectation for prisoners given long or life sentences.[90] The practice of release was so common, and languishing in prison so exceptional, that in the 1950s Governor Earl Long (1956–60) created a one-hundred-person Forgotten Man Committee, similar to Mississippi governor Johnson's effort a decade earlier, to identify prisoners who had failed to get clemency because of "personal inabilities and the lack of friends and relatives" and thus had been "literally forgotten by the rest of the world." Long's aim was to proactively "find freedom for deserving inmates."[91] In the wake of a 1951 incident in which at least thirty-nine prisoners at Angola cut their own Achilles tendons to protest intolerable prison conditions, relieving despair took on particular urgency.[92] As one journalist reported, the governor's committee would seek out "prisoners wasting away extra years because of sentences that were too harsh, the little guys with no legal help."[93] The committee, operating under the assumption that 90 percent of all of the prisoners at Angola could be safely released, found and commuted the sentences of 107 prisoners.[94] These included Charles Frazier, who was originally serving eighteen to twenty-eight years for a bank robbery, then given a life sentence in connection with the shooting death of a prison guard during an escape attempt. Governor Long said he thought Frazier, now sixty-eight years old and nearly blind, had been in Angola long enough.[95] By the time he left office in 1960, Long had signed a total of 1,605 pardons and commutations.[96] The total prison population in the state of Louisiana that year was 3,749.[97]

All prisoners reasonably expected that they would receive some form of discretionary release, as even those sentenced to life in prison might be freed on parole or good time—time off a sentence for good conduct in prison—well before they had served ten years and six months. One prisoner account claims that "only the nobodies, which in Louisiana translates into those without political pull," were incarcerated for that long.[98] There were few limits on who might apply for clemency, or how often. People incarcerated at Angola complained in 1953 that the Louisiana Board of Pardons was "clogging the wheels of mercy" when it considered limiting pardon applications to one per prisoner per year.[99] To put that in perspective, in 1994, Louisiana lawmakers introduced a bill to require a ten-year waiting period between a petitioner's clemency applications.[100]

After every quarterly meeting of the Board of Pardons, the editors of the *Angolite* produced an extra edition of the paper to announce the names of those granted clemency, as well as "also-rans." The day the decisions were made public, prisoners at Angola converged at the *Angolite* print shop, pressing their noses against the glass partition, where they awaited the news. According to reporters at the *Angolite*, "Negroes and whites . . . came in rags and tatters, in white shirts and well-tailored trousers . . . their shoes muddy and bearing trademarks of the field."[101] After its August 1954 meeting, which was according to the *Angolite* the "most lenient on record," the Board of Pardons recommended various forms of clemency for eighty-three people. A few months later, the board recommended clemency for 110, out of a total prison population of about twenty-nine hundred.[102] Despite the performance of deference that the clemency process required, prisoners insisted they were sincere in their efforts to improve themselves and expected state officials to live up to their end of the bargain. The 10/6 clemency policy was so entrenched that in a 1971 case commuting a defendant's death sentence to life imprisonment, a dissenting judge argued, "A death sentence is converted into one that really means imprisonment for only ten years and six months. No true life sentence exists in Louisiana law."[103]

The story of prisoner Will Gray, recounted sympathetically by the *Angolite*, reveals the enduring legitimacy of clemency in the Jim Crow South. In 1955, Gray, who had escaped from Angola in 1930, was arrested and sent back to prison after having remained at large for nearly twenty-five years.[104] A Black man who was twenty-eight when he was sentenced to life for murder, Gray slipped away from his job as a kitchen trusty one evening and managed to evade the bloodhounds. Crossing through thickets, he came upon a dilapidated skiff, paddled with his hands, and made it across the Mississippi River, where he changed into old clothes that he found in the trash. Gray was eventually employed by a Black farmer, did a series of odd jobs, and made his way to Camden, Arkansas, where he earned a good reputation as the night watchman for a sawmill.[105] He rebuilt his life in comparative happiness until a jealous rival turned him in. According to the *Angolite*, the police who brought him back to the prison "did everything we could to reassure the poor old fellow, but he seemed to even be afraid of our kindness." As he arrived at Angola, Gray's "frail old body" shook with terror at the harrowing memories that came flooding back. But soon he shed "tears of relief" as he experienced humane treatment: "His bent back would feel no stinging whip"; he was given a long shower with plenty of soap; instead of "well-remembered grits and foul gravy," he was served meat and potatoes. The Angola warden, Maurice Sigler, stated that no disciplinary action would be taken against him; because Gray had lived an exemplary life for twenty-five years, Sigler predicted he would be granted clemency. In October 1955, Gray's sentence was commuted to time served, and he was released.[106]

* * *

Throughout the first half of the twentieth century, governors in Mississippi and Louisiana granted clemency as a matter of course. Clemency enhanced the authority of the governor and reinforced social hierarchies and the subordination of labor. The paternalism that constituted the nervous system of the South, fortified by the musculature of Jim Crow, made clemency into a limit on incarceration that prisoners could reasonably expect. Undeterred by a fear of crime that might result from lenient clemency practices, state officials and the press supported discretionary release as an implicit bargain between the keepers and the kept that ensured, rather than challenged, the social order.

At the crest of the civil rights movement, a bizarre episode in Alabama delineated the parameters of gubernatorial paternalism and the compatibility of mercy with white supremacy in the Jim Crow South. In 1963, US marshals tried and failed to serve Governor George Wallace (1963–67) with a subpoena directing him to appear at a federal court hearing regarding his interference in the desegregation of the University of Alabama. When the marshals served papers on Martha Davis, a mansion servant who had been convicted of second-degree murder, Wallace argued that the subpoena was null because Davis was "civilly dead."[107] Governor Wallace's comment was a reminder that, however intimate the relationship with those in the state's highest office, prisoners still suffered civil death. The faithful mansion servant was an object of benevolence, but not a member of the polity, even in her subordinate capacity. As Black southerners and their allies rejected the deference that had been the glue of white supremacy, the foundations of the clemency process began to shake.

2 Freedom Struggles

Clemency Hangs in the Balance in the Wake of the Civil Rights Movement

In 1962 a "white married male registered voter and home owner" who referred to himself as a "dyed-in-the-wool segregationist and states righter" appealed to Mississippi governor Ross Barnett (1960–64) for an unconditional pardon for Dewey McCormick. According to Lewis B. Hopper of Laurel, Mississippi, McCormick was "a negro man unjustly convicted" of grand larceny on the false testimony of "two teen age negro thieves." Hopper assured Barnett that he had known and trusted McCormick for fifteen years, and that McCormick did not smoke, drink, gamble, carouse, or use profanity. Referring obliquely to the unwelcome political unrest of the moment, Hopper implicitly contrasted McCormick with "uppity negroes," describing him as "a white folk's negro of the type of my wife's black mammy, who knows his place and has no use for people trying to push the negro out of his place." Granting clemency to such a compliant Black person would reinforce the social order, not disrupt it. Hopper asserted that he knew some of the men on the jury that convicted McCormick and declared, "I would trust McCormick and believe what he says sooner than I would some of that jury." Referencing James Meredith's recent effort to desegregate the University of Mississippi, Hopper added that McCormick "has no more business in the penitentiary than Meredith has at Ole Miss."[1] Governor Barnett gave McCormick an indefinite suspension on June 10, 1963.[2] Grand larceny by a "white folk's negro" was more forgivable than demanding equal access to education.

The harmony between white supremacy and mercy resounds in the appeal of Lewis B. Hopper. But, when the civil rights movement struck a discordant note, white southerners who supported segregation framed their attacks on civil rights in criminological terms. In the 1950s, the white supremacist Citizens' Councils network stated that Black people "possessed genetically determined 'criminal tendencies,'" and Mississippi segregationists released a piece of propaganda titled "Crime Report Reveals Menace of Integration."[3] By the late 1960s, the South's white conservatives began to deploy supposedly color-blind jargon advocating freedom of choice regarding school placement, the limitation of welfare programs, the imposition of law and order, and the strict enforcement of sexual morality. In her analysis of the Citizens' Council movement in Louisiana, Rebecca Brückmann argues that the movement "tapped into public moral panics about (the intersections) of civil rights and anti-war protests, the women's liberation movement and changing sexual mores (including the US Supreme Court verdict in *Loving v. Virginia*, which rendered Louisiana's 'intermarriage' laws unconstitutional), the welfare (state) expansion of [President Lyndon] Johnson's Great Society, and fears of riots, increasing crime rates, and a supposedly impending 'race war' run by Black Power advocates."[4] These moral panics called the policy of gubernatorial clemency into question.

Southern governors continued to grant clemency in high numbers throughout the 1960s, most reliably to those Black prisoners who served in the executive mansion. But clemency began to decline in the generation after the legislative and judicial successes of the civil rights movement. Oddly, as implied in Hopper's appeal to Barnett, those who had been convicted of violent crimes seemed less threatening to white people than those protesting in the streets. But as civil rights activism came to be equated with crime and the New Jim Crow replaced the old, possibilities for early release were increasingly foreclosed through the imposition of longer sentences and the politicization of clemency. As political scientist Naomi Murakawa has argued, in the postwar period "the U.S. did not confront a crime problem that was then racialized; it confronted a race problem that was then criminalized."[5] If, as one future warden of a Mississippi penitentiary concluded immediately after the Civil War, "emancipating the negroes will require a system of penitentiaries," then the Black struggle for freedom was met with a hardening of penitentiary walls.[6] Governors were relatively willing to grant clemency when the architecture of Jim Crow was enough to keep former prisoners in check. With the dismantling of Jim Crow, prison would constitute a more permanent exile and site of containment.

This hardening was interrupted, however, by the reality of prison overcrowding. In the American South, as the formal mechanisms of Jim Crow were replaced by sentencing laws that produced more prisoners, the resulting overcrowding created a crisis, which was then addressed by various forms of clemency and early release. For a brief moment, gubernatorial clemency became a check on the growth of the prison system. In the face of fiscal constraints, Louisiana's corrections officials urged leniency to alleviate overcrowding at the state penitentiary, and the governor warned against "stockpiling" human beings. In the early 1980s, in the wake of court rulings mandating relief of overcrowding in Mississippi's prison and jails, the governor, along with numerous corrections professionals and state legislators, turned to clemency to reduce the prison population.

Yet this reversal proved short-lived, and the practice of clemency waned over the longer term. In the 1970s, white conservatives promoted white fears that desegregation would lead to racial violence by appealing to stereotypes of Black criminality. Led by District Attorney Harry Connick Sr., Louisiana legislators and prosecutors promoted the assumption that those convicted of violent crimes were perpetually dangerous and that rehabilitation was impossible. The Louisiana State Legislature passed mandatory minimum sentencing and three-strikes laws, reducing the latitude for judicial discretion. At the same time, the rise in sentences for life without the possibility of parole after the abolition of the death penalty rendered gubernatorial clemency—now increasingly politicized—the only avenue for release. The same venom that drove harsher sentences infected clemency, and a generation of prisoners who had pled guilty with the understanding that they would be released after ten years and six months watched the promise of freedom dissolve before their eyes. Now facing the possibility of dying in prison for the first time, these prisoners regarded the state's abandonment of the so-called 10/6 rule as a "revolution." The foreclosure of any realistic possibility for release led to low morale, individual acts of resistance, and the potential for collective unrest. Thus, clemency became a battleground between prisoner advocates and tough-on-crime politicians.

MERCY AND ITS CRITICS IN MISSISSIPPI

The combination of white supremacy and the lenient use of clemency was traditional in Mississippi. Governor Ross Barnett, who used Parchman Farm, the Mississippi State Penitentiary, to break the spirit of those who organized challenges to Jim Crow, was relatively generous about granting clemency. Civil rights workers had heard of the notorious Parchman Farm and perceived it as a site of struggle. As Freedom Riders descended on Mississippi with what Senator John Stennis called "the intent to incite riots or create breaches of the peace," they began to crowd the jails.[7] These "misguided knuckleheads" composed of "agitators and pink-to-red minorities" were eventually transferred to Parchman, where "they [would] get a taste of real heat in sunshine that is made even more brilliant when a hoe handle is fitted firmly in their hands."[8] Fred Jones, the warden who advocated the temporary release of certain Black prisoners to record a musical album, warned the Freedom Riders, "We have niggers on death row that'll beat you up and cut you as soon as look at you."[9] In the end, the hoe was not put in the Freedom Riders' hands. Governor Barnett insisted that they be isolated from the other prisoners and subdued by brutal conditions instead.[10] In response to the media's exposure of the protestors' horrifying treatment at Parchman, Barnett retorted, "When people come here and deliberately, willfully and obstinately break the law, you don't expect them to be treated as if at a Saturday afternoon tea, do you?"[11]

Barnett's contempt for the transgressive actions of civil rights activists did not translate into a spiteful punitiveness toward all incarcerated Black people. In contrast to the "agitators" confined at Parchman, Barnett regarded prisoners who worked at the governor's mansion as "white folk's negroes," trusted for their loyalty and subservience. In fact, one source suggests that mansion trusties were offered a pardon if they assassinated civil rights leader Medgar Evers, but instead the trusties sent messages to Evers warning him that he was in danger.[12] By the 1960s, as southern conservatives were railing against activists' efforts to dismantle Jim Crow, the Barnett family defended the use of prison labor at the mansion and presented it as evidence of the affectionate relations between trusted Black people and their white superiors. His wife, Pearl Barnett, insisted that her mansion servants were contented with her gentle supervision, and went so far as to imply that her benevolence disarmed whatever violent proclivities these Black women may have had:

> I got so tired when Ross would make talks in Northeastern colleges, where they would say why do you treat niggers like you do. I had two maids who were convicts in for murder and I would take them to a lake at least four miles from anyone and I frequently get my line tangled when I am fishing and they have to be cut. I did not have a knife. I would tell one of them to bring a sharp knife from the kitchen. They

could have cut me to pieces and I would never have been found but they didn't. If I had treated them badly what do you think they would have done.[13]

Ross Barnett shared more heartwarming stories about his relationship with his mansion servants that suggested his kindly rapport with them. In one interview he said that a "colored servant" told him that the previous night, in their basement room, the trusties had "passed some resolutions" that the governor should wear a white hat a foot taller than anyone else's, so "when you walk in a crowd everybody can see your hat and they will know you are governor. And he said you ought to get some wide silk neckties and put diamonds in them. And when you walk up to people, they will sparkle." The mansion servants knew how to flatter Barnett, and Barnett played his role in return. These trusted servants, who according to Barnett were "practically members of the family before it was over with," were all freed at the end of his term.[14] In keeping with typical defenses of Jim Crow, the Barnetts romanticized their relations with their Black servants; the fact that these servants had all been convicted of killing people magnified the family's generosity and confidence in their own invulnerability.

By the end of his term, Ross Barnett had granted over one thousand ten-day holiday suspensions to prisoners and a total of thirty-two pardons, 268 indefinite suspensions, and eighty-one commutations.[15] In response to criticism from a group of Mississippi attorneys general, Barnett argued that "every civilized country . . . has . . . provided for the power to pardon and . . . grant suspensions to be exercised as an act of grace and humanity. Without such power of clemency to be exercised by some department or functionary of government it would be most imperfect and deficient in its political morality, and in that attribute of the Deity whose judgments are always tempered with mercy."[16]

By the mid-1960s, white conservatives, including political hopefuls and members of law enforcement, expressed mounting discomfort with the governor's godlike prerogative of granting mercy. Increasingly worried about social unrest, critics of gubernatorial clemency stoked the fear of crime and promoted the discourse of law and order. Policemen and sheriffs complained that "quickie releases by pardon or suspension" threatened law enforcement.[17] Civil disobedience was equated with lawlessness, and protestors with "street-roaming thugs."[18] One Mississippian deplored "social slobberers who insist on compassion being shown to the junkies, the dope fiends, the throat slashers, the beatniks, the prostitutes, the homosexuals and the punks. Today, the decent man is practically off the reservation."[19] Governor Paul B. Johnson Jr. (1964–68) echoed fearmongering rhetoric in 1966, denouncing the alleged anarchy unleashed by civil rights protests and the "small bands of hoodlums, Negros and whites, who . . . spawned the whirlwinds of dissension and division, and which caused death and destruction to persons and property."[20] This position did not impede Governor Johnson from releasing every one of his mansion servants at the end of his term, all of whom had been convicted of murder, manslaughter, or armed robbery.[21]

Equally significant is that, throughout the 1960s, Mississippi corrections officials continued to advocate for prison reforms that aimed at rehabilitation, which included practices that allowed for early release. In a 1967 report, Parchman superintendent C. E. Breazeale argued for a more generous use of "good time" and education and job training services for those discharged from prison. Perhaps optimistically if not disingenuously, corrections officials praised their colleagues for shifting attention "from 'punishment' to the rehabilitation of inmates. No longer is the institution operated with economic motivation as the guiding principle," they proclaimed. They looked forward to a day when the prison would no longer be a "'whipping boy' for political campaigns."[22]

In the 1970s, amid a moral panic about drugs, clemencies for drug users were more controversial than those of violent offenders, revealing the fluidity of notions of risk and danger. When Governor John Bell Williams (1968–72) freed twelve first-time offenders who were incarcerated on drug convictions in 1971, the *Clarion-Ledger* argued that in these cases clemency was an insult to law enforcement and described "dope pushers" as "the lowest form of criminal and deadly enemies of society."[23] Williams responded, "I felt these boys were worth saving."[24] Echoing cries for law and order, a grand jury urged the state legislature to "eliminate the practice of swinging open the gates at Parchman at the end of every administration and flooding society with convicted criminals."[25] According to a 1972 poll, 83 percent of Mississippi respondents believed that the power to pardon should be removed from the governor and placed in the hands of an elected board.[26] But the editors at the *Delta Democrat-Times* defended the governor's actions, saying that drug laws, especially as they pertained to users rather than "pushers," were excessively punitive.[27] At the end of his term, Williams granted full pardons to the workers at the governor's mansion, all of whom had been convicted of murder or manslaughter and most of whom ended up serving fewer than ten years in prison.[28]

Wisecracks made about this practice reveal that clemency now signaled poor judgment rather than noble humanitarianism. When Williams assumed office, he quipped that his new home should be called Pardon Me, presumably to take a jab at Barnett's magnanimous pardon policies. After Williams granted clemency to the drug offenders, one journalist joked that the mansion should be called Pot Luck.[29] Although these barbed witticisms were entertaining, other rhetoric was dead serious, as when a conservative politician condemned a later governor's "bleeding heart [i.e., liberal] programs" of "leniency to criminals." The politicization of clemency meant that its days were numbered, even in Mississippi.[30]

ENDING LOUISIANA'S 10/6 RULE

In Louisiana, moral panics about drugs, crime, and desegregation lit a brushfire that scorched the terrain of the clemency process. At the height of the sit-in movement, the administration of Governor Jimmie H. Davis (1960–64) helped to ensure that the Black struggle for freedom would produce more criminals by introducing new bills explicitly aimed at "Negro sit-downs," such as laws that broadened the definitions of resisting an officer and "criminal mischief," as well as making it a crime to enter property "after having been forbidden to do so" or to "obstruct public passageways."[31] Arguing that the Civil Rights Act of 1964 had exacerbated crime, the Citizens' Council of Greater New Orleans and the Southern Louisiana Citizens' Council warned that desegregation would unleash attacks on white girls by Black boys and urged Governor John J. McKeithen (1964–72) to "sign the death warrants for all convicted rapists now confined to death row at Angola," the Louisiana State Penitentiary. Those would be "the only hope we have of being able to walk the streets again without fear of bodily harm."[32] Yet Edwin Edwards (1972–80) was elected governor with the campaign promise that he would sign any clemency recommendation made by the Louisiana Pardon Board.[33] Clemencies continued apace under Edwards and were not at the forefront of public scrutiny, but during the 1970s the reactionary political climate motivated the Louisiana legislature to construct new barriers to prisoners' freedom, closing off avenues of release long before it became politically fashionable in other states.

Clemency had been so common in Louisiana that it was considered a "legalistic ritual." The practice began to be eroded after the Supreme

Court's 1972 decision in *Furman v. Georgia*, which declared the death penalty, as it was practiced, unconstitutional.[34] As a result, people on death row were resentenced to life without the possibility of parole. State officials would not take the risk that someone who had been on death row would be released after ten years and six months, so they abolished the long-standing rule.[35] Meanwhile, according to criminal justice scholar Burk Foster, "the Louisiana legislature was finding new ways of insuring that these men would have plenty of company growing old."[36] Determined to halt the "early release" of prisoners, Louisiana prosecutors, led by Harry Connick Sr., lobbied the legislature to pass increasingly punitive sentencing laws.[37] In a trend that was repeated around the nation, prosecutors, adopting a popular "tough-on-crime" stance, became a well-organized and powerful political force.[38] They translated a punitive ideology into concrete changes in sentencing by raising the specter of criminals on the loose. Connick warned, "Early release is assured to each inmate, regardless of who he is or what crime he committed, regardless of his criminal record or his dangerous, even homicidal propensities."[39] A report authored by the Louisiana District Attorneys' Association argued that the "credibility of our system is damaged by what appears to be a systematic early release of prisoners," adding, "We believe that many people sentenced to Angola can never be rehabilitated in or out of the system. . . . It is our position, therefore, that the system should be based on the theory that sanctions should be imposed with punishment and/or incapacitation in mind."[40] As a result of suspended sentences and commutations, not enough people were serving enough time in prison; discretion was tantamount to freedom for dangerous criminals. District Attorney Rick Bryant declared that clemency for Wilbert Rideau, the award-winning editor of Angola's magazine, the *Angolite*, would "send a message loud and clear to every inmate that all you need to do is be rehabilitated, regardless of the crime. Sentences would mean nothing anymore."[41] In sum, rehabilitation was simultaneously impossible to achieve, too easy to achieve, and a ruse manipulated by undeserving prisoners.

In quick succession, the state legislature adopted a series of sentencing laws that increased the number of crimes punishable with a mandatory life sentence without the possibility of parole from two to seven; eliminated parole eligibility for anyone with a life sentence; and provided that second-degree murderers would not be eligible for parole for twenty years, which it then raised to a minimum of forty years. By the late 1970s Louisiana was the most parole-restrictive state in the nation. It was one of only five states with a general ban on parole for lifers, and it had excluded parole for a wider range of offenses than any other state.[42]

Connick and his followers pushed through habitual offender laws, colloquially known as three-strikes laws, which imposed draconian punishments on those with a second or third conviction for any offense, including minor crimes such as shoplifting or drug possession.[43] He portrayed incarcerated people as preternaturally dangerous and the public as their future victims: "We know that when a career criminal comes out he's going to revert to his former way of life. And that means dead people—dead innocent people. It means victims of armed robbery. It means victims of rape."[44] His position was the antithesis of the rehabilitative ideal, as well as an admonition that prison walls were the only guarantee of safety against mortal danger. Connick advocated a law that the "good time" habitual offenders accumulated by keeping a clean record while in prison could not be used to reduce their sentences. State Senator William Brown, who supported the law, upended the assumption that good behavior should lead to early release: "I resent the thought that if we don't treat them with what they think is proper respect they'll be bad prisoners. I'd rather them be all bad prisoners in the prison than pretty bad citizens on the street."[45] In rejecting the customary practice of 10/6, Connick asserted that "'career criminals'" were using a string of loopholes to "form a 'corridor to freedom.'"[46] By closing such corridors, Connick and his allies essentially resentenced prisoners by both extending their incarceration indefinitely and negating their personal development.

As the legislature blocked prisoners from release with mandatory sentencing, longer sentences, and reduced opportunities for parole, gubernatorial clemency became all the more important for prisoners. In 1978, 84 percent of those seeking commutation did so because they were ineligible for parole.[47] State Representative Johnnie A. Jones of Baton Rouge lamented these changes at a banquet hosted by the Lifers Association at Angola: "An eye for an eye is one thing, but keeping a man locked up behind bars forever, and ever, and ever . . . is something entirely different. It was never intended to be this way."[48] Even the relatively liberal Governor Edwards of Louisiana, who served for a total of sixteen years between 1972 and 1996, became more cautious about granting clemency, a finding that the Governor's Pardon, Parole, and Rehabilitation Commission attributed to his "political accountability." Although a 1978 study found that the Pardon Board recommended clemency in 60 percent of cases and the governor approved 61 percent of them, it said that Edwards's "hesitancy to grant clemency . . . indicates that he is very sensitive to public opinion and does not appear to be greatly influenced by factors other than the seriousness of the crime."[49] Prisoners expressed concern about the politicization of clemency. "We're all aware that most self-righteous citizens of Louisiana think of us as menaces to society, not individuals," commented an Angola journalist; he worried that the Pardon Board would succumb to pressure and "become overly cautious."[50] As early as 1974, prisoners noticed that clemency requests were increasingly being rejected. Of the 104 petitions submitted in January of that year, eighty-three were "flatly denied." "This is ridiculous!" Robert Jackson of *The Lifer* exclaimed, but at least, "for the first time in the history of the state, equal treatment [is] rendered to all prisoners, black, white, rich and poor. The Pardon Board did not give anyone a damn thing . . . and everyone the same thing—disappointment."[51]

Conservative white southerners propagated the fear of crime by expressing their views in extreme language. Members of law enforcement were particularly sensational in their claims. In 1980, a district attorney alleged that as a result of the clemencies of Mississippi governor Charles Finch (1976–80), "murderers, armed robbers . . . are being put back on the streets of Mississippi," and the press portrayed the governor as a "wild man hopped up on pills, totally out of touch with reality, issuing incredible edicts and orders like the Mad Hatter."[52] But the state attorney general supported the governor, arguing that clemency was a tradition in the state and, moreover, explaining that it was precisely crucial to public safety: "If you are going to work prisoners in the governor's mansion, they've got to have a way to get out. That's their reward. It's not safe otherwise."[53]

AN "EXTREME PUBLIC EMERGENCY": OVERCROWDING
AND THE POLITICS OF CLEMENCY

During the 1970s, correctional systems and criminal justice in Mississippi and Louisiana were, as Lydia Pelot-Hobbs notes about Louisiana, "pulled back and forth between the competing ideologies of liberal reformism and law and order."[54] While some politicians and law enforcement officials expressed a growing skepticism of clemency, the issue had not yet become the third rail of politics. Southern governors still granted clemency regularly, and they began to consider liberal prison reforms in response to the mounting problem of prison overcrowding. Though calls for law and order were becoming increasingly strident, neither the public nor government officials perceived constructing more prisons as an obvious solution to the ballooning prison population. Throughout the country, fiscal conservatism and the tax revolts of the late 1970s and early 1980s rendered additional prison construction unpopular and untenable.[55] This tension between get-tough politics and fiscal austerity reveals contingencies that interrupted a seemingly inexorable shift toward mass incarceration. In sum, "putting people in prison was easy, but building [prisons] was not."[56]

Nationally, between 1975 and 1985, the imprisoned population increased more than it had during the previous fifty years. Significantly, by 1981, prisons in thirty-six states were operating under court orders or engaged in litigation related to the conditions created by overcrowding. Citing malnutrition, poor health care, violence, and other indignities, prisoners and their lawyers throughout the United States successfully argued that the "totality of conditions" in these prisons amounted to "cruel and unusual punishment," which was banned by the Bill of Rights. Although it was difficult to prove direct causal links between overcrowding and other prison problems, prisoners and their lawyers convinced judges that overcrowding revealed or aggravated underlying problems in prison operations. Overcrowding became a useful lever to challenge a suite of abuses and forced judicial intervention in prison management.[57]

Prisons in the South were no exception. Beginning in the 1970s, a number of southern states were facing court orders to remedy those conditions, producing a crisis in penal administration.[58] When a 1975 federal court ordered Parchman to alleviate its overcrowding, the state legislature approved the aggressive use of parole and modest executive clemency to reduce the number of prisoners.[59] This solution did not sit well with all penal officials, some of whom fought to tighten furlough rules.[60] But throughout the 1970s discussions of the problem were as likely to urge early release and decriminalization as they were to call for more prison construction.[61] By 1983 at least twenty-one states had adopted early release, work release, and alternatives to incarceration to reduce their inmate populations.[62] Some scholars have argued that the corrections professionals had much to gain by increasing prison capacity—not only more funding, but the growth of their own bureaucratic power. But calls for decarceration came from prison officials as well.[63] According to the *New York Times*, southern prison administrators urged their governors to adopt liberal reforms in order to relieve the crisis, and unanimously endorsed recommendations to release "inmates not considered dangerous" and to decriminalize minor offenses such as drunkenness, drug use, and prostitution. William D. Leeke, the director of the South Carolina Department of Corrections, admitted, "Many of you won't like this, but the hard line in law enforcement is forcing us into more liberal policies." These professionals asserted their belief in a "correctional" rather than "punitive" approach to criminal justice and suggested that police, prosecutors, and courts were insufficiently concerned with prison conditions. An economist at the convention declared, "The system's clients cannot vote, and the society it serves probably does not care. Perhaps even worse is the facile exploitation of the crime issue by politicians."[64]

Mississippi was relatively successful in using clemency to relieve prison overcrowding, in large part because Governor William Winter (1980–84) defended the practice as common sense. From 1904 to 1970, Parchman had housed between eighteen hundred and twenty-five hundred prisoners; by 1995, its population was sixty-five hundred.[65] In 1979, when the state legislature approved an $18 million construction budget to build modern prisons, Ron Welch, the lawyer representing the prisoners in the long court battle to improve conditions, lamented, "We've gone from feudal to fortress."[66] "We can't keep building up at Parchman," warned Lula C. Dorsey, a Black woman who grew up in a family of sharecroppers and became a civil rights activist before serving as associate director of the reform-oriented Southern Coalition of Jails and Prisons.[67] Faced with the overcrowding crisis, circuit judge Darwin M. Maples wrote to Governor Winter, "I would have no objection to you and the Department of Corrections *releasing any person I have ever sentenced*," and a state senator suggested that the governor release people sixty years of age and older.[68]

In 1980 the Mississippi legislature relaxed parole laws to ease overcrowding and approved a $650,000 program to provide job training and placement to four hundred prisoners released early.[69] In 1982 Governor Winter observed in a speech to the Southern States Correctional Association that spending money on corrections did not attract much public support and asserted, "We can no longer deny certain realities—the old philosophies of 'out-of-sight, out-of-mind' and 'warehousing' of inmates are simply too costly." Winter argued that every effort should be made to reduce the number of people entering prison in the first place, reduce their length of stay once incarcerated, and to "try to stop this illogical wasteful building of a super prison system . . . so that we can raise further the level of skills held by our people and give them the types of jobs they deserve to enjoy the quality of life that is available in our section of the country."[70]

In Mississippi the most vocal resistance to early release came from sheriffs and prosecutors. "I'll never agree . . . and I don't believe many sheriffs will," proclaimed one county sheriff.[71] When nearly half of the 230 prisoners Winter released between 1981 and 1982 were found to have been originally convicted of violent crimes, a state senate committee urged the governor to consider prisoners' criminal backgrounds more carefully before authorizing their release.[72] Mississippians critical of gubernatorial clemency complained, "What about our rights as law-abiding citizens?" Winter responded firmly, asserting that he was not "coddling criminals."[73] Instead, he insisted, his interest in prison reforms, such as alternatives to incarceration, was aimed at making more room for incorrigible and violent offenders.[74] Rather than indulging or fanning fear, however, Governor Winter methodically explained the state's predicament. Faced with court orders to remedy prison overcrowding, he explained, "we have done the only responsible thing we could do, and that is to work with judges and district attorneys to determine which prisoners can most safely be released early." Echoing assumptions that were commonplace throughout the twentieth century, Winter rejected the idea that releasing prisoners posed a risk to the public. "We shall undoubtedly make some mistakes. . . . Of the 300 or so inmates to whom I have given suspensions in the last year and a half, only two have had to be sent back to the penitentiary for the commission of a subsequent crime. That is probably a better percentage than you will find in the population as a whole."[75] When a constituent accused Winter of "early release for rapists, murderers, and armed robbers" after a formerly incarcerated person committed assault and burglary, the governor replied, "I checked in to see how one of these criminals got out of Parchman and found that there had been no parole or early release. He served the time the court had given him."[76]

Corrections professionals in Mississippi advocated reducing the prison population through sensible approaches to decarceration. In 1981, Governor Winter held a three-day symposium, Mississippi's Prison Problems and Opportunities, which attracted nationally known, reform-minded criminologists from outside the South to consider the question, "What new legislative proposals can be passed to reduce the prison population while at the same time not excessively endangering the safety of the citizens of Mississippi?" On the table were alternatives to incarceration, work release, and restitution sentencing. The chairman of the Mississippi State Parole Board expressed disapproval of the law that denied "good time" to "habitual offenders." Startlingly, from today's perspective, the Mississippi

Department of Corrections issued a statement that "prison space must be viewed as a limited resource" and that alternatives to incarceration must be created so prison populations did not exceed capacity. Participants at the symposium were generally opposed to expanding the facilities at Parchman; if new facilities had to be built, they should be "constructed near urban centers."[77] Criminologist M. Kay Harris, who studied and recommended alternatives to incarceration, suggested that "the authority of Governors to commute sentences or issue pardons could be utilized more extensively," as had already been done in at least ten states across the country.[78] Notably, prisoners, too, tracked this trend; the *Angolite*'s editors argued that "against the backdrop of the rest of the nation's penal practices, the exhaustion of Louisiana's resources . . . in the name of achieving safety by literally sealing away every offender is reduced to little more than the pursuit of an expensive illusion."[79]

In Louisiana a crisis in prison overcrowding was the backdrop for the increasing politicization of clemency, but the fate of the practice remained uncertain. Angola had been designed to house twenty-six hundred people, but by 1975, it housed four thousand. As sentences were lengthened and the number of people who were paroled declined, Louisiana's prisons became increasingly crowded. The director of corrections, Elayn Hunt, estimated that the prison population was growing by 20 percent per year.[80] In June 1975, federal district judge E. Gordon West ordered massive changes to Angola and prohibited new transfers there. Declaring that the penitentiary was in a state of "extreme public emergency," he argued that its poor medical care and religious and racial discrimination, as well as overcrowding, not only "shock[ed] the conscience" but flagrantly violated constitutional requirements. The court ordered that Angola's population be reduced to its original capacity.[81] The legislature initially chose not to provide more housing at Angola, opting instead to fund the expansion of the Louisiana State University football stadium, but injections of federal funds through Law Enforcement Assistance Administration grants and the growth in state revenues due to a jump in oil prices made monies available.[82] The Department of Corrections advocated for a decentralization plan that would open smaller "regional prisons" focused on work release and educational and therapeutic programming and would be located closer to urban centers in order to attract qualified staff and provide greater access to family and friends; the department even envisioned closing Angola.[83] The state scrambled to find new properties, but local communities protested, fearing that dangerous criminals "would not only make their communities unsafe but would also lower their property taxes."[84] "We cannot continue to just stockpile human beings in one huge prison," Governor Edwards insisted; "to do so is not in the best interests of the public, the employees, or the inmates."[85] Lifers at Angola urged the early release of prisoners and expressed hope that Governor Edwards would abide by his promise to pardon "any prisoner recommended by Mrs. Hunt, with very few exceptions."[86] Like corrections administrators in Mississippi, members of Edwards's Pardon, Parole, and Rehabilitation Commission reiterated that sentences were too long and incarceration should be the "sentence of last resort," even for those convicted of violent offenses.[87]

Prison officials, too, favored decentralization and release over constructing new facilities at Angola. Associate Warden Lloyd Hoyle was emphatic: "We've never had any idea of expanding. It's too d——big now."[88] Superintendents and wardens supported the liberal use of clemency, arguing that they observed prisoners' behavior and personal growth and understood the practical problems resulting from low prisoner morale. When delegates from the state legislature visited Angola in 1974 to hear a presentation by a panel of men serving life sentences, the visitors asked how they could be guaranteed that former prisoners would not commit more crimes on release. It was the warden, C. Murray Henderson, who responded, "Guarantee? Who can offer guarantees? Hell, I can't even guarantee that I myself won't commit a crime in the next moment . . . and you can't either." He advised that sentences should not exceed than five or ten years.[89] As Angola's prison population continued to swell, prisoners urged Louisiana state officials to follow the example of Mississippi and establish a review board to determine which prisoners could safely be released early. They regarded this measure as "a solution for the political game-playing plaguing the system."[90] Ross Maggio, the warden of Angola from 1975 to 1984, did not let the fact that he had been recently taken captive at knifepoint by prisoners attempting to escape dissuade him from his conviction that "if someone told us that they want to release, let's say 400 people, then we could do that."[91]

To support the argument for early release, Rev. James Stovall, a reformer who served on the Pardon, Parole, and Rehabilitation Commission, reminded Governor Edwards that "such an approach is not without precedent in Louisiana." Under the 1958 Forgotten Man Committee of Governor Earl Long (1956–60), "several hundred inmates were released. There was no outcry against this policy and no effort to reverse the decision."[92] A lifetime advocate of civil rights, Stovall, head of the Louisiana Interchurch

Conference and eventual director of the Louisiana Coalition against Racism and Nazism, had the governor's ear. In 1984 Edwards heeded Stovall's advice and appointed a new eighty-member Forgotten Man Committee of his own to study the cases of the approximately fourteen hundred people then serving life sentences and recommend criminal justice reforms to the Louisiana State Legislature, in part to provide political cover and begin removing the governor from the pardon process. Referring to Earl Long's commission a generation earlier, Edwards remarked, "Out of that came new and fresh voices speaking up for those whose voices had been silenced by years of incarceration, despair, and isolation."[93] Judge Matthew Braniff pointedly criticized this position when he sentenced a purse-snatcher to forty years in prison: "I'm tired of all this talk about forgotten men. The forgotten men are the victims in these cases."[94] In an effort not to alienate conservative voters, Edwards used the language of fiscal responsibility: "My concern is that if we don't get away from this lock-'em-up business, we're going to go bankrupt. That's what's bringing about this consideration for change. It's not do-gooders."[95] By the 1980s over half the people confined at Angola were barred from parole. They understood that the hostile political climate had put the clemency process into a "state of paralysis"; it had become a "sensitive political issue, a development that has ended its role as a meaningful release mechanism and contributed significantly to prison overcrowding."[96]

So why did these initiatives to decrease prison populations in Louisiana, Mississippi, and other states outside the South come to naught? The personal discretion that was the engine of clemency came under attack from both the Left and the Right. In 1984 the US Congress passed the Federal Sentencing Reform Act, which ended the indeterminate sentences that had allowed early release based on assessments of rehabilitation. The law was originally supported by prison reformers because it aimed to create fairness, consistency, equality, accountability, and transparency in sentencing federal offenders. Conceived in a "kinder, gentler time," it had been developed by "liberal advocates" who protested racial disparities in sentencing and suspected "that judges used their lavish discretionary power in prejudiced ways."[97] But in practice the mandatory sentencing guidelines ignored or rejected prisoners' capacity for rehabilitation, adding more bricks to the prison walls.[98] As Naomi Murakawa explains, the act "did not contain a philosophy of punishment; it merely distributed punishment uniformly for all like cases."[99] In other words, it responded to disparate critiques of discretion as harsh, lenient, or arbitrary. Between its inception and its final form, it "had become encrusted with provisions added at different times, reflecting diverse ideological and political beliefs, and sometimes pointing in different policy directions."[100] Rigid sentencing guidelines reflected not only a fear of crime but a suspicion of the discretion that is essential for early release.[101] By prioritizing greater predictability and uniformity of sentencing over increasing prisoners' chances of being freed, politicians chose the equality of the graveyard over the equality of the vineyard.[102]

Changes in federal sentencing laws and in public sentiment reinforced political shifts on the state level. In 1984 Mississippi tightened its parole law. The same year that Governor Winter released hundreds of inmates, half of whom had been convicted of violent crimes, the Mississippi Legislature killed a bill to speed up inmates' release. By the mid-1980s, discussions of prison overcrowding shifted almost entirely toward building more prisons, and rehabilitation and early release were pushed off the list of potential solutions.[103] Whereas prisoners' rights advocates viewed overcrowding as a problem of too many prisoners rather than too little space, punitive hard-liners exploited the problem of crowding as an opportunity to build more prisons and put even more people behind bars. As policies that were later incorporated into conservative Republican Newt Gingrich's Contract with America were proposed and publicized, white Mississippians increasingly linked putative leniency toward people convicted of crimes with liberal social welfare policies.[104] A veterinarian from Biloxi wrote to the *Sun-Herald*, "The government has been telling people for generations now that they are not responsible for taking care of themselves. Witness the ever-expanding entitlement programs, teenage pregnancy, and certain segments of society saying that because of the color of their skin, society or government should be taking care of them and require nothing in return."[105] Although the crime rate actually decreased between 1975 and 1985, 84 percent of Americans polled believed it was rising.[106] In a fallacy of circular reasoning, the exploding prison population was now portrayed as objective evidence of growing criminality rather than the result of increasingly harsh sentencing.[107]

A turning point came in 1983, when clemency was a central issue in Louisiana's gubernatorial campaign. Edwin Edwards, the liberal Democrat who had served as governor from 1972 to 1980, was running against incumbent Republican David Treen, who had been parsimonious with clemency and had no intention of changing course. Republicans, seizing on a topic that fit into their campaign message of law and order, exploited Edwards's vigorous use of clemency. They suggested that he was too liberal in granting pardons and corrupted the process by signing pardons as favors to political supporters and lawyer friends. When Treen first campaigned in 1979, he raised the specter of career criminals on the loose. The contrast with Edwards was immediately apparent. The Board of Pardons' approval rate went down to less than one-third of what it had been just a few months before.[108] Jack Wardlaw, a columnist for the *Times-Picayune*, noted, "The framers of the state constitution gave the governor the right of clemency for good reason: to prevent injustices. Treen is right to use it cautiously and with regard for public safety. He would surely be wrong not to use it at all." When Treen signed only five of the three hundred applications the Pardon Board had approved, Wardlaw called him to task. While clemency had the potential to be corrupted, "going to the other extreme can also be an abuse of constitutional power."[109] Rev. James Stovall asserted that Treen's inaction was a failure of duty: "When the Pardon Board makes recommendations based on their comprehensive, systematic study, they have fulfilled their purpose. It seems to me the governor should then exercise his constitutional authority and grant a significant number of their recommendations."[110]

Treen harped on Edward's clemency record and instructed his staff to expose whatever new transgressions were committed by those to whom Edwards had granted clemency. Treen's campaign advertisements listed offenders by categories, such as "124 murderers, 62 rapists," and then reduced the emotionally charged issue of clemency to a neat score: "Edwards, 1,181; Treen, 34."[111] This emphasis on clemency took a strange and tragic turn when Nolan Edwards, an attorney and the brother of candidate Edwin Edwards, was murdered by a former client, whom Governor Edwards had pardoned in the last days of his second term. The client, who had been convicted for a drug offense, had been free on parole on a drug sentence when Edwards had granted him clemency. Despite the murder of his brother, Edwards defended clemency: "The greatest man-god who ever walked on this earth died on the cross to pardon people's sins."[112] Edwards won the election with 60 percent of the vote and the support of the Police Chiefs Association, suggesting that a liberal clemency record was not a fatal political liability.[113] According to Angola lifer Wilbert Rideau, for "perhaps the first time in history" the entire prison population and staff watched the gubernatorial election results on television. For a moment, the "seething despair eating away at the Louisiana State Penitentiary was quieted overnight as hope, the balm of the prison world, was restored."[114]

Prisoners worried about the ramifications of the rightward swing in political rhetoric and vigorously contested it. While conservative legislators and their constituents equated the gains won by the civil rights movement with crime, prisoners and their allies equated their struggle for release with those of freedom fighters. Rev. Caton Brooks, a veteran civil rights activist and a close associate of Martin Luther King Jr., spoke to a group of lifers at Angola in 1974. In spite of the sentencing laws that were erecting more barriers to release, Brooks proclaimed that "the men and women shackled behind bars throughout this nation can, through unity, prayer and effort, like Samson, bring these walls down and be free at last. Just imagine . . . free at last!"[115] As they witnessed the erosion of clemency, imprisoned people protested the precarity of their futures.

3 The House of the Dying

The Decline of Clemency under the
New Jim Crow

The case of Wilbert Rideau, the award-winning editor of the *Angolite*, the magazine of the Louisiana State Penitentiary at Angola, embodies the mercurial nature of risk and redemption, the limits of mercy, and the shift from paternalism to punitiveness. At the age of nineteen, Rideau was convicted in 1961 for the Lake Charles, Louisiana, murder of a white woman named Julia Ferguson during a bank robbery gone wrong. An all-white jury convicted him of first-degree murder, and Rideau was sentenced to death.[1] Rideau appealed twice, first on the grounds that his confession had aired on local television before the trial, then because the prosecution had eliminated twenty jurors who expressed discomfort with the death penalty.[2] District Attorney Frank Salter claimed in 1964 that the crime was "the most cold-blooded, brutal, maddog murder I have ever known."[3] At Rideau's third trial in 1970, another all-white jury took eight minutes to sentence Rideau to death.[4] After over a decade on death row, Rideau's death sentence was commuted to a sentence of life without the possibility of parole (LWOP) as a result of the US Supreme Court case *Furman v. Georgia*, which declared the death penalty to be cruel and unusual punishment, and he and forty-five others on Angola's death row were released into the prison's general population.[5]

During his decades of incarceration at Angola, Rideau became the first Black editor of the *Angolite*. In 1977 Billy Sinclair, a white prisoner and jailhouse lawyer whom Rideau had met while they were both on death row, joined Rideau as coeditor. Under their leadership the monthly went from "the equivalent of a boarding school newsletter" to an unflinching and rigorous piece of muckraking journalism.[6] Since then, the *Angolite* has won seven nominations for a National Magazine Award and Rideau has won numerous honors for his journalism, books, and a documentary film. Due to his good behavior and accomplishments, Rideau was allowed to speak to public audiences around the state and to appear on television; most remarkably, he and Sinclair interviewed Warren Burger, the chief justice of the US Supreme Court, on ABC's *Nightline.*[7] In 1993, a *Life* magazine journalist called Rideau "the most rehabilitated prisoner in America."[8]

Throughout these years, Rideau fought for clemency, his only chance at freedom. He applied for the first time in 1973, pointing out that he was already overdue for release based on the custom of the 10/6 rule, the commutation of a life sentence after an inmate had served ten years and six months. As he remained confined in prison, other lifers were freed.[9] When his fifth petition was denied, Rideau had been incarcerated for more than thirty years. By then the normative outlook on clemency and rehabilitation had shifted, and Rideau's fate was defined not by his growth, good deeds, or remorse but by the moment of his original offense. Governor Buddy Roemer (1988–92) stressed that "rehabilitation without freedom may be all that Rideau can ever hope for. . . . So far, this crime was worse than what happened to Wilbert Rideau. He's still alive."[10]

Rideau recognized that penal policies and practices had changed dramatically over time. "When I came into the prison system, they were stressing rehabilitation. I've done everything they've asked. I've served more time than 99 percent of the inmates in this state, and I've accomplished more than all of them. But now society has changed the rules. I'm being judged according to the guy who robbed a supermarket yesterday."[11] Rideau emphasized that he was not the same person he had been when he committed the crime: "The only violent act of my life . . . was done when I was a teenager."[12] Focusing on the "nature of the crime" left little room for considering rehabilitation and revealed the plasticity of prison's central purpose. If the "heinousness" of the crime, a classification that cannot be objectively determined, was the primary metric for assessing a prisoner's chance of release, then any proof of rehabilitation would be futile.[13] Indeed, District Attorney Rick Bryant said matter-of-factly, "When it comes to murder, . . . then rehabilitation is not an issue."[14] Dora McCain, a surviving victim of Rideau's robbery, contended that Rideau "wasn't sent [to prison] for rehabilitation. He was sent there for punishment until the day he dies."[15]

As Angola's long-termers came to realize that they might die in prison, they challenged the decline of clemency and urged mercy. The individualized nature of clemency, its demand for supplication, reliance on benevolence, and emphasis on the self-improvement of the petitioner over structural critiques of the prison system might make it seem an unlikely object of political organizing. Black radicals in the 1970s, who considered all incarcerated African Americans to be political prisoners, were suspicious of a process that required personal testimonies of remorse and transformation. "The prison cannot gain a victory over the political prisoner because he has nothing to be rehabilitated from or to," wrote Huey Newton.[16] But at Angola prison, men who saw the customary practice of clemency dissolve before their eyes collectively mobilized to demand clemency as an entitlement. As Angola turned into a "graveyard for the living dead," prisoners understood the potential permanence of their incarceration as a fundamental and catastrophic change in the state's carceral regime and sought to restore clemency. What had been discretionary was now demanded as a right.

THE USABLE PAST: PRISONERS ORGANIZE
FOR CLEMENCY IN LOUISIANA

People incarcerated in Louisiana paid close attention to the shifts in political winds. Initially, 1972 appeared to be a year of hope for those confined to prison. In 1971, after four Angola prisoners filed a civil lawsuit protesting the lack of medical services, unsanitary conditions, racial segregation, and abuse by guards, conditions inside Angola began to improve. Elayn Hunt, a progressive reformer who was appointed to direct the Louisiana Department of Corrections, eliminated the use of inmate guards, closed the notorious solitary confinement "hot house," and relaxed restrictions on prisoners' correspondence.[17] But as conditions within the prison became more humane, the chances of release began to recede. Until the 1980s clemency had been a commonplace practice used by both segregationist and liberal governors.[18] Then the passage of draconian crime bills eliminating parole signaled lawmakers' determination to reverse course. As criminal justice scholar Burk Foster puts it, "within less than a decade Louisiana went from turning all lifers loose in ten-and-a-half years to keeping virtually all of them in prison for their natural lives."[19] Prisoners were aware that their chances at freedom were being snuffed out by "get-tough" life sentences meted out for political rather than penological reasons.[20] In this context, clemency became a unique and crucial tool; increasingly, applications for clemency were for the shortening of a sentence for those who were no longer eligible for parole.[21] It was an uphill battle. Asserting that it was "too easy to avoid punishment," Governor David C. Treen (1980–84) declared when he assumed office, "It's going to be tough to get a pardon from me." Significantly, Treen acknowledged that "he wasn't worried about tradition."[22] During his term he issued only 181 acts of clemency.[23] When asked whether his reluctance to use the clemency power would result in more violence within the prison, he responded, "I would rather have the danger within prison walls than on our streets and in our communities."[24] Together with legislative changes, Treen's policy led to an exponential rise in the number of lifers at Angola. In 1972 Angola held only 193 prisoners serving for their natural life; by 1982 the number had multiplied to 1,084.[25]

Given the suddenness of this reversal, many prisoners at Angola, sharing the collective memory of a different epoch and conducting historical research to validate their claims, mobilized for executive redress. They mined the penitentiary archives to show the long tradition of clemency in Louisiana. The *Angolite* editors quoted a letter penned by Henry L. Fuqua in 1917, when he was the prison's general manager, declaring that clemency was a long-standing policy, "interwoven" with the criminal legal system, and constituted a "bilateral contract." Although Rideau described Fuqua as "more like a kindly slaveowner than a prison warden," his account provided a usable past that could serve the future for those incarcerated at Angola.[26]

Significantly, although no wrongdoer has a legal right to clemency, Angola prisoners who were aware of the earlier custom argued for it as though it were an entitlement. In pointed reference to what had been Louisiana tradition under previous governors, members of Angola's Lifers Association, including Walter Watson who had gone on tour with the Traveling Ambassadors musical group back in 1968, formed a Forgotten Men Committee that invited legislators and the state attorney general to speak with prisoners about their plight.[27] Prison journalists tracked changes in state laws and walked their readers through the labyrinth of new obstacles to release. Lifer Ron Wikberg described the "unique" situation of these sentenced to LWOP who "have no law governing their sentences—while ALL other prisoners have laws governing and providing for their incarceration." Almost all of these lifers were originally sentenced under the old 10/6 rule.[28] This "rare class" of prisoners, whom Wikberg described as cast outside the law, had no possibility of release. Significantly, Wikberg identified "forgotten men" as a *class* rather than as isolated individuals, and until the decline of clemency they were relatively few.[29] A piece in the *Angolite* featuring the long-termers argued,

> Society undoubtedly has a right to expect its full measure of punishment and retribution—and it created a justice system to carry out that right. But in so doing, it created a fundamental responsibility for that system to adhere to its own law. . . . The 10/6 law was part of the Louisiana justice system for 53 years. The legislature of 1926 did not contemplate the mood of the public today or the political mileage that would be made off law 'n order politics of this era. . . . Laws are made to be durable, not changed like soiled underwear.[30]

Prisoners asserted that, far from being an example of lawlessness and corruption, clemency was part of the long-established and legitimate legal system. Prisoners contended that the state had "ignored all testimony, documentation, and statistical showings that the practice of releasing lifers after ten years and six months was so ingrained in Louisiana, so much a traditional part of the criminal justice system, that every defendant pleading guilty to a life sentence had a clear and undeniable reasonable expectation to be released after serving 10½ years," at least if that person had been sentenced before 1972.[31]

Echoing the language of Fuqua, prisoners considered clemency the fulfillment of a contract. They documented cases in which prisoners such as Joseph White were told that if they kept their nose clean, they'd likely be released after ten years. White, convicted of murder in 1962, worked in the cannery, then as a clerk in the education department; he acquired a high school diploma, participated in inmate organizations, and was trusted to be an outside speaker. A prisoner-journalist framed the situation in contractual language: "The system urged White to do good and achieve, and he would be rewarded with release from prison. That was the bargain struck between the two. White lived up to his end of the bargain but the system didn't live up to its end."[32] After going before the pardon board several times, White's life sentence was reduced to sixty years, of which he would now have to serve twenty in order to be considered for parole. "I feel that

I had a reasonable expectation to freedom after serving 10½ years under the old law," White said. "After all, that was the law. You kept a good conduct record and tried to accomplish something and the state rewarded you. . . . I was waiting for the doors to open. But they never did."[33] Herman Smith, who eventually became one of Angola's most respected jailhouse lawyers, challenged his own protracted incarceration in similar terms: "I did what was expected of me and now I feel the system is obligated to respect the law no matter how uncomfortable they feel the law may be. . . . The law means nothing unless the system has the guts to enforce it. That's the law. I believe in it. I've paid with 15 years of my life for violating the law. The system is now abusing me by violating the law itself."[34] Prisoners cast themselves as following the law and state officials as disregarding it.

Those who argued that the lengthening of sentences was a betrayal of traditional practices emphasized that they had fulfilled their end of the bargain by keeping good conduct records and improving themselves. The language they used for rehabilitation was not "top-down rhetoric that promotes individual responsibilization," as critics of rehabilitation models proposed by prison authorities have suggested; rather, prisoners articulated self-improvement as a form of personal fulfillment and collective betterment, a way of finding meaning and purpose as well as a modicum of control over their chances of release.[35] In this context, personal transformation was a means of self-determination. Prisoner Bill Brown asserted, "Since the inmate has to spend a certain amount of time in the institution, he would be showing a degree of intelligence by making time serve him instead of serving time."[36] Rideau and Sinclair observed,

> We unfortunately find ourselves caught in a period of time in which the mood of the public is ugly and vindictive and the cry is to literally bury us all beneath tons o[f] concrete cemented by hate, a cry that presupposes that we are all irrevocably evil and dangerous and incapable of ever being anything different, beyond redemption and not even worth the effort. There is little, if any, compassion in the way they see and feel about us as a class of people. We can cry, plead, rant and rave all we want to, but the reality is that there is little hope for us until there is some improvement in the way they view us.[37]

In doing what they could to challenge the view that prisoners were irredeemable, prisoners tried to seize agency by demonstrating that far from being beyond redemption, they had earned the right to clemency.

"Probably the most curious aspect of the hard-headed public mood is how quickly it developed and then how firmly it took hold," explains Burk Foster.[38] Buddy Roemer was the first governor since 1892 not to grant a single clemency during the holiday season.[39] As Rideau and Wikberg explained, hope of receiving clemency from the governor was the "universal perception that locks most into decades of responsible and productive behavior, striving to 'earn' a second chance at life." Governors, "who control Hope, have generally understood this and traditionally kept hope alive. But there has been a revolution in Louisiana, the Roemer Revolution."[40] Those skeptical of gubernatorial clemency complained of the wide discretion it allowed and urged greater objectivity instead. But prisoners argued that the reaction against clemency reversed the long-standing principle of being "rewarded for doing well," which "is the American Way of doing things."[41] With the clemency system "in a state of paralysis, crippled by sensational journalism and law-and order-politics," prison administrators "dread the day when the longterm inmate population arrives at the collective realization that there is to be no future for them beyond prison walls."[42]

Predictions that prisoners with no hope would resort to acts of desperation came true. In 1988 the suicide rate among Angola prisoners was particularly high, which Angola journalists attributed to years of "anxiety, loneliness . . . frustration and despair stemming from long 'hopeless' prison sentences in a maximum-security environment."[43] In 1989 US district court judge Frank Polozola declared a state of emergency at Angola because of a series of escapes, stabbings, and suicides that year. All of the eleven people who attempted to escape were serving long-term sentences for murder, rape, or kidnapping.[44] The "state of emergency" justified shakedowns and lockdowns, but Rideau saw these actions as political theater.[45] While the judge, the governor, and investigators attributed the escapes to mismanagement of the prison, budget cuts, and low morale among the guards, those incarcerated offered a different interpretation. Prisoners agreed that budget cuts affected every aspect of prison operation, from food to recreation, but they charged that the primary cause of unrest was "the sense of hopelessness resulting from disappointment over the clemency and parole policies of Governor Buddy Roemer."[46] Model prisoners with something to lose would not commit suicide. "It's the hope of release that generates faith in the system," Wikberg explained. But he also warned that despair could ignite unrest. "When an inmate loses faith, you have a ticking time bomb."[47] In response to the startling number of prison suicides, Warden C. Paul Phelps averred that anyone working in corrections would recognize that the hope for release was "the most important thing to run a safe, constitutional prison. "Without hope," Phelps warned, "it's just a matter of sheer physical force."[48]

Stories of prisoners' desperate efforts to flee recalled the long tradition of runaway slaves who sought refuge from bloodhounds in the woods. After watching Governor Roemer articulate his harsh stance toward clemency on national television, Francis "Corky" Clifton, a "model prisoner" trusted to handle the prison's bloodhounds during his twenty-seven years of confinement for murder, suddenly escaped.[49] Clifton had expected to serve a 10/6 life sentence, but was repeatedly denied clemency despite recommendations from the pardon board. After hiding in the woods for a week with no food or money "and not wanting to steal," Clifton surrendered. He was placed in indefinite isolation, which prisoners and their advocates understood as a form of torture.[50] Clifton explained, "To think you're going to die [at Angola], it just gets to you."[51] After giving himself up, Clifton told reporters of his suicidal thoughts; taking his own life seemed to be "the most humane way out of a prison I no longer care to struggle in."[52] "One doesn't need a degree in psychology that even the most law-abiding of men will be moved to irrational and desperate behavior if hope is removed from their existence," Rideau and Wikberg remarked; "prisoners are no different."[53] Wallace McDonald, one of a group of incarcerated men who slashed their own Achilles tendons in 1951 in protest of the inhumane conditions at Angola, was uniquely qualified to discuss the varying forms of barbarism that characterized Angola in the twentieth century. He observed, "Now you got better living conditions, don't work as hard and got no corporal punishment, but you ain't got no hope. You can just forget it. Before, at least you had a chance to get out."[54] But when asked whether hopelessness resulting from his meager clemency record was to blame for prisoners' despair, Governor Roemer replied, "I don't think that's a problem; I think that's an excuse."[55]

While the free world seemed to regard them as an indistinguishable and disposable mass of criminals, prisoners understood that many of those who attempted to escape had done what they could to hold onto hope and demonstrate their trustworthiness. After twenty years of confinement, Donald Fink attempted to escape, an act which a fellow lifer interpreted as suicidal. "There was nothing to live for anymore. Hell, he just gave up! We all could see the dust flying as the bullets hit all around him." Another prisoner, John Ortego, said, "I feel Louisiana has taken away all of the hope and closed all the avenues of possible release." "What Donald did—that was nothing more than a kamikaze move."[56] Prison officials concurred. Warden Hilton Butler, a tough-minded "career security man" who served at Angola for forty years, insisted that when a prisoner "shows he has been rehabilitated or just gotten too old for his continuation of crime, something needs to be done for him. . . . If we don't, the situation is going to eat us alive."[57] While Butler conceded that there were prisoners who should never be released, he averred that "there are men at Angola who deserve clemency and they'll never be back."[58]

Numerous studies have demonstrated that those convicted of first-degree murder have startlingly low rates of recidivism: a 2013 paper found that among those who sentences were commuted in Louisiana, recidivism involving new crimes was just over 4 percent for those convicted of first-degree murder, and zero for second-degree murderers.[59] Other states had similarly low rates. In Michigan, *none* of the 268 first-degree murderers paroled between 1959 and 1972 returned to prison for any type of crime. A report examining parole in California went so far as to recommend that many of the state's eleven hundred prisoners serving sentences for murder or manslaughter should be reclassified as nonviolent because there was so little probability that they would ever again resort to violence.[60] Moreover, research by criminologists demonstrated that people "age out of crime" and that criminal activity peaks during one's early twenties.[61] But the public now perceived even elderly prisoners as immutably dangerous.

An additional challenge faced by aging prisoners, according to Warden C. Paul Phelps, was that the "older you are in prison, the fewer people you have left on the outside who cares for you [*sic*] or are in a position to do anything about taking care of you." District court judge Bob Downing remarked of his visits to Angola, "It's embarrassing to see all these old men that the State of Louisiana is scared of."[62] These were men whose time inside and hope of release had garnered them more responsibility within the prison. "Having accumulated enough age and seniority to avoid true hard labor," they tended rose bushes on the grounds. Over the years, they had lost their family members and friends. One man had had only seven visits in thirty years; another had had no visits in twenty-eight years. For the oldest and most isolated, hopelessness turned into resignation. Wikberg and Foster wrote, "After hearing accounts like these, one begins to sense how estranged from the outside world the long-termers feel, how they come to think of prison as their natural home, and how they gave up on a free world that long ago lost interest in them."[63]

Angolite editor Wilbert Rideau was committed to profiling the stories of Louisiana's thirty-one prisoners who had been confined the longest. "We were certain they would die in prison in anonymity unless we brought their stories to light," Rideau explains.[64] James Poindexter, a seventy-year-old prisoner who had been incarcerated since 1954, lamented, "They said if you kept a good record and go up, the people'll try to hep you. . . . Had I known Ah'd been heah dis long, Ah'd been run off. But Ah can't do it now."[65] Angola's associate warden, Peggi Gresham, echoed slaveholders' arguments against emancipation when she rhetorically asked, "If they have nobody in the world to help them and they're old men, unable to care for themselves, wouldn't it be better to just leave them here? Throwing them out would perhaps be more cruel."[66] Rideau retorted, "It's kind of late in the game to begin worrying about cruelty after you've taken a man in his youth, stripped his entire existence of meaning and purpose and converted his life into a nightmare, until he's old too do anything more than wait to die."[67]

Many men incarcerated at Angola rejected the notion that prison should be their "natural home" and refused to give up on returning to the free world. While long-termers were highly invested in improving prison conditions, they mobilized in the electoral arena in order to push for clemency and solidified their collective identity in the process. According to Lydia Pelot-Hobbs, "Having the collective memory of a different era in the state's attitude towards incarceration and believing it could change again," Angola activists—mostly inmate-lawyers led by "counsel substitute" Norris Henderson—formed the Angola Special Civics Project in 1986, which focused on getting them free.[68] Henderson explains, "We'd gone from helping individual guys fight their cases to helping everyone by working on policy."[69] They grasped the structural causes of their predicament and identified state officials, especially the governor, as "the real site of power." With a governor's race ahead, prisoners engaged in a letter-writing campaign to organize their families and friends on the outside to vote as a bloc to reelect Edwin Edwards, who had demonstrated his willingness to use his clemency power more regularly. In lobbying for political support outside the prison, the Angola Special Civics Project had the support of prison wardens, who "recognize the reality" and "respect the need of these lifers to try and do something to address their situation."[70] These activists conducted research into life sentencing, drafted legislation, held press conferences, and disseminated information to allies on the outside that exposed the cost of expanding Louisiana's prison system while starving social services.[71] The lived experience of these prison activists informed their understanding of the political and structural causes of their continued confinement and their insistence on their collective freedom. As part of that effort, they resurrected the memory of the state's historical tradition. But, as Burk Foster has observed, "In the early 1980s, when the public, the media, and the legislature were confronted with evidence that lack of prison space was indeed a serious problem, it was as if they no longer remembered the old days of leniency. That part of corrections history had been erased from the collective memory. People did not want to hear about old alternatives, new alternatives, or any alternatives at all."[72] Theirs was an uphill battle against historical amnesia.

A CORRIDOR TO FREEDOM: THE MISSISSIPPI GOVERNOR'S MANSION

As opportunities for clemency reached a vanishing point, working at the governor's mansion was one of the few corridors to freedom remaining for prisoners in the South.[73] The practice of using convict labor at the mansion, despite racially coded demands to contain criminals, suggests that whatever white people's assumptions about Black criminality, the governor's family did not believe that living in close quarters with convicted murderers would put them in danger. Mississippi governor Paul B. Johnson Jr. (1964–68) declared that those who were amazed at the arrangement didn't realize that "these people are not in the murdering business."[74] According to Carroll Waller, whose husband, Bill, was the governor of Mississippi from 1972 to 1976, those who were convicted of murder acted in the heat of passion and were not incorrigibly dangerous: "They kill their sweethearts and wives, not other people."[75] In fact, those convicted of property crimes were considered less trustworthy than those convicted of murder. The practice continued even after one mansion servant was charged with the murder of another.[76]

Corrections officials supported domestic service in the governor's mansion as a vehicle for rehabilitation. While their arguments might unwittingly echo defenses of slavery as a "school" for uncivilized brutes, they also drew on the language of mercy and the possibility of personal growth. In 1967 the chairman of the Mississippi Probation and Parole Board claimed, "We're gradually getting away from the idea that if we punish a man enough he'll be good. It's simply not true. A man needs help." He pointed out that not one person who had been pardoned had been returned to Parchman Farm, the Mississippi State Penitentiary.[77] The warden at the Louisiana State Penitentiary at Angola also claimed that "murderers are actually the best prospects for working outside the prison" because they "have the lowest rate of recidivism of any group of offenders." During her sixteen years in the Louisiana governor's mansion, Elaine Edwards, the wife of Governor Edwin Edwards, insisted that mansion staff be drawn from those who had committed violent crimes.[78] The former governor of South Carolina, John West (1971–75), has described his family's use of prison labor as "good therapy. My wife just recently ran into one of the upstairs maids, who saw her and hugged her and said, 'I've been going straight ever since I left the mansion.'"[79]

While one Louisiana journalist scoffed at the "long string of governors whose idea of opening government to blacks was to bring down some trusties from Angola to wait on tables at the Mansion," prisoners saw these assignments outside the prison as an opportunity.[80] One mansion trusty, Frank Gholar, had his life sentence commuted in 1988 by Mississippi governor Bill Allain (1984–88) after serving only six years; otherwise he would have had to wait fifteen years to be considered for parole. After he was released, Gholar, a former oil field worker, was hired by an oil company whose owner he met while at the mansion. "The program at the mansion gives you a chance to prove yourself," he said. "Everybody ain't against you. They'll trust you."[81] His new employer was a friend of the governor and an appointee to the Louisiana Pardon Board. Although the situation appears to resemble that of favored house slaves, the reporter for the *Hattiesburg American* claimed that Gholar, who is Black, "feels anything but a racial slight for being selected as a mansion servant, and concluded that he was "just glad it has removed the stigma of being an inmate."[82] In Louisiana the mansion was the most coveted work assignment. Lifer Wilbert Rideau explains that prisoners were willing to bow and scrape if it meant they would be released in just a few years' time.[83]

Former Angola prisoner Forest C. Hammond-Martin, arrested at the age of seventeen for murder and attempted robbery and sentenced to life in prison, recalled that when he was assigned to the mansion, "I was smelling freedom on the other side of the front gate." As he left Angola, he rolled down the car window to shout, "Goodbye, Angola! Kiss my black a——, you bastard." After his escort took him to a barber to get his Afro cut off, to a store to buy appropriate clothes, and to a McDonald's drive-through, "I was starting to feel human again. I had forgotten I could feel this way."[84]

Hammond-Martin soon realized that being part of the "Krewe of da Mansion" was far from freedom. In exchange for a chance at release, he was subject to demeaning treatment and constant surveillance. When he was selected to be butler to Elaine Edwards, he recalled, she instructed him with a "soul-piercing stare": "Never at any time initiate any greetings, conversations, or questions to the governor. The governor has enough to be concerned with in dealing with the business of running this state to be entertaining your trifling concerns. Is that understood? Speak when you are spoken to, answer when you are questioned, be present when you are summoned, and leave when you are excused. Is that understood?" In front of her eight-year-old grandson, Elaine Edwards admonished Hammond-Martin that if he failed in any of his duties, "then you will, without any hesitation on my part, be sent back to Africa—Angola, no questions asked. Understood?" He thought to himself, "She has her grandson there as a lesson to watch her humble a great Angola-African warrior. *What the f——? Slavery wasn't abolished. It was just hidden!*" Observing the other mansion trusties, Hammond-Martin recalled, "I felt I was watching the slaves who had been in America long before I arrived. They knew the white man's language and habits. I was fresh off the slave ship, having just come from Angola."[85] He had moved from the plantation fields to the Big House.

As enslaved people who worked in their white masters' mansions may well have done for many generations, mansion trusties used their positions and proximity to powerful people to their advantage. For example, Bobby Turner, the chef at the Louisiana governor's mansion, secured cash tips from the governor's wealthy guests. "Everybody who came to the mansion represented potential dollars for Bobby," recalls Hammond-Martin admiringly. When visitors tried to solicit inside information from Turner about the governor's doings, Turner expected to be paid. If someone asked Turner about the governor without offering proper compensation, he would "go into his *Amos 'n' Andy* routine, pretending to have lost his memory."[86]

All of the mansion trusties understood that faithfully executing their duties would result in a pardon. But Hammond-Martin's chances for a pardon seemed to slip away when he was accused of absconding to a girlfriend's house one night. After the incident, District Attorney Ossie Brown warned the governor, "He's a threat to society. If he stays here at the mansion another day, my office will be the platform for the most massive public protest that this state has ever known." Governor Edwards was unmoved, asserting that "sending him back to Angola is like convicting him of a crime he hasn't committed." But Hammond-Martin's pardon was not assured. In his final interview with Hammond-Martin, the governor exasperatedly recounted a series of problems he and his wife had with men whom he had pardoned and the family continued to employ. Edwards admitted that many people opposed Hammond-Martin's release. But, he said, "my decision is not based on . . . who you were then, but who you are now." With Hammond-Martin standing before him, Edwards signed, stamped, and sealed the executive order and said, "You've suffered a lot and paid for your mistakes. . . . You're free to go."[87] Released after serving six years of a life sentence, he was employed as Edwards's maintenance man at his private law office.

This decision was decried by the widow of the druggist whom Hammond-Martin had been convicted of killing (although Hammond-Martin did not pull the trigger), as well as by members of Baton Rouge's Pharmaceutical Society, who argued that, given the profits to be made by selling stolen drugs, "pharmacy crimes have been of epidemic proportions for several years."[88] Other critics argued incorrectly that early release "is the main reason why our crime rate goes up, up, and up." That Hammond-Martin was a minor when he was convicted was of no consequence. One constituent from Baton Rouge thought it so obvious that the youth of an offender was irrelevant that he asked rhetorically, "Would it have made any difference if Hammond was 23, 45, or 80 years old?"[89] On leaving office, Edwards stated that he couldn't understand why he should be criticized for his pardon record given the clarity of custom and law, adding, "In most cases, we are only following the spirit of the constitution. . . . Those inmates who work at the mansion have traditionally been pardoned at the end of [the governor's] term." While he acknowledged that some clemency decisions might distress people in the community, he said that he and his wife had worked closely with mansion trusties and had full faith in them.[90] As for the fearmongering media, he declared that "the press should not review" pardons; "it is none of your business."[91]

By the 1990s, the personalism of gubernatorial clemency, most pronounced in the paternalistic South and most literal in the context of mansion trustees, came to be seen as suspect. The abandonment of discretion was the result of an intersection of liberal and conservative approaches to crime and punishment. The liberal desire for fairness and equity coincided with the punitive turn against rehabilitation and second chances. This convergence, brilliantly analyzed by Naomi Murakawa, was observed by Wilbert Rideau as far back as 1978.[92] In a discussion of parole, he explained that mass incarceration was the offspring of both liberal reform and retributive reaction:

> Two divergent and contradictory forces prompted this [decline of parole]. One was the public's alarm over the continued rise in crime and violence and the criticism that parole release undercuts the deterrent effect of criminal law. . . . The other force evolved from discontent with the arbitrary and inequitable way in which parole is issued, the wide disparities in prison terms, and the unfair treatment accorded the many prisoners whose requests for parole are denied as arbitrarily as others' are granted. Thus, the assault on parole has come from the combined efforts of law-and-order advocates and reformists—two usually opposing forces.[93]

Rideau's lived experience taught him that, however imperfect and paternalistic, clemency was the last defense against permanent, unqualified exile.

NEITHER MERCY NOR CONTRACT: PERPETUAL CONFINEMENT

By 1994, when the bipartisan federal crime bill was passed, Mississippi was in the process of dramatically scaling back parole even further. State Senator Brad Lott summed up his constituents' views of criminals: "When they go to jail, leave them there until they rot and bring them out in a body bag."[94] In 1994, following the example of Louisiana, the Mississippi Legislature voted in a landslide to end parole for those convicted of murder, armed robbery, carjacking, drive-by shootings, and sex offenses. In that same session, the legislature prohibited the use of televisions, radios, and stereos in the prison and approved $52.9 million for over four thousand new prison beds.[95] In 1995, in the only law in the country that applied "truth-in-sentencing to all crimes," the state legislature mandated that all felons serve 85 percent of their sentences before being eligible for parole; prior to that year, they had to serve 25–33 percent. Governor Kirk Fordice (1992–2000), who wanted Mississippi to be "the capital of capital punishment," applauded the legislation.[96] He declared, "I will fight with every breath in my body to see that the criminals we take off the street serve their time, and if that means we have to build a bigger jail house, then hand me a shovel." The permeability that had characterized Mississippi's prison system early in the twentieth century was now sealed. As Fordice put it, "All I want is four thick walls and a few big men to keep Mississippi's worst away from Mississippi's best."[97]

Overcrowding came to be interpreted as a problem of crime, not a problem of overzealous incarceration. According to the state attorney general, Mike Moore, those who considered themselves law abiding should be poised in a state of constant vigilance: "This is a public safety crisis. Residents should be fearful for their property and their lives."[98] This panic was based on a fundamental public misunderstanding and the fabricated trope of "revolving door prisons." In 1993, when six hundred Louisiana voters were asked whether they believed "a person convicted of murder sentenced to life in prison without benefit of probation or parole or suspension of sentence . . . would live out his natural life and die in prison or . . . might be released at some time," 71.3 percent believed he or she would be released.[99] In fact, by the mid-1990s, roughly 90 percent of Angola's long-termers weren't going anywhere.[100] Their confinement was reinforced by the decision of Governor Mike Foster (1996–2004) to stack the Board of Pardons with crime victims. "Louisiana is the first state to have a crime-victim majority on its pardon and parole boards," imprisoned journalist Douglas Dennis noted. "Lost in the blather about 'fairness' is the fact that fairness is arrived at through impartiality."[101] Between 1975 and 1989, of over one thousand lifers who applied for commutations in Louisiana, 718 were granted a hearing, 538 received favorable recommendations from the Pardon Board, and governors approved 224. From 1987 to 1991, Governor Roemer commuted the sentences of only twenty-three prisoners serving life.[102] The remaining twenty-four hundred lifers were left to die in prison.[103]

Thus, while Governor Haley Barbour correctly invoked "Mississippi tradition" when he issued a torrent of clemencies in that state in 2012, the tradition had been interrupted by tough-on-crime policies. Now clemency was denounced by both liberals and conservatives. On the conservative side, crime victims felt betrayed, law enforcement felt undermined, and the public felt anxious about its own safety. Barbour's office was flooded with angry letters, particularly about his treatment of Michael Graham, who had been sentenced to life for having shot his ex-girlfriend, Adrienne Klasky. When Barbour granted Graham, a former mansion trusty, a suspended sentence in 2008, a friend of the victim's family wrote, "Your decision is wrong, wrong, wrong! If Michael David Graham deserves a 'new life' or 'fresh start' then death row should be emptied, and the doors of every prison in this state thrown open to allow anarchy to have its full and ugly sway over the good people of Mississippi who elected you to office."[104] Another constituent offered a strained but subversive analogy that reflected the jumbled politics of clemency, comparing Barbour's alleged interference in the justice system with the vigilantism of the Jim Crow era: "You have sent our state back to the day of executioners taking the law into there [sic] only hands. Medgar Evers, Emmitt [sic] Till, and Adrienne Klasky."[105] In this passionate missive, the governor's act of mercy for a white man who murdered a white woman was equated with terrorism against Black civil rights activists by white supremacist vigilantes. The governor's executive prerogative, previously regarded as a constitutional duty, was now equated with lawlessness. The bottom note in this dissonant chord was the belief that anyone convicted of a violent crime was immutably dangerous.

In the aftermath of these acts of clemency, several Mississippi legislators drafted bills to reduce eligibility for sentence reductions for trusties, and Barbour's successor, Phil Bryant (2012–20), pledged to phase out the practice of prisoners working in the mansion, though six prisoners were transferred to the mansion on his inauguration.[106] The favored status of a prisoner was seen as evidence of treachery rather than trustworthiness; a pardon for a trusty was framed as corruption rather than compassion. As State Senator Michael Watson explained, "We want to make sure that those people don't have any avenue to build a relationship with governors and wives that may lead to a pardon."[107]

Haley Barbour, by contrast, saw his personal relationships with those who served in the mansion as the foundation of his belief in their trustworthiness. His confidence in these men, whom he allowed to play with his grandchildren, was influenced by his own childhood experience. When his grandfather, a judge, lost the use of his legs due to a neurological disease, a nineteen-year-old man named Leon Turner, serving time for two counts of murder, was assigned to help him. Barbour had seen the power of a second chance and what it did for Leon Turner. "Christianity teaches us forgiveness and second chances," he explained. "I believe in second chances, and I try hard to be forgiving. . . . Leon helped take care of us. . . . He was our playmate, our friend."[108] Like his predecessors in the twentieth century, Barbour's conservative stance on crime was a rebuttal to the rehabilitative ideal. On the other hand, his Christian faith and his sense of hierarchy and obligation emboldened him to make generous use of his discretionary power.

The petitions for clemency that Barbour rejected are equally revealing. Gladys and Jamie Scott, African American sisters and young mothers from rural Mississippi with no prior criminal records, were each given a double life sentence in 1993 for their participation in an armed robbery at a mini-mart in which no one was injured and only eleven dollars was stolen; the jury took only thirty-six minutes to reach a verdict.[109] Neither sister had wielded a weapon; the alleged coconspirators who actually held the gun took plea bargains and testified under duress against the Scotts in return for reduced sentences.[110] The Scotts appealed their convictions, and for over a decade their mother agitated for a review of their case. By the time the Scotts petitioned Governor Barbour for early release with the help of Chokwe Lumumba, an attorney, activist, and later the mayor of Jackson, they had already served sixteen years in prison and Jamie Scott was in poor health due to kidney failure.[111] Facing public pressure from advocacy organizations about the miscarriage of justice, Barbour finally agreed to release them only on the condition that Gladys donate a kidney to her sister, whose kidney failure was a result of undiagnosed diabetes and poor medical care in prison.[112] While Barbour admitted that the two women were "no longer" a threat to society, he neither acknowledged that their sentence was excessive nor expressed sympathy for the critically ill woman. The sisters did not fit his mold of mercy because they did not show remorse and "did nothing to redeem themselves."[113] Using language befitting his Christian outlook, Barbour explained, "You can't ask for redemption until you admit that you've sinned."[114]

Although Barbour insisted that Gladys's offer to donate her kidney to her sister was entirely voluntary and Gladys herself reportedly said that the governor "didn't even have to put that in the order 'cause I was going to do that anyway," medical ethicists expressed concern that the commutation was contingent on organ donation. As Michael Schapiro, chief of organ transplantation at a Hackensack University Medical Center in New Jersey, asserted, "If the sister belongs in prison, then she should be allowed to donate and return to prison, and if she doesn't belong in prison, then she should have her sentence commuted whether or not she is a donor."[115] Linking release from prison with organ donation was a violation of both prisoners' and patients' rights. Lumumba argued that merely suspending the Scott sisters' sentences rather than granting them full pardons "is an act of injustice. They will continue to have to look over their shoulders, afraid that their freedoms will be snatched from them at the first infraction."[116] *New York Times* columnist Bob Herbert points out that Barbour had recently asserted "that there was hardly anyone in prison who didn't deserve to be there. It's an interesting comment from a governor who has repeatedly demonstrated a willingness to free prisoners convicted of the most heinous crimes."[117] Barbour's comfort with releasing those convicted of murder after he had developed personal relationships with them in the mansion did not translate into a structural critique of excessive sentencing or the routine violence of mass incarceration. As bioethicists Aviva Goldberg and Joel Frader explain, "By suspending [the Scott sisters'] sentence on medical grounds instead of pardoning them outright, Barbour can remain 'tough on crime' while acquiescing to the sisters' supporters and saving the state about $200,000 in daily dialysis costs."[118]

Barbour also refused to posthumously pardon Clyde Kennard, a decorated Korean War veteran, Sunday school teacher, and civil rights activist who had been framed by law enforcement and the Mississippi Sovereignty Commission for having tried to integrate the University of Southern Mississippi in the 1950s.[119] According to Monte Piliawsky, a political science professor there, "Because there was a law in Mississippi that prohibited a felon from being admitted to a state school, Mississippi officials determined that Kennard had to be turned into a felon."[120] In 1960 Kennard was wrongfully convicted of stealing twenty-five dollars' worth of chicken feed by an all-white jury after ten minutes of deliberation and was sentenced to seven years of hard labor at Parchman. Mississippi NAACP leader Medgar Evers, who spent his own short life investigating racist murders, knew and loved Kennard and considered Kennard's treatment "one of the long wracking pains" of his own years as field secretary. Evers himself was fined for contempt of court when he spoke out against the verdict.[121] Despite Kennard being diagnosed with colon cancer after complaining of abdominal pains, prison officials instructed prisoners to literally carry him to Parchman's cotton fields to work in the scorching heat each day.[122] In 1963 Kennard was freed early by a reluctant Governor Ross Barnett on compassionate release due to the severity of his illness, and he died just six months later at the age of thirty-six, weighing less than a hundred pounds. Kennard's last words, as recounted by John Howard Griffin, were, "Be sure to tell them what happened to me is less terrible than what this system has done to that warden, because it has turned him into a beast and it will turn his children into beasts."[123]

When the only witness who testified against Kennard recanted in 2005, Mississippians of all stripes, including senators, judges, and administrators from the very university that had denied him enrollment, advocated that he be pardoned posthumously. As civil rights veteran Julian Bond urged Governor Barbour in 2006, "Mississippi has long suffered because of its segregationist past. You have the opportunity to erase yesterday's shame through your action. I hope you have the courage to take it."[124] It was Mississippi that needed to atone, not Kennard. Barbour acknowledged that Kennard was actually innocent, and even presided over the proclamation of Clyde Kennard Day in 2006. But he refused to clear Kennard's name. In his feeble estimation, "If he were living, I think he would have already been pardoned," but "as far as I know, there's never been any dead person pardoned in our state."[125] Barbour's clemencies of his trusties alongside his failure to pardon Kennard and the Scott sisters suggest that his mercy was motivated more by paternalism than by justice and that political activism for democratic rights was still a greater crime than murder. Pardoning Kennard, even posthumously, would require wrestling with the ugly side of "Mississippi tradition"—the history and persistence of white supremacy. As Jamie Scott put it, "My grandma used to tell me . . . slavery is not dead in the south, it's called the law now."[126]

Across the Mississippi River, Angola Farm is perceived as a relic of another time. Its origins in slavery and its plantation have made its horror evidence of backwardness and racism. But the expansion of Angola, the permanent exile of its residents, and the aging of its population are all a modern creation. Whereas in the 1950s only 2 percent of Angola's prisoners died there, by 2016, 86.6 percent were serving life sentences.[127] As of early 2020, the number of people serving life sentences in Louisiana is almost three times larger than the entire state prison population was in 1970.[128] The personalism that characterized white supremacy in the Jim Crow South was different from the hyperincarceration of the current era. Liberal disavowal of anything that smacked of the Old South tainted the mechanisms of the past that could be redeployed to abolitionist ends. Without historicizing the decline of clemency, prisoners themselves might not acquire "the determination of a fanatic, the adeptness of the master politician, and the tough fighting ability of a seasoned mercenary" required to endure the rigors of a long prison sentence.[129] As Pelot-Hobbs points out, "Over time the era of the 10-6 life sentence has been wiped from the collective memory of Louisiana prisoners. Increasingly, the people housed at Angola have only known an institution with thousands of lifers who have no expectation of release."[130] This generational shift reminds us that we must take into account the life course of prisoners, the length of their sentences, and their experiences of changing carceral policies from *inside* prison. For them, the prison system did not just expand; their confinement had gone from a temporary condition to a perpetual one. (See figure 3.1.)

Lifers of all ages at Angola, whether they have been incarcerated since the days of the 10/6 rule or not, are determined to demonstrate that they

3.1 Headstone for Lee Wright, inmate #429061, who died at age forty-one while serving time at Angola. Photo courtesy of Giles Clarke.

are not the same people they were when they were convicted and that they deserve freedom. They continue to mobilize in an effort to gain release not just as individuals but as a constituency with political interests. Arthur Carter, a lifer who organizes inside and outside Angola, explains, "The only thing you can possibly live for is the possibility of making pardon. The possibility of a law passing" that will restore parole eligibility and ease the clemency process. "That alone is what I do every day." Carter considers it his "civic duty" to educate his fellow prisoners so that they are not daunted by the baroque nature of the legal system. "'Cause I could die tomorrow. We need guys in here who understand law, 'cause we're not rich, we're not going to buy lawyers or nothing like that."[131] Danny Sermon, a veteran incarcerated at Angola, has used his connections with veterans on the outside to vouch for him before the Board of Pardons and Committee on Parole.[132] Darren James educates fellow lifers on pardon and parole practices and coaches people as they prepare for their appeals.[133]

But many are overwhelmed by despair. While prisoners like Aaron Brent "strive to do better and get better" through GED programs, counseling, and work opportunities, they are discouraged by the fact that clemency remains out of reach.[134] Ron Hicks described the possibility of clemency as "dangling a carrot in front of the rabbit or whatever running the track and the dog running behind."[135] Joe White, who arrived at Angola in 1962 and saw his expected release vanish, was interviewed in 1990 by National Public Radio. White described serving life in prison as being "buried alive. . . . This is a graveyard. A graveyard of time." He began to sob as he recounted, "It's as if you don't exist, it's like you in a spirit and everything around you is alive, and you can't touch, you can't reach, you can't do anything but just look. We can't touch people's lives, we can't touch their lives. That's what tears us up, we can't touch their lives."[136]

That prisoners and free people could not touch each others' lives became the natural state of mass incarceration. By the 2000s, the personal interactions between governors and the incarcerated were seen as a residue of a bygone age, untrustworthy measures of a prisoner's virtue, or retrograde examples of paternalism.[137] But for some observers, personal relationships are precisely what provides a window into a prisoner's humanity and potential. As minister and therapist Randy Weeks put it, Barbour was a law-and-order governor, and "then it seems he spent a little time with some convicted criminals and something changed between them. . . . Over the years of his administration, as he had contact with the trusties at the governor's mansion, Barbour got to know these men as people—not just convicts. He saw beyond the crimes they had committed to the other aspects of their personhood. . . . I have had my share of second chances, and I won't begrudge them theirs. Sounds a lot like grace to me."[138]

At the beginning of his term, Phil Bryant, Barbour's successor, vowed to end the "archaic" system of having trusties work in the governor's mansion.[139] This move would satisfy both liberals who interpreted the practice as a vestige of slavery and Jim Crow and conservatives who bristled at the sloppy sentimentality it could engender. As discretion increasingly came to be seen as arbitrary and the administrative quality of punishment became more important than the purpose of punishment, gubernatorial clemencies were attacked by both liberals and conservatives as simultaneously too capricious and lenient, an abuse of power by an executive both soft-hearted and corrupt.[140] Whereas "modernizing" Mississippi's penal system during the 1940s meant introducing parole as a vehicle for individualizing justice and providing a path toward rehabilitation and release, "modernizing" Mississippi's penal system at the turn of the twenty-first century meant disabling discretionary release, the only check on increasingly punitive carceral machinery. A governor's personal relations with prisoners became uniformly suspect and mercy a slippery slope to lawlessness.

PART II. STRANGE BEDFELLOWS

Conjugal Visits, Belonging, and Social Death

4 Southern Hospitality

The Rise of Conjugal Visits

In November 2020 Ryan Adams, a white man serving two consecutive life sentences without the possibility of parole for murdering Chris Domingue and Domingue's girlfriend Stacie Boudreaux, went before the Louisiana Board of Pardons and Committee on Parole to make his case for clemency. During his thirty-one years in prison, he had earned his GED, participated in vocational training programs, and arranged funerals for deceased prisoners. An official from the Louisiana State Penitentiary at Angola testified that Adams, who had only six disciplinary infractions over his entire time in prison, had "given back to the state" and was not a risk to the public.[1] Adams tearfully avowed, "There is simply no excuse for what I did." Then he distanced himself from the person who killed Domingue and Boudreaux: "There was an eighteen-year-old kid that did something that was unimaginable." But, taking responsibility, he stated, "I betrayed what I believed in, I knew what was right and wrong." As he pounded the table for emphasis, Adams declared, "The one thing I can't change is the fact that I killed. . . . But I have changed every other thing I could, and that's exploring those defects growing up and making sure that I never compromise my values. That kid just doesn't exist anymore." Adams's adult daughter insisted, "We are excited to welcome him into our home. . . . We as his family have the utmost confidence that he will be productive." Gary Frank, the former athletic director at Angola, affirmed that Adams had paid for his crimes and added that he would be "proud to have Ryan Adams and his wife next door to me. . . . I wouldn't feel any danger whatsoever."

The victims' family members had a starkly different perspective. The brother of the murdered woman expressed the pain that the family continued to suffer: "My mother still dreams of finding her daughter and pulling that telephone cord away from her neck and trying to make her come back to life. This should be about punishment." He argued that Adams "has a wife and child now. My sister will never have a child. She's gone."[2] Louisiana prisons do not allow conjugal visits, which confirms the informal knowledge that Adams's daughter was conceived during an illicit encounter with his partner somewhere on the prison grounds. The grieving brother's contention that Adams had a child while the murder victim could not implied that no one should have what the victims had been deprived of: vocational programs, maybe, but not a family. But Adams acted on his human desire for love, physical affection, and family, even at the risk of severe punishment. Prisoners regularly took advantage of the gazebos in Butler Park, a relatively secluded picnic area set aside for prison trusties and their visitors, to steal intimate moments with their loved ones.[3] Adams's wife and daughter struggled to maintain meaningful ties with him during his confinement, but without conjugal or family visits private interactions were impossible. In the end, all but one member of the Board of Pardons voted to commute Adams's sentence. But because clemency decisions must be unanimous, Ryan Adams's petition was denied.[4]

Conjugal visits mattered to prisoners because they helped to sustain incarcerated people's intimate relationships, enabling them to avoid unmitigated exile and social death. The rise and fall of conjugal visits and the debates around permitting or forbidding them serve as a window into prison practices and the changing relationship between "inside" and "outside." Whether, how, and for what reasons they would be allowed involved questions of risk, redeemability, and belonging. The answers to these questions varied across states and changed over time.

Conjugal visits began not as a rehabilitative tool but as an incentive for hard labor and a safety valve for discontent. Such visits were first instituted at Mississippi's Parchman Farm, the Mississippi State Penitentiary, by those who regarded Black people as lacking in morality and self-control. In the 1950s, facing increasing national concern about prison unrest and prison homosexuality, coupled with a growing interest among social scientists about the potential of rehabilitative programs to modify prisoners' behavior, corrections administrators, elected officials, and penologists began to study Mississippi's conjugal visit system. At the same time that Mississippi segregationists used Parchman as a site for violent retribution against civil rights protestors, they touted their conjugal visit program as a model of progressive penology. Deodorized of its racist history, the policy was adopted in more than a dozen states to quell prison unrest, reduce homosexuality, and maintain normative family ties. Prison authorities' interest in averting prison unrest intersected with prisoners' interest in maintaining their intimate social relationships. Precisely because these visits meant so much to incarcerated people, they could be used as disciplinary tools as well as a means of human connection.

Part II of this book begins with this chapter, which traces the roots of conjugal visits in Mississippi, then proceeds in chapter 5 to follow the spread of the practice to California, New York State, and Washington State. Throughout the 1970s and 1980s, corrections professionals across the nation adopted conjugal visits in a response to prison unrest, since visits could be used as a reward for compliance. But if conjugal visit programs were aimed at promoting order and normative behavior, by the 1990s they came to be regarded as promoting lawlessness and pathology. Chapter 6, the final chapter in part II, analyzes the development of a new ideology of penal harm that reshaped the purpose of prison: to make incarcerated people experience pain. According to this ideology, espoused and dramatized by the increasing reliance on victim testimony, the perpetrator can never really pay for his crime as long as he lives, because the persistence of suffering by the victim's loved ones means that the crime never ends. The perpetrator must not only be permanently excluded from free society but must endure perpetual deprivation. Thus, the family of Ryan Adams's murder victim expressed disgust and despondence at the fact that Adams had a daughter while he was incarcerated; her existence itself was an affront to them. If prisoners should suffer, then the indulgence of conjugal visits was an insult to the victims' loved ones. As states, including Mississippi, curtailed and abolished conjugal visit programs, prisoners demanded them as a human right and fought for them in the courts.

DOWN IN THE DELTA

Conjugal visits began at Mississippi's Parchman Farm. In 1969 sociologist Columbus B. Hopper said that Parchman "has the most liberal visitation and leave programs of any state penitentiary in the nation."[5] This policy was consistent with the state's traditionally vigorous clemency practices. Although by the 1960s conjugal visits were hailed by a substantial proportion of sociologists and penologists as innovative way of normalizing the lives of incarcerated people, conjugal visits at Parchman were rooted in the racism that has always pervaded Mississippi's penal system.[6] Hopper remarked that "one would expect that if conjugal visiting developed any-where in the United States, it would do so in a prison with a philosophy of rehabilitation and treatment and in a state noted for liberal develop-ments."[7] As journalist and diplomat John Barlow Martin observed, "Most northern prison men"—that is, officials and experts—"consider the South a benighted land of darkness."[8] But Hopper pointed out why conjugal vis-its developed on Mississippi delta soil.

Far from being an aberration from otherwise conservative mores, Hopper explained, "a prison not only operates within a given culture, it is, in fact, part of that culture."[9] And Mississippi culture was shaped by white supremacy. Over a century before, Frederick Douglass had satirically de-scribed how his enslaver's belief in the moral incapacity of Black people of-fered enslaved children a peculiar kind of freedom: "The slave-boy escapes many troubles which befall and vex his white brother. He seldom has to listen to lectures on propriety of behavior. . . . He is never reprimanded for soiling the table-cloth, for he takes his meals on the clay floor. . . . He is never expected to act like a nice little gentleman, for he is only a rude little slave. Thus, freed from all restraint, the slave-boy can be, in his life and conduct, a genuine boy."[10]

Without Douglass's sense of irony, Hopper asserted that "although the Negroes' position as members of the 'lower caste' had its disadvantages, it did relieve them of the moral restraints which the white society imposed on all whites, including white prisoners."[11] As histories of Parchman Farm have shown, prison practices during the Jim Crow era were influenced by the belief that the supposedly promiscuous, voracious sexual appetite of Black male prisoners had to be satiated in order to boost their morale and productivity; sex workers were more likely to visit these prisoners than wives.[12] In contrast, conjugal visits were not allowed to white prisoners until the 1930s, and until 1972 they were denied to women for fear of pregnancy.[13] Conjugal visits were originally conceived at Parchman not as a vehicle for rehabilitation but as an inducement for producing cotton. "There is a class of negro convicts at Parchman among whom discipline cannot be established by any other means," a reporter asserted in 1919.[14] This viewpoint persisted into the 1960s, when one sergeant at the prison farm stated, "If you let a n——have some Sunday, he will be ready to go out and do some work for you Monday."[15]

Hopper uncritically located the tradition of conjugal visits in a long history of arrangements that were required to maintain order and elicit productivity from plantation laborers, both enslaved and incarcerated.

He contended that in large-scale agriculture, the chain of command depended on "an accommodative relationship between the landlord and the laborer, whether he is a slave, a sharecropper, cash tenant, or even a prisoner." Rather than being solely a site of violence and exploitation, Hopper argued, "the penal plantation may be viewed as a prison adaptation in which the sexual needs of inmates will be given more consideration." He implied that there was something necessary or natural about this hierarchy of command, ignoring its racialization, and posited that it was sustained by consent rather than coercion. In this agrarian context, Hopper interpreted tolerance for conjugal visits as an extension of southern paternalism and personalism. The informal, "direct face-to-face relations" of the rural South, which were implicitly contrasted with the bureaucratic formalism of the North, led to "unusual developments and concession to inmate needs."[16]

At Parchman, conjugal visits initially took place in prisoners' own quarters; the men secured whatever privacy they could by hanging up blankets around their beds.[17] In the 1940s prisoners built small houses for visits out of scrap lumber; giving them a coat of red paint—hence their moniker, "red houses"—lent some respectability to the practice despite their spartan furnishings and haphazard appearance.[18] They established systems to ensure orderliness and privacy, such as placing a board in front of each red house indicating which rooms were in use.[19] The prisoners improved these structures in their spare time, constructed slides and swings for visiting children, and looked after children while the children's parents retreated to seclusion.[20] By 1960 the cottages had three rooms and a shower (see figure 4.1). A man imprisoned at Parchman described conjugal visits as "the most important thing in the lives of married men," and another remarked that prisoners "would rather lose an arm than lose this privilege."[21] Those who did not receive conjugal visits because they were unmarried also supported the practice, asserting that the influx of visitors relieved their sense of confinement. One man remarked, "I like to see other people's families—children, women. . . . It makes it seem less like a prison on visiting days when the free world people come in." The visits were organized informally: participants were not required to fill out any paperwork, and prisoners managed themselves without supervision. The rural setting allowed for picnicking and strolling, with no concern about "inmates hiding in corridors or slipping over walls, for these do not exist."[22]

Hopper admitted the cynical and self-serving motives for the program but emphasized that the "economics of the penitentiary and its compatibility with conjugal visiting does not rule out the more constructive

4.1 A conjugal visit at Parchman Penitentiary, 1959. Courtesy of the Associated Press.

aspects of the practice and other motivations behind the granting of the privilege." He was aware that the program was not necessarily replicable throughout the country, as the nature of these visits derived from the specific features of Parchman itself. In the 1960s, most prisons in the United States were not rural, their economic motives were not so explicit, and correctional personnel could not easily segregate prisoners by race or ethnicity "to circumvent whatever taboos might exist in regard to their interaction." Yet Hopper argued that, given their success at Parchman, conjugal visits should not be discounted as an exercise in rehabilitative penology. Although he thought that the main source of public disapproval was the fundamental notion of prisoners having sex, he was optimistic that "many, perhaps the majority of Americans, now accept sex as a natural part of human existence," so they might consider it improper to "deny both husband and wife the 'rights of marriage' when the husband is in prison." Parchman was in a peculiar position; while its "plantation system is . . . more associated with the past than with the future in the United States," its practices were worthy of emulation.[23]

In the early 1960s Parchman began to move from toleration to official support of conjugal visits and touted the benefits of its program. In 1964 a Parchman administrator claimed, "We have never had any criticism from the general public who understand how visiting is handled. . . . We have been permitting these visits for quite a long time and have not had any regrets or adverse experiences." Instead, he maintained that the visits were helpful in keeping families together and providing prisoners with an incentive to conduct themselves well.[24] In 1965, among a series of improvements that included the introduction of a library and the elimination of a disciplinary lash known as "Black Annie," a camp for first offenders had space for conjugal visits incorporated into its design, along with a chapel.[25] Parchman officials recognized the need to improve the family visitation facilities for the other camps and supported larger and more attractive units with greater privacy.[26] "I couldn't even kiss a woman in there," said one member of the prison board of a red house containing nothing but a mattress and with a window that had broken glass.[27] A visiting Colorado prison official was unimpressed, remarking that a conjugal visit at Parchman was "the equivalent of a night in the red-light district."[28] Despite these charges, a staff member at Parchman declared, "I know one thing for sure, I wouldn't want to be around this place if the conjugal visit were taken away. It would be the greatest blow to the morale of the inmates which I can imagine."[29]

In 1972, under fire for its otherwise brutal practices, Parchman's officials allowed the married women among its fifty-five female prisoners to have conjugal visits. Tom Graf, the prison psychologist, explained that "this was to be a total family identification program rather than just a sexual outlet."[30] Superintendent John A. Collier emphasized, "We are establishing conjugal visits for our married women inmates because we are convinced it is a vital step toward fulfilling our moral obligation to attempt to preserve the marriages of our inmates."[31] When the "revolutionary program" was first established, the visits took place in the prison dispensary due to lack of funds.[32] Parchman's newly hired public relations official convinced the Illinois Central Railroad to donate an eighty-five-foot Pullman car, dubbed *Lady Champagne*, containing six bedrooms and air-conditioning, for the women's conjugal visits.[33] It is ironic that the very railroad that had served as an "Overground Railroad for slavery's grandchildren" during the Great Migration parked one of its cars at Parchman so that prisoners could reunite with their families.[34] Or, perhaps, the railroad that symbolized freedom to Black southerners was precisely the appropriate place for prisoners' seeking temporary refuge in intimate companionship.

Given Parchman's policy of allowing hundreds of prisoners to go home over the holidays, it makes sense that officials referred to the program in the language of moral discipline rather than risk of danger. Those who expressed skepticism about conjugal visits worried about indecency rather than security. In the face of criticisms that Parchman was running a whorehouse, prison officials proudly declared that the program was "moral in every way," and just as important, that it was successful at keeping prisoners in line.[35] In 1974, visits were extended to three days, and accommodations included televisions, stereos, and furniture donated by prisoners' families and local merchants.[36] By 1985, conjugal visits took place at the "Family House," a brick building that resembled a motel. Every two months, married inmates could spend three full days in its apartments with their spouses, children, and other close relatives. Over five hundred visits were scheduled a year, with a long waiting list. Jean McBride, who oversaw the visits in the 1980s, joked that she was the "madam of the penitentiary," but family visits were more than just an opportunity for sexual pleasure. Prisoners treasured the chance to cook or have a meal lovingly prepared for them; to help their children with homework; and to go fishing or feed the ducks at the lake with their families.[37] Bill Habig's wife and small child visited him twice a month through the program. When an editorial in the Memphis, Tennessee, *Commercial-Appeal* denounced the red house as a sexual "playpen," Habig protested, "Conjugal visiting in the Mississippi State Penitentiary is probably the one most rehabilitating factor that no other penitentiary in the whole country has at the present time."[38] Given the backbreaking labor that characterized most days at Parchman, the possibility of reclaiming one's body as part of a family unit rather than a cotton-picking gang must have felt essential for psychic survival.

"THE SEXUAL JUNGLE": PRISON REFORM AND THE PROBLEM OF PRISON SEX

In the 1960s Parchman began fielding inquiries from academics and corrections professionals outside the state who were interested in prison reforms that facilitated rehabilitation. Their concerns did not originate mainly in criticisms of prison conditions, although there were plenty of those; rather, they grew out broader postwar anxieties about perceived social decay. A moral panic about the criminal proclivities of adolescents was signaled by the establishment of the Senate Subcommittee on Juvenile Delinquency in 1954.[39] The wartime influx of women, especially mothers, into the paid workforce was not reversed in the 1950s, despite efforts to shore up a heteropatriarchal gender order with male breadwinners and female homemakers, raising alarms about undisciplined boys and wayward girls.[40] As historians have shown, juvenile delinquency was first portrayed as a "universal problem with psychological roots"; then, by the late 1950s, "as deindustrialization eroded the economic base of the Great Migration, the national media started to depict juvenile delinquency as an urban problem with racial overtones."[41] In response to rising fears about violent crime and nascent calls for "law and order," corrections professionals, penologists, and sociologists advocated prevention and rehabilitation. The failures of current correctional programs were underlined when fifty-three prison disturbances, ranging from self-mutilations to strikes and uprisings, erupted across the country between 1951 and 1953. The American Correctional Association concluded that the unrest was a response to overcrowding, a lack of meaningful programming, and arbitrary and brutal treatment of inmates by guards.[42] Government and correctional officials, supported by journalists, urged a more humane environment in order to turn offenders into well-behaved citizens. According to Edgardo Rotman, postwar penology "was permeated by a general rehabilitative thrust caused by the international reconstructive optimism and the relative prosperity of the 1950s. . . . Enthusiasm for psychological treatment . . . increased the input of behavioral scientists in the correctional system."[43] Throughout the United States, penologists generally agreed that the purpose of prison should be rehabilitation through individualized treatment.

Scholars and activists have persuasively exposed the fallacies of the treatment approach to criminal deviancy popular in this period and its deployment as a form of disciplinary power. According to Michel Foucault, the "medico-juridical remedy" promised by a psychological approach to crime and rehabilitation was the "ultimate alibi behind which the prevailing system will hide in order to remain unchanged."[44] Jessica Mitford, a radical journalist, Communist Party member, and staunch supporter of the civil rights movement, pointed out that the range of constituencies who supported this medical model included "liberal reformers, prison administrators, judges, prosecutors, law enforcement officers, and those indefatigable experimenters, the 'behavior modification' experts." These practices of mind control further reinforced class differences, offering "convenient and scientific-sounding explanations for the difference between Us (the upright white middle-class citizens who run the criminal justice system) and Them (lower-class lawbreakers and other 'deviants' who fill the juvenile reformatories, jails, and prisons—for if there *were* no essential difference, how should the former justify what they are doing to the latter?"[45]

Mitford's views were not widely shared when she penned this critique in the early 1970s after three years of in-depth research on the imprisonment of predominately Black activists. However hypocritical, manipulative, and authoritarian the treatment model may have been, it opened the problems of prison life to fresh scrutiny and encouraged experimentation regarding prisoners' amelioration. In exploring the potential of rehabilitative programming, social scientists and prison reformers paid a significant amount of time tackling the "sexual problem" within prisons. They concluded that riots were caused not only by "mandatory boredom, a sense of injustice . . . bad foods, brutality, [and] unfair or capricious treatment" but also by "sexual privations."[46] By the late 1950s, penologists and corrections practitioners envisioned conjugal visits both as a means of curbing sexual frustration, violence, and homosexuality and as a means of maintaining prisoners' contacts with the outside world.[47] Conjugal visits, which began as a necessary concession to the supposedly voracious sexual appetites of Black men, were reinterpreted as rehabilitative by social scientists both inside and outside the South.

Previously prison reformers had discussed "sexual privation" and its supposed corollary, sexual perversion, very cautiously. The preface to Joseph F. Fishman's 1934 book *Sex in Prison* reads, "We are living in a frank and realistic age, yet the subject of sex in prison—so provocative, so vital, so timely . . . is shrouded in dread silence." The author, a former federal inspector of prisons and academic criminologist, offered his book as a corrective to the "unenlightened world." Fishman found that although his students were nervous about asking questions "because of the quaint and rather ridiculous American attitude on all matters relating to sex," many thought that "the greatest punishment a prisoner can undergo is the deprivation of normal sex gratification."[48]

In the post–World War II period, most American psychologists saw sexuality as natural and healthy for all males. Thus, penologists began to consider conjugal visits beneficial, although they recognized potential resistance from correctional officials. Psychiatrist Benjamin Karpman published a particularly candid discussion of sexuality in prison in 1948, asserting that the main source of many "psychoses" that were the result of incarceration was men's deprivation of "normal sexual outlets." He lamented this institutionally induced pathology, chastised prison doctors who assume "a puritanical attitude," and reproved prison officials who would not "let a prisoner's wife visit . . . and spend an intimate hour with him." The idea of providing sex, he pointed out, seems "less reprehensible when we recall that every army of soldiers is followed by its army of prostitutes and the generals know how inefficient an army would be otherwise." Karpman charged that sexual deprivation was a metonymy for the cruelty of a "system that brings about as a result, if it did not have it for its original purpose, the brutalizing and degradation of the human being called criminal."[49] Sexual activity was so elemental that its denial was a mark of prison's intrinsic inhumanity. The only solution, according to Karpman, was to abolish prisons all together.[50] While his abolitionist position confirms his own admission that he was "at odds with the legal profession and most of psychiatry," Karpman was in the company of mainstream social scientists in his belief that the taboo against sexuality was not only retrograde but harmful and that the rejection of this taboo must extend to prisons.[51]

Although sex was increasingly being considered a "natural part of human existence," as Hopper claimed in 1969, that view did not apply to same-sex relations. Despite evidence that since the inception of the prison, social reformers had been concerned that it might breed rather than correct immoral behavior, including sexual deviance and rape, the belief that homosexuality is a raging presence in prisons is of more recent vintage.[52] As Regina Kunzel has asserted, "Although same-sex sexual acts have long been part of prison life, they have been understood in radically different ways and have provoked varying responses at different historical moments."[53] Early prison reformers, followed by Progressive Era social scientists, believed that the free world was more corrupt than prison and that prisoners' isolation from the contaminating dangers of the outside world was key to their rehabilitation. This "environmentalist" view of human behavior, combined with the concurrent understanding that sexual orientation was more fluid than fixed, meant that the notion that homosexual sex was rampant in prisons was not yet taken for granted. According to historian Brian Stack, Progressive Era reformatories were meant precisely to turn "sodomites into citizens." Corrections officials "judged those who had committed crimes of sodomy not by attributing a permanent sexual identity to them but by viewing their sexual desires as behaviors that could be corrected."[54] While this faith had its detractors and same-sex desire was pathologized, it was not yet a common assumption that prisons would create permanent moral depravity. The vices and temptations of a corrupt, urbanized world could cause young men to "fall" into homosexuality, but the reformatory and the penitentiary would turn them into productive, law-abiding citizens.[55]

By the 1920s and 1930s, however, prisons came to be seen as incubating degenerate sexual practices.[56] While a new generation of psychologists and sociologists, as well as pioneers of the emerging field of sexology, debated the exact source of same-sex attraction, it became common to accept Havelock Ellis's claim in 1928 that "homosexual practices everywhere flourish and abound in prison."[57] As historian Margot Canaday has argued, between the time of the Progressive Era and the New Deal, the state constructed policies that increasingly defined homosexuality as outside normative citizenship.[58] By midcentury, legislators, journalists, and the public were in the midst of a full-blown moral panic about sex, a scare that functioned as a proxy "for other postwar social anxieties: about the hypermasculinization and potential violence of returning veterans, the wartime dislocation of sexual and gender norms, Cold War threats to national security, and the heightened visibility of postwar gay and lesbian urban subcultures."[59] World War II had unsettled the gender division of labor and brought men into intimate, homosocial environments, fraying normative ideas about gender and sexuality.[60] Medical discourse lent scientific justification to increasingly punitive legislation criminalizing nonnormative sexual behavior.[61] In Cold War culture, "domestic containment" meant curtailing "sex crime" and deviant sexual practices as well as communists.[62] A *Collier's* magazine editorial ominously warned, "Who knows where or when the next psychopath or hoodlum will strike? In your town? In your street?"[63]

As legislators sought to contain "perverts" in prison, corrections professionals and social scientists grappled with the meaning of same-sex relations within prison walls, arriving at sometimes contradictory conclusions. They conducted numerous studies of the sexual "subculture" inside prisons, offering taxonomies of sexual types and a range of perversions that all linked criminality and sexual deviance.[64] On the one hand, observers and incarcerated people matter-of-factly reported that same-sex relations in prison were a reasonable and temporary adaptation to the absence of heterosexual partners and did not necessarily indicate a deterioration of morals or a permanent shift in sexual orientation. In what was called situational homosexuality, the peculiar constraints of prison life encouraged "normal" prisoners to engage in same-sex relations to satisfy their natural biological needs.[65]

On the other hand, observers—sometimes the same ones—asserted that long-term confinement in such unnatural conditions produced permanent psychic damage from which "normal" prisoners were unlikely to recover. Psychologist Robert M. Lindner referred to prison as a regressive institution, halting and reversing the natural progression of healthy sexual development: "Like some vampirous creature, prison literally drains its wards of all that makes for maturity."[66] Tortured by pent-up sexual desires and pressured by "true homosexuals," incarcerated men experienced a "disintegration of personality" that doomed them to reenact the "abnormal practices established while in confinement."[67] Corrections professionals voiced similar opinions. Clinton T. Duffy, the former warden at San Quentin State Prison in California, acknowledged that there was plenty of sexual activity in prisons, "but it's the wrong kind. No inmate, no matter how good his intentions, is entirely spared homosexual advances, and many succumb. Some can never resume a normal relationship. What they believe to be a temporary expedient in prison becomes a permanent problem when they get out."[68] Duffy asserted that "one of the worst tragedies of long-term prison life is the not infrequent transformation from heterosexual to homosexual preferences"; he argued that "the principal cause of prison outbreaks isn't discontent with *living* conditions. It's discontent with *sexual* conditions. If men in confinement could satisfy their urges in a normal manner, most prison rebellions—even escape attempts—would be a thing of the past."[69] Notably, Duffy singled out Mississippi as "the only state that 'squarely faces the fact that prison violence is triggered by men who can no longer stand the lack of conventional sex.'"[70] Whether prison sex was regarded as an unremarkable release of biological urges or a source of terrifying violence, observers agreed that prison homosexuality was largely situational, so corrections professionals suggested conjugal visits for married men as a way of preventing it from doing permanent damage.[71] In their eyes, the American penal system should no longer be, in the words of columnist Reverend Lester Kinsolving, "a collection of sodomy factories."[72]

Conjugal visits gained traction in the late 1960s and early 1970s with the revelation that homosexual rape frequently occurred in prison and jail. The most devastating exposé of this phenomenon, known as the Davis Report, led by the Philadelphia district attorney's office and the city's police department, was released in 1968. Chief Assistant District Attorney Alan J. Davis was ordered by Judge Alexander F. Barbieri to conduct an investigation after a youth was assaulted by other prisoners in a sheriff's van.[73] A dogged labor negotiator with a background in psychology, Davis was well suited to the task.[74] His capacity for outrage was equally notable. After an intellectually disabled auto theft suspect was sexually assaulted multiple times while in jail, Davis announced that because the sheriff and correctional officers were unable to protect the inmates in their custody, he set the suspect free until trial because "it is cruel and unusual punishment, under the circumstances, to keep this boy locked in prison."[75] On the basis of interviews with over three thousand Philadelphia prisoners and 560 prison employees, as well as polygraphs and written statements, Davis found that sexual assaults were "epidemic" in the Philadelphia prison system and attributed this violence primarily to lax guard supervision, idleness due to a lack of inmate programs, poor design of the physical plant, and ineffective disciplinary procedures. "After a young man's body has been defiled, his manhood degraded, and his will broken, he is marked as a sexual victim for the duration of his confinement," Davis concluded. "He eventually returns to the community ashamed, confused and full of hatred." The report suggested that if prisoners "were permitted conjugal visits, many family relationships might be saved, tensions relieved, and a higher morality introduced into the prison social structure. Such a program would require the construction of security cottages where man and wife could spend time privately together. It has been accomplished in as primitive a state as Mississippi; it can and should be done in Philadelphia."[76]

Adding to the alarming representations of rape in prison was the contention that most rapes were committed by Black prisoners on white prisoners.[77] As Regina Kunzel has argued, the prison "jungle" in which Black men purportedly dominated white men "evoked a racialized narrative, deeply embedded, of black degeneracy and specifically of the predatory black male rapist." Prison was a world turned upside down, not just because of the prevalence of same-sex relations but because of its supposed inversion of racist hierarchy. "Negro Rule" in prison was, according to Kunzel, a "story of black aggression and white victimization . . . that resonated in the larger cultural context of this period, in the wake of the civil rights and black power movements."[78] Sociologist Leo Carroll attributed these assaults to this cultural context: "The prison is merely an arena within which black males may vent a rage developed through 300 years of oppression at individuals perceived to be representatives of their oppressors." A Black prisoner told him, "You guys (whites) been cutting our balls off even since we been in this country. Punking whites is just one way of getting even."[79] These lines of argument demonstrate Naomi Murakawa's insight that both liberal and conservative whites equated acts of violence by Black people with lawlessness and crime.[80] In this case, liberals attributed Black prisoners' sexual assaults on white prisoners to Blacks' understandable resentment and anger, and conservatives ascribed the same sexual assaults to bestial qualities supposedly intrinsic to Black men. Both arguments are variations on a theme long articulated at Parchman: Black male prisoners needed to be controlled through the safety valve of sex.

Exposés about prison rape were accompanied by sensationalized books that fomented and reinforced homophobia, such as *Terror in Prisons: Homosexual Rape and Why Society Condones It* by sociologists Carl Weiss and David James Friar.[81] The press described "caged men" fighting "jealously for each other," while men sold their bodies for cartons of cigarettes.[82] Theater, novels, and films dramatized prison rape so that "rape came to be understood as the defining practice of sex in men's prisons."[83] This cultural trend, which encompassed genres from social science to fiction, simultaneously exoticized the prison as a world apart and generated sympathy for rape victims.[84] But the literature assumed that homosexual behavior was a concern in itself; consensual gay sex was as deviant as if it had been coerced.

Kunzel contends that by "reducing sex in prison to rape and conceiving of it as motivated by a drive for dominance rather than desire, the story of prison sexual violence as it emerged in the 1970s effectively disaggregated prison sexual expression from its troubling relationship to sexual identity." This separation tended "to cordon . . . off" the prison, effectively isolating its implications from the larger culture."[85] Yet this isolation was not complete either materially or ideologically. For penologists, academics, legislators, and corrections officials throughout the United States, this cordoning off was precisely the problem. They sought to cure the sexual pathologies of prison by opening the gates.

FROM "PRIMITIVE" TO "PIONEERING": MISSISSIPPI AS MODEL

Penologists from around the United States turned to Mississippi, where they noted the apparent paradox that racist paternalism begat humane prison practices. African American jurist Raymond Pace Alexander observes, "The intriguing aspect of the Mississippi experience is that what began as a rather primitive and barbaric practice has developed into a pioneer trial in prison reform."[86] Even though liberal northerners regarded southern prisons as the most backward and brutal in the country, they saw Parchman's conjugal visits as humane and forward thinking. In 1959 the Fourth Annual Southern Conference on Corrections devoted an entire panel, "A State Experiments with the Conjugal Visit," to Mississippi's policy.[87] As Parchman superintendent Bill Harpole explained, "When a man is deprived of normal sex activities, he seeks a substitute. . . . These cause fights and even killings."[88] An expert from the New York Institute of Criminology concurred that a less puritanical outlook on the part of penal officials as well as the public would allow for "a healthier sex activity program within our penal institutions." While acknowledging that Mississippi deserved criticism for many of its prison practices, he asserted that "it is far ahead of even the most progressive state in the conjugal visit."[89]

Whether conjugal visits were primarily an attempt to pacify prisoners and extract their labor or an earnest show of respect for family ties, Mississippi's penal officials touted conjugal visits to counter Parchman's critics. Since scholars have demonstrated that the rise of mass incarceration was part of a concerted effort to contain the civil rights movement and punish Black activists, it has been difficult to recognize that in this respect Mississippi officials persuasively presented Parchman as a laboratory for progressive penology. At the same time that the rest of the nation regarded Mississippi as the "singular site of political authoritarianism and racial extremism in 1960s America," it was especially strategic for Mississippi boosters to showcase selected features of their penal system to improve its image.[90]

At the same time that Parchman's spokespeople publicized its liberal visitation policies, the prison appeared in the national news as a torture chamber for Freedom Riders and other Black and white civil rights activists. Governor Ross Barnett (1960–64) and his segregationist supporters believed that sending protestors to Parchman would break their spirits if not their bones.[91] Organizers and demonstrators were incarcerated by the hundreds throughout the 1960s and subjected to abuses such as being stripped naked, forced to consume laxatives, crowded into steaming-hot cells, and denied bedding.[92] In a strange twist, Mississippi's corrections officials countered these revelations by foregrounding what had been the most taboo aspect of prison life—their frank treatment of prison sex—to distract from the depravity of the prison as a whole.

These tensions and discrepancies between reform and reaction reveal a moment before civil disobedience and violent crime had become synonymous in the minds of law enforcement. According to Parchman superintendent Fred Jones, "The most troublesome prisoners ever held at Parchman were not the convicted murderers on 'death row,' but the freedom riders who chanted stirring 'freedom songs' instead of work songs after being placed in solitary confinement."[93] Freedom fighters, too, implied a distinction between their acts of political protest and the transgressions for which Parchman's other prisoners were convicted. *Jet* magazine reporter Larry Still asserted that Parchman was a place where "citizens [Freedom Riders] seeking their rights in the state are placed in solitary confinement and convicted prisoners are given an unusual amount of freedom."[94] Though Still's assertion was tongue in cheek, the juxtaposition between protestors and "convicted prisoners" who "get sex privileges" suggests that disorderly conduct was not a *real* crime and that lumping them together was itself an indignity. While historians have recently established the direct and reciprocal connections between the civil rights and prisoners' rights movements, Richard Lott, a white man who was incarcerated at Parchman, expressed irritation that approximately $4 million, "plus numerous injuries and two deaths," had been spent trying to enroll James Meredith at the University of Mississippi and asked pointedly, "Why couldn't just a small amount of this money be spent on food, clothing, shoes, vocational training programs, instructive literature, etc. at Parchman?"[95]

Revelations about the presence of maggots and rats, raw sewage, routine floggings for refusing to work, and poor medical care at Parchman and the litigation that followed culminated in the landmark case *Gates v. Collier*, led by the indefatigable thirty-one-year-old attorney from New York City, Roy Haber, on behalf of plaintiffs alleging that their confinement deprived them of rights guaranteed by the First, Eighth, Thirteenth, Fourteenth, and Fifteenth Amendments to the US Constitution.[96] The decision, the first ever supported by the US Department of Justice, condemned the conditions at Parchman prison as a violation of both the Constitution and of modern standards of decency. US district judge William C. Keady ruled that living conditions were not fit for humans; Black prisoners were segregated, subject to harsher treatment, and excluded from certain vocational training programs; cruel corporal punishment was regularly used; and armed trusties were in charge of guarding other inmates. He issued a sweeping order for "immediate and long-range relief."[97]

As evidence that civil rights agitation was perceived as not only tantamount to but more dangerous than felonious crime, a Parchman sergeant warned a potential litigant that "he was on the bad list" and "would never be paroled if he continued to 'fool around with those fucking civil rights people.'"[98] Racist resistance reared its head in the face of the court's ruling; state legislators denounced Keady for "taking over Parchman" and complied with the court's mandates only grudgingly and with token gestures.[99] For example, prison administrators addressed the court's requirement to desegregate prison camps by placing a single Black prisoner in an all-white camp and a lone white man in the all-Black camp.[100] Meanwhile, prisoners complained that "goon squads" were beating dozens of prisoners during retaliatory rampages.[101]

In the face of this judicial intervention and state officials' efforts to obstruct it, Mississippi's segregationists simultaneously claimed that their prison brought enlightened treatment of offenders while criminalizing people engaged in civil disobedience. While Bill Zeman of the John Howard Association, a correctional oversight group, pointed out that "a prison can't claim to be a modern, progressive institution just because it allows conjugal visits and has prisoners riding herd over the other inmates," Parchman officials used their prison both as a weapon against protesters and as a source of defiant pride in the face of northern contempt.[102]

Curious about this peculiar coexistence of inhumanity and innovation, outside experts descended on Parchman, which they described as "virtually a kingdom unto itself."[103] A man who went by the name of Flip who was incarcerated there reported that "modern penologists, newspapermen and magazine writers have been contacting the Superintendent of this backward institution and requesting that they be allowed to study us and the workings of this sprawling penal farm. There passes hardly a week when someone isn't coming through asking how we like this or that."[104] Parchman officials welcomed these investigators with an official tour in 1972, just as Judge Keady declared its conditions unconstitutional.[105] During a public relations campaign on behalf of the prison, Jack Reed, the superintendent, told the Jackson, Mississippi, Lions Club that despite the inaccurate and hostile media reports, there were "positive things—things you've never heard of"—taking place, and singled out conjugal visits that boosted inmate morale.[106] Governor William Waller (1972–76) pointed to the prison's "innovative programs such as conjugal visiting, compassionate leave, work release and Christmas furloughs." He did not mention the raw sewage standing on the ground adjacent to sleeping quarters, and when a photographer asked to take a picture of the scene, Waller accused the photographer of "witch-hunting."[107] Claiming the high moral ground was disingenuous in the face of federal intervention to remedy the prison's deplorable conditions and inhumane practices. At the height of law-and-order backlash against civil rights agitation, however, it is significant that Parchman's boosters lauded the fluidity of Parchman's boundaries without having to reassure the public about criminals on the loose.

In the face of public scrutiny of Parchman's horrors, prison psychologist Tom Graf maintained that Parchman could become a model for the nation. While critics referred to Parchman as less a prison than a "farm with slaves," Graf praised its relatively "small population and ample space, [with] nearly autonomous prison camps scattered around the plantation."[108] Columbus B. Hopper, too, regarded the southern prison as suited for reform because of its openness; Parchman was "not deeply entrenched with the 'cellblock psychosis' as in other prisons." In contrast, prisons outside the South confined people in mass cell blocks, and "mass cell block systems will always have most emphasis on security and will remain unwieldy and resistant to change."[109] While Hopper's comments at best betray a naivete about the history of crime and punishment in the Jim Crow South and at worst express white supremacist attitudes that rationalized customary ways of keeping African Americans in their place, we can understand why some prison reformers regarded Parchman in this light. In the mid-twentieth century, psychologists and sociologists warned of "institutional neurosis" caused by total institutions and advocated decentralization and deinstitutionalization. In his analysis of mental hospitals, for example, Erving Goffman warned against the dehumanization caused by "the barrier to social intercourse with the outside world and to departure that is often built right into the physical plant," such as "locked doors" and "high walls."[110] The most promising feature of plantation prisons was that they were "more open institutions" that allowed more "prisoners outside the walls" and were more likely to let free people inside as well.[111] Harry Woodward Jr., the director of correctional programs for the reform-oriented W. Clement and Jessie V. Stone Foundation in Chicago, concluded after visiting over three hundred prisons in the United States and the world that Parchman was "one of the easiest places I have seen to turn into a model prison, and the most important reason to me is that they allow conjugal visiting."[112]

Mississippi suddenly became an unlikely model of progressive penology. The *Delta Democrat-Times* reprinted the approving words of Douglas E.

Kneeland of the *New York Times*: "The Mississippi state Penitentiary here, long a symbol of the worst in penal servitude, has taken long strides into the 20th century in the last four years."[113] In this light, opposition to conjugal visits was retrograde, a vestige of "the age-old theory of punitive rather than rehabilitative custody." Conjugal visits appeared to be common sense, part of the "preparation of an offender for successful re-entry into the community, the prevention of the deterioration of marriages and family life, and stimulation of the desire to be a useful and productive member of society."[114] The practice could be grafted onto a rehabilitation-oriented penology outside the South.

Those who retained the idea of the farm as a profit-making institution found more liberal visitation policies consistent with productivity. Whereas prison psychologist Tom Graf recommended that Parchman needed employees who were committed "to restructuring a human life instead of committed to getting in another crop," George John Beto, a Texas penologist hired as a consultant by the prison, affirmed that its land "could result in an improvement in the feeding program for the inmates and at the same time serve as a resource for a constructive work program."[115] But Beto also praised Parchman for being "the only penitentiary in the United States that recognizes the reality of sex."[116]

Conjugal visits were hailed by strange bedfellows for a wide range of reasons: as a means of sustaining normative behavior, as a way of restoring patriarchy and a sense of manly responsibility, as an incentive for generating greater productivity among imprisoned laborers, and as a safety valve to prevent violence and unrest. Rather than promoting permissiveness, conjugal visits could shore up discipline, heteronormativity, and compliance. Strikingly, they demonstrate the multivalent nature of prison reform. The views of Norman Carlson, director of the Federal Bureau of Prisons, illustrate this point. In 1977 Carlson, who backed furloughs for married inmates in order to restore family ties, also pushed to ban all communist, Black, and gay literature inside prisons.[117] This distinction was not a matter of hypocrisy but a reminder that notions of danger, risk, and belonging are neither fixed nor absolute. "Security" was not yet a blanket defense against any penological innovation; in fact, liberal visitation—at least when it upheld patriarchal norms—was instituted to preserve order rather than upend it. As Dan Berger and Toussaint Losier have asserted, during these tumultuous decades the future of prisons was "'up for grabs.' Liberals, conservatives, and radicals all battled over the future of American prisons."[118] But what they were fighting for overlapped in surprising ways.

5 "It's Something We Must Do"

The National Reach of Conjugal Visits

Soon after Raymond Pace Alexander, a Philadelphia judge and former criminal defense attorney, read the 1968 report revealing the extent of sexual violence in the city's jails and prisons, he spoke out in favor of conjugal visits. Alexander was brought up in the cosmopolitan New Negro movement, graduated from Harvard Law School in 1923, and spent his legal career fighting discrimination in public accommodations, education, employment, and housing.[1] In an address to his colleagues on the bench, he praised the courage of city officials in revealing the extent of sexual violence in carceral institutions and urged that they show the same courage in initiating new approaches to corrections. "The inmate who is isolated from society learns to distrust the values of the outside world," Alexander explained. "He is exposed to an inmate culture which supports anti-social attitudes." Conjugal visits would "make the convict's life worth living."[2] Opposition to the practice based on its alleged immorality seemed to him puritanical and hypocritical. Without providing healthy outlets for prisoners' sexuality and fostering connections to their families, Alexander noted, "We'll still be sending monsters out into the community."[3] In 1972, while recognizing that the proposal might seem revolutionary, Alexander predicted "that in five years, normal sexual relations in prisons, properly supervised, will be the practice in many states." "It's not something to joke about," he stated; "it's something we must do."[4]

While Alexander's views were supported by psychologists, prisoners, and their families, others condemned Alexander as a tool of "the Communists and the Devil." One indignant letter he received called for bread-and-water diets in prison and attributed crime to the "kid gloves and red carpets" that "Jack ass judges" like Alexander promoted. A prison sentence was turning into "a vacation—best of food—entertainment—and now women." The US quagmire in Vietnam informed this sense of disgust. Another critic moaned to Alexander that "it is as dangerous to live in Philadelphia as it is in Saigon"; another recommended that, instead of criminals, "our fighting men" in Vietnam should receive conjugal visits from their wives. Alexander's critics, like many conservative white people, linked social services to congenital interpretations of crime; conjugal visits would "add to the babies on welfare—breed more thieves, rapists, and murderers. How much more can you coddle criminals?"[5] Pathologizing the families of incarcerated men was common among criminologists as well. Donald R. Johns, a correctional official in Washington State, attempting to present the facts as "objectively as possible," asserted that conjugal visits would increase the number of children born to "inadequate families."[6]

Despite the concurrent law-and-order counterrevolution against the "decline in morality, religiosity, and righteous living" allegedly caused by the freedom struggles of the 1960s, the practice of conjugal visiting spread.[7] The rightward turn of American politics seemed incompatible with extending any liberties to prisoners. Scholars have generally agreed that this period marked what Francis A. Allen has called the "decline of the rehabilitative ideal."[8] But this declension narrative obscures the unevenness of this development and the level of experimentation government officials were willing to attempt. As in Mississippi, they did so for a complex and sometimes contradictory mix of reasons.

In California, according to historian Lisa McGirr, by the late 1960s "conservatives' concerns with 'law and order' as well as morality, and their critiques of 'liberal elites' and 'coddling criminals'—shorn of their apocalyptic, extremist tendencies—had become a part of the dominant political discourse."[9] Yet in 1968 California became the first state other than Mississippi to establish conjugal visits. Even prison officials recognized the incongruity. Raymond K. Procunier, director of the California Department of Corrections (DOC), who touted recent reforms in the state's prison system to a congressional committee in 1971, said that he would have thought he was dreaming if he had been told ten years before that California would have the nation's largest program of family visits. "Correctional agencies are supposed to be the epitome of conservatism when it comes to change," Procunier noted, "but this is a busted myth in California."[10]

According to criminologist Joseph P. Conrad, the goal of prison reform was taken up by people of all political stripes during the 1960s and

1970s as "the revulsion felt by liberal humanists for the degradation imposed by the prison coincided with the realization by fiscal conservatives that the costs of custody, even without attempts at programs, were escalating to levels of absurdity." Optimistic reformers provided a counterpoint to the fearmongering calls for law and order. Even as legislatures adopted increasingly severe sentencing laws in order to appease, as Conrad noted, the "accumulated anger of the public against the criminal whose predations epitomize so much of our collective discontent," prisons from California to Connecticut adopted the practice of conjugal visits.[11]

THE CALIFORNIA EXPERIMENT

In the 1950s, California was regarded by experts in criminology as the nation's leader in penology.[12] When it opened in 1951, Soledad State Prison in Monterey County was described as "California's model." Officials stated, "The policy of the California State Board of Prison Directors is based upon the concept that there can be no regeneration except in freedom." In the 1940s, Governor Earl Warren (1943–53) had called for a complete reorganization of the state's prison system and appointed progressive penologists and sociologists to overhaul the state's classification and treatment programs.[13] Clinton T. Duffy, who advocated education, sports, religion, and psychiatry for incarcerated people, was appointed warden of Soledad. "With a flair for public spectacle" he gained national attention through positive coverage of his reforms in magazines such as *Reader's Digest* and *Life*. As was the case with social scientists concerned with stamping out sexual pathology more generally, Duffy's efforts to soothe and socialize prisoners with vibrant programming also aimed to stamp out any form of sexual perversion.[14]

By the 1960s California's penal officials were experimenting with "therapeutic penology," rehabilitative practices designed to convert "criminals into useful citizens." Equipped with the information provided by the newly formed Correctional Research Division, the California penal system was regarded as "the world's most foremost laboratory for the development of new methods to rehabilitate criminals."[15] In 1966 eminent psychiatrist Karl Menninger, who argued that the vengefulness of the justice system constituted a crime in itself, was lavish in his praise: "The California correctional system . . . has been far out in the lead among the states, with excellent programs of work, education, vocational training, medical services, group counseling, and other rehabilitative activities." He emphasized that all of these innovations "constitute a systematic effort along scientific principles."[16]

If the walls of San Quentin State Prison could talk, they might have whispered that they had heard these nostrums before. In the 1940s, warden Clinton Duffy advocated what was then called the New Penology: reformation rather than punishment, short sentences and liberal clemency practices, kindness from guards.[17] As Angela Y. Davis points out, "If the words 'prison reform' so easily slip from our lips, it is because 'prison' and 'reform' have been inextricably linked since the beginning of the use of imprisonment as the main means of punishing those who violate social norms."[18] Michel Foucault concludes, "Prison 'reform' is virtually contemporary with the prison itself: it constitutes, as it were, its programme."[19]

In the 1960s and 1970s, prisoners straddled hope and despair as they expressed their grievances through litigation and rebellion, anxiously awaiting reforms that would put rhetoric into practice. John Irwin, who served time in San Quentin, recalled that prisoners "were led to believe that if they participated in prison programs with sincerity and resolve they would leave prison in better condition than they entered and would generally be much better equipped to cope with the outside world."[20] But they quickly became disillusioned with the "arbitrariness and authoritarianism" of those in charge, and professionals who looked beyond the puffery argued that in California prisons, "physical degradation is replaced by psychological degradation."[21] Some prisoners ultimately concluded that "adopting a treatment model of criminal deviancy had unforeseen consequences that transformed the treatment staff into custody officers of sinister, Orwellian character."[22] As Volker Janssen and Eric Cummins have shown, prisoners recognized new therapeutic strategies as tools of control and tried to redirect them to their own advantage. For all of the talk of rehabilitation, California prisons were still mismanaged and dehumanizing.[23] Seemingly progressive reforms reinforced fears of sexual deviance. Duffy's pathbreaking prison theater program, aimed at using the arts as a form of rehabilitation, banned any expressions of alternative gender identities on or off the stage. Guided by the new spirit of "treatment," Duffy invited Alfred Kinsey to analyze the "sex criminals" at San Quentin.[24]

The seeds for conjugal visits in California were sown in 1952 when the warden at the California Institute for Men changed the facility's visiting policy from noncontact visits that lasted one hour to outdoor visits every Sunday from 11:00 a.m. to 3:00 p.m., when participants were allowed to touch and embrace and share lunch at a picnic table. A prisoner re-marked that as a result of this change, his wife "hasn't missed a Sunday in 19 months"; visiting kept the couple together and helped him to "feel like a man again." His wife reflected on the difference this policy change made. It took her fourteen hours to travel five hundred miles to see him. "You can't think of anything to say in one hour," she complained; "I was half scared and we just sat and looked at each other across a counter."[25] This feeling might help to explain why 43 percent of spouses who visited their husbands for just one hour during their first year of incarceration had stopped visiting by the second year.[26]

The reform-minded former warden of San Quentin, Clinton T. Duffy, had been closely watching Mississippi and Mexico as models of conju-gal visitation. He was particularly struck when a penologist jibed, "You in California, with all your modern rehabilitation movements, schools, trades, church cooperation, medical facilities, psychiatric therapy and hu-mane treatment of inmates, are still behind Mexico in prison reform. You won't begin to catch up until you accept sex as a fact of life instead of turning your back and acting as if it isn't there."[27] Conjugal visits were an experiment in adopting a new outlook toward sex, bolstered by the Kinsey Report and the sexual liberation movement. Supporters of conjugal visits saw outdated thinking about sexuality as their main obstacle, yet most had no tolerance for homosexual conduct. A letter to Raymond Pace Alexan-der expressed the prevalent idea that allowing heterosexual expression in prisons would be "the remedy to overcome the frightful conditions ex-isting in the prisons; i.e. using the common vernacular, homosexuality."[28] In 1962 Duffy argued that "if men in confinement could satisfy their natural urges in a normal manner, most prison rebellions—even escape attempts—would be a thing of the past."[29] A year later California assem-blyman Tom Carrell proposed a study of conjugal visiting "or other means of alleviating the sexual and other problems incident to separation of a criminal offender from his family."[30] Although the legislative committee preferred home furloughs to spousal visits at the prison, the California DOC launched a pilot program for conjugal visits in 1968.

Governor Ronald Reagan (1967–75) publicly endorsed conjugal visits as a measure to promote strong family ties and support systems after re-lease. On the one hand, in the wake of unrest in Berkeley and in the Watts neighborhood of Los Angeles, he famously endorsed law and order, rail-ing against riots, crime, and the "permissive attitude which pervades too many homes, too many schools, too many courts."[31] On the other hand, he subscribed to the idea of California as a "creative society" strengthened by experimentation, individual freedom, and restrained government. Reagan was influenced by a paper submitted by public relations consultant Rus Walton that argued that conjugal visits would both alleviate homosexuality and help families remain intact.[32] Reagan had a canny sense of the latitude that a conservative politician might have to experiment with ideas that made sense, pointing out that "no one can accuse me of being a bleeding heart."[33] Allan F. Breed, director of the California Youth Authority, recalled the governor's response to Breed and Procunier's memo recommending conjugal visits: "He had a little twinkle in his eyes and he said, 'This is a very liberal issue.' We were both quiet and he said, 'No liberal could possibly support it. But a conservative could, if it's the right thing to do.' Then he talked a little about this concept that there are some kinds of changes that can be made that people will support from a conservative that they wouldn't necessarily support from a liberal."[34]

Announcing his support for conjugal visits, Reagan couched his opinion in patriarchal and heteronormative terms, saying that they would help "alleviate instances of homosexuality and help to keep the family unit intact while the head of the household is incarcerated."[35] These aims fit squarely with conservative values. As an official at the California Correctional Institution in Tehachapi put it, "A broken family in all probability becomes a permanent welfare case."[36] The conservative desire to curb homosexuality, welfare, and prison unrest intersected with liberal notions of rehabilitation, nourishing prisoners' dignity and connection to their families.

The first full-fledged conjugal visit program in California, called the Family Visiting Program, was established in 1968 at Tehachapi, a medium- and minimum-security facility for men in a remote area 150 miles north of Los Angeles. The prison was already experimenting with "community living" units focused on vocational training, group therapy, and some measure of self-government.[37] Married inmates were eligible to spend two days with their wives, children, siblings, and parents, in a three-bedroom apartment outside the prison fence that used to function as staff housing.[38] According to Superintendent G. P. Lloyd, these visits were an "attempt to bridge the gap between institutional and home life."[39] In this first incarnation, conjugal visits were narrowly framed as a means of preparation for freedom; to be eligible for them, men had to demonstrate six months of good conduct and be within three months of their release date.

In contrast to the severe architecture of the main buildings, designed to control behavior, the family visiting units at Tehachapi might have felt something like freedom. Superintendent Lloyd emphasized that the apartments were a site of patriarchal domesticity, featuring fireplaces that "symbolize . . . domestic stability," which offset the perils of a homosocial institution. The prison constructed a playground for children, and visiting family members provided their own food. Each visit lasted two nights and most of three days—a total of forty-six hours. A prisoner at Tehachapi told the superintendent that these visits penetrated the membrane of prison and of his identity as a prisoner: "It was a return to reality, a shedding of the 'skin' of prison-oriented thinking, if only briefly. Now I know that this skin is not irremovable."[40]

California's prison spokespeople explained the program in the language of family ties rather than sexual release. Lawrence E. Wilson, the deputy director of the DOC in 1970, clarified that "California does not want conjugal visiting. California wants *family* visiting aimed at preserving the family relationship and helping families grow stronger."[41] Sex was portrayed as incidental. The DOC's information officer explained that "we are trying to treat the sex part of it as just one factor and not euphemize it. The important thing is the family integration—living together, doing the cooking and housekeeping together."[42] Declared an unqualified success, the program spread to almost all state penal institutions in California by 1971. Until 1996, even those with life sentences were eligible for visits.[43] Approximately half of the state's adult prisoners took part in the program.[44] The DOC proudly announced, "The nation's largest prison system officially accepted and endorsed family visiting at a time when most other states were still debating the issue."[45]

Sociologists followed these developments closely. Upon visiting Soledad State Prison in the early 1970s, social scientist Jules Burstein described conjugal facilities—trailers, A-frame cottages, stucco bungalows, and apartments—just outside the prison perimeter. "Once inside," he observed, "the only reminder that one is in prison grounds is the site [*sic*] of the guntower 20 feet away, visible from the kitchen window." Although it was theoretically possible for an inmate to walk off the prison grounds, escapes were extremely uncommon. Burstein gathered data from participants, both incarcerated and free, comparing the conjugal visiting experience with that of regular, supervised, short visits. In the brief visits inside the prison, "the circumstances and setting cause more anguish than joy. The basic humanity of both the prisoner and his visitor are sharply reduced by the inability to ever touch each other." The noise, surveillance, and glass partition between husband and wife made many feel that the encounter was more painful than no visit at all. An incarcerated man lamented, "There's no privacy, no contact. It's like a torture chamber. It's better to communicate by letter." Burstein concluded that family visits "are progressively more humane" and "tend to create an atmosphere in which the captive state of the inmate is temporarily reduced, and where it becomes possible for the visit to truly alleviate the abiding loneliness and solitude of incarceration."[46]

Other social scientists applauded the program and urged its expansion. Norman Holt and Donald Miller recommended extending visits to common-law wives and placing people in correctional institutions near their homes to facilitate more frequent contact. They also suggested that extended family visits should prioritize those who were disqualified for temporary leaves, such as "chronic parole absconders, perpetrators of very violent crimes such as murder, or inmates who need to work out marital problems in a more structured setting than is provided by the home."[47]

Prison officials were matter-of-fact in the face of public skepticism, which tended to focus on security risks. When asked about objections such as unnecessary cost and moral indecency, Leah Bradshaw, a correctional counselor and the coordinator of the conjugal visit program, responded, "I see those reasons essentially as rationalizations" for inaction. When letters to the editor published in the local newspaper questioned the practice, Associate Superintendent E. A. Peterson asserted, "The best way to educate people is through outside contacts with interested public-spirited citizens like the speaking engagements of my community awareness group which includes inmates participating in the family visiting program." In addition, Peterson sponsored tours of the facility "to see how different the men in here are from what their notions of them might be."[48] By 1981 more than ninety conjugal visiting units were provided at California's twelve corrections institutions.

LOVE IN BONDAGE: PRISONER ACTIVISM FOR CONJUGAL VISITS

People who were incarcerated fought for conjugal visits through agitation and litigation. Throughout the prison unrest of the 1960s and 1970s, prisoners across the country who rebelled against oppressive conditions frequently listed conjugal visits among their demands.[49] For male prisoners, emotional support was at least as important as sexual release, and both reinforced their sense of visibility and virility.[50] They used the prevalent rhetoric of rehabilitation and "treatment" to argue for liberal visitation policies, wishfully claiming that conjugal visitation was "certainly not an unrealistic idea in this present age of social enlightenment."[51]

For prisoners to reintegrate into free society successfully, correctional practice would have to shed its repressive assumptions and punitive habits. Addressing the notion that the lack of heterosexual outlets led to sexual deviance, Piri Thomas, a Black Latino writer who had been incarcerated as a youth, reflected, "All the substitutes for heterosexual relationships in prison do not make the inmates perverted. It is the society that is perverted by perpetuating this negation of normal expressions of love."[52] Prison activists argued that depriving prisoners of love and family ties and denying them the "right" to feel and express emotions damaged their personalities. Gil Leano, a Filipino American incarcerated in Washington State after a narcotics conviction, contended that his estrangement from his children and his wife's potential infidelity hurt the public as well as himself: "What archaic notion permits you, the public, to think that men who have committed unlawful acts against society will return to their communities as better citizens after being dehumanized in a cage for a given period of time? You deny men sexually, you make them units and numbers rather than humans, you remove all form of humanity, self-respect and dignity, and then you think that a token program of rehabilitation . . . should be sufficient." He was willing to do time as the consequence of his actions, but he believed that the prison conditions created by "moral prudishness and a lust for vengeance" were "the most errant foolishness for the social order."[53]

Prisoners' arguments for conjugal visits trafficked in homophobia, as well as despair about the prison's capacity to simultaneously require hypermasculinity and impose emasculation. Louis X. Holloway, a Black "model prisoner" and activist serving a twenty-year sentence at Parchman Farm, the Mississippi State Penitentiary, contended, "A man *needs* a woman, and life without her, therefore without essence, is totally miserable."[54] He explained, "It is against the very nature of Man to be confined . . . together with other men, and denied the association of women. Such a system will *always* breed hatred, animosity, resentment, frustration, inferiority complexes, homosexuality, and general inhumanity to man."[55] With all "normal" avenues for demonstrating manhood foreclosed, "Is he *still* a man after years and years of incarceration? How can he prove it, and to whom can he prove it?"[56] As Gil Leano realized, conjugal visits could be a means of controlling the sex lives of prisoners' wives; another Parchman prisoner remarked that the program "helps to stop wandering on the part of married women" since "they know that they can be with their husbands as often as they please."[57]

Incarcerated men complained of prison rape as well as the denial of sexual expression. Although same-sex relations may not have been as "rampant" as researchers argued, rape and fear of rape were defining features of prisoners' experiences.[58] Angola lifer Wilbert Rideau frankly discusses this "deadly serious affair in the world behind bars," arguing that it is "always a matter of power and control—and often, of life and death" but insisting that "sexual violence has little to do with 'heterosexuality' or 'homosexuality' and is generally not the work of sex-crazed perverts." He attributes rape among prisoners to the dehumanizing conditions they endure, which destroys their sense of self-worth. In an effort to validate their masculinity, male prisoners "channel all of their frustrated drives into the pursuit of power, finding gratification in conquest and defeat, the domination and subjugation of each other." Rideau indicts the authorities who resisted the introduction of conjugal visits because they regarded sexual deprivation as a necessary feature of prisons: "So, while politicians play politics, the 'experts' theorize, and penal authorities censor Penthouse and Hustler to prevent a possible 'obscene' influence on the inmates, the nation's jails and prisons continue to be incubators of violence, abuse, murders, suicides, and warped psyches."[59]

In addition to arguing that conjugal visits would prevent homosexuality, rape, and violence, incarcerated men argued that the sexual deprivation they experienced in prison was a form of cruelty in its own right. Countering the tut-tutting that conjugal visitation would encourage carnality, prisoners emphasized love rather than sex and insisted on belonging rather than accepting disappearance. Piri Thomas suggested that intimacy with a woman was a foretaste of freedom: "By being able to treat each other as peers . . . we would retrieve our identity as human beings."[60] Prisoners relished having private conversations with their spouses and quotidian activities such as helping their children with homework. As sociologist Columbus B. Hopper puts it, conjugal visits allow the prisoner "to keep the self-image of a man who is still important to others."[61] Through sustaining their bonds with loved ones on the outside, those who were incarcerated reclaimed their sense of identity and humanity beyond bare life. By severing inmates' ties with and responsibilities to significant others in the free world, prison purposely stripped people of their sense of self and belonging.

Prisoners insisted on the benefits of intimacy even when conjugal visits were forbidden. In 1953, the editors of the *Angolite* magazine at the

Louisiana State Penitentiary at Angola asserted that prisoners themselves knew best what they needed to improve their conditions: "Progress in any penal institution STARTS FROM THE INSIDE." With the support of a former penitentiary physician, they proposed dances where those in the men's and women's camps could mingle and enjoy companionship. Angolites were savvy enough to make their case in rehabilitative language; such occasions would "teach again the fundamentals of social conduct and group behavior."[62]

After Mississippi's conjugal visitation program became widely publicized, a Louisiana state legislative subcommittee recommended conjugal visits to combat homosexuality and improve rehabilitation by giving prisoners "a touch of family life."[63] In 1970 Representative Francis Bickford proposed a bill that would allow conjugal visits to married prisoners, including those in common-law marriages.[64] He commented, "I would consider it as cruel and inhuman to deny conjugal visits as much as it would be cruel and inhuman to deny them food to survive. . . . We are actually breaking up families when we send a person to prison."[65] Bickford stressed that the main purpose of the bill was to prevent homosexuality, although he used the language of love rather than depravity: "Some of these men have fallen in love with other men and that's the real basis of this bill."[66] Debates over the bill were interrupted with wisecracks and snickers. Opponents contended that criminals should pay their debts to society, not carry on their regular lives. Foreshadowing a view that became common a generation later, a legislator asked, "If this bill passes, won't it be something like a summer resort out there at Angola?"[67] The bill failed. A decade later, Angola's wardens and administrators pushed for conjugal visits "simply because they recognize the human texture of prisoners and feel the prisoners should have it." But, an Angola journalist noted, "the question will ultimately be decided by politicians and bureaucrats far removed from us."[68]

CONJUGAL VISITS AS CARROT AND STICK

Corrections professionals advocated conjugal visits as a response to prison unrest, and in several states the visits were adopted as a means of pacifying rebellious inmates. These administrators believed that conjugal visitation could serve multiple goals simultaneously: promote rehabilitation, encourage normative heterosexual behavior, and shore up prison discipline. As prisoners staged uprisings around the country, those on both the left and the right recognized a revolutionary new breed of prisoner. For those on the left, prisoners constituted the heroic vanguard of broader radical movements. As Daniel Berger and Toussaint Losier conclude, when prisoners awakened to the structural origins of their brutal conditions and as "the revolt happening in inner cities in the mid-1960s migrated to prison," "some prisoners became activists, some activists became prisoners."[69] Members of the public, as well as policymakers, equated protestors with thugs who threatened to decent society with radical ideas and lawlessness. This prisoner was no longer the "'ordinary' robber, rapist, or slayer." Both liberals and conservatives imagined this militant prisoner as a Black man who "believes he is a victim of a racist society, a condition that can only be corrected, he feels, by wiping out that society"—that is, white society.[70] According to this interpretation, while prisoners became politicized in prison, their politicization was fueled by the turmoil in the urban communities from which they came. If prison agitators had not already been infected by Black militancy before their incarceration, the contagion spread from sources both inside and outside prison walls. "Even though an institution is physically remote," the American Correctional Association observed, "it is not insulated from this unrest. Reports in the press and on radio and television keep inmates well informed."[71]

Given these concerns, it seems surprising that policymakers considered expanding visiting as part of the solution to prison unrest. Throughout the 1970s, governmental officials blamed the turmoil in prisons on outside agitators—radical lawyers, prisoners' rights groups, firebrand hippies, and liberal do-gooders—who allegedly corrupted prisoners with their inflammatory politics and literature. When California corrections officials learned that prisoners were involved with the radical leftist organization the Symbionese Liberation Army, for example, the officials traced the connection to radicals who came into the prison under the auspices of a community relations program.[72] Environmental psychologist Robert Sommer, in contrast, points out that it was odd to surmise that prisoners who are otherwise impervious to all manner of behavior modification would be so easily duped by a few hours of contact with outsiders: "To suggest that prisoners who have effectively resisted the exhortations and authority of social workers, priests, and shrinks have suddenly crumbled and been brainwashed by a few hippie longhairs seems absurd." As a result of this "contagion theory," programs bringing community members into prisons were being curtailed.[73]

Yet opportunities for *family* visitation, seen as pacifying rather than agitating, were increased. On the national level, elected government officials, social scientists, and activists debated the merits of the demands emerging from the increasingly restive prison population and sought methods to quell unrest as well as reduce recidivism.[74] At hearings on prisons, prison reform, and prisoners' rights, members of the US Congress inquired about conjugal visits and listened to testimony in their favor. Thomas O. Murton, a criminologist, described such visits as an element of good penological practice and noted that, in contrast to California, "the prison authorities in Mississippi consider this a right and not a privilege and one does not have to have served a great deal of time and to be black or white . . . in order to be eligible for it."[75] Louis Randall, who had been incarcerated and now directed the St. Leonard's House, a halfway house in Chicago, advocated conjugal visits as an aid to a prisoner's readjustment after release: "The adoption of conjugal visits . . . would reduce the psycho-sexual warping of the offender's personality and the effects of exile, through enhancing the communication between the inside and outside 'worlds.'"[76] Legal scholars Norval Morris and James Jacobs have submitted that visitation policies should be as liberal as possible, and cited California as a model: "Sexual deprivation and disintegration of family were never intended to be a part of punishment and should be ameliorated when possible rather than exacerbated."[77] These comments revealed an essential contradiction in American imprisonment: its stated intent was to promote the resocialization of the prisoner, but the conditions of imprisonment maximized his social isolation.

Corrections officials were split on the issue of conjugal visits; according to a 1969 poll of the Florida Department of Corrections, 49.2 percent were in favor and 50.8 percent were opposed.[78] But psychologists continued to advocate for them. Psychiatrist Robert Sheldon reiterated the shared view that "complete isolation of men and women from all sexual activities of a heterosexual nature is completely unrealistic and results in homosexual behavior or in other displacement of the sexual drive in hostile, aggressive, and sometimes dangerous behavior toward other inmates and prison personnel."[79] Marital stability, community reintegration, the prevention of homosexuality, and the reduction of violence in prison were stock arguments for the practice.[80]

In 1973, after a series of widespread prison protests and rebellions, the National Advisory Commission on Criminal Justice Standards and

Goals called for conjugal visits in state prisons, arguing that correctional authorities should not only allow but also promote and subsidize the visits by providing transportation and privacy. Corrections professionals considered contact visits to be "essential" for maintaining family relationships and submitted that neither the length of the visit nor the number of visitors should be limited, except in cases of substantiated security risk.[81] After decades of studying prisoners and their rehabilitation as an academic and as the research director for expert commissions, sociologist Sol Chaneles argued that extended private visits should include "sweethearts, common-law parties and intimate friends." Taking a view that was unusual in 1975, he added that "for those whose mode of sexual behavior is homosexual, homosexual relations should be permitted among consenting prisoners as well as with homosexual partners from outside of prison. For those whose only means of finding sexual expression is through the payment of prostitutes, male or female, prostitutes should be allowed to practice their occupation" in prison.[82] With funding from the Law Enforcement Assistance Administration, Robert Sommer drafted proposals for the physical reorganization of prisons that included "pleasant apartment-like rooms" for family visits.[83]

For the next two decades, states instituted conjugal visits as part of a suite of reforms. In New York State, as *Newsweek* put it, "the disaster at Attica . . . drew attention, in the most dramatic possible way, to the incendiary conditions of many American prisons."[84] While the prison uprising at the Attica Correctional Facility in upstate New York fueled a "historically unprecedented backlash against all efforts to humanize prison conditions in America," historian Heather Ann Thompson points out that, "Janus-like," the uprising and its brutal suppression also generated significant reforms. New York State implemented many of the protestors' central demands, hiring more Black and Spanish-speaking correctional officers, allowing "greater religious and political freedom, banning censorship of all mail and newspapers, and providing more counseling and additional rehabilitation services."[85] Prisoners could receive visits from almost anyone, without prior approval and as often as desired. The screen in the visiting room was removed so prisoners and visitors could embrace or hold hands.[86] Voicing views that were common in predominately white upstate New York, where correctional facilities were thought to be filled with depraved and dangerous nonwhite strangers from urban centers downstate, a resident of Minoa complained that removing the protective screen "facilitates the passing of dope, guns and ammunition to the poor underprivileged prisoners."[87]

In 1976, New York was the first state after California to adopt extended visits for legally married male prisoners.[88] The program was initially established at Wallkill Correctional Facility, a prison that had been founded in the 1930s in the style of a college campus.[89] About five hundred residents, of a total population of approximately two thousand in the hamlet of Wallkill, signed petitions in protest. One resident, assuming that families of the incarcerated were criminals by association, worried about visiting family members shopping in the hamlet.[90] The state corrections department refused to let local resistance obstruct the program, and within a year, 2,091 visitors—including mothers, children, fathers, and other relatives of prisoners—made a total of 838 visits to Wallkill. By 1978 the program had reached three more prisons in the state, including the Attica Correctional Facility, where mobile homes were parked under a gun tower.[91] Inmate Freddie Ferraro was dubious: "Imagine what everybody's going to think of your wife when she walks out of one of those trailers."[92] Another prisoner complained that a guard walking his wife to a trailer degraded her with snide remarks.[93] Most participants simply enjoyed themselves. "We're people here with human feelings," Daniel Paulino insisted; "we're not all a bunch of animals and psychopathic killers."[94] Jane, whose husband was incarcerated at Wallkill, hadn't seen him in four years, and she worried that the guards would hassle her. "But they didn't. They left us alone. My husband told me that it was the most beautiful day he had, and he didn't get teased by the other men."[95]

In Washington State, conjugal visits began in 1980 at the recommendation of Anthony Travasio, head of the American Correctional Association, who saw it as a solution to a decade of unrest. Prisoners had been advocating conjugal visits since at least 1971, when the Washington State Reform Coalition was founded by both free and imprisoned people. In 1969 the superintendent outlined his intention to move away from a more authoritarian, custodial model toward rehabilitating prisoners for reentry into society.[96] Perhaps the most radical aspect of this shift was an experiment in prisoner self-government. A month before the Attica rebellion in New York State, observers worried that the Washington State Penitentiary at Walla Walla was a ticking time bomb. Some attributed unrest to the excessive protections of prisoners' rights and the power of "militant blacks," while others argued that the situation required more "'sensitive' treatment" by correctional officers, including "inmate councils to deal with prisoner grievances and upgrading of rehabilitation efforts," as well as conjugal or family visits.[97] After the prison had been locked down for almost a month because of the stabbing of a guard, 230 prisoners tore sinks and toilets from their cell walls and attempted to break through their cells, demanding showers.[98]

In 1981 the Washington State Penitentiary began its Extended Family Visit Program, through which family members and the incarcerated could enjoy eighteen hours of complete privacy. According to both prisoners and guards, calm descended on the prison in anticipation of visits.[99] One man enthused, "I've been waiting three long years for this."[100] Another, serving a thirteen-year sentence for armed robbery, emphasized that the visit was not just about sex. He described the joy he felt putting groceries away together, eating a home-cooked meal, and doing the dishes. "We did a lot of laughing and finally had a chance to smooth a few things out that had been troubling us. It was just a good escape from the prison for a few hours."[101]

During the 1970s and 1980s, other states seriously considered instituting conjugal visits, and a dozen did so.[102] After four years of debate, New Mexico established conjugal visits in 1983 in the wake of a deadly riot in which visits were among inmates' demands.[103] A grand jury investigation recommended the program "to combat friction among inmates and reduce their idle time"; prisoners asserted that "physical contact is important in making them feel like human beings."[104] Across the country, the value of conjugal visits was one policy on which corrections officials and prisoners agreed. But beneath it lay the threat of force on both sides. Many correctional officials considered the program "untouchable" because prisoners had openly stated that they would riot if the visits were ever taken away.[105]

In 1977 psychologist Jules Burstein found that family and conjugal visits contributed to rehabilitation and promoted marital and family stability. But, he asserted, visits should be recognized as a human right. "We now understand that torture, exile, and mutilation are no longer acceptable in this culture," he reasoned. Thus, "conjugal visits ought to exist, not only because they may be instrumental in producing valuable individual and social benefits, but because making them available is the *right thing to do*."[106] Corrections officials did not agree that such visits constituted a right. Derral Byers, who coordinated the family visiting program at the Soledad State Prison in California, forthrightly explained to Burstein why he saw conjugal visits as a privilege rather than a right: "As an administrator I always look for ways of controlling a man's behavior. Having rights would do away with such means of control."[107]

In 1984, a Gallup poll found that 61 percent of Americans approved of conjugal visits in "special weekend guest houses within the prison grounds."[108] Jean McBride, who oversaw visiting at Parchman Farm, the Mississippi State Penitentiary, said that "we kind of take pride in the fact that we had [conjugal visits] first" and noted that they had attracted little controversy. Making a claim that appears disingenuous given the program's racist origins, she declared, "Mississippi is a really family-oriented society, and so it's socially acceptable."[109] That same year, advice columnist Anne Landers remarked that it was "unfortunate" that conjugal visits were only allowed in seven states, because "for too long our prisons have turned out vengeful, bitter, hostile inmates who were not rehabilitated but become only more angry and more dangerous. Conjugal visits cut down on rapes and violence."[110] While corrections officials across the nation were still divided, with 46 percent indicating strong approval and 47 percent expressing disapproval, 69 percent agreed that visits help strengthen family ties, 53.3 percent believed they improve inmate morale, and 57.9 percent thought that conjugal visits were not only "here to stay" but would increase over the next ten years.[111] By 1993, seventeen states permitted conjugal or family visits.[112]

"TO MAKE LIFE IN PRISON JUST LIKE HOME": PRISON LITIGATION AND THE RIGHT TO INTIMACY

Prisoners took their insistence on their visibility and humanity to the courts. Until the mid-twentieth century, federal courts generally refused to hear cases regarding the internal operation of prisons. This position, which came to be known as the "hands-off doctrine," emerged from an 1871 Virginia case that declared that prisoners were "slaves of the state"; they were "civilly dead" and had no claim to protection by the courts.[113] Courts maintained this largely hands-off approach toward prison practices for almost a century on the grounds that judges lacked expertise in penology and that interfering with established practices could threaten the security of prisons. As legal scholar Stewart M. Bernstein puts it, "The wall which thereby was erected between the courthouse and the jailhouse served to isolate the prisoner from society to a greater degree than his incarceration did."[114] But in the 1960s and 1970s, extending a judicial trend of reforming public institutions and addressing the rights of minority groups, courts issued a series of opinions expanding the constitutional rights of prisoners.[115] As Keramet A. Reiter has shown, with the expansion of habeas corpus rights and the ability to bring challenges against prison officials on the grounds that prison conditions violated prisoners' civil rights as well as protections against cruel and unusual punishment, "prisoners suddenly had a whole new litigation toolbox. And they used it." Within two decades of the landmark 1964 *Cooper v. Pate* decision that established a Muslim prisoner's right to access a copy of the Koran and participate in Muslim religious services in an Illinois prison, there were eight thousand pending prisoner lawsuits challenging conditions of confinement in twenty-four states.[116] In 1979, prisoners filed 11,195 petitions in federal courts, more than quadruple the number in 1970.[117] Many litigants believed that these suits would be a means toward decarceration. In the words of a jailhouse lawyer in Atlanta, "Prisoners' rights litigation is a process of subversive guerilla warfare—aimed at overthrowing the most despicable manifestation of the corrupting effects of absolute power exercised absolutely."[118]

Although prisoners and their families pursued a range of approaches to litigating their claims to conjugal visits, the case law reveals an "almost unanimous refusal on the part of American courts to declare that any class of incarcerated persons is entitled to conjugal visit rights."[119] Sheldon Polakoff, incarcerated in Atlanta, tried and failed to establish that the denial of conjugal visits constituted cruel and unusual punishment prohibited by the Eighth Amendment; he was told that his deprivation did not sufficiently "shock the conscience."[120] When others argued that the lack of conjugal visits produced such emotional stress as to constitute cruel and unusual punishment, courts found that the need for institutional security and the deterrent value of incarceration justified their denial.[121] In *Lyons v. Gilligan*, male prisoners and their wives argued unsuccessfully that the denial of conjugal visits infringed on their constitutional right to privacy. The court rejected the idea "the state is obligated to create private places for the conduct of marital relations. . . . Imprisonment of persons convicted of crimes is not tantamount to an intrusion of the prisoner's home."[122] Courts found the state's interest in incarceration to be fundamentally incompatible with the sanctity of the marital bed: "One cannot be both in prison and in the sanctum of one's bedroom. The state is under no constitutional obligation to create such a sanctum within the prison walls."[123] As legal scholar Richard Singer has asserted, "The prison is, almost by definition, a place where the resident has lost his privacy, and his identity, and has become a number."[124]

Despite discouraging outcomes, prisoners from Texas to Wisconsin sued for the right to have conjugal visits.[125] Rather than accept the theft of intimacy and privacy as inevitable, they insisted that, as a discrete, insular, and vulnerable class, they were entitled to the court's protection.[126] They savvily drew on the outpouring of social science literature in support of their claims, lending professional legitimacy to their experience of "tension, frustration, and anguish." Columbus B. Hopper, who became the nation's expert on conjugal visits through his study of Parchman, served as expert witness in the case *United States Ex Rel. Wolfish v. Levi*, testifying to the importance of the visits for psychological health.[127]

Although these suits failed in the courts, agitation for prisoners' rights helped to sustain a movement with adherents both inside and outside prison. The very notion that prisoners were persons with cognizable constitutional rights whose claims could be heard "destroyed the custodians' absolute power and the prisoners' isolation from the larger society."[128] Moreover, legal activism by and on behalf of prisoners engendered legislative support, and state legislatures moved to codify some of the standards established by landmark court cases. In 1968, the same year he approved conjugal visits, Governor Ronald Reagan signed what became known as the Inmates Bill of Rights. Extending California's rehabilitative agenda, the bill's author, Alan Sieroty, a Democrat from Beverly Hills, explained, "We are defeating our purpose by depriving inmates of so many rights that they lose their self respect and no longer regard themselves as citizens who can make a meaningful contribution to society."[129] The Inmates' Bill of Rights, enhanced in 1975 by companion legislation signed by Governor Jerry Brown (1975–83), guaranteed those incarcerated in state prisons the right to read any published materials, to marry or enter into any other contract, to confidential correspondence with a public officeholder or lawyer, to inherit property, and to receive personal visits.[130] Pete Wilson, then a Republican assemblyman from San Diego, voted for the measure.[131] State Senator Dennis Carpenter, a Republican from Newport Beach, objected, "This is part and parcel of the effort to make life in prison just like home."[132] Although prisoners critiqued the "treatment" model as both empty and coercive, they benefited from the recognition of the suffering they endured, which was usually invisible to most of the public, and were emboldened by the cracks in their walls.

At the same time, the increasing visibility of prisoners suggested to many conservatives that judges were liberal busybodies giving aid and comfort to criminals with nothing better to do than choke the courts with frivolous lawsuits. In the 1980s and 1990s conservative politicians, correctional unions, victims' rights groups, and the press spread anecdotal accounts of prisoners suing over bad haircuts, chunky peanut butter, and melted ice cream, constructing a framework that pit prisoners' well-being against the rights of "law-abiding" citizens.[133] In 1984 a stunning escape by six men on death row from Virginia's maximum-security Mecklenburg Correctional Facility fueled conservatives' ire over prison litigation and the threat it purportedly caused to public safety. A supporter of Governor Chuck Robb (1982–86) wrote to him, "I did not vote for Chan Kendrick [the head of the American Civil Liberties Union, ACLU] as either governor or director of prisons. The ACLU would turn them all free if the choice were theirs. ACLU would house them in country clubs."[134] By the mid-1990s, at the crest of tough-on-crime legislation, the image of prisons as country clubs prompted a bitter attack on conjugal visits. After all, as the court established in *Lyons v. Gilligan*, "the absence of conjugal visiting . . . is merely a customary concomitant of the punishment of incarceration." Conditions might be uncomfortable, but such were the "wages of incarceration."[135] Because conjugal visits were a "privilege" and not a "right," they could be taken away. As a criminal justice professor observed, "No matter how conservative a warden is, you'll find that most of them tend to be much more liberal in regards to rehabilitation-type programs because that allows them control. . . . They can take it away from them."[136] The termination of these visits strained the already tenuous ties between incarcerated people and their loved ones in the outside world.

6 "Daddy Is in Prison"

The Decline of Conjugal Visits and the
Strange Career of Family Values

In 1993 Dorothy A. Bush, a resident of southern California, expressed her disgust that incarcerated people were allowed to marry. Weaving together her concerns about crime, welfare, immigration, race, AIDS, and taxes, she fumed,

> The conjugal visits should be done away with. Are these people not in prison as punishment? One of several offenders is Tex Watson of the Manson family. He married while in prison and by conjugal visits has fathered three children, all courtesy of the welfare system. His wife is now pregnant with their fourth child, and again who pays? We should stop all welfare and medical care to immigrants and non-American citizens. To the bleeding hearts who want to bring HIV-infected Haitians into our country for treatment and help, put your money where your mouth is and get them help someplace else, but not with my tax dollars.[1]

Even as jurisdictions around the nation established conjugal visits throughout the 1970s and 1980s, the practice was a subject of constant controversy. Although both liberal prison reformers and conservatives had tentatively agreed that conjugal visits provided prisoners with an incentive for good behavior and compliance with family norms, tough-on-crime rhetoric destroyed this common ground during the 1990s. According to psychologist Craig Haney, "In the past, society's commitment to rehabilitation served as a vague but still effective moral restraining edge that indirectly limited the amount of prison pain that could be openly delivered and would be publicly tolerated."[2] Socially conservative hard-liners' brand of moralism set aside preventing homosexuality in prison and maintaining the patriarchal family unit and instead advanced the goal of inflicting pain on lawbreakers. Politicians embarked on a substantive and symbolic crusade to demonstrate their toughness in the face of crime, and in the words of historian Mona Lynch, "the standards for the treatment of criminal offenders spiraled down to a new low over the last two decades of the twentieth century."[3] Throughout the nation, legislators, governors, sheriffs, and commissioners of corrections eliminated prison "frills" such as college classes, hot meals, and conjugal visits.[4]

As prisoner-activists and their allies on the outside successfully mobilized to win some concessions from their keepers and the courts, conservatives framed prisoners' gains as losses for "decent citizens." According to this logic, Jonathan Simon explains, lawmakers cast the law-abiding public as "victims and potential victims," defining "the crime victim as the idealized political subject, the model subject, whose circumstances and experiences have come to stand for the general good."[5] Conservatives regarded incarcerated people as incapable of rehabilitation and thus incorrigibly dangerous. Whereas the spread of conjugal visits had reflected a belief that humane treatment produced public safety, now the ruthless degradation of prisoners was advocated as a method of crime control.[6]

In contrast to the 1970s, when feminists and women of color organized against violence by establishing rape crisis centers, emphasizing mutual aid, and protesting the criminal legal system as a site of violence, a more punitive victims'-rights constituency "viewed the rights of victims as a zero-sum game predicated on tougher penalties for offenders."[7] By the 1990s the victims' rights platform extended these penalties into the walls of the prison itself, eroding prisoners' hard-won benefits. With the ascendancy of the "no-frills" or "penal harm" movement, elected officials, prosecutors, and journalists told "law-abiding citizens" that their tax dollars were funding prime rib dinners and yoga classes for prisoners.[8] These tropes resonated with concurrent attacks on welfare and the racialized discourse of a pathological underclass of "undeserving poor" feeding at the trough of federal largesse. In 1995 Representative Dick Zimmer, a Republican from New Jersey, introduced the No-Frills Prison Act, which would ban cable television; movies rated NC-17, R, and X; martial arts; weight-lifting equipment; and electronic musical instruments from federal prisons. "At a time when many Americans are struggling to make ends meet and Congress is struggling to reduce federal spending," he maintained, "we should not be spending money to pamper those who neither respect nor obey our laws."[9] Stripping allegedly "luxurious" prisons of "frills" served as a spiteful authorization of fiscal austerity in the free world.

Winning conjugal visits had been a success for prisoners who longed for intimacy and privacy with their family members, but, as many prisoners predicted, their victory contained the seeds of its own demise. Without a commitment to conjugal visits as a right rather than a privilege, visits could easily be framed as an excess that should be eliminated. As conservatives consolidated their power in the 1990s, conjugal visits became a target of particular animosity. Despite opposition from prisoners and their families, as well as many corrections professionals, longer sentences and fewer opportunities for release were followed by deliberately cruel prison conditions. A war on crime became a war on prisoners.[10]

THE PAINS OF PRIVILEGE

The debate about conjugal visits was a referendum on the nature of crime and the purpose of prison. The 75 percent of Americans polled in 1971 who believed that criminals were let off too easily could be readily persuaded that decent prison conditions suggested a tolerance for lawlessness.[11] Not grasping that forced removal from one's community was itself a devastating punishment, a corrections official scoffed, "If we are going to place them in individual cells with clean sheets every night, feed them family style, work them short hours under ideal conditions, provide hours of recreation every day and frequent conjugal visits with their respective spouses, I can see no particular reason for containing them at all." In the 1970s and 1980s, however, even with the rise of law-and-order discourse and policy, there was still no political consensus that prisons should be designed for suffering rather than rehabilitation. Most opponents of conjugal visits did not frame their arguments in a penal logic of "just deserts" or security but claimed instead that the practice would humiliate prisoners' wives and inspire jealousy among ineligible prisoners. One prison warden contended that "the unselfish prisoner who respects his wife would not subject her to the conditions under which conjugal visits must be practiced. Sex is, or should be, a private matter. The sexual relationship must take place in the sanctity of the house and not in a prison cubicle."[12] As if to remind the public that the debate was over decency rather than security, many correctional officials preferred home furloughs instead.

Although their voices did not dominate the debate about conjugal visits in the early years of their establishment, opponents linked conjugal visits with racially coded critiques of welfare, suggesting a causal connection between indulging prisoners and breeding pathological dependence among the nonwhite poor. Placing the issue in a quasi-eugenic perspective, a penal administrator told a sociologist, "One who has not been an asset to society, has many common law wives, has produced many bastard children should not be permitted to increase society's burden just to satisfy the nature of man." He assumed that conjugal visits were purely physical outlets for carnal impulses, not the opportunity for privacy and intimacy that participants cherished. Another critic opined, "Prisoners are not considered to be good prospective parents. If birth control were not required, the size of families of prison inmates might be increased, resulting in a possible increase in hereditary defects, children growing up with fathers frequently absent in jail and subject to the stigma of a father who has served time." Offspring from these liaisons would swell welfare rolls, end up in broken homes, and "grow up to be delinquent or emotionally disturbed."[13]

Prisoners who supported conjugal and family visits understood that as long as such visits were considered a privilege, and not a right, these programs were another weapon in the arsenal of penal officials. Louis X. Holloway at Parchman Farm, the Mississippi State Penitentiary, acerbically conceded that the sexual and emotional needs of heterosexual prisoners were "taken into consideration by the slavemasters at Parchman and their political co-conspirators in Mississippi. They know that conjugal visits *are* a way of equalizing the balance of nature. They know that conjugal visits *can* be a vital asset in the rehabilitation of the prisoner." But, he charged, "the conjugal visit is just one more tool used to further the interests of prison officials." He added, "Let us not forget the model we are dealing with: a plantation. Let us also not forget the objective: economic exploitation of prisoners' labor." Holloway recounted a 1972 episode (just as district judge William Keady was declaring Parchman unfit for human habitation) during which nearly one hundred prisoners refused to work in protest of their horrid working conditions; Superintendent John Collier came out to the fields and proclaimed that "if you don't go back to work, the first thing I'm going to do is take your pussy and your watermelon." In Holloway's view, the public's increasing intolerance for Parchman's notorious "terror tactics" meant that prison officials resorted to "more sophisticated forms of oppression." Prisoners were pacified in insidious ways; Holloway said he had seen prisoners pathetically subservient for weeks on end so they would remain eligible for an upcoming conjugal visit.[14]

Many prisoners concurred that conjugal and family visits were essentially a bribe.[15] Prisoner-activist Alvin Gilchrist emphasized that conjugal visits were the result of "a long hard united struggle" and that "the state never gave us anything." Yet he acknowledged that the privilege could be used to pacify prisoners.[16] Mark LaRue, an activist incarcerated at the Washington State Penitentiary at Walla Walla, saw penal officials' institution of conjugal visits as "a reactionary scheme to control prisoners by using their families and children more directly as a form of punishment."[17]

Drawing strength and ideas from the gay rights movement, radical prison activists critiqued the heteronormative assumptions that drove conjugal visits. Ed Mead, who spent twenty years in prison for his involvement in the George Jackson Brigade and formed a group called Men against Sexism inside the Washington State Penitentiary, asserted, "It should go without saying that homosexuality is a healthy form of sexual expression, the consensual practice of which will serve to combat heterosexism within the population and to make prisoners more whole human beings."[18] Tom Kennedy of the Prisoner Solidarity Committee criticized the magazine *United Families and Friends of Prisoners* for adopting the language of "perversion among prisoners" as a reason for supporting conjugal visits. As to the assertion that programs such as those at Parchman "curtailed homosexuality," Kennedy wrote, "Curtailed! Gay men and lesbians have been curtailed enough by self-righteous straights. Gay prisoners who suffer from behavior modification programs, parole denial and discrimination, masculinist attacks (psychological and physical), out and out rape, forced prostitution and harassment from guards and other inmates know what real curtailment is about. The 'problems' attributed to homosexuality within prisons are equally related to male supremacy, masculinism, heterosexism and straight chauvinism." Turning the common allegation that homosexuals "flaunted" their sexuality on its head, Kennedy implored prison activists to consider the pain experienced by gay prisoners and their loved ones who "are forced to sit in cold tension during prison visits, unable to comfortably share their affection and love while straight inmates and their wives, lovers, and girlfriends are wrapped around each other flaunting their heterosexuality and wallowing in their heterosexual privileges."[19] Those fighting for conjugal visits should support the human rights of everyone, not just straight people. Gilchrist agreed. In 1981, activists inside the Washington State Penitentiary drafted a statement of principles for a prisoners' union that, based on their commitment to "international class struggle" against "racism, sexism, and fascism," included a demand for "the right of all confined peoples to visit with their loved ones in full privacy."[20]

Prisoners and their advocates sought to navigate the tension between specific reforms and transformative change. Angela Y. Davis captured the contradiction by acknowledging that "the prison system attempts to completely rob the prisoners of their own humanity . . . of the ability of a man to love a woman, and for a woman to love a man. But conjugal visits now are rewarded to the prisoners who keep their mouths shut . . . who acquiesce to the brutality that goes on. So what appears at first to be reform is used to uphold the existing repression."[21] In 1981, after Washington State instituted conjugal visits, Mead and Gilchrist declared, "The bribe of conjugal visits will . . . depend upon the effectiveness of the program as an efficient control mechanism."[22] Prisoners and their allies cautioned against the liberal tendency to see improvements in prison conditions as goals in themselves. While they insisted on their right to conjugal and family visits, they contended that "the state has thrown out a few more crumbs to pacify and divert us, and uses these crumbs as another tool to keep us in line and competing and squabbling among ourselves." While reforms "may allow us to survive a little longer," they could ultimately be used "to strengthen and perpetuate the prison system."[23] Mark LaRue argued, "The only way the state created *privilege* of conjugal visits can be made into a productive, rather than divisive, tool, is for it to be extended or elevated to the level of a democratic *right* available to all prisoners."[24] This view was correct: since extended private visits were a privilege and not a right confirmed by the courts, they could be terminated.

FROM CARROTS TO STICKS: REVENGE VERSUS RIGHTS

In 1994, California, the first state in the postwar era to initiate conjugal visits, enacted the nation's most severe three-strikes law. Governor Pete Wilson (1991–99), who had already trumpeted the law-and-order theme and signed a succession of anticrime bills, advanced the law after the kidnapping and murder of twelve-year-old Polly Klaas by Richard Allen Davis, who was out on parole after serving half of his sixteen-year sentence.[25] According to this measure, defendants with two or more previous felony convictions would be sentenced to a mandatory minimum of twenty-five years to life on a third felony conviction. Between 1993 and 1995, twenty-four states introduced three-strikes laws. The logic behind such initiatives was that "habitual offenders" were unresponsive to incarceration as a form of correction and that imposing lengthy sentences would remove them from society and deter felons from committing more crimes. Although the political stage for this penal extremism was set in the 1970s and 1980s, the 1990s saw a "frenzied lawmaking atmosphere where politicians from both parties dueled to write and advance ever-more draconian policies."[26] As states overhauled their criminal codes and raised their law enforcement budgets to increase the number and length of prison sentences, legislatures and governors cut off release mechanisms such as parole and clemency. Central to the "just deserts" ideology that drove these policies was the proposition that people should be sent to prison in order to experience pain.

Lawmakers advocating tough-on-crime measures justified changes in penal policy that were qualitative as well as quantitative; longer sentences were eventually accompanied by the adoption of deliberately harsh penal techniques that lacked even the pretense of rehabilitation. In California, Governor Wilson promised to end conjugal visits, portraying any comfort or privilege extended to a prisoner as an offense to crime victims and a danger to public safety.[27] This ideology of "penal harm," according to sociologist Todd Clear, is a "planned governmental act, whereby a citizen is harmed, and implies that harm is justifiable precisely because it is an offender who is suffering."[28] Advocates of penal harm used conjugal visits to tap into disaffection with the perceived excesses of the rights revolution and the expansion of social welfare services. This movement, coinciding with disenchantment with correctional rehabilitation, advocated punishment as its own reward. A generation earlier, departments of corrections recognized the sexual and emotional needs of prisoners by establishing conjugal visits. The movement of the 1990s did not represent a dismissal of prisoners' needs; instead its leaders acknowledged those needs but insisted on their deprivation. Conjugal visits were a key issue around which people could define who was entitled to humane treatment and who was beyond human belonging. Radicals' critiques of conjugal visits were prophetic: the carrot was replaced by the stick.

Journalists and politicians portrayed the growing number of prisoner lawsuits in the 1970s and 1980s as a series of impudent and petty complaints made by freeloaders. The highly publicized case of Ray Cummings, a prisoner at San Quentin State Prison in California, was a litmus test for the issue. Cummings sued for the right to have conjugal visits with his girl-friend. If she were his spouse, he would be allowed conjugal visitation with her, but he preferred not to marry her, declaring to a reporter that "marriage is like being in a prison."[29] Prison regulations directed administrators to make family visitation available "to as many inmates as is possible commensurate with institutional security" but also stated that overnight visits were only allowed to "immediate family" of the prisoner, defined as a legal spouse, children, parents, grandparents, siblings, and others related by blood, marriage, or adoption.[30] The crux of Cummings's argument was that his relationship with his girlfriend Susan and her daughter, which had begun seven years before his arrest, constituted an "alternative family" and that regular overnight visits posed no threat to the security of the institution. The courts denied his claim, arguing that the restriction of such visits was reasonable rather than arbitrary; since "prison officials may ban overnight visits with inmates altogether, then certainly they may limit those visits." After reiterating dryly that "compelling institutional considerations" justified intrusions on prisoners' rights, the court's opinion took a more scolding tone in its conclusion: "We discern no valid public policy requiring California's taxpayers to provide overnight housing accommodations and security supervision for a prison inmate with his or her paramour. In our view, such a program would represent both social folly and fiscal extravagance at a time when penal funds are much needed for more critical purposes. . . . Finally, we note from the record that petitioner is serving a life sentence for first degree murder. Susan herself has a criminal record. The potential volatility of such a situation is obvious."[31] In his statements to the press, deputy state attorney general Karl Mayer discredited Cummings by calling him "a pimp, heroin dealer and self-styled hitman."[32] Another account turned the murderer into a legal charlatan whose opportunism revealed weaknesses in the criminal justice system: "He was not smart enough to stay out of prison, but he has learned how easy it is to clutter up the courts with far-fetched lawsuits."[33]

Sylvia Riddle of Spokane articulated an outlook typical of those who assumed that prisoners' lawsuits had turned the world topsy-turvy. She repeated a common refrain: "We are . . . sick of criminals getting free attorneys while the victims are left to pay the damages. Sick of criminals being pampered in deluxe prisons which even include apartments for conjugal visits. Sick of repeat offenders, many of them of the most violent type." Her facetious solution was to lock up the liberals "with these criminals who are given sympathy and multiple chances to reform themselves."[34] Riddle was clearly influenced by journalists' sensational accounts of prisoners manipulating the legal system to indulge their sinful appetites for gourmet meals, pornography, and velvet upholstery. In a particularly disparaging and widely reprinted account, Lidia Wasowicz referred to "convicted murderers, rapists and thieves" who were allowed to "dance under flashing disco lights and arrogantly threaten guards with lawsuits." "Armed with legal rhetoric learned at court-mandated prison law libraries," inmates were suing in shockingly large numbers and at increasing taxpayer expense.[35] Worse, each added civil right allegedly increased the chances of violence, both within the prison and on the streets. "You've got these turkeys filing suits and these wacky judges ruling in their favor," complained Don Novey, president of California's Correctional Officers' Association. "The laws are becoming so liberalized, our lives are in danger."[36] It was bad enough that "frivolous" lawsuits clogged the courts; according to commentators, the improved prison conditions that sometimes resulted supposedly led to a rise in violent crime.

This ideology presumed that making prisons more humane negated the rights of law-abiding and taxpaying citizens. As Julily Kohler-Hausmann argues, "This zero-sum understanding of rights suggested an inverse relationship where those with full citizenship had their rights constricted when they were accorded to new groups."[37] Governor Pete Wilson's 1996 statement when he signed the law restricting visits encapsulates this logic: "For far too long inmates have seemingly had more rights than their victims. We must make it clear to those who commit crimes that prison is a place for punishment."[38] Vocal members of the public, alongside law enforcement and elected officials, asserted that, as one angry Mississippian put it, when prisoners "committed their crimes, they forfeited all their rights."[39] Echoing the post-Reconstruction argument that convicts had no more rights than slaves, a Californian insisted that because incarcerated people had committed crimes, "complaints about cruel and unusual punishment don't apply."[40] Prisoners should not only remain excluded from free society for longer periods but should be excluded from the dignities and protections of citizenship.

The counterrevolution against prisoners' rights culminated in new obstacles to prison litigation. The 1995 Prison Litigation Reform Act (PLRA), signed by President Bill Clinton, limited the ability of prisoners to file suits to address their grievances. Senator Orrin Hatch, a Republican from Utah and chair of the Senate Judiciary Committee, introduced the PLRA by saying, "Jailhouse lawyers with little else to do are tying our courts in knots with an endless flood of frivolous litigation." Misleadingly equating prison litigation with prisoners' release, he continued, "It is past time to slam shut the revolving door on the prison gate and to put the key safely out of reach of overzealous Federal courts."[41] Senator Spencer Abraham, a Republican from Michigan, asserted that judicial intrusion into the prison system obstructed the real purpose of prison—"hard time." "By interfering with the fulfillment of this punitive function," Abraham claimed, "the courts are effectively seriously undermining the entire criminal justice system."[42] Bars to prison litigation ensured that prisoners serving longer terms would have fewer opportunities to complain.

If prisoners were understood as having no rights, any meager comfort during their incarceration could be framed as an indulgence. Those who recited the script about their tax dollars going to subsidize television sets for prisoners were unaware that prisoners had to pay for televisions themselves.[43] A Mississippian betrayed his ignorance of Parchman's plantation operations when he jibed, "Put the inmates in the field and give them a shovel and see how badly they want their TVs, radios and air conditioners."[44] Politicians spread misinformation about prison conditions by championing laws that would symbolize their tough-on-crime bona fides; for example, a Mississippi law in 1994 banned "personal air conditioners for prisoners" despite the fact that not a single prisoner had one.[45] In fact, corrections commissioner Burl Cain—the former warden of the Louisiana State Penitentiary at Angola—announced in 2022 that Parchman would receive air-conditioning for the first time in its 121-year history.[46] Those arguing for harsher punishments linked recent but exaggerated gains made by prisoners to luxurious conditions and closed the loop by saying that cushy prison conditions led to more crime. As a Californian put it, "The American Civil Liberties Union has made jails and prisons so comfortable and enjoyable that the inmates don't mind going back: color TV, telephone privileges and conjugal visits."[47]

It was not enough to serve more time; prisoners had to serve *hard* time. Politicians used their megaphones in the press to exaggerate the amenities available to prisoners. California's deputy attorney general, Karl Meyer, warned that prisoners were "getting more sophisticated and successful in their demands" and aimed "to make middle class neighborhoods out of prisons."[48] He echoed what the British utilitarian Jeremy Bentham called the "principle of least eligibility": prisoners should not be given material comforts, programs, or services that were better than those of the lowest classes of the noncriminal population.[49] Mayer embroidered his point by falsely claiming that prisoners enjoyed better conditions than the average law-abiding American. If prisoners should do nothing in prison but suffer, then behavior that would be considered normal or even desirable in the free world was pathologized as sinister, parasitic, and deviant. In his *Reader's Digest* article "Must Our Prisons Be Resorts?," which drew on his television talk show and was regularly cited by law-and-order politicians, conservative reporter Robert James Bidinotto stated that "today's correctional facility is an expensive, even enticing, hybrid of camp, clinic, and community college" and "American taxpayers are forced to provide programs and 'perks' without charge to those who rob, rape, or kill them."[50] The incarcerated audience of the *Reader's Digest* refuted Bidinotto's demonstrable falsehoods and compared him to Joseph Goebbels, the Nazi minister of propaganda in "Must Society Be Misled?," an article published in *Prison Life*. The author described being forced to sleep on kitchen floors due to overcrowding; a prisoner who lost a foot to gangrene because the facility's medical staff couldn't properly cut a toenail; cells as cold as fifty-two degrees; and food infested with vermin. "If our prisons are such resorts," he noted, "simply open the gates and see how many run out . . . and how many walk in."[51] "The intellectual and bureaucratic forces that have turned prisons into 'resorts' are deeply entrenched," alleged the conservative Princeton University sociologist John DiIulio, who also coined the term *superpredator*.[52] It would be more accurate to say that the stock images of prisons as country clubs, resorts, and vacation spas were becoming deeply entrenched.

Armed with this grab bag of sensationalized motifs, the state legislatures, governors, and sheriffs—claiming to be responding to the public will—eliminated a wide range of prison programs.[53] In 1995, 60 percent of corrections departments in forty-six states reported the elimination of some "privileges," including hot meals, personal clothing, and the use of gym weights; others reported greater restrictions on the privileges that remained.[54] Some jurisdictions added hardships and humiliation. In 1994 the Mississippi Legislature required that prisons replace denim uniforms with black-and-white striped clothes with the word CONVICT printed on the back. Representative Mack McInnis, a Democrat, explained, "We want a prisoner to look like a prisoner, to smell like a prisoner, and taste like a prisoner. When you see one of these boogers a'loose, you'll say 'I didn't know we had zebras in Mississippi.'"[55] When legislators lambasted the corrections commissioner for not implementing the change more quickly, he explained that it would cost about $1 million to produce and distribute the new uniforms.[56] In the 1990s Alabama's Department of Corrections (DOC) reinstituted chain gangs; in Maricopa County, Arizona, Sheriff Joe Arpaio put pretrial detainees in tents in the 110-degree weather and made them wear pink jockey shorts; Massachusetts governor William F. Weld (1991–97) terminated all art, music, vocational training, and college courses available in state prisons. To Craig Haney, psychologist and researcher on the Stanford Prison Experiment, these trends bespeak a "crisis of cruelty" that "has ripped us from the ethical moorings that once held this punitive system in check."[57]

When critics targeted conjugal visits, they used a well-worn vocabulary about a parasitic poor dependent on welfare. Severing ties between "offenders" and their communities would not only increase the pain of imprisonment but prevent prisoners from procreating and burdening the welfare rolls. Mississippi state legislator Bennett Malone, a Democrat, said, "A lot of us don't think it's right they go up there and get in a family way and then have a baby that goes on welfare."[58] Some of these arguments smacked of eugenicist thinking: Kelly Rudiger, the executive director of the Doris Tate Victims Bureau, averred, "This is not a segment of society that needs to be procreating."[59] At a forum on three-strikes legislation, Fred Goldman, whose son Ron had been slain along with Nicole Brown Simpson in 1994, favored tightening the rules for conjugal visitation: "We're going to let them pass on their gene pools? Am I crazy, or is something wrong?" Prosecutors gave Goldman a standing ovation.[60] Just as the attack on prison weight lifting cautioned against producing "a super breed of criminals," obstructing prisoners' ability to procreate would advance public safety. Eugenicist arguments found fertile ground in the era of the "superpredator" scare.[61]

As the AIDS crisis began to gain public attention, debates over whether condoms should be provided to male prisoners raised more questions about conjugal visits. In the late 1980s the Mississippi DOC considered whether to provide condoms to prisoners, although officials worried that it would appear to condone homosexuality. Journalist Sid Salter quipped that Parchman's superintendent had "secured his place in the Taxpayer Outrage Hall of Fame" for entertaining such a proposal. Salter argued that distributing condoms was tantamount to subsidizing conjugal visits and homosexual acts behind prison walls, a proposition that drew on the zero-sum logic that pit prisoners' well-being against that of law-abiding citizens and equated prisoners' health with criminal acts: "But ask yourself, is the grocery owner whose business is robbed, whose property damaged or whose employees are shot or maimed really obligated to provide 'safe sex' for the criminal in prison who chose to perpetrate the crime?"[62] An argument for condom distribution came from a prison hospital administrator who assumed that his patients had criminal habits: "These people are in prison for not obeying the rules.... I'd rather have the expense of providing condoms as opposed to dealing with AIDS patients at the hospital."[63]

These arguments were not based on the contention that prisoners were not human beings; it was the very recognition of their human needs that lent purpose to their deprivation. According to this ideology, meeting prisoners' needs robbed the taxpayer while enabling the continuation of the social ills caused by liberals. That prisons began eliminating events such as Family Day along with banquets for veterans' clubs and lifers' organizations underscores the drive to inflict emotional pain as well as physical discomfort.[64] As California Democratic gubernatorial candidate John Garamendi put it, "It's time to move lawbreakers from the Hotel California to Heartbreak Hotel."[65] These "devolving standards of decency" classified conjugal visits as excessive and immoral. Conjugal visits had been justified as an effort to preserve families, but the decimation of these programs in the 1990s made clear that conservatives' brand of "family values" did not extend to families with incarcerated members. These families were not worth preserving. The fact that Governor Ronald Reagan (1967–75), champion of family values, had initiated the program in the 1960s was all but forgotten.

KEEPING PRISONERS AND THEIR FAMILIES WHOLE

Although Mississippi's conjugal visitation program remained robust throughout the closing decades of the twentieth century, state legislators attempted to shrink its scope. Beginning in the 1980s, Parchman warden Eddie Lucas issued a directive that only legally married prisoners would be allowed private visits with their spouses. The authorities would no longer recognize common-law marriages, as they had since the program's inception. Prisoners responded by producing fake marriage licenses in the print shop. A delegation of incarcerated men explained to Lucas that the majority of people confined at Parchman were Black and not legally married but were nonetheless committed to their partners.[66] They pointed out the length and stability of their relationships, as well as the children who were the products of these unions. "We have paid rent, bought food and clothes for our women and children before the law sent us here to Parchman, and we had and shared the same responsibilities as any married man with a marriage license," they insisted. "Now it seems that you would take the respect, responsibility, and our manhood from us." For administrators, mutual obligations of care needed the imprimatur of the law: "We're trying to get them to live within the bounds of laws set by society and definitely, a legal marriage is one of those as it exists in Mississippi," argued a prison warden.[67] A program that had been touted as a vehicle for rehabilitation was now placed outside the law.

In California, legislators chipped away at conjugal visits by attacking the very premise of prisoners' rights. In the 1990s political candidates and their constituents focused their indignation on the Inmates' Bill of Rights signed by Ronald Reagan in 1968. When a bill to eliminate it was introduced in the legislature in 1994, the California Correctional Peace Officers Association (CCPOA) asked rhetorically, "Tired of 72-hour unsupervised family (conjugal) visits and quarterly packages fueling the underground prison drug railroad?" That the CCPOA attributed security breaches to conjugal visits (and compared the Underground Railroad to drug smuggling) reflected the racialized demonization of incarcerated people's efforts to sustain human connection. In fact, a state DOC study showed that of the twenty-six thousand conjugal visits in 1992, officials found only ten incidents involving drugs.[68] The CCPOA explained that eliminating the Inmates' Bill of Rights would grant correctional officials the "legal ammo to impose 'any legitimate penalogical [sic] interest' to control inmate activities. . . . Those privileges aren't rights any longer."[69] State Assemblyman Dean Andal, with the support of Governor Wilson and the California Correctional Officers' Union, as well as victims' rights groups, inserted language in a 1994 budget act that would eliminate family visits for prisoners convicted of murder, spousal abuse, or a wide array of sex offenses and prohibit extended family visits for those who were sentenced to life.[70] As with clemency, the nature of the original crime, not behavior during incarceration, determined a prisoner's entitlement to contact with loved ones. Parroting tough-on-crime rhetoric, a reporter flippantly explained, "Inmates who are not getting out don't have to worry about getting along with family members on the outside and so don't need special time to maintain family ties, which is the department's rationale for having conjugal visits."[71] Signaling the bipartisan consensus on punitive policies, California Democratic gubernatorial candidate Kathleen Brown advanced a thirty-three-point program for "fighting crime" that included incarcerating first-time drug offenders and graffiti vandals as well as ending all conjugal visits. "We must stop the abuse of taxpayers and the correctional system," she asserted.[72]

When conjugal visits came under attack in California, prisoners and their families mobilized to protect them. Anita Hartman, whose husband was serving a life sentence at the California Correctional Institution in Tehachapi, was among the many who testified at the California State Legislature. With her five-month-old daughter—conceived during a conjugal visit—on her lap, Hartman accused critics of demonizing incarcerated men: "My husband Ken is not a crime, or a slobbering beast."[73] Clyde T. Gambles, serving a fifteen-year sentence for second-degree robbery, had enjoyed extended visits with his family for a year before the new restrictions prohibited him from participating. He had a misdemeanor conviction for sex with a minor when he was an eighteen-year-old high school senior and the girl was fifteen. Now Gambles was forbidden any contact with minors, including his own children. Raymond Shipley's wife drove six hundred miles for a visit with "guards hovering over him like insolent chaperones." He lamented, "The . . . visit with my wife is my whole life, and every time the guards ruin it, the pain is excruciating. . . . The state is the antithesis of close family ties. They do everything in their power to hinder our relationships at every given opportunity."[74]

Activist groups such as FamilyNet and Pro-Family Advocates galvanized a campaign, including one thousand incarcerated people, that barraged policymakers with opposition to any curtailment of extended visits. They launched a lawsuit, *Pro-Family Advocates et al v. James Gomez*, to challenge these restrictions in court. When Judge Peter Allen Smith issued an injunction against the new regulation prohibiting several classes of people from participating in the family visit program because it constituted an ex post facto law, Governor Wilson complained, "Once again a liberal judge has ignored the feelings and wishes of the victims and their families[,] siding with rapists, child molesters and murderers."[75] In 1996 an appeals court reversed Judge Smith's injunction, ruling that because a prisoner's right of association was necessarily affected by confinement, because extended family visits were a privilege and not a right, and because restricting visits had "legitimate, nonpunitive governmental purposes," the state was within bounds when it prohibited family visits to specific categories of prisoners.[76]

Prisoners took matters into their own hands. In March 1995, some one thousand men incarcerated at the maximum-security California

State Prison, Los Angeles County in the city of Lancaster participated in a general strike, refusing to come out of their cells even for meals, to protest proposed changes to visiting. "What you're doing is creating a desperate sub-class with nothing to lose," said Martha Riley, whose husband was serving thirty-six years to life for murder.[77] Over a year later, between one hundred and two hundred prisoners at New Folsom Prison, formally known as California State Prison–Sacramento, rioted; when the violence ended, one prisoner was dead and ten were hospitalized. Governor Wilson attributed the incident to rival gangs, but family members of the prisoners interpreted it differently. "It's all about the rights they're taking away from inmates," said Kathleen Burdan, whose husband was incarcerated. "This is the only way to get their [officials'] attention."[78]

Prisoners and their families pushed back against efforts to curtail conjugal visits and pointed to the hypocrisy of expecting "good citizenship" from prisoners while destroying their families. In Washington State, prisoners' loved ones gathered to protest proposed restrictions on the Extended Family Visit program (EFV). The program, established in 1981, excluded from eligibility only those who had recent drug-related infractions or had assaulted staff or other prisoners. Incarcerated journalist Paul Wright reported that under a proposal spearheaded by representative Ida Ballasiotes, a Republican, prisoners who "refused" to work or to enroll in educational programs would be ineligible for the EFV program and any child conceived during an EFV would be ineligible for welfare benefits.[79] Ballasiotes exemplifies an emerging type of anticrime activist whose family members had been victims of violence; she advocated three-strikes laws and sex offender registries after her daughter was murdered by a sex offender who was out on work release.[80] Conversely, the family members of those who were incarcerated opposed of the proposal because limits on the EFV program violated the rights of innocent people by depriving them of "quality time" with their loved ones. Prisoners at the Washington Corrections Center for Women in Purdy staged a one-day strike to protest the law. A participant remarked that if programs that help prisoners cope with prison life and retain social skills and social connections were ended, "you might as well lock them up for life."[81] Incarcerated activist Paul Wright called out the larger political situation succinctly: "Rather than focus on societal problems the fascist right wing is targeting the weakest segments of society, single mothers, immigrants and prisoners as scapegoats for the failures of capitalism."[82]

Washington State legislators forged ahead over the objection of corrections officials. King County prosecutor Norm Maleng supported the bill, arguing that work requirements and spartan conditions would usher in a "rediscovery of old values."[83] Some critics, in contrast, smelled hypocrisy: "That EFVs are being targeted by the so-called 'Family Values' crowd is just another of the many ironies in . . . America."[84] Others pointed to the state legislature's refusal to provide the $40 million it would require to offer adequate work and education programs to prisoners, revealing the catch-22 that forged fiscal austerity with penal cruelty: work and education programs were a condition of conjugal visits, but the state would not fund education or vocational programs.[85] Corrections secretary Chase Riveland, who had a background in social work as well as the military, was confounded by legislators' disregard for commonsense notions of incentives and opportunities for rehabilitation: "Almost nothing they are proposing has anything to do with crime or violence or drugs. It's all rhetorical stuff."[86] Law-and-order politicians dismissed him as a "relic of the touchy feely 1960s," and journalist Jim Brunner added to the chorus of mockery and contempt by describing Riveland as an aging hippie who "believes in summer camp for drug dealers, weight-lifting contests for murderers and cable TV for rapists."[87]

On the one hand, the passage of the PLRA signaled a return to a "hands-off" ethos regarding the internal operation of prisons, theoretically an act of deference to corrections professionals. On the other hand, the politicization of prison operations meant that "legislative micro-management of the DOC [was] now enshrined into law" and undermined the expertise and authority of corrections professionals.[88] By obstructing prisoners' ability to challenge their treatment in court, the federal legislation made visits especially important for bringing prison conditions into view. Emma Childers, representing the Friends Committee on Legislation, a Quaker lobbying group, emphasized, "If they are able to keep the public out, no one is going to know what is going on inside."[89] The editors of the *North County Times* agreed: "By allowing the families of prisoners to visit, the rest of society can keep an eye on how prisoners are treated."[90] In response to the litigation that exposed harsh penal conditions to the public, DOCs around the nation restricted the ability of journalists to interview specified prisoners face-to-face. The California DOC defended its restrictions as an effort to protect the "emotional well-being" of victims.[91] After all, according to Oceanside resident George H. Cullins, "The right to converse with the news media ... should be the same as my murdered daughter's from her coffin—none."[92]

The peak of this movement coincided with the twenty-fifth anniversary of the uprising at the Attica Correctional Facility in upstate New York. Prisoners and their allies around the nation took stock of what had changed since then. Jaan Laaman, a leftist organizer who had participated in the Attica rebellion, recalled it "as a bright light, a searing beacon showing that even the most oppressed in the tightest conditions can rise up." Although it was followed by torture and more bureaucratic forms of state repression, "it also brought about longer-term changes, including some meaningful ones, like family/conjugal visits throughout NY State prisons."[93] Black Panther Sundiata Acoli wrote in 1997 that "numerous ... rights that are taken for granted today" were established in Attica's D Yard, but "many of these hard won gains have been taken away."[94] Whether prison officials had granted conjugal visits cynically or sincerely, by the 1990s the practice was being denounced for encouraging crime.[95] Eric Martin, incarcerated at Pelican Bay State Prison in Crescent City, California, reminded readers that "issues of censorship, sex publications and visitation were all litigated and fought over in the '60s and '70s. Many prisoners and CDC [California Department of Corrections] staff died or were hurt before the system realized there was a better way to treat incarcerated human beings. But the toll of prison uprisings from New York to California "has apparently all been forgotten or ignored now," Martin noted.[96]

THE END OF THE MISSISSIPPI EXPERIMENT

In 1989 Columbus B. Hopper claimed that conjugal visits were an obvious benefit to prisoners, correctional officials, and the public.[97] A few years later, he warned that "if you cut off all the privileges an inmate has, it makes them feel like slaves."[98] Even when Mississippi state legislators and corrections officials extended sentences, they did not limit conjugal visits. But there were signs of things to come. "I think the whole program stinks," griped the district attorney of Sunflower County, where Parchman is located, in 1994: "The prison is not a country club or a motel. Where else can you go to have free medical attention and all the comforts of home including meals and sex?"[99] A program meant to reduce recidivism was now seen as luring career criminals back to prison.[100]

Less than a generation later, after Governor Ronnie Musgrove (2000–2004) appointed Chris Epps as the state's corrections commissioner in 2002, the conjugal visit program was scaled back. Visits were allowed only to prisoners who were legally married, housed in minimum security, exhibited good behavior, and were not at risk for transmitting HIV or other sexually transmitted diseases. By 2010 the Mississippi experiment was focused crudely on sex rather than on sustaining family ties: prisoners were given one hour, along with soap, condoms, tissue, a sheet, pillowcase, and a face towel.[101] A knock on the door served as a five-minute warning.[102] No longer would incarcerated people at Parchman be able to take their children fishing at the lake on the grounds and teach them how to clean and cook their catch. Ruth Anderson recalled that on the night after her son was born, back in 1995, a family visit allowed the infant Naeem to sleep between his mother and his incarcerated father.[103] "It was more like you were at home," remembered Victoria Phillips, whose husband is incarcerated at Parchman. "It was more freedom."[104] The practice of conjugal visits had previously aroused concern because it might be "demeaning to women," but now it seemed demeaning to everybody.

In 2014 Commissioner Epps unilaterally terminated conjugal visits. By then fewer than two hundred people (less than 1 percent of the twenty thousand incarcerated in the state) were eligible, yet Epps alleged that the program was too burdensome and costly.[105] Since Epps conceded that the policy reduced recidivism and prison violence and helped to keep families intact, one journalist suspected that Epps's motivation was more political than financial.[106] One of Epps's explanations was especially telling: "Even though we provide contraception, we have no idea how many women are getting pregnant only for the child to be raised by one parent."[107] Separating spouses was a way to prevent the couple from reproducing, not a way to save the family.

This sudden change, announced in a memorandum taped to the prison's visiting room wall, required a "radical reshaping" of the lives of incarcerated people and their families.[108] Relatives formed Mississippi Advocates for Prisoners to fight this shift in policy. They cherished the privacy afforded by extended family visits and protested being scolded for a hug that lasted too long. They found the justifications for eliminating extended visits disingenuous and argued that the program was worth the limited costs it entailed. They were insulted by the insinuations Epps made about the families involved. "I am not on welfare or anything like that," said C. J. Page, whose husband was imprisoned.[109] Glendia Mason, who conceived two children with her husband while he served a long sentence for aggravated assault, asserted that how those children were conceived was none of the commissioner's business.[110] Naeem Anderson, the child conceived during a conjugal visit in the 1990s, proclaimed, "God gave me this life. Some people in there may never get out, and they need another piece of them out here living."[111] The same year that Commissioner Epps terminated conjugal visits, he was indicted on forty-nine counts of bribery and misallocation of funds involving hundreds of millions of dollars and sentenced to twenty years in prison.[112]

Whereas in 1990 seventeen states allowed extended private visits, by 2015 the number had shrunk to four.[113] The war on prisoners and their families erected barriers to belonging and created new weapons of state-sanctioned degradation. Across the country, corrections professionals, legislators, social scientists, and incarcerated people and their families had concurred that allowing prisoners to re-create briefly the sanctuary of home and marriage—and even to conceive a child—was instrumental for surviving prison life and facilitating the transition to life outside. But humanitarian claims did not survive the punishment wave of the late twentieth century, when dehumanization, or what scholar Colin Dayan has called "soul death," became the purpose of prison.[114] In response to a ban on contact visits in Michigan, a federal court stated that it "goes to the essence of what it means to be human; it destroys the social, emotional and physical bonds of parent and child, husband and wife, body and soul."[115] Although the Michigan DOC was referring to institutional security when it defended the ban for "legitimate penological interest," the bitter taste of harm was baked into this policy.

Nonetheless, those who are incarcerated sustain, and are sustained by, their persistent material, bodily, and psychic connections to their loved ones. As historian Heather Ann Thompson points out, the argument that incarcerated people and their partners should not have children—implicit in the ban on conjugal visits—is nonsensical: "What we're really saying is that we don't believe that prisoners, people who have 'offended,' should have the right to have children or the right to parent their children."[116] Susan V. Koski, an assistant professor of criminology and criminal justice at Central Connecticut State University, welcomed the disappearance of conjugal visits, voicing the conventional concerns about smuggling, gang activity, communicable diseases, pregnancies, and single parenting that abetted the permanent exile of incarcerated people: "The notion of being able to have sex on the public dime, while you are supposed to be punished, is a politician's/legislator's nightmare." Koski expressed alarm about family members of the incarcerated moving to prison towns to facilitate visiting, which was formerly seen as a healthy development. Instead of interpreting efforts to preserve the family as a goal people across the political spectrum had espoused for decades, she turned it on its head: allowing conjugal and family visits "promotes a culture, which normalizes that 'daddy is in prison.'"[117] This view blames conjugal visits, not hyperincarceration, for normalizing this pathology. Policies that had been defended on the ground that they promoted family unity were now dismissed as breeding grounds for the wrong kinds of families. As journalist Elie Mystal perceives it, the ban on the practice is not about prison expenditures but about "black people having babies." Looking back to the origins of conjugal visits at Parchman, he concludes, "Conjugal visits started as stupid racism with no basis in fact. It's ending because of stupid racism with no basis in fact."[118]

PART III. WEEKEND PASSES

Furloughs and the Risks of Freedom

7 "To Rub Elbows with Freedom"

Temporary Release in the Jim Crow South

Prison walls face both directions, inside and out, and what those walls have signified in penological thinking has changed over time. In the early years of the northern penitentiary, incarceration was intended to isolate offenders from the tempting vices of urban life. Social reformers concluded that the causes of crime and poverty lay in the chaos, mobility, and anonymity that characterized rapidly growing cities. Surrounded by brothels and taverns, the honest but naive young man needed to be "like a vigilant soldier, well-trained to guard against temptation." But many fell victim to corruption. The solution was the prison, usually in a rural setting, which would isolate offenders from vice-ridden communities and rehabilitate them through strict discipline and solitude.[1] These prison schemes aimed to prevent all contact with the outside world. As a 1976 federal report stated, "Disciples of [early penitentiaries] would never have thought of suggesting that an inmate be allowed to visit persons outside of the institution—with or without an escort." During the early republic, leaving the prison would have been self-defeating—not because the prisoner was dangerous but because society was.[2]

In the Progressive era, reformers reversed the guiding principles of their forebears. Following British politician William Gladstone's belief that "it is only liberty that fits men for liberty," the gradual release of prisoners and their integration in the community came to be a penological goal. Early twentieth-century critics found the regimentation, imposed silence, and isolation of the penitentiary degrading, demoralizing, and ineffective and instead advocated practices that would foster moral regeneration and self-respect. Fixed sentences were removed and replaced by programs, such as parole, that conditioned release on good behavior.[3] These reforms reflected the rise of social science, trust in an expansive state, and faith in the use of official discretion.

This trajectory was not followed in the South, where prisons were introduced primarily as a means of policing and exploiting labor and Jim Crow foreclosed the possibility that people of African descent would ever enjoy full citizenship. Mississippi memoirist David Cohn captured the prevailing ideology among southern whites when he opined in 1935 that "crime is the normal state of being" among Black people and that the "negro community" had "become accustomed to murders and mutilations, to stabbings and cuttings, to the severing of heads with axes and the beating out of brains with clubs." There was no point in aiming for rehabilitation of a Black convict, as "he is rarely a victim to the gnawing pains and terrors of remorse which so often make living a bitter unbearable reality to the white man who has killed a human being."[4] Without any pretense of a rehabilitative goal, southern penality was not bound by moral restraints. According to historian Mark Colvin, "the prevailing moral order, based on white supremacy, gave further justification to the brutal treatment of prisoners who overwhelmingly were Black. Thus the moral force of white supremacy combined with the profit motive to shape the southern penal system."[5] The plantation prison was not meant to prepare prisoners for citizenship but to enforce and perpetuate their subordination.

The plantation prison in the Jim Crow South was woven into a fabric of surveillance and control, a treacherous terrain of discipline and punishment. But precisely because the entire region resembled an armed camp, white people could tolerate some fluidity between the prison and the outside world.[6] Free white citizens could always be counted on to terrorize or supervise wayward prisoners of African descent. As Cohn observes, echoing the "Mississippi tradition" of clemency, "In the Delta these oscillations between severity and leniency are feudal survivals."[7] Prisoners regularly left the prison on temporary furloughs to visit relatives at Christmas, to labor, or to perform entertainment for civic organizations. The practice was celebrated by the press, prison officials, and elected leaders as evidence of the benevolence of the southern penal system. When a prisoner absconded during a furlough, critics did not sound the alarm of danger but raised questions about corruption and cronyism. If prisoners failed to return, they were dishonoring promises rather than terrorizing law-abiding citizens. In a context where "degrees of freedom" and paternalistic culture provided a normative structure for society as a whole, allowing prisoners to be released temporarily as a reward for good behavior made perfect sense. A governor trusting a prisoner to honor his "man-to-man" promise could always rely on bloodhounds and lynch mobs to handle those who transgressed. But for those who were captive on the penal farm, degrees of freedom were consequential. Just as in slavery, incarceration fixed people in place, denying mobility as well as connections with kin. Prisoners treasured furloughs as an opportunity to maintain their ties with the outside world.

By the mid-twentieth century most Americans outside the South viewed the region's penal system as exceptionally barbaric. Federal measures to advance civil rights were accompanied by efforts to reform penal conditions. Revelations of brutality and punitive practices aroused concern among professional penologists.[8] Despite their defensiveness about the peculiarities of their region, southern prison officials were open to "modernizing" their programs by participating in national professional organizations, listening to experts from outside the region, and implementing some of the changes those experts suggested. As the rhetoric of reform and rehabilitation penetrated the South, the customary fluidity between the plantation prison and the free world came to take on new meaning. In the 1950s and 1960s penologists advocated for the integration of correctional institutions into the free community. As we have seen in the case of conjugal visits, the "open" plantation prison came to be seen as a viable site for rehabilitative practices. Southern prisons were unimaginably cruel, but, as with clemency, they also had traditions that could be adapted to new purposes. As the region's penal system cracked open to national scrutiny, prisoners seized on the rhetoric of rehabilitation to argue for better treatment and acceptance into the free community.

As in part II on conjugal visits, part III begins in the South, where prisoners were allowed to leave prison regularly and the white public supported the practice despite the occasional fugitive. As much as these furloughs represented the surveillance and paternalism characteristic of the Jim Crow South, they were also cherished by incarcerated people as opportunities to maintain ties with kin and community and eventually regarded by professional penologists as a useful rehearsal for reintegrating prisoners into society. Chapter 8 looks at the national spread of furloughs under the rubric of *community corrections*, with a particular focus on Massachusetts, where prison activists persuaded political leaders and corrections administrators to establish one of the most liberal furlough programs in the nation, allowing furloughs even to those serving life sentences for murder. Chapter 9 is a close reading of the moral panic that politicians and the media created in the aftermath of the Willie Horton scandal. It examines the politicization of furloughs by conservatives who sensationalized the furlough practice to promote the perpetual disappearance of putatively incorrigible offenders for the sake of crime victims' families and free society. The "Horton effect" constitutes a hybrid of hoary stereotypes of the bestiality of Black people and a new common sense that cast the public as perpetual victims, whittling faith in discretionary release of any kind. By looking at states both in the South and outside it, we can see clearly how central white racism was—and still is—to the current carceral regime.

THE CHRISTMAS SPIRIT IN ALABAMA AND MISSISSIPPI

In his autobiographical writings, Frederick Douglass describes the complex ways in which enslavers enhanced their power through their holiday beneficence. Planters' suspension of work schedules and their flamboyant bestowal of gifts required slaves to smile and bow gratefully in return. Some enslaved people took advantage of slack times to secure passes to visit their families for several days. In 1831 South Carolina enslaver and politician James Henry Hammond told the enslaved laborers on his plantation that they could "go where they pleased during the holidays."[9] This latitude and relaxed discipline provided the opportunity for escape. Jermain Loguen plotted flight over the Christmas holiday, confident that a travel pass conferred by the master and the holiday itself would provide him cover: "Lord speed the day! Freedom begins with the holidays!"[10] Escape was a risk that enslavers were willing to take because paternalistic rewards were a means of fracturing solidarity, ensuring obedience, and improving productivity. Thus, as Douglass discerned, this generosity was a psychological tool of the slave master. One white overseer remarked that giving gifts to enslaved laborers was a more effective tool of control than physical violence: "I killed twenty-eight head of beef for the people's Christmas dinner. I can do more with them in this way than if all the hides of the cattle were made into lashes."[11] Douglass perceived that the excess of Christmas indulgences, such as rituals encouraging enslaved workers to binge whiskey, "appears to have no other object than to disgust the slaves with temporary freedom, and to make them as glad to return to work, as they were to leave it. . . . These holidays serve as conductors, or safety-valves, to carry off the rebellious spirit of enslaved humanity."[12]

After emancipation, Christmas leaves from plantation prisons reiterated many of the same features. In December 1937 over five hundred Alabama prisoners, Black and white, went home for Christmas, pledging to return in ten days. Among them were Daniel "Puddin' Foot" Clenny, serving a life sentence for killing a sheriff, and Jim Germany, who hobbled through the prison gates on legs "off at the knees," "looking for my folks."[13] Governor David Bibbs Graves (1935–39) had initiated the practice during his first term, ten years earlier.[14] Using his clemency powers, the governor allowed "Christmas paroles" to prisoners recommended by prison officials as a reward for good behavior. Most were long-termers—which by definition included people convicted of murder—because Graves believed that he should extend the privilege only to those who had already served at least a decade.[15] Despite protests and warnings that these "old hardened convicts" would never come back, Graves took the view that anyone who had been able to "so demean himself or herself as to get by any and every criticism of every guard or warden put over them was fit to be trusted."[16] The prisoner was bound only by honor to return. A columnist for the *Miami News* mused, "It is curious to find in a state of the South, whose prison-camp and chain-gang justice is so severe, this opposite extreme."[17]

In the first half of the twentieth century, granting holiday leaves was common in prisons in the American South. These furloughs could last for weeks, enabling selected prisoners to go home to their families. During the Christmas season, governors across the nation offered pardons and commutations in especially large numbers.[18] But temporary leaves, theoretically earned through good behavior and allowed to hundreds of prisoners, were granted in only a handful of states, mostly in the South. While observers occasionally warned of the potential for favoritism and corruption, no one questioned the belief that holiday furloughs were an important custom, even when the occasional prisoner went AWOL. Governors and corrections officials tolerated a certain degree of risk in temporarily releasing prisoners into the free community. Moreover, they defined the failure to return on time not as a risk of future crime but as a betrayal of trust.

Throughout the 1930s the Alabama press followed the fates of lucky parolees closely, seeming to take a sentimental pride in the extension of benevolence to worthy unfortunates.[19] Newspapers depicted parolees with pity, betraying no sense of danger. Positive press coverage generated curiosity, and eventually a film company created newsreels of the men leaving Alabama's prisons for the holiday with a voice-over narrative by Governor Graves.[20] Graves then selected a white prisoner, J. E. Duskin, serving a sentence of thirty-six to sixty years for embezzlement, to "tell the world" about the furlough program on a national radio broadcast.[21] The white-collar criminal testified that the governor "has a reputation of being kind to those behind prison walls."[22] Criticism of the program was directed at Duskin's supposedly exaggerated tales about brutality in Alabama prisons; he represented himself as having emerged from "a world of living dead" for the first time when he had in fact been given temporary release at least six times, for a total of 240 days.[23] While Alice Fogleman, one of Duskin's victims, disparagingly referred to Duskin's furlough as a "joy ride," her main concern was that "the right impression was broadcast in regard to the treatment of our State prisoners."[24] Governor Graves was scolded more loudly for choosing such a poor spokesman for the prison system than for being soft on criminals.

When twenty-three of Alabama's roughly six hundred Christmas parolees, including eleven who had been convicted of murder, failed to return to prison on time in 1938, Warden Hamp Draper was confident that they would be "picked up later" and expressed no anxiety about public safety.[25] Governor Graves used the biblical analogies of betrayal to both call on Christian principles and underplay the significance of the escapes. "There was one Judas in 12 disciples picked by Christ himself," he commented.[26] The Alabama press and prison administrators supported the continuation of the furlough program.[27]

When the state legislature reformed the clemency process in late 1939, it standardized the permanent release of prisoners through a modern, bureaucratic system of parole and postrelease supervision, removing the taint of politics and favoritism from discretionary release.[28] The new State Board of Pardons and Paroles restricted temporary leaves to emergencies such as critical illness or death within the immediate family, ending the Christmas furlough program.[29] The board reasoned that the earliest system's reliance on personal sentiment and paternalistic obligation made it less likely to be fair. "An emotional spurt of the spirit of benevolence at a time when the gift can serve no constructive purpose except an expansive feeling of generosity on the part of the donor is unwise," a board member explained; the rehabilitative benefits of maintaining community ties were not part of its consideration. The board members who traveled to prisons to explain the new clemency system reported that prisoners were disappointed: "Lawdy, I sure was expecting to get out for Christmas."[30] But the board believed that prisoners who could be trusted to leave for fifteen or twenty days would be a good risk for permanent release. In short, Christmas paroles in Alabama were ended not because of a fear of criminals on the loose but in order to prevent officials from "playing politics with the Yuletide spirit" and institute a more rational and standardized administrative process for permanent release.[31]

Alabama's furlough practices were watched closely throughout the South. One Mississippi journalist appreciated how few prisoners who were temporarily released absconded: "The ratio of convicts who kept faith and returned is probably higher than the percentage among ordinary citizens who could be trusted under similar circumstances."[32] Mississippi officially adopted a policy of Christmas leaves in 1944, at the same time it set up its parole bureaucracy.[33] The warden who initiated the program at Parchman Farm, the Mississippi State Penitentiary, farmer and businessman Marvin E. Wiggins, established reforms in order to boost the plantation's productivity, arguing that proper incentives would ensure good behavior and industrious labor. In Wiggins's outlook, according to historian William Banks Taylor, "convict laborers and free laborers were no different."[34]

Each winter Wiggins sent more than a quarter of Parchman's prisoners home.[35] Tom Ambrose, an African American man sentenced to life for "kill[ing] a negro," was granted a Christmas leave despite a 1935 escape that lasted for seven years until he was captured.[36] When Wiggins was warden, a prisoner's flight was not equated with an increased likelihood of future crime. Nor was the nature of a prisoner's original crime indicative of his trustworthiness or dangerousness. "Our murderers and manslaughters are our best releases," explained a Parchman official who served on the Christmas Leave Committee, because those crimes were usually "a one-time deal." On the other hand, "the burglars, arsonists, and armed robbers are the worst, because they're repeaters."[37] The mixed reviews of Parchman's new administration reveal the limits and internal contradictions of Wiggins's reform program. The *Clarion-Ledger* applauded the move, noting, "Instead of wearing a ball and chain in a dark dungeon and having a diet of bread and water," the typical prisoner "finds comparative freedom behind the bars in the Mississippi State Penitentiary program of work, recreation, and most of all, reformation."[38] Frank Smith, a journalist and eventual congressman, contended that "Parchman would take no prizes for scientific penology from modern criminologists, but it receives few complaints from the taxpayers of Mississippi" because of its profitable cotton production.[39]

By the 1950s Parchman was under fire from local newspapers and politicians, as well as national experts and reformers. The Mississippi Press

Association stated that the penal system should emphasize "rehabilitation of the prisoner rather than money making," and the Mississippi Bar Association recommended hiring a manager with expertise in the science of penology rather than agriculture.[40] Some state legislators concurred, while others defended the prison's traditional practices. In this contentious climate, Christmas leaves were one of the few features of life at Parchman that met with the approval of both the prison's defenders and detractors. Just over a decade after the practice began, more than 3,204 prisoners had enjoyed ten-day furloughs during the Christmas season, with only three remaining at large.[41] Superintendent Bill Harpole reminded Governor James P. Coleman (1956–60) that prisoners had returned nearly 100 percent of the time, although "as you know, I cannot make a definite promise as to what these people would do."[42] The governor granted leaves to at least 275 of the twenty-two hundred prisoners at Parchman in 1957.[43] That year, prisoners were no longer required to serve additional days at the end of their sentences to compensate for their holiday leaves.[44]

As in the case of other forms of clemency in the Jim Crow South, upstanding white citizens initiated furlough requests or endorsed a prisoner's temporary release. Mrs. Howard Weeks wrote to Governor Coleman on behalf of Robert House, "a colored person" who had worked for the Weeks family and demonstrated his reliability and trustworthiness: "He was left alone with a big sum of money. We know he never took a bit of it." House's labor was needed at the Weeks household because Mr. Weeks had been disabled by a back injury. In addition, Mrs. Weeks made a plea for House's "family of six children at home waiting for him" and vouched that his wife was a devoted mother: "She doesn't run around and she has the children in school every day." The white woman concluded, "I know they are colored, but I think they deserve some consideration" for a two-week leave at Christmas.[45]

The press praised these temporary releases and announced them annually.[46] Furloughs provided "joy and comfort" while "maintaining and improving penitentiary discipline and morale."[47] A reporter for the *Delta Democrat-Times* wrote an approving piece that featured a prisoner convicted of murder who had gone on Christmas leaves seven or eight times, and he quoted the prisoner as saying, "Not once have I given a thought to not coming back. I'm trying to make a good record and I appreciate the trust put in me."[48] Newspapers repeatedly expressed sympathy for prisoners' innocent family members who missed their loved ones.[49] When two prisoners were still unaccounted for one Christmas season, the *Clarion-*

Ledger asserted, "The escape of these two is a cheap price for the State to pay for the benefits accruing from this program."[50]

To be sure, the furlough incentive was a form of coercion that extended across the boundary between the prison plantation and the free world; the entire Jim Crow South was a carceral space for people of African descent. But holiday leaves also represented real benefits to prisoners. Incarcerated people looked longingly toward home, as reports in Parchman's magazine, *Inside World*, attested. Robert George interviewed his friend O. P. Ferguson about his recent six-day furlough. "Just the goin' did me a lot of good," Ferguson said. "Just lookin' at all them pretty things like streets, roads, cars, and people and stuff like that done me a lotta good."[51] When Fred McGinnis returned from his ten-day furlough, he advised his incarcerated readers that "some of the old landmarks have moved so that you may have a bit of trouble finding your way around for a couple of days," but "let me tell you it can sure make you realized [*sic*] what the true meaning of freedom means."[52] "Seems like all the fellows are talking about is going on ten days," wrote Ozie Lee Townshend, another prisoner, wistfully. Observing the smiles on his friends' faces in anticipation of their upcoming furloughs, John Keith wondered if he would ever hit the Christmas "jackpot." "Could happen," he mused; "I have 40 chances left."[53]

Holiday freedom did hold dangers for those who were released. Getting back to the prison on foot or by hitchhiking was unreliable and treacherous, especially for prisoners of African descent. In Alabama, those who failed to return on time were flogged or put in solitary confinement; one tardy prisoner was lashed into unconsciousness on his return.[54] Another prisoner hopped a freight train back to the prison, but lost his leg when he fell under the moving train. From a hospital bed in Tuscaloosa, he begged doctors to let the prison authorities know that he had been "delayed."[55]

TROUBLES WITH TEMPORARY RELEASES IN MISSISSIPPI DURING THE 1950S AND 1960S

By midcentury the Mississippi press considered the few prisoners who violated trust to be a negligible and acceptable feature of the furlough program. In the few escapes that were widely publicized, the main characters were portrayed as daring outlaws rather than dangerous monsters.[56] Throughout the 1950s, Mississippi's newspapers lauded Parchman's Christmas leave system.[57] In the early 1960s, when a series of people absconded from their furloughs under unusual circumstances, the press, state officials, and the public began to scrutinize the program more closely.[58] Yet, while wondering about the wisdom of decisions made in specific cases, they continued to express support for temporary leaves. Escapes were not in themselves alarming, a Mississippi reporter explained, since even a trusted prisoner might "obey an impulse and head for the hills. Parchman's long succession of superintendents have not felt compelled because of the abuse of the privilege by a few, to abolish the system, *and in this we think they are correct*."[59]

The case of Kimble Berry, a twenty-four-year-old "blond and blue-eyed" young man who had been sentenced to Parchman for manslaughter, seemed alarming, since while he was on furlough he had inadvertently been used as a pawn by another incarcerated man for a robbery scheme. When he turned himself in to the authorities in his home state rather than commit a crime, he told a reporter he was terrified that if he returned to Parchman he would be killed: "It's a school for criminals. It's not a rehabilitation center. It just teaches men to hate."[60] Readers could sympathize with Berry and still criticize the furlough system. The legislative committee investigating this case found that it exposed corruption and failures of judgment, as men who had committed serious crimes were frequently granted leaves.[61] The policy could be redeemed, the lawmakers argued, if decisions were placed in the hands of a board so the governor would "not be harassed and pressured by families of prisoners and 'influence peddlers' seeking release of inmates from Parchman."[62] Still, the *Clarion-Ledger* concluded that it was unfair to blame the program for violations by a few "rotten apples": "The system has otherwise proven most successful and has guided prisoners back to useful lives" while reducing the state's expenditures.[63]

The 1966 case of Robert Everett Rawls was more alarming, and thus potentially more damaging to Mississippi's leave program. Rawls, a white twenty-seven-year-old who was serving two consecutive life sentences for rape and murder, was on a ten-day leave when he purchased a rifle from Sears and planned to find a girl on Dixie Road in Hattiesburg whom he could "butcher." Finding no one to attack, Rawls hid the gun in a ditch, where it was found and traced back to him. Hattiesburg journalist Elliott Chaze argued that the case exposed the need for more rigorous controls on the leave system, "because next time hunting might be better on the Dixie Road." Yet Chaze averred that the majority of people convicted of murder had killed "in the heat of anger" and that "it was reasonable to assume that if the penitentiary turned one loose on leave he would not go shopping around for someone to murder in the manner of a man picking out a new hat."[64] The Mississippi Legislature suggested that the furlough program was too informal. As Senator Howard McDonnell put it, at Parchman "they have a good classification system for livestock, mules and hogs, but not for prisoners."[65]

Yet the practice of Christmas leaves continued. Mississippi legislators suggested more careful screening of those eligible for temporary release, but concluded that the system should not be condemned for one mistake.[66] In the late 1960s furloughs became the rule rather than the exception in US prisons.[67] In 1974 Mississippi governor William Waller (1972–76) approved holiday leaves for 13 percent of the Parchman population.[68] Despite legislators' concerns that Parchman was an "antiquated penal institution" with a "disregard for rehabilitation," the corrections commissioner supported the Christmas furlough system.[69]

"WE EXTEND TO YOU, OVER THE WALL, OUR HAND!"

Even as plantation prisons in the Mississippi delta were extensions of enslavement and the bulwark of southern apartheid, prisoners identified incarceration as a distinct condition, characterized by physical and social isolation, as well as brutality. Compared with the situation today, however, incarcerated people had numerous opportunities to interact with those in the free world. By traveling beyond the prison, mingling with visitors, and publicizing their accomplishments and anxieties through prison newspapers and magazines, prisoners fought against invisibility. From inside the Louisiana State Penitentiary at Angola, the editors of the *Angolite* magazine proudly announced that when over two hundred people representing the evangelical Christian organization Gideons International mingled with over seven hundred prisoners during an event, "NOT ONE UNTOWARD INCIDENT MARRED THE DAY!" The authors surmised that the "old die-hards" would have people believe that Angola was ripe for "murder, riots, and mayhem," but the happy occasion proved that prisoners would respond as "HUMAN BEINGS IF TREATED AS SUCH!"[70]

As Ethan Blue has shown, inmate sports could serve as a form of discipline, but also that prisoners' "experiences of bodily pleasures exceeded, in complex ways, the networks of prison control."[71] Prisoners in Louisiana and Mississippi particularly relished the custom of playing free world teams in athletic competitions because "it would give the outside a clear view of inmate sportsmanship. The men who play on our local college teams will probably be leaders in our state one day."[72] Parchman athletes welcomed a semiprofessional baseball team from Greenwood, Mississippi, "not only as ballplayers, but as men who are interested in our welfare, and as friends." After courteously explaining that the Parchman team only won the game because it was accustomed to the facility's rough ball diamond, they concluded, "We extend to you, over the wall, our hand!"[73] The prisoners of Parchman's Camp 5 wrote to the team from Clarksdale, "Thanks for the fun, and for the chance to rub elbows with freedom."[74]

Playing at musical events outside the prison was an occasion to showcase talent and foster goodwill.[75] In 1960 Parchman superintendent Fred Jones hired Wendell Cannon, a professional musician and former bandleader for Ross Barnett's (1960–64) gubernatorial campaign, to assume the position of musical director at Parchman. He organized two prison bands, one white and one Black, that performed regularly both inside and outside the prison. Cannon said that the program boosted morale and taught skills; not only would it help "people on the outside know our situation" but association with people of "good character" would be "a positive influence on inmates."[76] Traveling in an old school bus painted with caricatures of prisoners, and outfitted in prison stripes, the Insiders and the Stardusters played at dances held by the American Legion, the University of Mississippi, and the Veterans of Foreign Wars.[77] Writing in *Inside World*, band members praised Jones's approval of the program as evidence that "we are now dealing with a gentleman who is interested in other things besides work and punishment."[78]

The positive publicity that the program garnered could offset the contemporaneous revelations of brutality at Parchman. Columnist Cliff Sessions expressed the hope that "after-dark sounds" of "rock 'n' roll and jazz from convict orchestras" would replace the "screaming of a convict being flogged, baying of bloodhounds and harsh orders of prison guards."[79] A journalist in a Memphis, Tennessee, newspaper acclaimed the bands for offering prisoners "a new avenue of complete rehabilitation, preparing them for the long journey back to the society from which they departed." Playing with his head held high, each musician tried "to reclaim the dignity that he had lost." Incarcerated musicians appreciated the faith that Cannon had placed in them. Blackie Boudreaux, a member of the white band the Insiders, told a reporter that the music program "has provided me with a lighted path to follow. I know now I want to make something of my life. I have somewhere to go, something I can accomplish."[80] These men hoped to create "understanding between men confined at Parchman and the free world. We can show that people here can succeed if given the chance."[81] A writer for *Inside World* asserted that the concerts "will tend to relieve the feelings of the public as to the kind of men we have here."[82] In the 1970s the prison bands continued to play at the Governor's Ball, music festivals, and elementary schools.[83] In 1976 an integrated Parchman band performed on a flatbed trailer at the Rosedale, Mississippi, Bicentennial Parade.[84] One former Parchman band member recalled performing close to two hundred engagements a year.[85] Ultimately, although the bands provided temporary and qualified freedom to only a handful of prisoners, they made a positive impression on the public. Though one effect of such performances may have been to sanitize life at Parchman by entertaining rather than frightening their audience, these musicians challenged the spatial control of the prison.[86]

For those who remained confined, the penal press was an essential vehicle for challenging stereotypes that stigmatized them. Just come inside and get to know us, Angola's imprisoned journalists pleaded with free-world readers. Visitors might realize that "they look just like human beings! *Not Lombroso's genus convictus, the low-browed degenerate. They are just like outsiders minus the out.*"[87] Prison journalists blamed the free-world press for exploiting the curiosity of "Casper Milquetoasts" by titillating them with exaggerated stories of crime.[88] Readers, prisoners charged, devoured sensationalist and simplistic headlines; "licking your lips you hungrily suck up all the 'Facts.'"[89] Desperate to be seen as people rather than convicts, Parchman's journalists implored, "MUST SOCIETY ERECT ANOTHER TYPE OF BARS WHEN CONVICTS HAVE PAID THEIR DEBT TO SOCIETY AND RETURN ONLY TO FIND THAT THEY ARE OUTCASTS?"[90]

Prisoners were particularly troubled by the likelihood that their criminal records would be a barrier to their reintegration after they had paid their dues to society. Parchman journalists reassured fearful readers that "no one wants to hurt you! All an ex-con wants is an even break." An incarcerated man had the potential to be an honorable citizen: "Chances are, he has worked far more hours while in the penitentiary . . . than any man in the free world." Prisoners objected to the persistent employment discrimination that former felons encountered. One accused the general public of being more forgiving to the Nazis and Japanese war criminals.[91] The editors of the *Angolite* advised former prisoners seeking employment to keep their past incarceration to themselves; their past mistakes were nobody's business, and their privacy should be honored.[92] From inside the prison, people took advantage of the programs offered to them, insisted on their visibility, and argued for their inclusion in society.

THE "OPEN INSTITUTION" AND THE PARADOX
OF SOUTHERN EXCEPTIONALISM

Southern plantation prisons have been characterized as both brutal and pastoral. Like apologists for slavery who portrayed southern bondage as a benevolent institution in comparison to the cold materialism of the North, some observers contrasted the twentieth-century plantation prison favorably with the northern institutional prison. In the 1930s Mississippi memoirist David Cohn, the son of a Polish-born Jewish immigrant who had a close friendship with the scion of an elite white family, romanticized Parchman, implicitly comparing it to the dungeons and fortresses that were found in northern cities: "This prison has no high walls of granite, no stink of fetid humanity, no cages of steel into which human beings are locked like wild animals." He continued, "Its walls are green trees; its roof is the blue sky; its floor is the rich earth." According to this idyllic view, the labor assigned to Parchman's prisoners did not represent "unfair competition with the labor of free men"; they picked cotton "under conditions of labor closely paralleling those that most of them had known in the 'free world.'" With its liberal visiting policies, plaintive work songs, and rural setting, Parchman was "closer by far to . . . the large antebellum plantation worked by numbers of slaves than to . . . the typical prison."[93] For Cohn, the prison's similarity to a slave plantation was a source of admiration.

The continuum between slavery and incarceration was not lost on prisoners, but they also identified prison as distinctly characterized by totalizing regimentation and antithetical to the relative freedom of world outside. Prisoners were not only anxious about their alienation from, adjustment to, and acceptance by the free world; they also chafed against their depersonalization and immobilization. They aimed to hold their keepers to the standards of rehabilitation that they realized the penal authorities were beginning to espouse. To counter the brutality for which plantation prisons were known, prisoners seized on the rhetoric of reform and rehabilitation to press for improved conditions. Scholars and activists have revealed that prisoners were skeptical of promises of rehabilitation, referring to their performance of requisite docility and compliance as the "rehabilitation game."[94] Yet according to John Irwin, a former inmate at Soledad State Prison in California and a sociologist, however coercive the "chickenshit routines" of treatment-oriented incarceration had been, "rehabilitation inadvertently contributed to mounting criticism of itself by promoting a prison intelligentsia."[95] Prisoners in the Mississippi delta, too, educated themselves on the theory and language of the latest penological thinking to insist on their humane treatment and preparation for return to free society.

In the face of Angola's heel-slashing scandal of the early 1950s, as well as a series of prisoner uprisings around the country, Louisiana governor Robert F. Kennon (1952–56) was eventually forced to bring in outside experts to reform the prison.[96] Kennon, a segregationist who preferred to spend oil money on highways rather than on schools for Black children, appointed a committee of prominent citizens to lead an independent inquiry and brought in James V. Bennett, the head of the Federal Bureau of Prisons, who believed that traditional prisons should be replaced with "open institutions."[97] Bennett was accompanied by Reed Cozart, the warden of the Federal Correctional Institution, Seagoville, in Texas, who had been assistant supervisor of classification at the Federal Bureau of Prisons.[98] Cozart's task was to implement the latest penological strategies and design a rehabilitation-oriented penitentiary that could turn "today's convict" into "tomorrow's citizen." Like Bennett, Cozart deplored the belief that "prisons should be operated as fortresses in reverse—to hold people inside."[99] Seagoville was known as a "prison without walls," designed as a set of cottages with unlocked single rooms arranged around courtyards.[100] In addition to regular contact with the outside world, prisoners enjoyed more autonomy in their daily routines; they could bathe when they chose and move about the facility relatively freely.[101]

Cozart warned that despite the shift in penological goals from punishment to rehabilitation, "there still remains, however, an element of vengeance, retribution and retaliation in our sentencing practices." Rather than regard the prisoner as an "enemy of society," society should treat him as "a fallen brother" and aim to "restore him to the brotherhood." Cozart insisted that security can be obtained "without iron bars and concrete" and instead with "faith in people rather than fear."[102] He thought that Angola's harsh, labor-intensive agricultural regime was ill suited to preparing prisoners for modern life; by midcentury, two-thirds of those incarcerated there came from urban areas, and "nothing will be gained by the state training these men to farm work."[103] While both apologists and critics understood the toil of the plantation as an extension of "normal" life for the laboring class in the Jim Crow South, Cozart, like many prisoners, emphasized the *abnormality* of the prison. "It looks rather nonsensical and incongruous to feel that abnormal persons can be placed in an abnormal environment and expect them to come out normal persons," he declared.[104] Cozart secured an $8 million budget to build new buildings; provide separate facilities for various classifications of prisoners; bring in social workers to institute "treatment" programs; expand educational, recreational, and religious activities; improve the quality of food and medical care; eliminate the use of trusty guards; order blue denim to replace prison stripes; prohibit whipping and sweatboxes; and authorize an inmate advisory council. According to the Louisiana Department of Institutions, these reforms constituted a "quiet revolution."[105]

In reforming Angola, Cozart focused on its physical environment. The new penology required a new architecture.[106] In the past, prison design had emphasized security, but these "gloomy, thick-walled bastilles inevitably produce mental attitudes and behavior patterns on the part of both administrators and inmates which militate strongly against the possibility of putting rehabilitation foremost."[107] Cozart oversaw the construction of a "modern central penitentiary," designed by New Orleans architects Curtis and Davis with a "branching plan" that featured natural light and greater air circulation. Thanks to the employment of prison labor, the new buildings were completed under budget.[108] Much as sociologist Columbus B. Hopper theorized that Parchman prison, with its open design, could shed its backward reputation and become a model of progressive penology, Cozart saw in Angola an opportunity to begin from a foundation that bore no resemblance to the northern industrial prison. Angola already had features of the "open institution": "The absence of very obvious security walls, gates, etc. adds more to a proper climate for rehabilitation than it detracts from a security program."[109] What appealed to Cozart and Hopper was the opportunity to avoid the "prisonization" and "cellbock psychosis" that they thought plagued other prisons.[110] As Hopper pointed out in the late 1960s, the small units that characterized sprawling plantation prisons could become an alternative to locked doors and high walls. "Mass cell block systems will always have most emphasis on security," he argued, "and will remain unwieldy and resistant to change."[111] Thinking along similar lines, Cozart razed the "dungeons" used for punishment at Angola—small concrete solitary cells lacking light and ventilation, with ceilings too low for most prisoners to stand upright in.

Prisoners at Angola cheered when these cells were demolished.[112] The new dormitory buildings had louvered glass windows, allowing light, ventilation, and views of the outside. As architect Arthur Q. Davis put it, "There are no prison walls and therefore the entire complex gave the impression of a series of buildings set into a great expansive openness." The new prison complex at Angola was lauded in architectural publications and received an award from the American Institute of Architects.[113] (See figure 7.1.)

Prisoners regularly stressed the abnormality of their daily lives in the pages of the *Angolite*. A 1954 editorial chastised prison officials who dispensed extreme punishments for infractions of "minor, pusillanimous rules" that "serve no purpose except to confuse and bewilder" and "force subservience and docility." Adopting the language of corrections professionals, the editorial stated that "the sooner the trend toward individual treatment for prisoners is put into effect, the sooner it will pay dividends in citizenship."[114] Another editorial called for the professionalization of prison employees and urged administrators to adopt a scientific approach to prisoners' treatment.[115] It is difficult to uncover prisoners' unvarnished opinions about the effects of Cozart's reforms because they carefully censored their statements to avoid offending the authorities, understanding that reformers were always on the defensive.[116] Although prisoners might well have supported a more radical interrogation of the criminal legal system as a whole, they endorsed reforms as small triumphs of modernity over barbarism. Progress was coming to the plantation prison, and those who would "turn backward the hands of the clock" would fail, "even at Angola." Those who were imprisoned there acknowledged that the new buildings did "rate encomiums. No more unsanitary eye-sores, rat-ridden and fire traps, in which rehabilitation was both unheard of and unknown."[117] The contours of Angola's modernization were revealed in a new mattress factory, where prisoners manufactured mattresses covered in discarded prison stripes.[118]

Prisoners were alert to the long history of prison reform and astutely interpreted Cozart's advances as a hybrid of southern distinctiveness and progressive modernity, "retaining all that was good and discarding all the bad of the old types." In an implicit critique of industrial prisons, as well as Angola, they pointed to the new recreation area in the Louisiana sunshine and fresh air, without the "odious window bars of current jails and prisons." But Angolites vigilantly tempered their praise with their indictment of incarceration as a whole. "Lest the conception rise that this new Angola is a rural retreat—it isn't. Although different, it is still a prison and

7.1 The cafeteria at Louisiana State Penitentiary, Curtis and Davis, architects. Courtesy of the Louisiana State Penitentiary Museum Collection, University of Louisiana at Lafayette.

will continue as such."[119] Although reforms over the past two years signaled that "humanity has replaced brutality" and promised "life instead of death," Angola prisoners contended that "a pink-silk boudoir can become no less a prison if the occupant is held against his will."[120] That is, there was no such thing as a good prison.

Through the penal press, prison libraries, and local grapevines, prisoners gained an understanding of the variety of prison practices around the nation, looking toward fellow prisoners with envy or sympathy according to their own values. In Mississippi, writers for the *Inside World* expressed their approval of Seagoville.[121] A Parchman author unromantically pointed out that his prison, too, was a "prison without walls," a fact that "has baffled many penologists." Why were there so few escapes without a "grey, sinister-looking wall to block the sunlight"? He suggested that the freedom to mingle and socialize with others, both inside and outside, allowed for mutual support and care, whereas a "cell block system" isolated the prisoner, which "leads a man to become melancholy and paranoid."[122] Prisoners understood their captivity as an extension of the South's peculiar institution, but sometimes they saw models to emulate within the South. Indeed, prisoners were among the first to perceive Mississippi's furlough program as an example of progressive practices. The editor of the *Angolite* admired the "unique and long established practice" of the Mississippi governor releasing hundreds of prisoners to spend the Christmas season with family and friends, citing it as a "tremendous incentive to morale." Why couldn't prisoners at Angola receive the same, even for just one day?[123] Prisoners in Mississippi, who already enjoyed Christmas furloughs, looked to Texas for another bold experiment in which incarcerated men, in civilian clothes, were allowed to leave the prison to watch high school basketball games or attend church services. The warden and correctional officers accompanying them wore civilian clothes as well.[124] As imprisoned writer Tom Runyon put it in 1959, "If it were frankly admitted that prisons were places for exacting revenge on the lawbreaker, convicts could understand. Instead its spokesmen talk piously of 'reformation' and 'rehabilitation' while advocating sterner laws. . . . Convicts despise hypocrisy above all things."[125] The rhetoric of rehabilitation provided a condition of possibility for prisoners as they searched for tools, both new and old, to serve their future.

By the late 1950s, prison spokespeople and their allies in the press cited the Christmas furloughs and clemency practices to counter criticisms of Parchman, even claiming that Mississippi was "traditionally first among states in pioneering many progressive achievements."[126] Articles trumpeting "improvements" mentioned medical examinations, educational programs, television sets, and baseball games, as well as solitary confinement for "unruly inmates."[127] Although the historical record demonstrates the limits of these improvements, such puffery reflects civic leaders' concern about the public image of their prison system and their belief that temporary release was a progressive feature of Parchman. Harpole spread his doctrines to his professional colleagues, touting Christmas furloughs and conjugal visits to his colleagues at the Southern States Prison Association conference. Of furloughed prisoners, he remarked colloquially, "I've only lost one since last June. If you place a little confidence in prisoners, they hate to betray it. After all, they are just folks like the rest of us."[128]

Penologists, too, looked for best practices that would aid in rehabilitation. When sociologists Eugene Zemans and Ruth Shonle Cavan conducted a comparative study of conjugal visits and furloughs around the world, they contributed to a discourse that, rather than seeing social isolation as a penal end in itself, regarded contact with people in the free community as essential to rehabilitation.[129] Along with isolation, sociologists and penologists rejected the regimentation characteristic of prison life, which led to "constriction and atrophy. The person . . . stops growing, learning, feeling. In short, confinement . . . prepares one only for confinement." Reform required "new methods with which the offender" could experience the "maintenance, even strengthening, of family and community ties."[130]

Ironically, the belief that prisoners were innately criminal and suited only to heavy physical labor, and thus neither worthy nor capable of rehabilitation, did not prevent governors and superintendents from trusting prisoners enough to allow them to leave the prison. Prisoners' contacts with the free world were taken for granted as part of the fluidity that characterized the boundaries between freedom and bondage in the Jim Crow South. Christmas furloughs were the natural offspring of the union between the southern customs of paternalistic deference and labor exploitation. Like conjugal visits, these furloughs began as a reward for compliance and an incentive for labor. They were justified in terms of Christian benevolence, sealed with codes of honor, and enforced with violence. For their part, incarcerated people cherished furloughs and other opportunities to interact with the free world as a means of securing their acceptance by society.

As the rhetoric of rehabilitation penetrated the South, both prisoners and professional reformers identified southern traditions that could be carried over into a rehabilitative program of reintegrating the prisoner into the community. At Angola, a prisoner facetiously described Cozart's reforms as a futuristic model of the rehabilitative promise: the prison now boasted "$6 million worth of streamlined steel and stone housing electronic humanitarianism and radionic brotherly love." It was a "hybrid of old and new, an admixture of what is half forgotten and that which is vaguely hoped for."[131] As reformers sought to bring southern prisons in line with modern penological principles, the paradigm of the "open prison" and mobility between the inside and outside found an unlikely precedent in plantation prisons. In 1967, *The Challenge of Crime in a Free Society*, the report of Lyndon B. Johnson's President's Commission on Law Enforcement and Administration of Justice, argued that the transition "from institution to community can be made less abrupt, and the resources of the community institutions drawn upon to help in rehabilitation." Citing Mississippi's furlough program and its miniscule escape rate as a pioneering example, it recommended similar practices to "prevent the deterioration of family ties," allow prisoners to apply new skills, and "test the insights they have developed in counseling experiences."[132] Mississippi prisoners, too, expressed pride in their long history of furloughs, publishing an open letter by a psychiatrist to the superintendent of the Washington State Penitentiary in support of them: "Your idea of furloughs is a good plan, though not in the least original, for Mississippi has been giving men 10 days a year at home FOR OVER 30 YEARS."[133] By the 1970s, nearly every study of furloughs cited Mississippi as the leading light of this innovative program.[134] Southern traditions were turned into a new, national common sense: prisoners should have more contact with the free world.

8 Conquering Prison Walls

Furloughs at the Crossroads of the
Rehabilitative Ideal

Los Angeles police officer Phillip J. Riley was only twenty-six years old when he was shot and killed with his own service revolver. It was October 1971, and Riley had stopped David W. Brenenstahl, who was reportedly driving a stolen car. After a chase through the Venice neighborhood, Brenenstahl wrested Officer Riley's gun from his holster and shot the officer twice in the chest. Brenenstahl had been sentenced to prison three years earlier on a burglary conviction and was out on a seventy-two-hour furlough. Two months later, John Lee Groeschel, serving a life sentence for kidnapping, was also out on furlough when he fatally shot seventy-two-year-old Rebecca Farber in her North Hollywood home. Los Angeles police chief Edward M. Davis wrote to Governor Ronald Reagan (1967–75) to express his disapproval of "freedom passes" for prisoners.[1] Davis, who had received national attention when he arrested Charles Manson in 1969, soon authorized the use of choke holds, covert intelligence-gathering on alleged radicals at the University of California–Los Angeles, racial profiling of suspected gang members, and raids on gay establishments.[2] According to Davis, furloughs were just another instance of letting "dangerous men into the Southern California community." He warned, "The Phillip Rileys and the Rebecca Farbers who are still alive cry out for someone to protect them from the murderous onslaught of the criminal army in this state which daily intensifies its warfare on society."[3]

Governor Reagan disagreed. Rather than taking the opportunity to remind the public of his get-tough bona fides, he boasted that the state's corrections system was "very progressive" and was "leading the nation in rehabilitation." "Obviously you can't be perfect," he shrugged.[4] Reagan's equanimity was shared by corrections officials such as Milton Burdman, the deputy director of reentry programs. Burdman lamented the recent killings but admitted, "There are going to be more. . . . No matter how good we are and how good the police are there are going to be terrible, tragic events." Reagan and corrections officials stressed that all the data indicated that the furlough program was a success.[5] A year earlier, the warden of San Quentin State Prison expressed doubt that furloughs led to crime. He proudly told a reporter, "There has been a great breakdown in the barriers between the inmate body and the free world. Today a convict is segregated from society—but not isolated from it."[6]

This defense of furloughs by Ronald Reagan, whose attacks on welfare, insistence on personal responsibility, and denunciation of urban Black and Brown communities as lawless jungles became notorious, should give us pause. Not only was the road to law and order a crooked one, but what law and order would look like was not foreordained. Reagan's support of furloughs reveals the contingency and malleability of notions of risk. Far from being scientifically measurable or objectively intolerable, *risk* was defined by proponents of furloughs as a necessary feature of a reintegrationist view of corrections—that is, the idea that prisons should give their residents the tools for their inevitable return to society. At the very moment when "crime in the streets" emerged as an elastic mantra that helped to fuel mass incarceration, prisons were temporarily releasing people onto the streets in the name of public safety. Moreover, as in the case of conjugal visits, the lens of furloughs provides a more precise view of the constituencies that built and opposed the machinery of mass incarceration. Law enforcement agencies supported Reagan's bid for governor, but soon found themselves at odds with him on the issue of furloughs. Chief Davis's claim that Americans faced a choice between the "law of the jungle, or the law of organized society" reiterated Reagan's position on crime.[7] On furloughs, however, corrections professionals and governors from both parties sided with prisoner-activists and their allies, often in opposition to prosecutors, police, and prison guards, as well as a fearmongering press.[8]

This crucial moment contained the seeds of prison expansion and the hardening of its architecture, but it also generated vigorous support for furloughs as a step toward decarceration. In the 1970s, debates about and defenses of furloughs, even for prisoners facing life sentences, reveal the primacy of reintegration of formerly incarcerated people as a correctional goal, which was based on the assumption that all prisoners should be treated as though they would eventually return to the free community. Supporters of prison furloughs were not always radical critics of incarceration, but they argued that rehabilitation, to the extent that it was a plausible outcome, would be most effectively done *outside* prison walls. In 1971 US attorney general John N. Mitchell predicted that in the near future, the "public's predominant impression of penology will be not of old walls but new doors."[9] It turned out that he was mistaken. But at this transitional juncture, because supporters of furloughs believed that prisons themselves perpetuated crime in the streets, the risk of keeping people in prison was seen as greater than the risk of letting them out.

"NOT OLD WALLS BUT NEW DOORS": FURLOUGHS AND COMMUNITY CORRECTIONS

Furlough programs spread nationwide after the US Congress's approval of a federal prison furlough program in 1965.[10] The federal statute functioned as a blueprint for states to implement their own furlough systems. The publication in 1967 of the report of Lyndon B. Johnson's President's Commission on Law Enforcement and Administration of Justice, *The Challenge of Crime in a Free Society*, led to a further expansion of prison furloughs. Colloquially known as the Katzenbach Commission, it recommended partial release and furlough programs as a method of rehabilitation and of facilitating a prisoner's transition back into the community. Noting the miniscule failure-to-return rate in the few states where prison furloughs were common, the report contended that implementing furlough programs could help to "prevent the deterioration of family ties," allow "offenders to try newly learned skills," and give them the opportunities to "test the insights" developed through counseling. The report promoted work and school release programs, which had been launched with favorable results in a number of states, along with "prerelease guidance centers." To facilitate those programs, it recommended that correctional institutions be located close to population centers and have cooperative relationships with schools, employers, and universities.[11] Established alongside other Great Society programs, furloughs were regarded sympathetically by the press and the public. One federal prisoner participating in work release was amazed that he could put on a suit and go through the steel gates for "an honest day's work," and he felt touched that "many, many times my co-workers have invited me to go fishing, go to their home for supper and meet their families. . . . I was a Mr. and not an inmate."[12] Lawrence Carpenter, the warden of the Federal Correctional Institution, Seagoville, in Texas, announced, "The walls of the old-line prison have finally been broken down."[13]

The Katzenbach Commission endorsed furlough programs as part of "community corrections," which emphasized transforming incarcerated people into "law-abiding citizens" through therapeutic treatment and reintegration into normal life.[14] Advocates believed that creating opportunities for prisoners to leave the prison and/or serve their time outside an institutional setting was most effective for rehabilitation.[15] Furloughs would enhance public safety by acclimating prisoners to life in the free world and providing them with the skills they needed to be productive members of society. Occasional and temporary release would allow prisoners to develop new identities other than that of prisoner; according to criminologist Elmer K. Nelson Jr., stereotypes such as "slum-youth, minority-group member, school dropout, unsuccessful employee, and law-violator" unjustly branded prisoners as "damaged goods."[16] *The Challenge of Crime* criticized "the fact that the correctional apparatus is often used—or misused—by both the criminal justice system and the public as a rug under which disturbing problems and people can be swept." Further, the report noted, "Institutions tend to isolate offenders from society, both physically and psychologically, cutting them off from schools, jobs, families, and other supportive influences and increasing the probability that the label of criminal will be indelibly impressed upon them. The goal of reintegration is likely to be furthered much more readily by working with offenders in the community than by incarceration." *The Challenge of Crime* deplored the "alienation and apartness of the inmate society" that obstructed reintegration by allegedly promoting "moral deterioration."[17] Concluding that most people in prison did not have to be there, advocates of community corrections argued for the establishment of halfway houses, more vigorous use of probation and parole, and intermediate sanctions rather than incarceration. Practitioners also began to experiment with electronic monitoring.[18]

The Katzenbach Commission's report had the backing of social scientists and attorneys. In 1972, lawyers and criminologists convened by the Roscoe Pound American Trial Lawyers Foundation concurred that the use of imprisonment as a sanction needed to be curtailed and that the majority of incarcerated people should be released and undergo rehabilitation through community-based services. Moreover, they argued, much of the behavior that led to incarceration could be decriminalized. Attorney and international law professor Gerhard O. W. Mueller explained that "imprisonment means the caging of human beings. . . . If there were the slightest scientific proof that the placement of human beings into boxes or cages for any length of time, even overnight, had the slightest beneficial effect, perhaps such a system might be justifiable."[19] While in retrospect it is clearer that the Katzenbach Commission's emphasis on reintegration actually implied a more expansive and comprehensive role of corrections in American society, the decline of faith in the prison as the best site for "correction" created an opportunity for flexible approaches to release.[20]

Discussions among architects about the physical design of prisons reflected the philosophy behind community corrections. Like Columbus B. Hopper and Reed Cozart, the Katzenbach Commission agreed that prison architecture was generally "grim and fortresslike, with tier upon tier of individual cells arranged chiefly with a view to security" rather than rehabilitation.[21] In the aftermath of the 1971 uprising at the Attica Correctional Facility in upstate New York, architecture critic Ada Louise Huxtable traced the prisoners' distress to the inhumane design of the prison itself and encouraged architects to create buildings that fostered human relationships rather than fear, anonymity, and degradation. She commended efforts to construct a "community-like" complex that "restores, rather than destroys, a sense of normal life situations" and praised designs that featured courtyards, glass, outdoor walkways, and visiting rooms without barriers. Open plans translated what Huxtable called the mandate to "conquer the walls" into material form.[22] In 1972 architect Alfred Gilbert, commissioned by the American Foundation's Institute of Corrections under the direction of the Law Enforcement Assistance Administration to tour over one hundred prisons and jails to evaluate their architecture, observed that correctional environments dehumanized inmates: "Dressed in white coveralls against a monochromatic gray background and in the artificial glare of fluorescent lighting, the men moved like laboratory zombies in a grade B. horror film. How will they move about in society upon release? Whose interests are thereby served?"[23]

Robert Sommer, an influential environmental psychologist whose research was also supported by the Law Enforcement Assistance Administration, railed against the effect of the so-called hard architecture that ensured prisoners' hard time. The fashionable style called brutalism was characterized by simple, functional forms in steel and concrete that lacked amenities, resisted vandalism, and refused human imprint. Those imprisoned in brutalist structures suffered both sensory deprivation and sensory assault. Sommer lamented that prison architecture typically lacked "permeability between inside and out." Connecting the recent design trend to the unrest of the 1960s, Sommer commented that it "had the avowed purpose of increasing security. Frequently this reason is a coverup for a desire to maintain order, discipline, or control."[24] From cement picnic tables to bulletproof glass and steel doors, hard architecture was based on a "security state of mind" in which "the potential enemy was the criminal."[25] "A building can make a good situation better or a bad situation worse," he contended. Hard spaces *produced* antisocial behavior, although prison rioters notably spared "television sets purchased with inmate welfare funds" and "paintings made by their fellow prisoners."[26]

Sommer and others proposed spaces that were responsive to their users and more permeable. A 1973 piece in *Architectural Forum* titled "Pushing Prisons Aside" argued that prisons should have natural light, visual stimulation, privacy, recreational areas, and personalized space. The best new experiments in prison architecture serve the prisoner's rehabilitation by seeking "to reinforce his personal identity and self-image through a permissive and supportive physical setting."[27] These design principles were in sync with the rationale for community corrections: greater permeability between the material structure of the prison and the surrounding community. As Gilbert concluded, "the denial that the interest of the individual inmate and the interests of the community are common to each other" was apparent "in the physical plant where elements presumably designed by the community are, to the offender, austere, impersonal, intimidating, sometimes terrifying, and seldom constructive."[28] Rather than causing isolation "as if there were no world outside," prison design should embody the notion that incarcerated people were ultimately members of the free community.[29]

At the same time, elected officials and corrections professionals urged a process of decarceration. As political scientist Naomi Murakawa emphasizes, reducing reliance on prisons was not "not on the radical fringe" at the dawn of "law and order."[30] For example, President Richard M. Nixon's 1973 National Advisory Commission on Criminal Justice Standards and Goals, composed of political leaders, law enforcement officials, and criminal justice professionals, recommended a ten-year moratorium on prison construction. Referencing high rates of recidivism, as well as the litigation that exposed the inhumane treatment of prisoners, the report stated that "the American correctional system today appears to offer minimum protection for the public and maximum harm to the offender," and it proposed reducing reliance on prisons.[31] Through more freedom and contact with the community beyond the prison, prisoners could develop abilities "often atrophied through institutionalization."[32] As the president of the American Foundation in Philadelphia, William G. Nagel—whose research resulted in the influential study *The New Red Barn: A Critical Look at the Modern American Prison*—asserted, "The prison, or call it by any other name . . . is obsolete; it cannot be reformed, and it should not be perpetuated through false hope of forced treatment. It should be repudiated and abandoned."[33]

With expert opinion moving in the direction of reducing reliance on incarceration and making existing prisons more open to the free community, corrections authorities began to authorize furloughs for work, education, and family visits. Unlike emergency leaves to attend funerals or to receive medical care, these furloughs were unsupervised and could last as long as ten days. One rationale for furloughs was that they provided a more viable alternative to conjugal visits. Those who were skeptical of conjugal visits recognized that preserving family ties served a crucial rehabilitative function; they preferred furloughs because they were less burdensome for the facility, avoided public criticism, and were "more normal" for the couples involved.[34] Since married prisoners were in the minority, home visits would benefit a wider range of people.[35] All in all, federal authorities agreed with Nelson's statement that providing incarcerated people with more access to the outside world and trying to "blur the line between confinement and life in the community, to make the boundaries of institutions more 'permeable'" resulted in an increase of public safety rather than a decrease.[36]

Throughout the 1970s states broadened the eligibility criteria for furloughs and expanded the accepted aims of furlough programs.[37] By 1976, prisons in forty-seven states, as well as the federal prison system and the District of Columbia, had furlough programs. In ten of those jurisdictions, there was no criminal conviction that would make a prisoner ineligible for a furlough.[38] The universality of the program led one criminal justice scholar to assert, "A restraining of rehabilitative zeal does not by any means necessitate the isolation of the offender from his family and the community. 'Reformed' or not, the inmate still may enjoy a brief respite from the pains of confinement. The humanitarian benefits of furlough continue to justify temporary release programs."[39]

Peter Makarewicz enjoyed planting tomatoes in the garden. After patting down the soil, he mowed the backyard lawn and sat down to breakfast with his mother and sister. He was not used to talking to women, but these ladies were family. It was a thrill to drink coffee out of a heavy mug emblazoned with "World's Greatest Uncle" and eat his eggs with real silverware. Once it was time to leave, Makarewicz had to steady himself as he maneuvered through the living room furniture. To him it looked like a hoarder's dollhouse; there was so much *stuff*, yet it all seemed tiny. He was used to wide spaces, long corridors, and empty rooms. Makarewicz walked to the corner store, screwed up his nerve, and asked to buy a pack of cigarettes, flinching when the bell on the door jangled as he exited the store. When he returned to his mother's home, she was waiting with her car running to take him back to the Massachusetts Correctional Institution, where he continued to serve a life sentence for murder.[40]

Makarewicz was able to spend the weekend at his mother's home in Foxborough, Massachusetts, because of the furlough program that the state Department of Corrections had established in 1972 as part of a suite of reforms advanced by the governor, Francis Sargent (1969–75), a liberal Republican who was reared in the "progressive Yankee reform tradition" and had professionally trained as an architect.[41] Upon his election in 1970, he endorsed a goal of deinstitutionalization, moving people out of big caretaking institutions such as mental hospitals and prisons. As his secretary of human services he appointed Peter C. Goldmark Jr., a thirty-year-old former city planner in the administration of New York City's liberal mayor, John Lindsay, ignoring Massachusetts' correctional officers' dismissal of Goldmark as a "hippie" and a "pinko."[42] In turn, Goldmark recruited twenty-six-year-old James Isenberg to serve as his special assistant for corrections.[43] While studying criminal justice at the University of California–Berkeley, Isenberg was schooled in the philosophy of community corrections and its practice in Europe.[44] Steered by his staff, Sargent was poised to address what he saw as the persistent horrors of the Massachusetts corrections system.

The governor was moved to act by a potent combination of public pressure and prisoners' protests. In late September 1971, confronted with news of the massacre at Attica, prisoners at the Concord, Walpole, and Norfolk prisons in Massachusetts organized peaceful demonstrations and engaged in work strikes in solidarity with their counterparts in New

York State. The Massachusetts prisoners, protesting the "depersonalized and inhuman conditions and treatment that we are subject to as prisoners in this institution," formed committees that drafted specific demands and began negotiations with the administration.[45] Meetings with prison administrators were open to reporters and widely publicized.[46] A memorandum from prisoners Lester J. X. Richard Jr. and Gilbert Hester of the Black Rights Committee reported that after four days of peaceful demonstrations, "we human beings here assembled have come to a reasonable conclusion," as officials granted many of their demands. "This historic meeting if implemented *might* prevent massacres such as Attica," they asserted, but only if negotiations continued in good faith.[47] In early October 1971, however, Superintendent Robert M. Moore ordered a lockup at the Massachusetts Correctional Institution–Walpole, charging that the protests did not represent the views of the majority of prisoners and instead were "caused by a small, hard-core group of agitators."[48]

Fearing another Attica, Governor Sargent agreed to introduce a prison reform bill and created the Citizens' Committee on Corrections to identify and analyze the prisoners' grievances and propose recommendations. He was aware that "people equate lawlessness with prison reform," but he was determined to address what he saw as the harms generated by excessive reliance on incarceration. In a speech at a church in Waltham, Massachusetts, Sargent declared, "We have developed over the years a sense of security by building large walls around our prisons. We have said we are safe as long as inmates remain behind the walls. But this is a fantasy. The walls may be a symbol, but they do not protect. Ninety per cent of our inmates behind these walls will someday be released."[49]

Composed of incarcerated and formerly incarcerated people, corrections professionals, and community organizers, the Citizens' Committee was led by Harry Elam Sr., the first Black chief justice of the Boston Municipal Court.[50] Its report, titled *Corrections '71: A Citizens' Report* and known colloquially as the Elam Report, expressed unequivocal sympathy for the protests and outrage on the prisoners' behalf: "The demands for change have infused the prisons as they have pervaded our society, and just as they cannot be repressed with brutality on the streets, neither can they be subdued with transfer and punitive isolation within the prison." After listening to prisoners' demands, the committee urged officials to develop a furlough program, among other reforms, so that prisoners could sustain ties those on the outside: "This would ease the shock of going in one swift move from inside an institution back to the community." In addition, the

Elam Report recommended that the legislature repeal the requirement that convicted persons serve two-thirds of their sentences before being eligible for parole, and establish parole eligibility after fifteen years for those sentenced to life (who otherwise would not be eligible without the governor's commutation to a term of years).[51]

The findings of the Elam Report and the tragedy at Attica emboldened Sargent's commitment to correctional reform. Peter Goldmark appreciated the possibilities of that moment. It was "a good time to try the reform . . . because the system was so rotten, and everybody's expectations were so conflicting and hot. So when whatever you do was going to be trouble, that's when you try and do something serious in government."[52] In July 1972 Sargent signed the Omnibus Corrections Reform Act, which repealed the two-thirds law, created community-based correctional centers, and established a furlough program in state prisons. To signal his attentiveness to the pleas of incarcerated people, Sargent signed the bill in the yard of the Massachusetts Correctional Institution–Norfolk.[53]

Sargent needed a new corrections commissioner who would be sympathetic to his reforms—preferably someone from outside the Massachusetts system.[54] The choice was John O. Boone, the African American superintendent of Lorton Reformatory, a federal prison facility in northern Virginia. A native of Atlanta, World War II veteran, and Morehouse College alumnus with a graduate degree in social work, Boone had moved up through the federal prison system first as a guard and then a casework supervisor. By 1972 he was a central figure in the shift toward community corrections on the national level, having been recognized by the US Department of Justice for "unusual success in the treatment of offenders" after he spent three years overseeing research on the administration of criminal justice in the South under the auspices of the Southern Regional Council, a multiracial organization that was famous for its longtime opposition to racial segregation.[55] Sargent warned Boone that he had three strikes against him: he was from out of state, he was a reformer, and he was Black. One aide to Goldmark, conscious of the political culture that dominated corrections' rank and file, remarked that Boone "was the first black man" guards "had ever seen who wasn't behind bars."[56] Before assuming his post, Boone was well aware of the turmoil in Massachusetts prisons; he embraced the position because he felt that there was a broad mandate to carry out reforms.[57]

Throughout his career Boone decried the "Iron Curtains" that shielded prisons from public concern and allowed "corruption, political intrigue and human degradation" to persist.[58] When he arrived at Lorton, prisoners welcomed a superintendent who recognized, according to one social worker, that they were "sons, brothers, husbands and fathers, and above all, citizens" and acknowledged that "we take on a burden when we put a man behind the walls. And that burden is to give him a chance to change, to reenter society."[59] Boone attributed crime to an economic system "which just as surely produces a handful of millionaires, secure in the protection of their property, person and privilege, because of their money, also produces millions of poor people who are unable to find a decent job, adequate housing and an equal opportunity because of their poverty."[60] He aimed "to give prisoners the maximum opportunity to control their own lives, both within the correctional institutions and without, through the minimum form and amount of institutional controls, custody, and supervision appropriate for each person."[61] While his ultimate goal was decarceration, he sought to improve the lot of prisoners inside and create pathways to release.[62] Goldmark's perception was that Boone "believed that for some of these people the best thing was just to be out."[63]

When Boone assumed his post in Massachusetts, the situation in state prisons was volatile. Prisoners had formed a chapter of the National Prisoners Reform Association (NPRA), a collective bargaining unit that could balance the powerful guards' union during negotiations with prison authorities. Walpole prison, where the interracial pair of Ralph Hamm and Bobby Dellelo was elected to lead the NPRA, had been convulsed by a tug-of-war of strikes and lockdowns since the massacre at Attica. Prisoners were particularly distressed that incarcerated leaders actively involved in negotiations with prison administrators were dragged from their cells in the middle of the night and transferred to other prisons in retaliation for their political activity.[64] Max D. Stern, an attorney for the NAACP Legal Defense Fund, argued that these transfers demonstrated that "prison security is maintained" by "a reign of terror." "However unpleasant in absolute terms," he argued, a prison was temporarily "as much a home as our communities are to us." Prisoners developed friendships, held jobs, engaged in programs, and organized for change. "Were they not prisoners," Stern said of those who were transferred. "we would say they were kidnapped."[65]

Prisoners continued to stage work strikes and demand that civilian observers be allowed into the prison. Guards retaliated by tear-gassing prisoners and engaging in violent shakedowns. One prisoner reported that guards put soap powder in prisoners' food and urinated in their beverages.[66] The most brutal lockdown, which lasted over three months, was initiated hours before a Kwanzaa celebration organized by the newly formed Black African Nations toward Unity. The celebration had been planned for months; prisoners had raised and spent $1,600 for the event; families and entertainers were already waiting in the visiting room for the event when they were turned away.[67] When two hundred correctional officers walked off the job in March 1973, Boone suspended them without pay, recognized the NPRA as a bargaining unit, and authorized an experiment with prisoner self-government. As detailed in *When the Prisoners Ran Walpole: A True Story in the Movement for Prison Abolition*, for the next several months the NPRA essentially ran prison operations; historians have called this the "most audacious experiment in prisoner governance" in the country.[68] One prisoner referred to life at Walpole during this brief utopian experiment as being "like a furlough."[69]

"THEY WANT TO SEE ME WITHOUT CHAINS ON": PRISON ACTIVISM

During the crisis in Massachusetts prisons in the early 1970s, prisoners tried various ways of making prison walls more penetrable. On a basic but crucial level, they insisted on their own visibility and on public scrutiny of what transpired inside. Thanks to a bill that allowed the press to meet directly with prisoners, prisoners spoke to reporters about their conditions and reprisals by guards.[70] Although skeptics wondered why people should take the word of a convict, the Massachusetts commissioner of youth services, Jerome G. Miller, explained that he tended to believe the stories of prisoners over those of the staff, not because "one group is made up of liars and sadists and the other more truthful" but because prisons were so "self-protective," "self-sealed," and "closed" that for prisoners to speak out against their conditions meant taking a great risk.[71] Prisoners contacted the press in order to testify about their own lives. One prisoner who was transferred from Norfolk to Walpole as a reprisal for his participation in the protests challenged the narratives of his keepers: "The public hears of what fear and what a dangerous job the prison guards have, but what about the fear and hardships that the inmate[s] are subject to?" He added, "The time has come for you, the public, and we, the inmates, to tear down these vast warehouses of human refuse and build a system that will have a more positive end result in terms of correction."[72]

Prisoners aimed to rehabilitate their image as productive and caring members of society. As Walpole prisoner Gerard Letellier explained, "People on the outside think we're just animals. We want them to know the truth. We feel, we love, we loved. We hope to do that again sometime."[73] To build ties with the community, Walpole prisoners hosted a cookout at the prison for elderly women residing at a nearby housing complex. For Charles McDonald, serving a life sentence, such events allowed him to see "another side to the world."[74] Newspaper readers might have been surprised to see a photograph of self-confessed "Boston strangler" Albert DeSalvo jitter-bugging with guests in the prison courtyard.[75] But prisoner Paul Durant told a reporter that "old-timers and convicts" had a lot in common: "We're both imprisoned and pushed away in a corner of society where no one really cares anymore. That's why we relate to each other so well."[76]

Incarcerated people knocked holes in the walls by organizing with allies on the outside. During the unrest, prisoners received support in the form of funds, letter-writing campaigns, and public demonstrations from groups as wide-ranging as the Black Panthers, the Boston Junior Chamber of Commerce, the Massachusetts Council of Churches, the National Association of Social Workers, the Southern Christian Leadership Conference, and Vietnam Veterans against the War. The Ad Hoc Committee on Prison Reform acted as a conduit between prison activists and the public, and prisoners invited civilian observers to pass through the "Iron Curtains." Rev. Edward Rodman, a former member of the Congress of Racial Equality and the Student Nonviolent Coordinating Committee, a prison abolitionist, and one of the Ad Hoc Committee's leaders, trained over one thousand students, clergy, labor organizers, and former prisoners to observe Walpole's daily operations and report abuses.[77] Rodman believed that these observers could act as a "third party nonviolent interventionary force" and provide information to the press that would counterbalance the biased narratives of correctional officers.[78]

The day after the civilian observers entered the prison, the correctional officers' union walked off the job and demanded Boone's resignation; prison guards were up in arms about the commissioner's reforms.[79] Guards understood the threat that his decarceration program posed to their jobs.[80] They taunted him by calling him "Boone the coon," and their union expressed disgust at his interference at Walpole.[81] Boone responded to the guards' walkout by suspending them without pay.[82]

Prisoners and their advocates, by contrast, sought to expand the state's furlough policy. Boone had championed furloughs at Lorton, but just before he arrived in Massachusetts, the program had been temporarily suspended.[83] Virginia's attorney general filed suit, arguing that furloughs constituted "a continuing danger to the health, safety and welfare of the citizens of the commonwealth."[84] Boone defended the practice by pointing to its success rate and its importance as a motivating factor.[85] He did not see furloughs primarily as a reward for good behavior within the prison but rather as a means of reintegrating prisoners with their communities and as an opportunity for them to demonstrate their capacity for self-determination.[86] Echoing the view of the Katzenbach Commission, the Massachusetts Department of Correction declared, "If a man is returned to society more embittered, vengeful, demoralized and incapable of social and economic survival than when he first came to prison, then we certainly will have failed in our obligation to protect society."[87] Like other advocates of community corrections, the department insisted that "the protection of society . . . involves much more than the inmate's isolation from the community."[88] The department allowed furloughs so that prisoners could obtain medical or psychiatric services not available inside the facility, contact prospective employers, secure a residence, and "for any other reason consistent with reintegration of a committed offender into the community."[89]

Incarcerated people supported the furlough program and urged its continuation and expansion.[90] When state legislators threatened to restrict eligibility, prisoners urged their allies on the outside to lobby on their behalf.[91] Prisoner Richard Roberts said that furloughs gave him something to look forward to. To Juan Matthews, serving a fifty- to one-hundred-year sentence, it was important to "keep the feeling of outside, to let a guy know that the outside is still there."[92] Leo Nolin had been incarcerated for fifty years when he told a prison journalist in 1977 that furloughs allowed him to "keep up to date."[93] There was a direct connection between furloughs and clemency: lifers at Norfolk prison knew that the governor would "not recommend commutation . . . without a positive furlough record" and argued that "the longer a human being is kept captive away from family and friends, the harder it is for him to successfully survive when released."[94] Thus, those whose furloughs were approved felt a responsibility not to jeopardize their privilege or the program for fellow prisoners.[95]

Some prisoners complained that the discretion involved in granting furloughs resulted in their unfair distribution. As in the case of conjugal visits, there were prisoners who disparaged furloughs as a tool of control. Leaders in the NPRA who were skeptical of anything endorsed by the state, the prison administration, or any other formal authority interpreted furloughs as "behavior modification." Ralph Hamm, for example, recognized that furloughs were an important way for prisoners to maintain ties with their families and communities, but "I also saw them as a coercive administration tool . . . as a lure and incentive to pull prisoners away from the philosophy of the NPRA, and break the unity and collective resistance."[96] Another NPRA member at Walpole told an outside observer that furloughs undermined prisoners' self-determination because the administration could withhold them at its whim; he expected the administration to offer furloughs to "inmate leaders" in exchange for compliance. If he were offered a furlough, "I'll tell him, stick your furlough."[97] On the other hand, Arnie King, sentenced to life for murder, cherished his opportunities to leave the prison. "Stick your furlough? No. I'm in." King's wife and family "want to see me beyond these walls. They want to see me without chains on. I owe them."[98]

The *Black Panther* newsletter charged that "troublemakers" were given furloughs to keep quiet, and the authorities "exploit the program as a means of behavior control."[99] Prisoners were conscious of the bargain they were making by accepting a furlough program. A prisoner in Washington State admitted that even those who were "left behind" while others went out on furloughs vowed to refrain from "radical activity" so as not to get those furloughs canceled. For him, self-restraint was not evidence of behavior control but solidarity with fellow prisoners.[100]

FAULT LINES

The debate about furloughs occurred amid the widely publicized unrest in Massachusetts prisons and was politicized from the outset. Most opposition came from the police, prosecutors, and sheriffs. If for prisoners Attica was a metonymy of American oppression, for hard-liners prison reform and prisoner self-government were indistinguishable from open rebellion and evidence of brazen criminals getting away with murder. As reports of people absconding during furloughs made the headlines before the 1974 elections, candidates for county sheriff and for district attorney advocated ending the program. This stance jumped party lines. Democratic member of the Massachusetts House of Representatives, Barr T. Hannon of Braintree, who was running for district attorney, linked Watergate, "corruption in government," "crime in the streets," "clogged courts," "juvenile delinquency," Walpole, and "prison furloughs."[101] The *Black Panther* accused

Democratic state representative Clifford Marshall of playing "on the public's fears of 'criminals on the loose'" in his campaign for Norfolk County sheriff.[102] On the other hand, Republican state representative Jonathan L. Healy opposed a bill that would bar furloughs for those serving life sentences, explaining that the program "offers one small thing to a lifer—that if you change, you have a chance to get out on furlough."[103]

The press was instrumental in sounding the alarms. The conservative *Herald-American* ran a piece about escapees with descriptions of the crimes for which they had been convicted, along with their mugshots. The "Norfolk Fourteen" included "heroin pushers and an assortment of thugs who had assaulted, terrorized and robbed their fellow citizens."[104] The *Lowell Sun* blamed prison unrest and violence on Boone's "free and easy" approach to prison reform. As with conjugal visits, critics of prison reform decried evidence that incarcerated people were allowed some semblance of normal life, such as "photos of prisoners lounging in the courtyard of Walpole with their wives and lady friends," which suggested a "scene more akin to a country club than it does to a maximum security prison." The paper said sarcastically that the prisoners would "reform themselves into more and more privileges, crime and disorder and eventually . . . reform themselves over the prison walls to freedom where they can continue to 'reform' law-abiding members of society into submission."[105] Allegations about the dangers posed by furloughs were not based on facts. Between November 1972 and March 1973, 2,966 furloughs, ranging from twelve hours to seven days, were granted to 968 prisoners out of a population of nineteen hundred. With only thirty-eight instances in which people failed to return on time, the program had a success rate of 98.7 percent.[106]

The incident most damaging to the Massachusetts furlough program in its early years was the flight of Joseph Subilosky. Convicted of first-degree murder, Subilosky escaped while out on furlough in March 1973, a temporary release that resulted from a bureaucratic error. Over a month later, Subilosky was captured in New Hampshire and charged with the armed robbery of a bank in Boston.[107] When questioned, Subilosky said that after serving thirty-six years in prison, he was "fed up with the whole thing." He had deliberately avoided becoming involved in prisoner organizing at Walpole, but he sympathized with younger prisoners who wanted "rights and freedoms and decent salaries" and predicted that the prison would erupt in riots if Boone were replaced by a hard-liner.[108] Juan Pagan, formerly incarcerated at Walpole, suspected that prison guards had released Subilosky on purpose in order to damage the furlough program and undermine Boone.[109] Boone believed that sabotage was a possibility, and directed prison officials to determine whether the furlough was human error or "actually an effort to undermine the furlough program at Walpole."[110]

While critics charged reckless permissiveness, Governor Sargent continued to support furloughs, and offered a calculation of risk that contrasted with that of the critics: "The stakes, the risks to public safety, are too high to abandon it." Sargent added, "You cannot pen an individual up in isolation from society and then one day open the gate, end the isolation, and expect him to be able to cope with all the forces of society."[111]

Nonetheless, the governor fired Boone in June 1973. Concerned about saving his own political hide, he deciphered that Boone had become a visible symbol of the disorder in Massachusetts prisons and thus a liability. In a televised address, Sargent made clear that Boone resigned against his own wishes and lauded his record of achievement: "John Boone is not the cause of the problem at Walpole, he is the victim of it. He must go because his effectiveness has been crippled by the onslaught of assault upon him."[112] Concluding that "there can be no reform without order," Sargent turned control of the Walpole prison over to the state police.[113] Boone blamed legislators and the press for turning the events at Walpole into political capital.[114] When Sargent defended using the state police to control violence in Walpole after Boone's departure, Boone objected: "Violence has always been a part and parcel of imprisonment, from slavery to Walpole State Prison. Justice, honest decision making and respect for human dignity are the only methods to reduce violence in a prison, or in any community."[115]

Incarcerated people and their allies protested Boone's firing. The sheriff of Middlesex County, John Buckley, a liberal Republican, declared, "The tragedy of the governor's capitulation to reactionary pressures is that now we have control without reform, which is right where we were 20 years ago."[116] The Black Panthers referred to Boone as a scapegoat.[117] The Ad Hoc Committee said it was "baffled," "appalled," "confounded," and "horrified" by Sargent's decision to fire Boone, charging that the governor had "literally handed Walpole to the State Police whose control represents the antithesis of reform." The committee added, "Massachusetts, which was a national model of progressive penal reform, now runs the risk of becoming a model for repression which we fear may be emulated in other parts of the country."[118] Robert Dellelo, president of the NPRA, interpreted Boone's firing as proof of the limits of reform: prisoners and progressive administrators worked to improve conditions, and "the administration shifts and it is all out the window." All of the programs that the NPRA members had risked their physical safety to achieve dissolved as soon as Boone left. "You can't give up," Dellelo said. "But you have to realize you can't depend on anything. This is really the best argument for prison abolition."[119]

Boone's successor as corrections commissioner, Frank Hall, was a white administrator from the North Carolina prison system. Defending reform, Hall acknowledged, "We are moving more slowly than we'd like. We are being more conservative than we'd like."[120] Hall, like Sargent, reasoned, "It's worth the risk. It's worth the flak, it's worth all of it in terms of the impact it has on people. . . . Just to watch a change in someone's feeling about himself—even a reduction in paranoia level, which is pretty high in a big institution—you get a feeling that it's worth every bit of it." He believed that furloughs were more effective than any other program, and stressed that its return rate was the same as that of the US Army's Fort Bragg, where he had once been stationed.[121]

The controversy ignited by Boone's reforms, particularly furloughs, was at its core about competing definitions of public safety. On one side, correctional officers, district attorneys, and some of the press equated prison reform with crime in the streets. On the other side, progressive prison administrators, a Republican governor, and incarcerated people and their allies argued that greater freedoms ensured greater safety. In the words of the Ad Hoc Committee, "The safety which must be ensured has larger dimensions than metal detectors, frisks, transfers of suspected inmates, and lock-ups—dimensions which security has and never and cannot achieve." The committee defined safety in a "broader and more enduring sense, for both those within prisons and in the community at large," which could only be justly achieved by combining "prisoners' rights" with "programs in the areas of mental health, training, education and employment."[122] A journalist summed up the confusion of the moment in an opening line: "The reformer is dead. Long live reform."[123]

"WE DO NOT ALLOW MEN TO DIE OF OLD AGE IN PRISON": FURLOUGHS FOR LIFERS

The controversy over the furlough of Joseph Subilosky raised the question of whether those serving life sentences should have access to furloughs.[124] The Omnibus Corrections Reform Act of 1972 allowed furloughs for *any* incarcerated person for periods of no more than three days and with a maximum of fourteen days per year. Lifers in Massachusetts left prison to testify before the legislature, participate in radio and television programs, get married, and make speeches before community groups.[125] Hank Powell—at the time the longest-serving prisoner in Massachusetts and, with a PhD in clinical psychology, probably the best educated—left prison to speak to eighty-two thousand schoolchildren each year.[126] Imprisoned fathers took their children shopping, ran into old acquaintances on the street, met with lawyers and police officials to advance their applications for commutation, and shared intimate moments with their partners.[127] Lifer George McGrath used a furlough from Walpole to hand deliver a clemency petition to the governor's office.[128] Professional boxer Chris Pina, sentenced to life for second-degree murder, was regularly allowed to leave the Norfolk prison to compete in matches.[129] But the rehabilitative ideal had a peculiar application to those serving life sentences without parole, since they had a harder time making the case that their inevitable release should qualify them as recognized members of the community.

Yet that was the very reason why furloughs were so crucial for lifers. For those serving life with no opportunity for parole who were excluded from work and education release programs, a successful furlough was indispensable evidence of rehabilitation when applying for clemency. The *Boston Globe* portrayed the plight of lifers sympathetically. "I'm a dead man," lifer Richard Cote explained to a reporter. "The only way I can get out is to have access to people who can help me get out, to have contact with people in the community to show them that I'm not a vicious animal."[130]

After the Subilosky affair, the Massachusetts legislature amended the furlough law to unequivocally exclude those facing life sentences for first-degree murder and allowed those second-degree lifers and those convicted of violent crimes to be eligible only when they were within twenty-four months of parole eligibility. The push came from State Representative Clifford Marshall, who was running for Norfolk County sheriff and had the vigorous support of the state attorney general, Robert H. Quinn, a candidate for the Democratic gubernatorial nomination.[131] The *Boston Globe* pointed out that of 184 furloughs granted to forty first-degree lifers, Subilosky's was the only one that resulted in escape.[132] Several studies of furloughs confirmed that those convicted of first-degree murder had the highest success rate, while those who had committed property crimes were *most* likely to abscond.[133] Lifers expressed their anguish at losing the opportunity to associate with people in the free world and the potential for clemency that successful furloughs enhanced. In the wake of the attorney general's declaration, one lifer exclaimed, "My God, he's just sentenced us to death."[134] James McAlister stressed the pain the end of furloughs would cause his loved ones: "It's like they want to extend the walls of the prison. It's like extending solitary confinement to your family, your wife and kids."[135]

In response to the new ban, Henry Arsenault, Arthur Devlin, Russell LeBlanc, Melvin Simpson, and John Spencer, all serving life sentences at Walpole, launched a lawsuit.[136] In 1973, the state's Supreme Judicial Court issued a decision overturning the ban on furloughs for lifers. Although life sentences generally excluded the possibility of parole, the court asserted, "We know that life sentences for murder in the first degree are from time to time commuted. . . . Because that barrier is not insurmountable, we see no justification for concluding that the temporary release of a 'first degree lifer' can never be 'consistent with . . . reintegration into the community.'" In fact, the furlough could provide information as to the capacity of that offender. The superintendent of Walpole wrote in support of the plaintiffs, "It is a historical tradition that we do not allow men to die of old age in prison."[137] This claim was borne out in 1975, when then governor Michael Dukakis (1975–79) commuted Arthur Devlin's life sentence.[138]

In this contested moment, prison administrators, governors from both parties, architects, social scientists, and incarcerated people fought for furloughs as part of a broader effort to create opportunities for prisoners—even those who had committed violent crimes—to move about in the free world. While many incarcerated people interpreted furloughs as a tool for pacifying protest, and supporters of law and order slandered furloughs as a dangerous indulgence, the era of community corrections ushered a new conventional wisdom that furloughs were essential to the outcome of prison: the reintegration of incarcerated people into the free world. Advocates of furloughs were confident that because furloughs provided demonstrable evidence that incarcerated people were not perpetually dangerous and could be valuable members of society, they could open the door to decarceration more generally. Even in the face of repression, fear, and sensationalism, lifers in Massachusetts, supported by elected officials and corrections administrators, won the right to be eligible for furloughs because they were seen as future members of the free community. One of those lifers was William Horton.

9 The End of Redemption

Willie Horton and Moral Panic

William "Willie" Horton took his duties at Quarterway House seriously. This institution for adults with developmental disabilities, affiliated with the Massachusetts Mental Health Center in Boston, accepted Horton as part of the Concord Achievement Rehabilitation Volunteer Experience (CARVE) program initiated by the Massachusetts Department of Correction (DOC). Incarcerated volunteers bathed and clothed the patients, brushed their teeth, and changed their diapers. Since 1968 the program had screened prisoners for work in state mental institutions to alleviate a staff shortage and prepare them for reintegration.[1] When Horton began his time at Quarterway House in 1985, he finally appeared to have turned a corner. After his conviction for the 1974 murder of a gas station attendant in Lawrence, Massachusetts, when Horton was twenty-three years old, his prison record was marred by infractions, and he had been placed in isolation for drug possession and gambling. By 1981 he was transferred from the Massachusetts Correctional Institution–Walpole to the medium-security Massachusetts Correctional Institution–Norfolk because of his improved behavior. Horton had taken up leatherworking, worked in the metal shop, and completed a culinary certificate.[2] His supervisors at Quarterway House observed that he was well groomed, followed the rules most of the time, and could be relied on to work without much supervision. The patients respected and trusted him.[3]

Being trusted to work at a state hospital was not the same thing as being free to leave prison; participants in the CARVE program were transferred from one state facility to another but remained in the custody of correctional officers. Horton wanted to go home. Because he demonstrated that he was a reliable worker and had served ten years of his sentence, he was approved for furloughs in 1985. His first was for twelve hours, which he had to spend with a sponsor approved by the DOC. Eventually he left the Norfolk prison for the Thanksgiving, Christmas, and New Year holidays, and he returned every time. He went to church; he went shopping; he took his teenage daughter to the movies. On his tenth furlough, in 1986, Horton fled. Of 8,896 furloughs granted to 1,645 Massachusetts prisoners that year, eight other prisoners failed to return, constituting an escape rate of 0.1 percent.[4]

Most Americans have heard the name Willie Horton, since the scandal that followed in his 1987 conviction for assault, armed robbery, and rape in Maryland while he was on furlough—for which he still maintains his innocence—contributed to Massachusetts governor Michael Dukakis's loss to George H. W. Bush in the 1988 presidential election.[5] When polls showed that Bush was trailing Dukakis by seventeen points, the Republican campaign seized the opportunity to paint the Democratic candidate as "soft on crime" with a television advertisement that went viral: "Dukakis not only opposes the death penalty, but he allowed first degree murderers weekend passes from prison. One was Willie Horton, who murdered a boy in a robbery stabbing him nineteen times. Despite a life sentence, Horton received ten weekend passes from prison. Horton fled, kidnapped a young couple, stabbing the man and repeatedly raping his girlfriend. Weekend Prison Passes. Dukakis on crime."[6] Bush defeated Dukakis, 53 percent to 46 percent. The advertisement, backed by a team including Roger Ailes and Lee Atwater, was a coded appeal to white voters' fears, replicating the racist myth that Black men want to rape white women, which was used to justify lynching.[7] When Bush brought up the issue in campaign speeches, he used it, along with Dukakis's opposition to the death penalty, as evidence that the Democrat represented "old-style sixties liberalism."[8] Horton himself offered a comprehensive analysis of the cynical exploitation of his transgression, locating its origins in the threat posed by social movements of the 1960s and 1970s. In a later interview, Horton argued, "All poor people and minorities are portrayed in a similar manner by people who exploit their woes in order to whip up public anger and fear. Obviously, many people resent the gains that blacks and poor people have made in recent years. If they had their way, they'd like to return to the good old days, when blacks and poor people had to shuffle for crumbs. Today, these bigots don't go out and beat up black people anymore. They do it with a paper and pen. And that's what happened to me."[9]

The "Horton effect" has shaped the politics of crime and punishment ever since. With the exploitation of the Horton case, furloughs became the theater for a proxy war on crime. The specter of "future Willie Hortons" signified that furloughs entailed an unreasonable risk and demonstrated the absurdity of rehabilitation. In the heyday of community corrections, the public was regarded as responsible for absorbing prisoners into the free world. Now politicians and the media figured the public as perpetual potential victims who required constant protection against the threat of violence posed by prisoners on furlough. Ultimately, the backlash led to the condemnation of discretionary release of any kind. In Massachusetts and across the nation, the demise of furloughs signaled changing calculations of risk, leading to the perpetual exile of incarcerated people.

"FIRST DEGREE MURDERERS KILL AGAIN"

William Horton grew up in rural South Carolina in the 1950s and 1960s. His father, a trash collector, struggled with alcohol abuse, and his mother did domestic work. Eventually Horton found work in the automotive factories of Lawrence, Massachusetts, an old mill town.[10] In 1974 Horton and two friends decided to rob a gas station. The body of the station's attendant, seventeen-year-old Joseph Fournier, was found in a trash can with nineteen stab wounds. In Massachusetts, district attorneys could pursue "joint venture" prosecutions—if more than one person worked together to commit a crime, the law would not distinguish among them, even if only one of them committed the physical acts involved. This practice was reinforced by the "felony murder" rule by which all participants in a killing could be charged with murder, regardless of who actually caused the death. Horton and his two friends were tried together, and although prosecutors could never prove that Horton stabbed Fournier, he was sentenced to life in prison without the possibility of parole (LWOP). When Horton became a household name more than a decade later, after the assault on a suburban Maryland couple while he was on furlough, Cliff Barnes and his fiancée, Angela Miller, during which Miller was also raped, the family and friends of Fournier joined the Maryland victims to mobilize against furloughs in Massachusetts and nationally.

Before Horton's escape became a presidential campaign issue, the *Lawrence Eagle-Tribune* had been following the story closely. When Horton was captured in Maryland after being on the run for over a year, a dogged young reporter named Susan Forrest, with the encouragement of the paper's editor, was determined to find out "how a cold-blooded killer ever got out in the first place."[11] The newspaper ran nearly two hundred stories on the Horton case over the course of a year, winning a Pulitzer Prize, much to the disgust of fellow journalists.[12] Unlike the more even-handed approach of the *Boston Globe*, which pointed out the success of the furlough program, Forrest's stories dismissed any defense of furloughs, stoking anger at corrections officials with headlines such as "There Is No Guarantee Killers Will Stay Jailed." The paper uncritically adopted the views of the police and of victims Cliff Barnes and Angela Miller. One article on Horton's furlough quoted Miller: "Why do monsters exist and why do civilized correction officials let monsters out?"[13] Barnes confessed his desire for revenge: "I'd love to get this animal alone in a room with me now, one-on-one with no weapons."[14]

Massachusetts corrections commissioner Michael V. Fair received newspaper clippings from sympathetic wardens about similar incidents from around the country that had received relatively little media coverage.[15] According to experts in the field, furloughs were "firmly entrenched in the scheme of correctional programming" and much of the original controversy over them had subsided by 1980.[16] But thanks to the *Eagle-Tribune*'s unrelenting attention to an exceptional case in Dukakis's home state, Republicans were able to gather plenty of ammunition to attack the Democratic presidential candidate. Cliff Barnes spoke regularly on television talk shows and at Bush campaign events.[17] Republican congressman Newt Gingrich read the *Eagle-Tribune*'s coverage out loud on the House floor.[18]

Suddenly the practice of granting furloughs, which had been common sense around the nation for the previous twenty years, was a source of outrage. In Illinois, registered voters received a pamphlet from the Republican State Central Committee stating, "ALL THE MURDERERS AND RAPISTS AND DRUG PUSHERS AND CHILD MOLESTERS IN MASSACHUSETTS VOTE FOR DUKAKIS."[19] The College Republican National Committee printed and distributed 100,000 yellow "Get Out of Jail Free" cards "Compliments of Michael Dukakis" in the style of those used in the Monopoly board game.[20] Far-right activist Phyllis Schlafly promoted a twenty-minute propaganda film titled *Justice on Furlough*, whose poster featured little more than a huge butcher knife.[21] George H. W. Bush claimed a cowboy-vigilante masculinity when he referenced Clint Eastwood's character Dirty Harry at a campaign event: "My opponent's answer is slightly different. His motto is: 'Go ahead, have a nice weekend.'"[22] Roger Ailes argued that Dukakis's endorsement of correctional expertise "reinforces this idea that he's lived in a Harvard ivory tower, looking at computer models of recidivism rather than understanding the terror of a crazy person attacking someone. It's like a guy from outer space, who walks and talks like us but doesn't feel the same things we feel."[23] That Ailes charged Dukakis as an unfeeling academic alien is disingenuous and spurious given that the Bush campaign relied precisely on fear and sensationalism rather than reason and evidence.[24]

As many news outlets pointed out, the campaign materials distorted the reality of furloughs.[25] The ads implied that furloughs were exceptional and confined to Massachusetts, when active programs existed in all fifty states as well as the federal prison system. Ron Wikberg, a prisoner at the Louisiana State Penitentiary at Angola, emphasized that in the previous year the federal prison system had granted furloughs to 23 percent of its population without incident.[26] The fearmongering tone and a follow-up ad about "revolving door prisons" implied that escapes were frequent and represented a violent threat: mostly Black and Brown prisoners walked in single file through a revolving door, as the words "268 Escaped" flashed on the screen to ominous music. "Michael Dukakis wants to do for America what he's done for Massachusetts," said the voiceover; "America can't afford that risk."[27] These ads deliberately avoided the fact that the Massachusetts furlough program had been instituted in 1972 under a Republican governor and widely endorsed by many across the political spectrum, including Ronald Reagan, then California's governor (1967–75). And the advertisements intentionally ignored how selective the furlough process had already become.

Beginning in 1981, Commissioner Fair had implemented more stringent controls over furloughs. The DOC regarded them as "a vital tool in minimizing the isolating effects of institutionalization, building or rebuilding solid ties between offender and community, and reintegrating offenders from prison to community life." Furloughs provided a way of "testing an individual's ability to adapt to increased increments of freedom."[28] Studies showed that participation in furlough programs reduced recidivism rates.[29] Corrections administrators asserted that furloughs were especially important for those facing long sentences, for whom there were few incentives for good behavior, but they instituted more stringent requirements. Fair increased the amount of time first-degree lifers had to serve before becoming eligible for furloughs from five to ten years and for second-degree lifers from three to seven years, established a central furlough board to review all applications of first-degree lifers, required that first-degree lifers remain with their furlough sponsors at all times, and required those on furlough to be available for random phone checks.[30] The number of furloughs granted between 1973 and 1980 had decreased by 36 percent.[31] But from the point of view of the individual prisoner, release was enjoyed, on average, seven times a year.[32] In 1981, 12.6 percent of the prison population was furloughed in any given month. By 1987 the number of furloughs granted had decreased by another 34 percent.[33]

Horton's escape and crime did not initially diminish Dukakis's support for the furlough program. As a group of protestors stood outside a Dukakis campaign event with signs reading "First Degree Murderers Kill Again" and "Lifers Are In for Life," Dukakis defended furloughs as an effective correctional tool. Moreover, he pointed out that prisoners' performance on furloughs provided essential information about their behavior and rehabilitation, which a governor could take into account in deciding whether to commute their sentences. But after meeting with legislators critical of furloughs, Dukakis agreed that the program should be reexamined.[34]

Grassroots political organizing by victims' groups, galvanized by the *Eagle-Tribune*'s coverage, put pressure on elected officials. Maureen Donovan of Methuen, Massachusetts, read in *the Eagle-Tribune* that on the night Horton escaped, the police had stopped him just a few blocks away from her house and then let him go. How could a murderer be roaming around? Worse yet, how could the police pull him over and not know that he was on furlough?[35] During the year that followed, Donovan partnered with Donna Cuomo, brother of the murdered Lawrence teenager, to found Citizens against an Unsafe Society (CAUS) to lobby the legislature to curtail the furlough program. The organization worked closely with Democrat Larry Giordano, who was already part of the Massachusetts House Committee on Post Audit and Oversight's investigation of the state furlough system. Giordano received hundreds of letters from outraged constituents and filed a bill that would ban furloughs for prisoners convicted of first-degree murder.[36]

Critics portrayed furloughs as unacceptably risky. A quotation from Cliff Barnes's testimony before the committee was chosen as the report's epigraph: "I think when you're dealing with people that are this dangerous and violent, anything short of 100% is not successful."[37] The committee was not satisfied that first-degree lifers returned from furloughs

99.9 percent of the time; according to opponents' interpretation, any of those men was a potential Willie Horton. "Truly, it is hard to determine who will be a non-repeater," the committee mused. In a bit of rhetorical alchemy, the committee recast Horton as typical rather than exceptional; the very fact that Horton could be released even when procedure was followed suggested that the entire program was dangerous. If any seemingly well-behaved prisoner could be a Willie Horton, then it was impossible to discern who was trustworthy and who was not. As the report put it, "Obviously DOC at present is not entirely capable of making this determination because the aftermath of the Horton furlough escape was heinous enough to counterbalance the good" that furloughs did for others.[38] This logic—a departure from the rationale for furloughs just a few decades earlier—established a new calculus: risk was not framed as a rational estimation of the likelihood of harm but as any exposure to the possibility of harm, no matter how remote. This desire to eliminate risk was foundational to a penal ideology that justified longer sentences and distrust of corrections professionals and ultimately led to increased surveillance beyond the prison. In the post-Horton world, penal politics were increasingly concerned with containing people perceived as immutably dangerous.[39] The kindling of this logic was not probable danger but fear.

Critics of furloughs expressed particular consternation at the volunteer program in which Horton had participated. According to participants and administrators, the CARVE program was a success. Medical professionals attested that "patients who almost never left their wards" were "showing a new interest in life" as a result of the personal attention offered by the prisoners.[40] Most volunteers considered the program an opportunity to give back to the community, improve their chances at release, and develop skills that might earn them more permanent employment.[41] David E. Johnson, serving a life sentence for murder, recognized that he and Allen, his "blind mute" charge, were a lot alike: "Both of us are confined, both dealt with as robots. We're misunderstood. People don't take the time, have the patience, to understand us."[42]

Skeptics were alarmed that people serving life sentences had been allowed to participate in the program at all. Despite Horton's positive work evaluations, opponents maintained that he was a "risk to the patients and the public at large" because he had been convicted of murder and had used drugs. Legislators asserted the novel claim that *all* people convicted of murder were permanently dangerous and intrinsically incapable of contributing to society. According to the committee's calculus, the

"Department of Mental Health's position of improved quality of care is not valid when weighed against the risk of placing patients in direct contact with convicted murderers." Proponents of CARVE did not draw such a bright line between "murderers" and "the rest of us." When pressed, the assistant commissioner of mental health admitted that he could not rule out the possibility that a prisoner would engage in a drug deal during his lunch break at the park across the street, but he emphasized, "There's nothing stopping an inmate *or any of our staff* from being involved in a drug deal."[43]

Committee chair Robert Cerasoli, a Democrat who opposed furloughs, not only equated past conviction with present character but likened those convicted of murder with those who committed genocide: "A multiple murderer may murder a family, just women, or just children; what really is the difference between murdering those of one religion, or seven nurses in an apartment in Chicago?"[44] What was not taken into account was the fact that 60 percent of people convicted of first-degree murder were first-time offenders; that a number of them did not actually commit the murder but were convicted because of the felony murder rule; and that lifers and those convicted of violent offenses against people were the *least* likely not to return from furloughs and had the lowest recidivism rates.[45] By warping remote possibility into imminent mortal danger, opponents of furloughs rendered Willie Horton the locus classicus for expressive punishment: rather than be tempered by rationality, guided by evidence, and promote rehabilitation, criminal justice policy should eternally express communal outrage.[46]

Legislators most critical of furloughs adopted the outlooks of crime victims and their advocates and were swayed by their robust political organizing. In Massachusetts, activists expressed the views of those whom Carrie Rentschler has called "secondary victims"—those who had lost a loved one. In their personal testimonies and public activism, these victim advocates depict victimization as "connective and vicarious, as transportable and transposable experiences."[47] Secondary victims spoke not only of their continued suffering in the face of loss, but acted as spokespeople for the dead by calling on officials to deny prisoners any benefit that could not be enjoyed by the deceased. In one case, for example, the widow of a police officer who was shot to death by someone who had been released on furlough thirty-three times saw furloughs as a privilege that her suffering denied her. She testified, "Isn't he lucky that he can go on with his life? How fortunate for him, and we are not allowed to. I have to live with it every day of my life to the day I die. I wish I could have a furlough . . . one

weekend . . . one hour."[48] The impulse to see prisoners suffer is the definition of retribution, but true retribution for murder is impossible unless a
defendant is put to death. Instead secondary victims would have to accept
the perpetrators' "death in slow motion," an unsatisfying emotional limbo
that would only be inflamed by the reminder of the perpetrator's stubborn
humanity.[49] Moreover, victim advocates argued that furloughs imposed
more anguish on "law-abiding citizens" by inevitably creating future victims. As conservative journalist Robert Bidinotto put it in his influential
Readers' Digest piece on the Horton case, "if armed guards can't keep 'very
dangerous' killers inside locked cells, how are unarmed citizens supposed
to deal with them?"[50] The couple whom Horton had assaulted stated
that as long as Massachusetts continued its furlough program, "people
throughout the country are not safe."[51]

Antifurlough activists were witnesses to trauma and loss, but also saw
themselves as victims of the criminal legal system itself.[52] To them, the constitutional rights of criminal defendants and the abolition of death penalty
rendered the criminal justice system "a perpetrator against a vulnerable
public besieged by inner-city criminal classes whose rights protections as
defendants accounted for the increasing problem of street crime."[53]

Among the supposedly undue rights that prisoners supposedly enjoyed was the right to privacy. In Massachusetts, this right was protected
through the Criminal Offenders Records Information (CORI) Act. Passed
in 1972, the act was intended to protect information regarding criminal
defendants' history and prisoners' institutional records from public dis-
semination. The original law was passed at the peak of community corrections as a means of aiding former prisoners' transition to the free world.[54]
The state asserted that the privacy of these records was essential to public
safety: "An arrest record, and . . . a conviction record, may be a serious
obstacle to employment, housing and credit, as well as being damaging
to a defendant's reputational and associational interests, on which access
to many of the other benefits of a civilized society may turn. Arrestees
and convicted defendants who are denied employment, housing, and/or
credit based on their records are at far greater risk for future criminal conduct."[55] Attorney Ernest Windsor argued that for reintegration to be successful, society "must offer criminals greater and greater degrees of privacy
as they near their return to society."[56] The law was uncontroversial until
the Horton case dramatized the issue.[57]

The CORI Act frustrated elected officials, their constituents, and journalists as they tried to pry open Horton's record for public scrutiny. The

editor of the *Lawrence Eagle-Tribune* complained that "we were stone-walled from start to end" in investigating the case.[58] Critics framed this law as protecting the inmate over the public.[59] In an article titled "The Law Criminals Love," Bidinotto depicted prisoner privacy in sinister terms: "Every day across the United States, convicted robbers, rapists and murderers are granted a special 'right to privacy' the minute they go behind bars. And when these criminals are released, often sooner than expected, many of their victims are not informed—sometimes with chilling consequences." The conservative journalist mocked the notion that an incarcerated or formerly incarcerated person might want or deserve a "clean slate." This "strange idea" had "emerged in the late 1960s, when reformers argued that criminals were victims of circumstance who committed crimes only because they lacked other opportunities. Once criminals were 'rehabilitated' in prison and released, it was unfair to saddle them with the 'stigma' of past transgressions." Conservatives portrayed a criminal's right to privacy as compromising public safety and sought its repeal.[60]

Over the two decades following the Horton incident, victim advocacy organizations, members of the press, and a growing number of politicians cast the public as potential victims, those with arrest records as perpetual criminals, and the situation as a zero-sum game between the rights of each group. "It's incredible," said Vivianne Rugierro. "The man who killed my husband has more rights than I do. A person could find out more about me than [about] someone in prison."[61] As the result of this outcry, the legislature passed nearly a dozen amendments to the original CORI Act, nearly inverting its original purpose. In 1989, for example, the decisions of the Massachusetts Parole Board, previously protected from disclosure under the CORI Act, were made public, and victims of crime were granted limited access to criminal records related to that crime. The transformation of the CORI Act from a law that protected prisoners' privacy to a law that enlisted the public as agents of surveillance helped to mark those ensnared in the criminal legal system as permanent outcasts.[62] Finally, in 1996, Massachusetts became the last state to adopt a version of the Violent Crime Control and Law Enforcement Act of 1994 (known commonly as Megan's Law and named for Megan Kanka, a seven-year-old who had been raped and murdered in New Jersey), which made public the criminal records of sex offenders and required the police to notify residents that a convicted sex offender lives or works in their town.[63] In this realm, crime was an inevitable and perpetual threat from which those outside the correctional system demanded total protection. The perversion of the original

CORI Act redrew the lines of public responsibility and constituted a new class of monstrous criminals who could never be rehabilitated, but only confined, regulated, and surveilled.

If family members of the murdered were also victims, then the state was the coconspirator of criminals against victims. Punctuating arguments against furloughs was the language of "secondary victimization," the notion that crime victims were victimized first by crime, and then by mistreatment by the state.[64] Debates about furloughs provided an opening for this discourse because, opponents asserted, they belied the promise of a true life sentence. The Massachusetts House committee's investigation confirmed that most defendants sentenced to life without parole served an average of eighteen years in prison before having their sentence commuted by the governor.[65] Legislators who opposed furloughs identified harsh sentencing as one of the entitlements that the criminal justice system owed victims. As committee chairman Cerasoli put it, "The law is being subverted. Life without parole does not mean complete confinement. If one can kill and eventually receive freedom, then the system cannot insure that those who have killed will serve their sentence."[66] State Senator John Houston, a Democrat from Worcester, jibed, "Should we change the name of the sentence and not fool the public?"[67] The very fact that prisoners were able to engage in any activities outside prison alarmed legislators. As Representative Richard Voke, a Democrat from Chelsea, declared, "You cannot say in the statute that you are going to put them away for life and then have them out going to law school. That was not the intent."[68]

"THEY COULD VOTE TO FREE THEMSELVES": THE STRUGGLE OVER BANNING FURLOUGHS

Corrections professionals continued to support the furlough program in the face of this outrage. The Massachusetts secretary of human services, Philip W. Johnston, admitted that he was ambivalent about granting furloughs to those convicted of first-degree murder but explained that additional revisions to the program would reduce the number of prisoners being furloughed and vigorously restrict their activities. Corrections commissioner Michael V. Fair defended furloughs unequivocally, urging committee members to distinguish between the Horton case and the furlough system as a whole.[69] But the committee would not separate the two issues.

After hearing Fair testify for three hours, the committee concluded, "He could not guarantee Committee members that another William Horton case would not occur."[70]

Representative John C. Bradford, a Democrat from Bristol, argued in his dissenting report that those convicted of first-degree murder are "human beings" who "cannot be lumped into one category or dehumanized in the name of justice." Since rehabilitation was possible, a conviction and a life sentence were not a reliable index of future danger. A defendant might be charged with second-degree murder in exchange for a plea deal, or (like Horton himself) with first-degree murder due to Massachusetts's felony murder rule.[71] The category of "first-degree murderer" included people who were juveniles at the time of the murder, those who participated in but did not commit the actual murder, and those who had spent decades in prison and were no longer a threat to society.

Prisoners followed these events closely and used every lever at their disposal to preserve furloughs. A few weeks after Horton's capture, the lifers' organization at the Norfolk prison wrote to lawmakers, "We ask that you treat [Horton's] case as it is, which is an individual case and does not and should not reflect on the innocent people who have accepted the responsibility for their actions . . . and are serving their time in a very positive and productive manner."[72] Lifer Omar Haamid Abdur-Rahim, who debated Horton's Maryland victims on television, questioned the logic of treating Horton's case as proof of lifers' incorrigibility: "If we are so deadly why hasn't there been an outbreak of violence and a mass flight out of the state?"[73]

While incarcerated people testified in public hearings, they organized both behind and beyond prison walls. Political scientists Amy Lerman and Vesla Weaver have defined the concept of "custodial citizenship" as the lived experience of people ensnared in the criminal legal system who were "constituted not as participatory members of the democratic polity, but as disciplined subjects of the carceral state." From inside this "custodial lifeworld," prisoners' "sense of the state" is control, hierarchy, and arbitrary power.[74] Yet Massachusetts prisoners made claims on the state. Most remarkably, they conducted a voter registration campaign inside the prison walls.

In Massachusetts, prisoners were allowed to vote by absentee ballot.[75] Furlough was both an electoral issue and a vehicle for political participation. Each year, the Penal Information Committee at Norfolk prison conducted a seminar for Legislative Awareness Day and invited legislators and their aides to attend.[76] With the Horton scandal posing a threat to furloughs for lifers, the committee invited legislators to speak with them about the issue. Legislators who supported furloughs, such as Royal Bolling Sr., a Black lawyer and prominent Democrat in the Massachusetts Senate, and Marjorie O'Neill Clapprood, a Democrat in the Massachusetts House of Representatives, were greeted with cheers when they arrived at Norfolk with Richard Shipley, the secretary of state, who was bearing absentee ballot applications. The chair of the Penal Information Committee estimated that if each of ten thousand prisoners could enlist ten relatives and friends, they could muster a voting bloc of one hundred thousand votes. One state legislator thought that prisoners having the right to vote was "crazy because . . . they could vote to free themselves."[77]

Dukakis had initially resisted changes to the furlough program, but in March 1988 he pledged to not to veto a ban passed by the legislature. This shift astonished people on both the left and right, but in his second term Dukakis had already begun to take a more punitive stance on crime. Forming the Governor's Statewide Anti-Crime Council even though crime rates were declining, Dukakis began mentioning crime in every major address to the legislature. He hired 250 more state police and requested $100 million for prison expansion, in contrast to $13.5 million in 1977.[78] Dukakis also supported the shift to sentencing models that limited judges' discretion by establishing narrow ranges of permissible sentences for particular crimes. The furlough ban, which the legislature passed and Dukakis signed in 1988, was part and parcel of this package of tough-on-crime measures.

Prisoners and their families were devastated by the furlough ban, which the *Berkshire Eagle* referred to as the Horton Law.[79] Weekend visits made it almost possible to feel "like you were a normal family," said the sister of a prisoner.[80] Julian Stone, a lifer at the Massachusetts Correctional Institution–Concord, maintained that with regular furloughs he had felt like "a part-time prisoner"; his baby daughter had been conceived while he was on furlough. Now he would have to endure watching officers search her diapers at the end of a prison visit.[81] One prisoner tried in vain to win a court injunction for an emergency furlough, first to see his dying mother and then to attend her funeral. Maureen Donovan, who spearheaded the antifurlough campaign, was unmoved. "He was the cause of a funeral himself," she remarked.[82]

While hard-liners saw furloughs as a slippery slope to lawlessness, prisoners and their allies considered the ban on furloughs for lifers to be a slippery slope toward longer and harsher confinement. Senator Bolling prophesied that the full backlash of the Horton escape had yet to be felt. John Bolgett, chair of the Penal Information Committee at the Norfolk prison, worried that "if they don't have us [lifers] to kick around anymore, who do you think they'll go after?"[83] Bonnie Gibson, the wife of a first-degree lifer, predicted that the attack on furloughs would produce a "domino effect." Soon they would attack work release, and then they would eliminate "any progressive reform that empower[s] prisoners and their families."[84] Kris Dodson, the sponsor of an imprisoned person who regularly stayed in her home while on furlough, mourned, "They are very frightened. So are we all."[85]

UNPARDONABLE CRIMES: THE DECLINE OF DISCRETIONARY RELEASE

The ban on furloughs for lifers sealed a new set of assumptions about risk and redeemability. By 1989 at least five states—Louisiana, Maryland, Michigan, Texas, and Virginia—limited their furlough programs, and some states closed the halfway houses that were the hallmark of community corrections.[86] Corrections commissioners saw these changes as politically motivated and restricted furloughs reluctantly. The attack on furloughs was an overreaction, they said, a result of short-term thinking and the politicization of corrections. Edward C. Morris, the deputy director of the Virginia DOC, frankly accused politicians of racism: "The fact that politicians can demagogically come forward at any time and scream law and order and put up the Willie Horton face—the black male murderer, rapist, every stereotypic horror nightmare of white America—and say, 'this is what the liberal agenda is' and lock them up and throw away the key, vengeance becomes the total basis of our criminal justice system."[87]

Given corrections administrators' steadfast faith in furloughs and states' authority over policy, the reduction in the practice was uneven and gradual. Prisoners in Mississippi, including those convicted of first-degree murder, continued to receive holiday furloughs following the Horton incident, although the state's DOC adopted a new screening process.[88] "You can't stop the world because of something that happened in politics," the Mississippi corrections commissioner explained.[89] Other Mississippians saw the attacks on Dukakis as a validation of their concerns and raised alarms about the continuation of furloughs. Reiterating the sentiment that murderers should enjoy nothing that their victims' relatives could not, a woman whose brother had been murdered wrote to the *Clarion-Ledger*, "My family would love to have my brother home for the holidays—but three men took his life for no reason and we will never have him with us again."[90]

In Massachusetts, furloughs dropped by another 33 percent in 1990, and the median number of furloughs granted any given prisoner per year fell to one.[91] The decline and disappearance of furloughs represented the repudiation of discretionary, expertise-based correctional practices rooted in rehabilitative principles. Instead, according to Representative Cerasoli, the sole purpose of prison was to separate vicious criminals from society: "Instead of depending on psychological and personal evaluation of the inmates in determining suitability for integration, let us depend on the *universally agreed upon method*, increased deprivation of freedom."[92] Joseph W. Casper, a staunch opponent of court-ordered busing for school integration, fumed, "It's about time that we sent the criminal element out with the tide, to an island without a bridge. We don't want some bleeding-heart furlough program, so that the glow worms can be back in the neighborhood for a weekend deal."[93] People convicted of murder existed beyond shared public space not only physically but morally.[94]

Grassroots activists, their representatives in the state legislature, and members of the media perceived furloughs to be "only part of the only problem"; the larger problem was discretionary release of any kind. Jonathan Simon describes the opposition to discretionary release as tethering "the correctional subject ever more tightly to his crime" by first curtailing furloughs and then curbing early release through gubernatorial clemency.[95] Columnists for the *Washington Post* warned that "Murderer Willie Horton is not the only skeleton in Democratic presidential nominee Gov. Michael S. Dukakis' closet" and detailed the case of Thomas Childs, who had received a pardon from Dukakis after serving time for armed robbery and then committed a murder in 1983.[96] The distinctions among penal practices and their applications were lost in the haze of sensationalism that characterized the Horton case. A member of a 1989 focus group explained that he would not vote for Dukakis because he "pardoned that guy that went out and killed someone."[97] Furlough and pardons, rape and murder, all blurred together.

Since Massachusetts sentenced people to LWOP, the only way for someone serving LWOP to be released was through the clemency process. Thus, the only way to *ensure* LWOP was to seal off possibilities for discretionary release.

In its investigation of the furlough process, the Massachusetts House committee condemned the policy of releasing "dangerous criminals" as a betrayal of victims and a threat to public safety.[98] Just as the ban on furloughs for lifers was sent to Dukakis's desk, another legislative committee proposed to extend the minimum number of years served before people convicted of murder would be eligible for clemency.[99] Victim advocates vowed that their next crusade was to restrict the governor's power to commute sentences.[100] Representative Cerasoli made the case by casting the denial of clemency as a means of protecting society from vigilante action. If a sentence for murder were not sufficiently harsh, then "individuals may be willing to pay that price to protect themselves from perceived threats." He believed that crime victims and their loved ones were only dissuaded from taking the law into their own hands by the promise that perpetrators would never see freedom again. Cerasoli mentioned Bernard Goetz, who shot several Black teenagers whom he believed were about to rob him in a New York City subway car, as an "early symptom" of what might happen if people came to feel that the justice system did not "protect them."[101] In other words, the state had to enact retributive justice on behalf of victims in the name of public safety.[102]

While the measure to curtail the governor's clemency powers did not pass, the Horton case effectively led to a decline in clemency in Massachusetts and shifted the social norms by which clemency operated in the decades that followed.[103] This shift can mostly be attributed to politics, but it was also a concrete by-product of the demise of furloughs, which had enabled incarcerated people to demonstrate their rehabilitation. Corrections officials disapproved of this trend: "Without commutation, there is no redemption; there is nothing a convicted murderer can do to pay back society except grow old, sick and feeble, and die in prison."[104] Horton himself told a reporter that furloughs helped incarcerated people "stay grounded in the real world" and "observe how law-abiding people behave" so that they can show that they are capable of change. Without such opportunities, clemency would be unwise: "If you treat someone like an animal, put him in a pen and feed him raw meat, then you shouldn't be surprised that when he's released, he will turn on his keeper and devour him."[105]

In the wake of the Horton scandal, Massachusetts guidelines for clemency became more stringent, and Dukakis's successors treated clemency as "an extraordinary remedy" for injustice rather than an integral part of the correctional process."[106] Lifers have been most profoundly affected by the decline.[107] In 2015 the revised clemency guidelines of Governor Charlie

Baker (2015–23) declared that "the nature and circumstances of the offense" was the "paramount consideration," paying particular attention to "the impact on the victim or victims and the impact of the crime on society as a whole." Moreover, Baker insisted that a prisoner "clearly demonstrate acceptance of responsibility for the offense for which the petitioner is seeking clemency"; appealing or challenging the original conviction was disqualifying.[108] These guidelines penalized prisoners for exercising their legal right to appeal against a miscarriage of justice.

The permanent stigma of the original crime now taints even the most extraordinary of clemency petitions. The case of Arnold King is a devastating example. In 1971 King shot and killed John Labanara, a law student and aide to Boston mayor Kevin White, during an attempt to buy drugs. King described himself as "an 18-year-old high school dropout who consumed drugs and alcohol every day" and shot Labanara in a drunken haze.[109] Nearly every article discussing the killing mentions that Labanara was shot just as he was celebrating passing the bar exam.[110] King was convicted of first-degree murder and sentenced to LWOP. Unfortunately, he brought his first clemency petition in 1987, just as Willie Horton's arrest in Maryland chilled the Dukakis administration's approach to discretionary release. When King's attorney Edward Berkin testified before the board at a 2007 clemency hearing, he detailed King's unsupervised monthly furloughs as evidence that he would be a law-abiding citizen if he were released. In addition to visiting with his wife, relatives, and friends, King spoke at churches and youth facilities "to counsel young people to be . . . positive in their families, positive in their communities, . . . in essence, telling them don't do what I did." After furloughs were banned, King consulted with youth agencies and parents on criminal justice issues, connected children with prisoners to present "the reality and consequences of becoming involved in criminal behavior," wrote articles and book reviews, and earned bachelors and master's degrees. "I am here today not as an 18-year old who in a moment of rage and stupor prevented John Labanara from living in our society and pursuing his goals and objectives," King told the board. "Rather, I am here today, this morning, 55 years old at the end of this year, to show that I've transformed my life" and "can be of greater service to the community. . . . I'm living my life in remembrance of who I was. But I don't want to be stuck there."[111]

Throughout the decades that spanned his nine clemency hearings, King received the support of the Massachusetts Black Legislative Caucus, academics, attorneys, clergy, formerly incarcerated people, community leaders, artists, and directors of social service organizations. Seventeen people testified in support of King at his 2007 hearing, including Charles Ogletree, a legal scholar who directed the Charles Hamilton Houston Institute for Race and Justice. Ogletree was himself a secondary victim of violent crime, as his sister, a police officer, was murdered in 1982. He urged the board not to judge King by his past, but to recognize the person he had become.[112] The only person testifying against commutation was the victim's sister-in-law. In the face of King's many accomplishments and extensive outside support, she remarked, "I don't feel that Mr. King has changed but is working to change his image to the public." She interpreted his life itself an affront: "Mr. King has had a lifetime, but because of his actions, John's lifetime was only 26 years." Despite these claims, the Parole Board unanimously approved King's 2007 petition with a vote of six to zero, but Democratic governor Deval Patrick (2007–15) rejected the recommendation.[113] Patrick cited "the egregiousness of the underlying offense, in which Mr. King shot an innocent stranger in the face, at point blank range, without provocation, only two days after another state had released him on parole for another violent crime," as well as the continuing anguish of the victim's family.[114] In 2010, as King's ninth clemency petition sat on Patrick's desk, another prisoner released on parole shot and killed a police officer. In response, the governor reconstituted the Parole Board with law enforcement officials, and in 2011 the board denied King's request for a new clemency hearing.

King still hoped that his clemency would "inspire other people to think of folks who have done things such as myself . . . in a different light." He was concerned, however, that the opportunities that furloughs might afford him to demonstrate his reformation no longer existed. Denied freedom, King continued to make amends with his service work and shared his thoughts in essays published with the help of people on the outside. In one, he expressed despair: "I am one of so many humans bound with chains around the wrist, waist, and feet. Much like my African ancestors, a peculiar institution (first slavery then prison) has launched a vicious attack to subdue and render me complacent. The triangular approach of physical, mental, and spiritual restraints intended to micro-manage my body and soul all echo Dante's message ["Abandon all hope, ye who enter here"]."[115] In another, he explained his struggle to find sanctuary through meditating and reading in his cell.[116]

The domino effect that knocked furloughs into clemency until all possibilities for discretionary release were toppled is an example of what legal scholar Sharon Dolovich has called a shift from a reintegrationist to an exclusionist system of penal policy. Implicit in this shift is a commitment to the ideology that "people in prison must and will be kept behind bars as long as the state can possibly keep them there." Incarceration marks "who is simultaneously outside society's moral circle and a perennial subject of state control." Willie Horton is the creation myth for this view.[117] While the Horton story trafficked in enduring stereotypes about the innate criminality of Black men, it was used to justify a departure from an equally long tradition that valued mercy and affirmed the possibility of rehabilitation. In the wake of the Willie Horton scandal, the possibilities for public recognition of personal transformation were radically narrowed. Marjorie O'Neill Clapprood, one of the state legislature's most vocal supporters of furloughs, captured the significance of the Horton case: "They wrapped the American flag around our necks and shoved Willie Horton down our throats and many politicians were swept away by the angry tides. Now we have paralysis. It is a frightening trend towards public policy-making by metaphor. Willie Horton became a metaphor in an angry environment when folks were looking for a quick and simple answer. . . . We have effectively blocked the outflow of those who are ready to reenter society.[118]

Those convicted of crimes lost not only their liberty but their status as human beings and citizens. In the course of their years behind bars, prisoners experienced diminishing contact with the outside world and declining possibilities for release. As prisoners were suspended in the amber of their original crimes, the physical mobility they had expected and hoped for had disappeared. Those serving LWOP sentences struggle with this paradox of self-improvement when the public imagination will not allow it. Lifers at Norfolk prison acknowledge the suffering of crime victims and their loved ones but assert, "Life is not frozen at the point of a murder. People move on, struggling to self-mend. The community is better served by recognizing and embracing such healing in perpetrators and their families and friends as it intends to do the families, friends and associates of the victims. It is in that healing that the community's social fabric can be rewoven."[119]

Epilogue

These walls are broken down and sent back to the quarry
when we transcend the places which attempted to hold us.
—**BEN HALL**, Columbia River Correctional Institution, 2019

On a sticky day in July 2000, men incarcerated at the Louisiana State Penitentiary at Angola gathered for the prison's first Longtermers Day, an occasion meant to honor those who had served sentences of twenty-five years or more. The occasion was sponsored by Angola's Human Relations Club, which had begun decades earlier primarily as a way to finance the pardon notices that were required to appear in newspapers; now it focused on providing support to elderly prisoners and overseeing the burials of those who died at Angola with no one to claim them. One hundred eighty of 274 long-termers attended the event, which featured entertainment by a local gospel choir, a performance by musician Aaron Neville, and jambalaya prepared by a renowned Louisiana chef.[1] Wilbert Rideau, the coeditor of the *Angolite* prison magazine, who had himself been incarcerated for forty years, stressed that the event was not a celebration. "Just the opposite," he clarified. "It's a day to recognize that you've endured this long, that you are still here after all this time, that things can change and need to change."[2] Many long-termers knew firsthand that things could change. Not only had *they* changed during the course of their incarceration; their very existence, notes prison journalist Kerry Myers, "as a group of people consigned to live, grow old and die in prison, [was] unprecedented in penal history." One such person had been incarcerated since the administration of President Dwight D. Eisenhower.[3]

The fluidity of the category *long-termer* reveals these changes over time. *Angolite* editors Wilbert Rideau and Ron Wikberg first used the term in 1977 to catalog what appeared to be a new kind of prisoner, "the guy who's been in prison for so long that he seems as much a part of the institution as the concrete that forms the walls." In mounting their investigation into this emerging class of prisoners, the first systematic study of its kind, Rideau and Wikberg defined a long-termer as anyone who had been locked up for a decade or more. After months of research, they identified 186 Angolites who had been confined for over eight years, eighty-eight of whom had been confined for ten to twenty-nine years. Five out of six (83 percent) were Black.[4] Eleven years later the *Angolite* revisited the topic in a thirty-nine-page spread, "The Longtermers," in which the writers redefined a long-termer as anyone incarcerated for longer than twenty years. In 2000 the category was revised again to include anyone incarcerated for over twenty-five years. Whereas at the first Longtermers Day in 2000 there were 274 long-termers, in 2009 there were 880.[5] In 2010 the *Angolite* featured a story about the men who had been incarcerated for forty or more years.[6] Long-termers were respected both by penal management and other incarcerated people because they traditionally served as a stabilizing force, having matured over time, served leadership roles, and mentored others.[7] But, an *Angolite* editorial lamented, "the context of their imprisonment has been altered drastically. Hope, the single most powerful control factor traditionally influencing the life expectations of longtermers, has been removed to an extent never before experienced in penal history."[8]

After emancipation, desperate for tractable labor and intent on disfranchising Black men, legislatures enacted black codes throughout the South that criminalized Black people both for "moving around" and for "staying still."[9] But mobility out of prison remained possible, either temporarily through furloughs or permanently through early release. By the turn of the twenty-first century, however, a growing class of people, a disproportionate number of them Black, were condemned to die in prison without ever having a chance to leave. With the increase in mandatory minimum sentences and the growing use of life without the possibility of parole (LWOP) as an alternative to the death penalty, the number of people condemned to die in prison has quadrupled since 1984 despite a decline in violent crime rates.[10] As of 2021, over two hundred thousand people, or one in seven US prisoners, is serving life—either LWOP, life with parole, or a virtual life sentence of fifty years or more.[11] Incarcerated activists and their allies refer to these extreme sentences as death by incarceration (DBI).[12]

Kempis "Ghani" Songster, who served thirty years of a DBI sentence at the State Correctional Institution–Graterford in Pennsylvania after being convicted for a murder he committed when he was fifteen, describes this retributive trend in sentencing as Procrustean:

> Procrustes was the bandit in the Greek tale of the hero Theseus. Procrustes would invite travelers to spend the night in his inn, but once they checked in, he would force them to lie down on his iron bed, binding them with chains. For those who were shorter than the length of the bed, Procrustes would stretch them on a rack until they equaled the length of the bed. For those who were too tall, Procrustes would cut off their extremities to make them fit the bed. In either case, the end result was death. In the same way, the U.S. criminal legal system ruthlessly forces everyone into the same mold of "criminal," "super-predator," "prisoner," and "inmate." It treats all of us the same without regard for our special circumstances and individual characteristics, effectively chaining millions to an iron bed and robbing them of the chance of redemption. That iron bed is manifest in our mandatory sentencing schemes, particularly mandatory life without parole.[13]

Because LWOP forecloses any opportunity for review, clemency is the only route to freedom for people serving these sentences. But as Songster and others have documented, clemency has been on the decline throughout the nation since the 1980s.

In 1977 the *Angolite* noted that nearly 90 percent of long-termers were seeking clemency.[14] By the turn of the twenty-first century, however, incarcerated people were giving up on clemency petitions, and, according to Angola journalist Lane Nelson, "an era of gloom settled over Angola like at no other time in the prison's long history and with it began a drop out rate for lifers who were giving up on freedom in exchange for a mysterious peace that can attach to accepting a lifetime behind bars."[15]

The decline in clemency petitions was due to hopelessness in the face of mounting obstacles to release. In 1995 Louisiana governor Mike Foster (1992–2004) appointed crime-victim majorities to both the State Pardon and State Parole boards. Tough-on-crime legislators pushed back against a move to consider parole after age sixty, or after thirty years in prison, asserting that making people sentenced to LWOP eligible for release was a betrayal of the public. The *Angolite* noted that it was prisoners who were "tricked" into thinking they would be eventually released. It reminded readers, "The once consistent pattern in Louisiana's clemency practices over the past century has been a rejection of 'real' life sentences. . . . Clemency and the prospect of a second chance were integral parts of 'doing life.'" During Rideau's thirty-nine years in prison, governors had commuted the terms of more than seven hundred people serving life sentences for murder.[16] In 2000 the Louisiana Board of Pardons imposed a new rule requiring clemency applicants to publicize their petitions more widely in local newspapers, pay higher fees for those notices, and request that citizens contact the board with any comments. Prisoners were frustrated, but the *Angolite* remarked that "the impact may not be that great, since far fewer prisoners are applying for clemency in light of the governor not having commuted a single sentence for a prisoner in four years."[17]

Louisiana governors' reluctance to grant clemency was consistent with changes around the country, from New York to Oregon. Clemency had been used robustly and frequently throughout the United States until the 1980s. In New York, clemency was routine. Despite vocal skepticism about the persistence of the governor's "royal prerogative" in a democracy, clemency survived every challenge of the early twentieth century, including a "crime news wave" that reflected and roused anxieties about communism, the migration of African Americans and immigrants to northern cities, and organized crime.[18] With the establishment of new mandatory sentencing laws in the 1920s, New York's governors continued to use their clemency powers to mitigate harsh punishments and relieve prison overcrowding.[19] In other words, governors used clemency to manage risk, not produce it. Between 1940 and 1949, New York governors granted 109 commutations; between 1970 and 1979, they granted 119. These commutations occurred when the state's total prison population averaged around fifteen thousand; this is a notable contrast to the decade 2000–2009, when New York State's prison population ranged from sixty thousand to seventy thousand and the total number of commutations granted was seventeen.[20] Significantly, until the 1970s, clemency in New York was most often granted to those convicted of homicide offenses. In the 1970s clemency became a useful tool for addressing unfair sentencing, and clemency for homicides began to decline. When the New York State Legislature amended the notoriously harsh Rockefeller Drug Laws in 1977 to reduce penalties for marijuana but stopped short of making the amendment retroactive, Governor Hugh Carey (1975–82) granted commutations to those sentenced under the old law to promote fairness by "limiting the unintended consequences of sentencing reform."[21] Notably, a *New York Times* journalist remarked that Carey was "continuing a Christmas tradition."[22] In Pennsylvania, in the thirty-five-year period between 1932 and 1967, 607 lifers were granted commutation.[23] In Oregon, governors granted clemency for a variety of reasons that included the petitioner's family's financial dependence, ill health, "services to the state," and "exceptional rehabilitation," and did so on the recommendation of district attorneys, judges, and juries. During his first two years in office, Governor Sylvester Pennoyer (1887–95) made ninety-seven grants of clemency at a time when the prison population did not exceed four hundred people.[24] In the 1970s, due to a change in the criminal code, Oregon governor Tom McCall (1967–75) used his clemency power to release people who continued to be incarcerated despite the fact that their conduct was no longer illegal. In doing so he was undoing "the inequitable disparities in the treatment of persons similarly situated."[25] In short, for most of the twentieth century, governors did not believe that the clemency power was one that should be used only rarely. Instead they regarded it as an essential mechanism to improve the quality of the criminal justice system, remedy deficiencies, exercise benevolence, or acknowledge a prisoner's rehabilitation.

By the 1980s legislation limited the consideration of these factors in sentencing. Fear of the perceived risk of becoming the victim of crime, rejection of the possibility of rehabilitation, and a desire for purportedly race-neutral standardization in sentencing led to mandatory minimums determined by "the mathematical analyses of the offense, the offender, and its effects, based on an array of predetermined categories." The result, explain legal scholars Aliza B. Kaplan and Venetia Mayhew, "was to dehumanize defendants and to apply uniformly harsh sentences that allowed for no individual discretion." This rejection of judicial discretion also chilled the use of clemency. The personalism that had characterized the clemency process was no longer seen as the normal workings of a complex system but as a concession to criminals, an irrational exercise of personal feeling out of line with modern bureaucracy, and an attack on the supposedly unimpeachable decisions of tough-on-crime prosecutors.[26] As gubernatorial candidate Dick Thornburgh put it in 1982, "We in Pennsylvania are paralyzed by indecision in dealing with violent criminals, who prey on innocent people in our streets and in our homes." The Republican nominee seamlessly linked his support of new mandatory minimum laws and new obstacles to attaining clemency: "Pardons and commutations should be issued in only extraordinary circumstances. . . . They are not good-conduct medals."[27] After Thornburgh's election, applications for clemency in Pennsylvania dropped dramatically, the Pennsylvania Parole Board became more stringent with its recommendations, and Thornburgh honored a total of seven clemency petitions in his eight years as governor.[28] In just the previous decade, during his eight years in office, Governor Milton Shapp (1971–78) had commuted 251 life sentences.[29]

In the 1990s Pennsylvania had its own Willie Horton–like scandal that eviscerated clemency even further. In 1994 Governor Robert Casey (1987–95) commuted the life sentence of Reginald McFadden, a Black man who had been convicted in 1969 of a murder committed when he was a juvenile. Within three months of his release, McFadden killed two people and raped and kidnapped a third. Despite the fact that he was only the second of over nine hundred paroled lifers since 1930 to commit murder, the media manufactured consent that early release was not worth the risk to public safety, and elected officials concluded it endangered their political careers.[30] In 1997, in swift response to the McFadden calamity, legislators amended the state constitution to require that the Parole Board be unanimous in order to recommend commutation of any life sentence to the governor, so that one board member has the unilateral power to veto an applicant.[31] Clemency grants in Pennsylvania have dwindled. Between 1967 and 1994, over 360 life sentences were commuted. Between 1994 and 2015 there were six.[32] In most states, the process is so opaque, prohibitive, and politicized as to make clemency nearly unattainable. In four states laws now *forbid* governors from granting clemency to prisoners serving LWOP. Four others explicitly exclude rehabilitation as grounds for release.[33] Songster and his coauthors, Terrell Carter (serving a DBI sentence) and attorney Rachel López, refer to this negation of human evolution as "legally codified condemnation."[34] In fact, the US Supreme Court's decision in *Graham v. Florida* that LWOP sentences for juveniles who did not commit homicide were unconstitutional rejected executive clemency as a sufficient protection from LWOP because it was so rarely granted.[35]

This permanent exile forces existential questions on prisoners, such as those imagined by philosopher Lisa Guenther: "Without a living relation to past and future generations, who am I? Do I still have a stake in historical time?"[36] Antonio, serving a life sentence in Florida, feels an urgency to "buck against the narrative imposed on me by the prison system," and grieves the fact that since his incarceration two decades ago, his "footprint on society has ceased."[37] And, for those in the free world, prison's spectacular invisibility freezes those beyond the walls as beyond historical time, arresting narratives of their development and instead defining them only by their worst act as permanently incorrigible. Carter and Songster, along with fellow lifers, struggled with what it meant to internalize the exclusion of incarcerated people from humanity: "We saw that if we continued to use others' definitions of who we were, then no matter how far removed we were from the people who caused so much pain, no matter how much we transformed, no matter the determination that we had to be the best versions of ourselves, no matter the certificates, the degrees, and the lives that we affected in positive ways, we could always be chained and shackled to the worst moments of our lives."[38]

According to Angola long-termer Kerry Myers, "Prison destroys relationships. A prisoner's world shrinks with time. Visits and communication with family and friends decline steadily. . . . Longtermers live in isolation, their world seldom extending outside the prison gates."[39] Previously, clemency petitions had involved regular contact between the imprisoned, members of parole and pardon boards, and the governor, who might visit "forgotten men." The demise of clemency sealed off this conduit of communication with authorities outside the prison.[40] The end of furloughs prohibited incarcerated people from contributing to their communities and challenging stereotypes; the end of conjugal visits closed the door to intimacy with loved ones and, for some, the chance to have children. As clemency, furloughs, and conjugal visits dried up around the nation, prisoners' isolation became even more acute. Daryl Waters, who has been incarcerated at Angola for twenty-four years, adapted by turning his sense of purpose toward his fellow prisoners: "Every time I invest my time in someone else, I free a part of myself." By counseling young men who enter Angola, he could transcend prison walls: "I want to impact them so strongly that I can't be confined. . . . I'm going to love people so passionately until a part of me will always live outside the gates of Angola."[41]

The forced disappearance of incarcerated people affects all of us. It has robbed communities of valued members. "If it takes a village to raise a child then I am absent of that village," wrote Clinton "Nkechi" Walker, serving a DBI sentence in Pennsylvania. Walker has wisdom and experience to offer, but locked away, he was compelled to "neglect my responsibilities and letting down those little ones that need my knowledge."[42] If we can no longer imagine prisoners taking classes on university campuses, as we could have in 1968; if our children cannot play in chess tournaments with incarcerated people; if we cannot hear testimonies of incarcerated people as invited guests at our houses of worship; if we cannot dance to the melodies played by incarcerated musicians, then we are robbed of the opportunity to test our faith that even those who have committed the most terrible acts can, in the words of the Supreme Court, "achieve maturity of judgment and self-recognition of human worth and potential."[43] Furloughs implicitly raise the question, If these people can be trusted to be free in the community and can even contribute to it, what justifies their remaining in prison at all? We have been severed not only from the human potential of our neighbors, but from the historical memory of an era when free people were confronted with that potential on a more regular basis.

Many incarcerated people are now subject to greater spatial and geographical isolation due to the recent trend of siting prisons in remote areas; all of the prisons built in New York State between 1982 and 2010, for example, are located in rural settings.[44] Rural prisons are not unprecedented. In the nineteenth century prisons were constructed on the outskirts of urban areas to remove supposed deviants from the corruption of city life; in the South, prison plantations maintained their agricultural orientation and spatial location. And in the 1960s, as we have seen, southern gulags were reimagined as templates for the "open prison." But prisons' rural locations now have different purposes and carry different meanings, serving as much-needed sources of employment in declining communities and as symbols of the state-as-protector. Paul Wright, an activist and journalist serving a sentence for murder at the Washington State Penitentiary, diagnosed the prison boom as a wishful performance of state legitimacy: "As the capitalist economy sinks even deeper into the morass of its own contradictions we well [sic] even greater attempts to distract the citizenry from the reasons behind this economic crisis, especially the role of Reagan/Bush in fomenting it. With the collapse of the Soviet Union as a credible menace, there is a need for something to distract the U.S. voter from his economic predicament."[45]

As scholars and activists have documented, the economic restructuring that began in the 1980s eviscerated the country's mining, farming, and timber industries, as well as its manufacturing, and hosting a prison emerged as a Faustian catalyst for economic survival.[46] While a disproportionate share of prisons are located in rural areas, a disproportionate share of incarcerated people come from urban areas. Researcher Tracy Huling describes this situation as a "fateful, symbiotic bond between depressed communities in urban and rural America."[47] The prisons are so far from the communities from which their inhabitants originate that visitation is extremely arduous. More than 63 percent of people in state prisons are incarcerated over one hundred miles from their families. Largely as a result of the institutions' inaccessible locations, fewer than one-third of people in state prisons receive a single visit from a loved one in a typical month.[48] Restrictive visitation policies create further barriers. Arizona, for example, charges visitors a onetime twenty-five-dollar background check fee; North Carolina allows only one visit per week for up to two hours; Washington State's Monroe Correctional Complex warns that visitors avoid being "excessively emotional," and those who "cause significant concern" may be banned.[49] Limitations on visits are justified as necessary for security, despite evidence that demonstrates that visitation decreases violence and facilitates rehabilitation.[50]

Incarcerated people are also increasingly likely to be isolated from fellow prisoners due to the rising use of solitary confinement. Whereas long stays in solitary confinement were rare until the late 1980s, the past few decades have seen the normalization of the practice as a permanent condition, most often imposed on young and Black prisoners.[51] Just as the criminalization of activists lent fuel to the idea that prisons were essential to ensure social order, the additional criminalization of people on the inside for their activism, beliefs, and personal associations has led to increased isolation and dehumanization within prison. The late 1980s marked the invention and proliferation of supermax prisons, where "problem" prisoners—supposed gang members, the mentally ill, the extremely violent, and political activists—are kept in lockdown for twenty-three hours per day with almost no human contact, under fluorescent lights that are never turned off.[52] If long sentences strangle possibilities for acknowledging change in a person over time, solitary confinement detemporalizes its victims even further by literally disrupting their diurnal rhythm. For Lisa Guenther, the supermax prison and solitary confinement give concrete shape to inmates' social death, which is produced and reinforced by law.[53] This permanent isolation has been defended as necessary to avert chaos, riots, and revolutionary uprising, especially in the absence of incentives for "good behavior" such as parole, furloughs, conjugal visits, and clemency.[54] Thus, according to Guenther, the historic promise of redemption and rehabilitation has been replaced "by neoliberal rhetoric of risk management, security, [and] efficiency."[55] Supermax prisons are the material culmination of the idea that prisons should inflict harsh punishment on offenders; sensory and emotional deprivation accompanies material deprivation. These supermax facilities are seldom endorsed by corrections officials, but for politicians they have become potent symbols of how tough on crime a jurisdiction has become.[56] The supermax prison is held up as a way to manage "the worst of the worst," the permanently dangerous *others* for whom regular prison is not enough. Guenther urges, "but they are *our* others, and a society that practices long-term, wide-scale solitary confinement cannot help but be shaped by our (non)relation to those who have been 'disappeared' but who remain among us, and sometimes return to haunt us."[57] Despite a consensus among psychologists, penologists, and human rights activists around the globe that solitary confinement longer than fifteen days is a form of torture, federal courts have maintained that these conditions are permissible for security reasons.[58] The actuarial logic of zero risk has legitimated the supermax prison as a means of preventing violence, but instead, the facility should be recognized as a site of state violence itself, adding insult to exile.[59]

* * *

Nonetheless, incarcerated people continue to struggle for their physical freedom and freedom from the stigma of their original convictions at every opportunity. Prisoner activist Norris Henderson cherished visits by college students in 2001. "When are we going to meet the inmates?" one student asked, to which Henderson responded, "You're sitting next to one. . . . They're all around the room." Prisoners found that taking students to see the prison hospice was instrumental in changing the minds of the young and free. "Why don't they let them go home if they are that ill or dying?" one college student asked Jerry Francis, an incarcerated hospice volunteer. "Because you don't want them out," Francis replied. "Maybe *you'd* let them go, but that's because you've seen . . . prisoners as real people. But what about your friends, your family, those who are 'society' who haven't seen what you've seen?"[60]

Darwin Willie, incarcerated at Angola since he was eighteen, explains that maintaining hope is itself a form of resistance. "To a certain extent we're rebellious," he admits, and in this situation, "it's what helps us survive" when "everything around you and surrounding you says there's no hope."[61] Change comes to incarcerated people whether politics admits it or not. In fighting for clemency, parole eligibility, better conditions, visitation, reconciliation with victims, and personal redemption, long-termers refuse to be passively swept along the river of time; instead they insist on being temporal subjects, making amends, finding purpose, testifying to their transformations, and organizing with people on the outside. As a man incarcerated at the Maryland State Penitentiary known as Q put it, "To me, time is like a dragon I have to slay. If I can master the present, I will have used my time to redeem time."[62]

Carter and Songster have chosen to redeem time by organizing for the right to redemption itself. In 2011 they joined with Wayne Battle, the president of the lifers' association at the Graterford prison, Lifers, Inc., to form a new group that would mobilize to secure parole eligibility for those serving LWOP or DBI. As they reckoned with their own accountability for the harms they had caused and defined their organization's goals and values, they "adamantly resist[ed] legally codified condemnation" by forming Right to Redemption, or R2R. Drawing on a human rights framework, R2R asserts that "all humans have the inner capacity to forgive and be forgiven[,] to transform and be transformed, and that the law should reflect these innate qualities—that all humans have the right to redemption."[63] By using the word *redemption* these men are not conceding to the notion that they are sinful creatures or that they bear sole responsibility for their actions. Carter, López, and Songster explain, "We contend that it is possible to recognize, as we profoundly do, that the criminal legal system is often racist and fundamentally flawed, while at the same time to wish that we were not shedders of anyone's blood." Carter and Songster want to make amends; they want to help the communities that they have harmed. But their increasing isolation obstructs atonement and belonging because the walls hardening around them announce that "we can never be trusted, that we will never be better than our worst actions, that we must therefore be separated from our communities to keep them safe." Right to Redemption insists that the state, "as the custodian of liberty, has the power to either obstruct, or, alternatively, to facilitate, a path toward redemption." Without regular reviews of sentences, Carter, López, and Songster assert, "we are forever locked into the box of the worst expression of ourselves."[64]

In Louisiana, a coalition of former prisoners and progressive prosecutors is reawakening the practice of mercy. But this time the state is also trying to atone. The Louisiana Parole Project, founded by Andrew Hundley and Kerry Myers, both formerly incarcerated at Angola, revived the Forgotten Man Committees of decades past and established the Forgotten Men Project to free people who have served many decades in prison.[65] Meyers and Hundley have the ear of Jason Williams, who was elected Orleans Parish district attorney in 2020 on a campaign promise to revisit unjust sentences. One of Williams's first acts as district attorney was the creation of a new Civil Rights Division to "unabashedly confront the ills of the past" by reexamining potentially wrongful convictions and excessively harsh sentences.[66] He stated that the abandonment of the 10/6 rule (the practice by which those with life sentences could see release after serving ten years and six months) in the 1970s "literally broke the promise that was made to these men in court, without explanation, without apology, without discussion." That these "forgotten men," most of whom were Black, were crippled by moving goalposts, is, explains Williams, "patently and clearly unfair."[67] One of these "forgotten men" is Lester Pearson, who pled guilty to a murder in 1964 because he was told by the district attorney that in the Jim Crow South pleading guilty was his best bet, as he would otherwise face the electric chair.[68] Another, Louis Mitchell, was sentenced at the age of nineteen in 1966 to two life terms for aggravated rape. He maintained his innocence, but at the time he would have faced capital punishment if convicted. He, too, was advised to plead guilty by his attorney, who assured Mitchell that he would be permitted release after ten years and six months of good behavior. Instead Mitchell served fifty-five years of hard labor before being released at age seventy-four.[69] When he was finally released, he admitted, "For me, it was like I fell from outer space."[70] District Attorney Williams, perhaps originally unaware of the history of clemency in Louisiana, was astonished to learn that there were so many elderly prisoners needlessly languishing in prison. "These were not mistakes," Williams declared. "The forgotten men is just one of the many broken promises to Blacks and minorities in the United States. It also sends a clear message that there is no bigger monument to white supremacy and racism than Angola state penitentiary."[71] In May 2022, Louisiana lawmakers passed a bill that will provide parole eligibility to some of the people who pled guilty because they had been told that they would have a chance at release after ten years and six months of good behavior. Most of them have now been in prison for at least fifty years, and a majority of them are Black.[72]

Implicit in the Forgotten Men Project is the fundamental principle that people change over time. Incarcerated activists single out this principle as constitutive of being human. The members of R2R, all of whom have been convicted of homicide, argue that the need to atone is so integral to human dignity that depriving someone of an opportunity for atonement is a violation of the Eighth Amendment to the US Constitution and beyond the pale of "evolving standards of decency" around the world. But making amends is not a lifetime of servility and self-flagellation; it is an insistence on being part of a community of care, of enacting the repair whose loving intentions might both mend harm and model an alternative to exile. These prisoners have been cast out from the social community of the free world, and fighting for redemption is a two-pronged battle of achieving one's transformation to satisfy one's own conscience and transforming the public view that prisoners are irredeemable. A key part of R2R's mission is to "tout the unsung wonders of the many men and women sentenced to life without parole, who have convicted themselves to a life of sacrifice and service and have become agents of restoration in the communities they have wounded."[73] For Felix Rosado of R2R, incarcerated in Pennsylvania since 1995, dispelling the myths about incarcerated people by fostering contact between inside and outside is crucial to the work of ending permanent exile. "It will take a total upheaval of the mindset in our society that the answer to every problem is banishment," Rosado avers.[74] Having concluded that "my freedom fight was inextricably tied to the liberation for all," Rosado asserts that collaboration between incarcerated and free people is not only strategic but a practice of collective liberation.[75]

In 2015, R2R joined with several other free-world organizations to organize a campaign to end DBI and formed the Coalition to Abolish Death by Incarceration, which pushes bills in the Pennsylvania General Assembly to make people serving DBI eligible for parole. Uniting with people on the outside is essential to this movement. Felix Rosado and Layne Mullett point out that "people locked away in hundreds of thousands of cages across the United States are the front line in this struggle and have been leading the way" for decades, but "the time, the resources, connection, and mobility of those on the outside is essential both for bringing that struggle to light and for amplifying its message." In this work, R2R has articulated that its movement is a collective struggle not just for individual freedom earned through personal transformation but for liberation for everyone. As Rosado and Mullett note, "We struggle because we are fundamentally opposed to injustice and state repression, not because we are desperate for freedom. Every prisoner, regardless of their sentence, wants to be free, for freedom is the natural disposition of humans. As conscious and politicized prisoners however, we connect our freedom to the need to struggle against societal injustice. Therefore, if we were released tomorrow, our struggle would not be over, we would continue to struggle against all forms of oppression." Thus, organizing inside and outside is an embodiment of the beloved community that the movement aspires to achieve. Since the past several decades have seen the thickening of prison walls, this approach penetrates the walls and shows that they are permeable. Rosado and Mullett write that unconditional confinement is "not the totalizing force that the state might like it to be. For we are not absent from each other when we struggle together, when we build community, family, and movement together, when we strategize, argue, and plan together, when we work together to bring people home."[76]

Significantly, both Rosado and Songster are also members of the Inside-Out Think Tank, a group of alumni of the Inside-Out Prison Exchange Program at the Graterford prison who coach prospective university instructors in the program's pedagogy.[77] Like Henry in my own Inside-Out class (see the introduction to this book), J. Michael Lyons and Felix Rosado hold that this "gathering of people who are never supposed to meet—people from inside and outside the prison walls—is 'radical.'" As the students engage with each other, they testify, "something revolutionary begins to unfold. Stereotypes shatter, walls come crumbling down. Jumpsuits, jeans, state boots, or sneaks—it all stops mattering. We're human beings, being human." These sessions are not just opportunities for a break in the monotony but an extension of the work incarcerated people are already doing to bring attention to mass incarceration and, according to Rosado, an opportunity "to transcend that wall and to come together and talk about what's really going on in these places and who's really locked inside them."[78] With such encounters, eye to eye, we chip away at the walls: "We're building bridges and pathways to the kind of society we want to live in," Rosado and Mullett explain. "And it's making those walls feel a little less concrete—until the day they come crumbling down."[79]

There are simply too many people in prison, and they are in prison for far too long. No one can predict how people will change and grow over the course of their time inside. Despite every new obstacle to hope, people incarcerated for decades have doggedly sought meaning and purpose in their lives. They point out that they are the least likely to commit rule violations in prison and the least likely to reoffend once released.[80] The LWOP sentences and governors' reluctance to grant clemency disregard these basic truths and instead entomb people who present no public safety risk for their own political gain. How many of us would wish to be defined forever by our worst act? Songster is emboldened to counter such potential abjection. Now free, he declares, "I have a responsibility to not be confined to my lowest and darkest moment. . . . I have a profound duty to discharge to the universe." Do we not have the same responsibility to ourselves, and thus toward each other? Songster recalls a revelation from behind the walls: "I *could* and *must* regain my humanity and moral rectitude. . . . No other struggle was more worthwhile. I could and must water the seeds that I knew were still in the soil of my soul. And those seeds could sprout and blossom into something, someone, worthy of being called community member, citizen, brother, friend, neighbor, advocate, husband, and now father."[81] Banishing our neighbors legitimates and exacerbates our worst traits: vengeance, fear, racism, and cruelty. In this sense, allowing incarcerated people their chance at redemption is a chance to redeem ourselves.

NOTES

INTRODUCTION

1   All students' names have been changed to protect their privacy.

2   I thank artist Emily Squires for devising this exercise.

3   Stevenson, *Just Mercy*.

4   Though CRCI is a men's facility, trans women are incarcerated there as well.

5   Davis and Roswell, "Introduction," 5.

6   On the demise of higher education in prison as part of a politics of austerity, see Yates and Lakes, "After Pell Grants," 61–70.

7   Jones, "Biographical Mediation," 500.

8   Rodríguez, "Abolition as Praxis of Human Being," 1576. As Gilmore, "Ruth Wilson Gilmore on Abolition, the Climate Crisis and What Must Be Done," notes, "abolition is life in rehearsal."

9   Vick, "Look at Me!," 155.

10 Henry [pseud.], Inside-Out reflection booklet, 2019, collection of the author, Lewis & Clark College.

11 *FYSK: Facts You Should Know* (Virginia State Penitentiary) 2, no. 1 (1982): 10, Library of Virginia.

12 DelSesto, "Norfolk's 'Model Prison Community,'" 127–46; Malcolm X, *The Autobiography of Malcolm X*, 212.

13 "Wallkill Prison without Walls a Success; Only Eight Break Trust in an Air of Freedom," *New York Times*, June 18, 1933.

14 Tyrone Werts, quoted in Pompa, "One Brick at a Time," 133.

15 "Avoyelles Manor Nursing Home News," *Cottonport (LA) Leader*, June 16, 1974; Nan Nadler, "Angola Cons Have Music, Will Travel to Perform," *Daily World* (Opelousas, LA), July 25, 1968.

16 "Viewpoint: Traveling Ambassadors," *Angolite*, June 5, 1968, 1.

17 "Traveling Ambassadors," *Rayne (LA) Acadian-Tribune*, June 27, 1968.

18 "Viewpoint: Traveling Ambassadors," 1.

19 John Leaer and W. W. Stagg, "America's Worst Prison," *Collier's*, November 22, 1952, 13–16.

20 "Those Westernaires," *Angolite*, September 30, 1968, 18.

21 "The Axe on Travel," *Angolite*, March 1, 1979, 16.

22 Wilbert Rideau, interview with the author, June 20, 2022.

23 Fairclough, *Race and Democracy*, chaps. 12–14; Strain, "'We Walked Like Men,'"43–62; Hill, "The Bogalusa Movement," 43–54.

24 "'Non-violence' Breeds Violence," *Shreveport (LA) Journal*, quoted in Brückmann, "Citizens Councils, Conservatism, and White Supremacy," 1.

25 "The Axe on Travel," 16.

26 Bergeron, "Second Place Isn't Good Enough," 124.

27 Jones, "Biographic Mediation," 489, 500.

28 Norris Henderson, interview with the author, June 24, 2022.

29 Harry Connick Sr., quoted in "D.A. Would Jail More Criminals," *Times* (Shreveport, LA), April 28, 1979.

30 Bergeron, "Second Place Isn't Good Enough," 126.

31 Jerry Moskal, "Furlough Programs Growing Stricter after Controversies," *Times* (Shreveport, LA), December 24, 1988; Jerry Humphries, "State Prisoners Now Get Few Furloughs," *Town Talk* (Alexandria, LA), October 24, 1988.

32 "The Axe on Travel," 20.

33 Ned Hicks, quoted in "The Axe on Travel," 21.

34 Rideau interview.

35 "The Axe on Travel," 22.

36 Marie Gottschalk, "Days without End: Life Sentences and Penal Reform," *Prison Legal News*, January 15, 2012, https://www.prisonlegalnews.org/news/2012/jan/15/days-without-end-life-sentences-and-penal-reform/.

37 Herbert Williams, quoted in Kerry Myers, "The Real Deal," *Angolite*, November/December 2000–January/February 2001, 35. As Bergeron, "Second Place Isn't Good Enough," 125, notes, "Unlike Louisiana's sentencing structure, which has become progressively more severe, prison conditions in Louisiana have actually witnessed a dramatic improvement."

38 Hilton Butler, quoted in "The Forgotten Men," *Angolite*, May 1, 1980, 24.

39 Chavez, "Aging Louisiana Prisoners."

40 Darren James, Visiting Room Project, video, 2021, https://www.visitingroomproject.org/archive/darren_james.

41 Daryl Waters, Visiting Room Project, video, 2021, https://www.visitingroomproject.org/archive/daryl_waters.

42 I thank Garrett Felber for this formulation.

43 Scholars who have centered the inside-outside relationship in their analyses include Pelot-Hobbs, "Organized Inside and Out"; and Janssen, "When the 'Jungle' Met the Forest."

44 Patterson, *Slavery and Social Death*; Price, *Prison and Social Death*; Cacho, *Social Death*.

45 Ayers, *Vengeance and Justice*, 63, 204–6; Oshinsky, *Worse Than Slavery*, 179–204; Miller, *Crime, Sexual Violence, and Clemency*; Wood, "Cole Blease's Pardoning Pen"; Garton, "Managing Mercy."

46 One excellent source on the history of clemency throughout the twentieth century focusing on one state is Seeds, "Governors and Prisoners."

47 Ogletree and Sarat, *Life without Parole*.

48 Seeds, "Life Sentences and Perpetual Confinement," 291.

49 I am borrowing this now well-known identifier, the New Jim Crow, from Alexander, *The New Jim Crow*.

50 Harvey, *The Shadow System*, 112.

51 For recent discussions of the relationship between sexuality and the modern carceral state, see Kunzel, *Criminal Intimacy*; Halperin and Hoppe, eds., *The War on Sex*; Lancaster, *Sex Panic and the Punitive State*; and Renfro, *Stranger Danger*.

52 Most studies of prison visitation have been done by legal scholars, criminologists, and sociologists and do not include a historical approach. See, for example, Boudin, Stutz, and Littman, "Prison Visitation Policies"; and Hensley, Rutland, and Gray-Ray, "Inmate Attitudes." On the effects of incarceration on prisoners' loved ones, see Harvey, *The Shadow System*.

53 Murakawa, *The First Civil Right*; Forman, *Locking Up Our Own*; Hinton, *From the War on Poverty to the War on Crime*; Taylor, *From #Black Lives Matter to Black Liberation*.

54 Gilmore and Gilmore, "Restating the Obvious," 145.

55 Chard, "Rallying for Repression"; Page, *The Toughest Beat*.

56 For the punitive turn, see Flamm, *Law and Order*. For how this punitive turn manifested and was amplified by popular culture and the media, see Macek, *Urban Nightmares*; and Sherry, *The Punitive Turn in American Life*. On links between liberal Great Society programs, welfare and opposition to it, and the rise of mass incarceration, see Murakawa, *The First Civil Right*; Kohler-Hausmann, *Getting Tough*; Hinton, *From the War on Poverty to the War on Crime*; and Weaver, "Frontlash."

57 Rosen, "Carceral Crisis."

58 Strange, *Discretionary Justice*, chap. 7, finds that executive clemency remained strong in New York State in the 1920s and 1930s despite a panic about crime and prisoner unrest.

59 Clear, *Harm in American Penology*.

60 For a close examination of the twin processes of social disinvestment and prison expansion—what Alex Lichtenstein calls "sunbelt penology," see Lichtenstein, "Flocatex and the Fiscal Limits of Mass Incarceration."

61 Gilmore and Gilmore, "Restating the Obvious," 158, emphasis in the original. See also Thompson, "Why Mass Incarceration Matters."

62 Paul Harvey, "Columnist Thinks Prison Life Getting Soft," *Daily World* (Opelousas, LA), December 28, 1980.

63 Theorists who have identified a carceral continuum include Wacquant, "Deadly Symbiosis." The concept of a "carceral archipelago," which includes other punitive institutions in addition to prisons, was introduced by the French historian and philosopher Michel Foucault in *Discipline and Punish*, 297. Further, this exile or banishment is related to and contemporaneous with Beckett and Herbert, *Banished*, 8, who point out that "increasing swaths of urban space are delimited as zones of exclusion from which the undesirable are banned."

64 See, for example, Lynch, *Sunbelt Justice*; Perkinson, *Texas Tough*; McClennan, *The Crisis of Imprisonment*; Gilmore, *Golden Gulag*; and Oshinsky, *Worse Than Slavery*.

65 Kennedy, "'Longtermer Blues,'" 307. For examinations of regional distinctions and commonalities in prison practices, see Thompson, "Blinded by a 'Barbaric' South"; and Kamerling, *Capital and Convict*.

66 I have been influenced by the scholarship of geographer Dominque Moran, which itself is in dialogue with Erving Goffman's work on the "total institution," Michel Foucault's work on the development of the prison and regulation of bodies, and Giorgio Agamben's work on "spaces of exception" and "bare life," among others. Moran suggests that "the 'carceral' is something more than merely the spaces in which individuals are confined—rather, that the 'carceral' is a social and psychological construction relevant both within and outside physical spaces of incarceration." Moran, "Linking the Carceral and the Punitive State," 166. See also Moran, *Carceral Geography*. Wang, *Carceral Capitalism*, 151, 17, analyzes both algorithmic policing and the "municipal plunder" by which cities rely on revenue generated by fines and fees and refers to this practice as evidence of the "predatory state." On electronic monitoring, see Kilgore, *Understanding E-carceration*. On the collateral consequences of incarceration, see Jones, "Biographic Mediation."

I have also been influenced by the scholarly and cinematic work of Brett Story, who looks at the prison as a set of relationships, tracking the entanglements of prison with broken windows policing in Detroit, the demise of coal mining in Kentucky, and the liminal space of the prison bus; see Story, *Prison Land*. Turner, *Prison Boundary*, 5–6, suggests that scholarship "has not yet interrogated the work of the boundary as a process in creating and stabilizing these categories," and that this boundary is "constituted as a *set of connections* that work to construct, reinforce, and transgress that boundary" (emphasis in the original).

67 Martin Sostre, "The Open Road Interview," by David Spaner, *Open Road*, Summer 1976, 12. I thank Garrett Felber for this reference.

68 Gilmore, *Golden Gulag*.

69 Wang, *Carceral Capitalism*, 82–83, emphasis in the original. For the use of the fear of crime as a mode of governance, see Simon, *Governing through Crime*.

70 Appreciation and analysis of how fear has shaped the design of the physical landscape can be found in Davis, *City of Quartz*; Sorkin, *Indefensible Space*; Zukin, *Landscapes of Power*; and Smith, *The New Urban Frontier*.

71 Gilmore and Gilmore, "Restating the Obvious," 144–45.

72 Fallacious assumptions that Black people were inherently criminal long predate the Willie Horton scandal; see Muhammad, *The Condemnation of Blackness*.

73 Simon, "The 'Hard Back' of Mass Incarceration," 202.

74 Gilmore and Gilmore, "Restating the Obvious," 154.

75 Dolovich, "Foreword," 254.

76 Bortz, "From the Editor," 2.

77 On the increasing reliance on risk assessment in criminal justice policy and its relationship to the politics of mass incarceration, see Scheingold, *The Politics of Street Crime*; Simon, *Governing through Crime*; Garland, *The Culture of Control*; Simon, "Wake of the Flood"; Harcourt, *Profiling, Policing, and Punishing*; Pratt and Anderson, *Criminal Justice*; and Baker and Simon, *Embracing Risk*. The ascendant strategy of risk-based criminal justice, in which one class of people is categorized as the primary threat to the other and thus must be controlled rather than integrated, has been called "actuarial justice"; see O'Malley, "Globalising Risk?"

78 Atkinson, *Do Not Resist*.

79 Allen, *The Decline of the Rehabilitative Ideal*; Phelps, "Rehabilitation in the Punitive Era"; Tonry, *Sentencing Fragments*; Grasso, "The Unity of Individualism and Determinism."

80 Reiter, *23/7*; Rhodes, *Total Confinement*.

81 Criminologist Christopher Seeds has examined the varying ways that people serving life and virtual life sentences have maintained hope and has urged more research in this area; see Seeds, "Hope and the Life Sentence."

82 As Steven Herbert has found in his interviews with people serving life sentences in Washington State, "Life-sentenced prisoners do good works because of the positive impact it can generate for others, but also because they can simultaneously write a new story about themselves, one that can provide a sense of both atonement and hope"; Herbert, *Too Easy to Keep*, 34.

83 Schenwar and Law, *Prison by Any Other Name*; Whitlock and Heitzeg, "'Bipartisan' Criminal Justice Reform."

84   Gilmore and Gilmore, "Restating the Obvious," 147.

85   Simon, "A Radical Need for Criminology," 10–11.

86   Fields, *Slavery and Freedom on the Middle Ground*, 39.

87   Guenther, *Solitary Confinement*, 60.

88   Henry [pseud.], Inside-Out reflection booklet.

89   Douglass, *My Bondage and My Freedom*, 90.

1. CLEMENCY IN THE AGE OF JIM CROW

1   Twelve percent of the clemencies, issued to twenty-six inmates, were for people who were in custody at the time of their release. Statement from the office of former governor Haley Barbour, quoted in Donna Ladd, "Barbour Finally Addresses Pardons; Insults Mississippians," *Jackson (MS) Free Press*, January 12, 2012, https://www.jacksonfreepress.com/news/2012/jan/12/barbour-finally-addresses-pardons-insults/.

2   "Haley Barbour May Try to Rewrite the Script for 2012 Presidential Race," *Washington Post*, March 21, 2011; "Questionable Decision by Outgoing Governor," *Meridian (MS) Star*, January 15, 2012, https://www.meridianstar.com/opinion/editorials/questionable-decision-by-outgoing-governor/article_ee43fd4d-ba10-55d9-a7d3-a8b8c6ac9768.html; Patrik Jonsson, "Haley Barbour's Pardons Put Southern Redemption on Trial," *Christian Science Monitor*, January 14, 2021, https://www.csmonitor.com/USA/2012/0114/Haley-Barbour-s-pardons-put-Southern-redemption-on-trial.

3   Haley Barbour, quoted in "Lawmaker Wants to Strip Governor's Pardon Power," *Sun Herald* (Gulfport, MS), July 27, 2008, reposted *Magnolia Tribune* (Flora, MS), https://magnoliatribune.com/2008/07/28/lawmaker_wants_to_strip_governors_pardon_power/.

4   The use of clemency had been routine at the federal level for most of US history until the administration of President Richard Nixon. See Love, "Fear of Forgiving."

5   Guenther, *Solitary Confinement*, xxi.

6   Ayers, *Vengeance and Justice*, 63, 204–6; Oshinsky, *Worse Than Slavery*, 179–204; Miller, *Crime, Sexual Violence, and Clemency*; Wood, "Cole Blease's Pardoning Pen"; Garton, "Managing Mercy."

7   Wood, "Cole Blease's Pardoning Pen," 148.

8   Myers, *Race, Labor and Punishment*, chaps. 6–7.

9   Wood, "Cole Blease's Pardoning Pen," 148–49, describes Governor Blease's use of the pardon power as "a modern, prebureaucratic approach to criminal justice" that "reinforced a dynamic of benevolence and deference between the governor and his supporters." Blease's

practices stood at odds with a "new penology" that sought not only to improve penal conditions but also to create pardon and parole boards "to operate as modern bureaucratic agencies, with accountability and transparency."

10   Scholars who have pointed out the uneven development of the rehabilitative ideal in the American South include Wood, "Cole Blease's Pardoning Pen"; and Kamerling, *Capital and Convict*. McLennan, *The Crisis of Imprisonment*, contends that by the late nineteenth century, prisons in the North and South came to resemble each other as both depended on prison labor as a means of economic control. Thompson, "Blinded by a 'Barbaric' South," argues that the regional difference in prison systems was more of a matter of degree than kind, and that the notion of southern prisons as exceptionally barbaric has impeded reform in prisons outside the South.

11   Carter, *From George Wallace to Newt Gingrich*; Airstrup, *The Southern Strategy Revisited*; Lassiter, *The Silent Majority*.

12   Garton, "Managing Mercy," 676. See also Ayers, *Vengeance and Justice*, 63, 204–6; and Oshinsky, *Worse Than Slavery*, 179–204.

13   For examinations of the waning use of executive clemency, see Rosenzweig, "Reflections on the Atrophying Pardon Power"; Love, "The Twilight of the Pardon Power"; Kobil, "How to Grant Clemency"; Barkow, "The Ascent of the Administrative State"; and Kaplan and Mayhew, "The Governor's Clemency Power."

14   See, for example, Morison, "The Politics of Grace," 1–2; Tait, "Pardons in Perspective," 134; and Kobil, "The Quality of Mercy Strained."

15   Hamilton, *Federalist No. 74*, 553.

16   George Washington first exercised the pardon power when he granted amnesty to those engaged in Pennsylvania's Whiskey Rebellion; Thomas Jefferson issued pardons to those convicted of crimes under the Alien and Sedition Acts; Abraham Lincoln used clemency to encourage desertions from the Confederate Army; see Ruckman, "Executive Clemency in the United States," 253–54. Presidents have granted clemency for public policy reasons, such as when President Jimmy Carter issued amnesty to those who evaded the draft during the Vietnam War.

17   Strange, *Discretionary Justice*.

18   Montgomery v. Cleveland, 134 Miss. 132, 98 So. 111, 98 So. 543 (1923).

19   Love, "Fear of Forgiving," 125.

20   Colorado Board of Pardons, quoted in Kaplan and Mayhew, "The Governor's Clemency Power," 1299.

21   Rapaport, "Retribution and Redemption in the Operation of Executive Clemency," 1503. See also Johnson, "Entitled to Clemency," 109–18.

22   According to a report for the National Governors' Association, "Clemency remains an [*sic*] valuable outlet for the repercussions of a system

in which human error remains a distinct possibility"; see Brown, Keiser, and Humphries, *Guide to Executive Clemency*, 10.

23 Wood, "Cole Blease's Pardoning Pen," 156.

24 Oshinsky, *Worse Than Slavery*; Blackmon, *Slavery by Another Name*; Perkinson, *Texas Tough*.

25 Perkinson, "Angola and the Agony of Prison Reform," 9. See also Carleton, *Politics and Punishment*, 3–84.

26 Woodfox and George, *Solitary*, 25, 34.

27 Wilbert Rideau, "In the Field," *Angolite*, September–October 1979, cited in Armstrong, "Slavery Revisited," 836.

28 Louisiana Department of Public Safety and Corrections, Annual Statistics, Demographic Dashboard, June 30, 2023, https://doc.louisiana.gov/demographic-dashboard.

29 Stephen Gettinger, "Mississippi Has Come a Long Way, but It Had a Long Way to Come," *Corrections*, June 1979, 5.

30 RG 27, Series 1840: Suspensions of Sentence, Box 12547, misc. folders, Records of the Office of the Governor, Mississippi Department of Archives and History (hereafter MDAH); "Ambassadors," *Angolite*, May 2, 1953, 5.

31 "Ambassadors," 5.

32 "Unreformed Freed Too Quickly," *Delta Democrat-Times* (Greenville, MS), August 24, 1958.

33 A. J. McLaurin, quoted in Bailey, "Please Don't Forget About Me," 70.

34 Walker Wood, "Capital Activities," *Winona (MS) Times*, February 1, 1935.

35 Taylor, *Down on Parchman Farm*, 54.

36 "Johnson Listens to Prisoners Tell Freedom Claims," *Clarion-Ledger* (Jackson, MS), December 18, 1940.

37 "Pardons and Pardons," *Delta Democrat-Times* (Greenville, MS), November 5, 1939.

38 "State Scored by Parole Authority for Prison System; Most Backward State in Parole Developments, Writer Affirms," *Delta Democrat-Times* (Greenville, MS), October 2, 1939; "Thames Suggests Parole Law for State Prisoners," *Clarion-Ledger* (Jackson, MS), September 28, 1939.

39 "First Steps Taken for Prison Reform; Senate Given Bill," *McComb (MS) Daily Journal*, March 14, 1944.

40 Editorial, *Inside World*, July 1958, 3, emphasis in the original.

41 William Waller, Suspension of Sentence to Nevada Atterberry, September 24, 1975, RG 27, Series 1840: Suspensions of Sentence, Box 12547, Folder 3, Records of the Office of the Governor, MDAH.

42 Memo from Bill Harpole, Superintendent, November 19, 1956, RG 27, Series 975: Paroles and Suspensions, 1956–1960, Box 1942, Sid Brethren Folder, Records of the Office of the Governor, MDAH.

43   John Herbers, "Coleman Out as an Enigma," *Clarion-Ledger* (Jackson, MS), January 17, 1960.

44   "Ohio Governor's Plan Killed on Death Penalty Abolition," *Deseret News and Salt Lake Telegram*, March 26, 1959. As Brown, Keiser, and Humphries, *Guide to Executive Clemency*, 8, note, "Governors, at the end of their terms, sometimes commute the sentences of inmates who have been working as their domestic help." Prisoners were also employed in the executive mansions in Louisiana and South Carolina. See W. D. Workman Jr., "Prison Trusty Use Is Defended by Hollings," *Greenville (SC) News*, December 8, 1959, 2; and Burk Foster, "Pardons and Politics: How It All Went Wrong," *Angolite*, January–February 1988, 33.

45   Haley, "Care Cage," 58–85.

46   Claudia Brewer Strite, "Biography: Earl LeRoy Brewer," manuscript, 1946, Z/0348.0001: Brewer (E. L.) and Family Papers, Folder 1, MDAH.

47   Sansing and Waller, *A History of the Mississippi Governor's Mansion*, 114, 115.

48   "Convicts Serve as Servants 4 Years; They Get Pardoned," *Hattiesburg (MS) Daily News*, January 12, 1916, 5.

49   Haley, "Care Cage," 69.

50   "Governor's Servants Are Bowed in Grief," *Jackson (MS) Daily News*, March 20, 1927, Governor's Mansion Subject File, MDAH.

51   "Governor Frees Bailey Servants," *Clarion-Ledger* (Jackson, MS), December 19, 1946.

52   "White Pardons Mansion Staff: Prison Trusties Given Freedom," *Clarion-Ledger* (Jackson, MS), January 11, 1956, 3.

53   Sylvester Wright, quoted in "Petition for Pardon," *Winston County Journal* (Louisville, MS), December 10, 1959, 6.

54   "Breathitt to Review Use of Civilian Labor at Mansion," *Advocate-Messenger* (Danville, KY), December 3, 1964, 9; "Mansion No Place for Prison Help," *Courier-Journal* (Louisville, KY), August 24, 1962, 8.

55   "Combs Will 'Consider' Ending Convict Labor," *Paducah (KY) Sun*, August 22 1962, 5B. The American Federation of Labor had long campaigned against the use of prison labor on the grounds that it was coerced and competed unfairly with free workers. These campaigns, which were often linked with anti-immigrant movements, trafficked in explicitly racist and xenophobic discourse. See Thompson, "Rethinking Working-Class Struggle"; and Jackson, "Prison Labor."

56   This point is made in Miller, *Crime, Sexual Violence, and Clemency*, and Garton, "Managing Mercy."

57   Grover C. Doggette to Hon. Ross Barnett, August 19, 1961, RG 27, Series 975: Paroles and Suspensions, 1956–1960, Box 2009, William V. Andrews Folder, Records of the Office of the Governor, MDAH.

58   Mrs. H. E. Barnett to Governor Barnett, September 19, 1963, RG 27,
      Series 987: Penitentiary Correspondence, 1960–1964, Box 2032, Folder
      L, Records of the Office of the Governor, MDAH.

59   James Moore to Governor Wright, February 8, 1947, RG 27, Series 938:
      Pardons and Suspension Files, 1948–1952, Box 1793, Sam Bland Folder,
      Records of the Office of the Governor, MDAH.

60   J. C. Bassett to Governor Thomas Bailey, November 29, 1945. RG 27,
      Series 985: Pardons, 1960–1964, Box 2009, Ben Arledge Folder, MDAH.

61   Eddie Campbell to Governor J. P. Coleman, March 1, 1954, RG 27,
      Series 975: Paroles and Suspensions, 1956–1960, Box 1942, L. C. Black-
      well Folder, MDAH.

62   J. C. Jourdan to Hon. Fielding Wright, September 23, 1949, RG 27,
      Series 985: Pardons, 1960–1964, Box 2009, Jim Allen Folder, Records
      of the Office of the Governor, MDAH.

63   Jourdan to Wright, September 23, 1949.

64   Gerald W. Chatham to Gov. Hugh L. White, January 2, 1939, RG 27,
      Series 917: Pardon and Suspension Files, 1936–1940, Box 1647, Parker
      Allen Folder, Records of the Office of the Governor, MDAH.

65   "Everett Deplores System of Exploiting Convicts," *Delta Democrat-
      Times* (Greenville, MS), July 6, 1952. See also Garton, "Managing
      Mercy," 683–85; and Meyers, *Race, Labor, and Punishment in the
      New South*.

66   "Everett Deplores System of Exploiting Convicts."

67   Mrs. R. L. Exum to Governor Ross Barnett, February 24, 1962, RG
      27, Series 987: Penitentiary Correspondence, 1960–1964, Box 2031,
      Penitentiary Correspondence Folder C, Records of the Office of the
      Governor, MDAH.

68   Thad Thomas to Governor Ross Barnett, November 19, 1962, RG 27, Se-
      ries 987: Penitentiary Correspondence, 1960–1964, Folder D, Records
      of the Office of the Governor, MDAH.

69   W. F. Turman to Governor Hugh L. White, October 6, 1952. RG 27,
      Series 975: Paroles and Suspensions, 1956–1960, Box 1942, Jim Abram
      Folder, Records of the Office of the Governor, MDAH.

70   C. B. Henley to Ben Walley, June 30, 1959, Series 974: Penitentiary
      Correspondence, 1956–1060, Box 1941, Folder 1, Records of the Office
      of the Governor MDAH.

71   K. S. Archer to Hon. Fielding Wright, April 16, 1949, RG 27, Series
      2801: Pardon and Suspension Correspondence, 1946–1952, Box 32256,
      Folder 1, MDAH.

72   Sheriff C. B. Busby to Governor Fielding Wright, February 11, 1946, RG
      27, Series 938: Pardon and Suspension Files, 1948–1952, Box 1793, Sam
      Bland Folder, Records of the Office of the Governor, MDAH, emphasis
      added.

73 Thelma to Tom [Bailey], December 21, 1944, RG 27, Series 938: Pardon and Suspension Files, 1948–1952, Box 1810, Rosalie James Folder, Records of the Office of the Governor, MDAH.

74 Robert H. Powell to Gov. Hugh White, December 12, 1939, RG 27, Series 917: Pardon and Suspension Files, 1936–1940, Box 1647, Lewis Aldridge Folder, Records of the Office of the Governor, MDAH.

75 James B. Sykes to Jack Hancock, Secretary to the Governor, February 11, 1938, RG 27, Series 917: Pardon and Suspension Files, 1936–1940, Box 1647, Cliff Adams Folder, Records of the Office of the Governor, MDAH.

76 M. P. Moore to W. R. Burris, Educational Director, Mississippi State Penitentiary, May 27, 1949, RG 27, Series 985: Pardons, 1960–1964, Box 2024, Arthur Lee Small Folder, Records of the Office of the Governor, MDAH.

77 Letter from M. P. Moore to Governor Wright, May 27, 1949; Letter from M. P. Moore to W. R. Burris, RG 27, Series 985: Pardons, 1960–1964, Box 2024, Alfred Lee Small Folder, Records of the Office of the Governor, MDAH.

78 Lottie Mae Nichols, Welfare Agent, West Bolivar County, to Catherine McFarlane, State Dept. of Public Welfare, July 22, 1948, RG 27, Series 938: Pardon and Suspension Files, 1948–1952, Box 1810, Rosalie James Folder, Records of the Office of the Governor, MDAH.

79 "Everett Deplores System of Exploiting Convicts."

80 Catherine McFarlane to Alex McKeigney, Executive Secretary, Governor's Office, July 26, 1948, RG 27, Series 938: Pardon and Suspension Files, 1948–1952, Rosalie James Folder, Records of the Office of the Governor, MDAH.

81 C. A. Varnado to Hon. Gov. Hugh L. White, December 10, 1938, RG 27, Series 917: Governor White Pardon and Suspension Files, Box 1647, J. T. Alsobrook Folder, Records of the Office of the Governor, MDAH,

82 Julian Bland to H. A. Boren, Executive Counsel to Gov. Barnett, June 27, 1963, RG 27, Series 985: Pardons, 1960–1964, Box 2009, Louis Ashwander Folder, Records of the Office of the Governor, MDAH.

83 Wood, "Cole Blease's Pardoning Pen," 163.

84 Nellis, *Still Life.*

85 This was not unusual in the United States. In the early 1950s researchers found that the average time served by someone sentenced to life in prison was 14.3 years in Pennsylvania, 11.4 years in Texas, and ten years in Kentucky. See Giardini and Farrow, "The Paroling of Capital Offenders," 93.

86 "Open Letter: The Star of Hope," *Angolite*, September–October 1989, 55. See also "Fuqua Writing Three Louisiana Anti-Klan Laws," *Town Talk* (Alexandria, LA), May 5, 1924; Fairclough, *Race and Democracy*, 197.

87 "Open Letter," 57.

88 Carleton, *Politics and Punishment*, 115; "Open Letter," 57.

89   Foster, "When Mercy Seasons Justice," 1.

90   Foster, "The Meaning of Life: The Evolution and Impact of Natural Life Sentences in Louisiana," *Angolite,* July/August 1995, 16–23.

91   "Ex-Governors, Long to Study Prisoner Aid," *Shreveport (LA) Times,* January 16, 1959.

92   Perkinson, "Angola and the Agony of Prison Reform"; Westbrook Pegler, "Fair Enough," *Wilmington (DE) Morning News,* July 4, 1951; "20 Steps to Improve Angola Asked by Group," *Shreveport (LA) Times,* April 20, 1951. Chase, *We Are Not Slaves,* 47–57, also documents a crisis of self-mutilation among Texas prisoners in the same era and reformers' efforts to prevent it.

93   James McLean, "Four Former Governors to Aid Study of Prison," *Shreveport (LA) Times,* September 14, 1958.

94   "Jones Sees New Rehabilitation Plan in Prisons," *Crowly (LA) Post-Signal,* August 27, 1959, 2; Wilbert Rideau, "Conversations with the Dead," in Rideau and Wikberg, *Life Sentences,* 61.

95   "Long Freeing Charlie Frazier," *Shreveport (LA) Journal,* May 25, 1959.

96   Compiled from Collection No. 1994-017, Pardons: 1944–72, Box 6, Louisiana State Archives.

97   Langan et al., *Historical Statistics on Prisoners,* 10.

98   Foster, "Ten-Six," 2.

99   "Don't Sell Us Short on Hope," editorial, *Angolite,* October 24, 1953, 4.

100   Nelson, "A History of Penal Reform in Angola, Part I: The Immovable Object," *Angolite,* September/October, 2009, 17.

101   "Extra Arouses All Angola," *Angolite,* October 31, 1953, 1–2.

102   "Pardon Board Okays 111!," *Angolite,* March 30, 1955, 1.

103   State v. Shaffer, 260 La. 605, 257 So.2d 121, 134 (1971).

104   "1930 Escapee from Angola Is Arrested," *The Shreveport Times* (LA), April 12, 1955.

105   "Run-Away Brought Back after 25 Free Years," *Angolite,* April 23, 1955, 1; "Convict Caught after 25 Years," *The Gazette* (Ville Platte, LA), April 21, 1955.

106   "Run-Away Brought Back after 25 Free Years," 5; "Time Served Is Granted Willie Gray," *Angolite,* October 26, 1955, 1.

107   "Wallace Refuses Subpoena Given to Servant," *Troy (AL) Messenger,* May 29, 1963.

2. FREEDOM STRUGGLES

1   Lewis B. Hopper to Ross Barnett, October 31, 1962, RG 27, Series 987: Penitentiary Correspondence, 1960–1964, Box 2032, Folder H, Records of the Office of the Governor, Mississippi Department of Archives and History (hereafter MDAH).

2 Parchman record of #29,067—Dewey McCormick, RG 49, Series 1567: Convict Registers 1874–1981, Book A-B, Microfilm Roll 15,223, Department of Corrections–Penitentiary Records, MDAH.

3 Murakawa, "The Origins of the Carceral Crisis," 238.

4 Brückmann, "Citizens' Councils, Conservatism and White Supremacy," 12.

5 Murakawa, "The Origins of the Carceral Crisis," 236. See also Murakawa, *The First Civil Right*; and Flamm, *Law and Order*.

6 Oshinsky, *Worse Than Slavery*, 35.

7 John Stennis, quoted in "Stennis Seeks Ban on 'Freedom Riders,'" *Clarion-Ledger* (Jackson, MS), May 24, 1961.

8 "Agitation Continues," editorial, *Greenwood (MS) Commonwealth*, June 13, 1961.

9 Fred Jones to Governor Ross Barnett, June 17, 1961, Series 987: Penitentiary Correspondence, 1960–1964, Box 2031, Folder Penitentiary Correspondence B, Records of the Office of the Governor, MDAH; Arsenault, *Freedom Riders*, 233–34.

10 Berger, *Captive Nation*, 44, argues that "mass arrests of political activists" in the South during the civil rights struggle "provided a dry run for mass incarceration" and notes that officials in Jackson "used civil rights activity to justify the purchase of new weapons—including a tank—for the city police force."

11 Ross Barnett, quoted in "Minnesota Heads, Barnett Confer on 'Freedom Riders,'" *Daily Advertiser* (Lafayette, LA), July 7, 1961.

12 Jerry Mitchell, "Activist Was atop Hit List, Confidant Says," *Clarion-Ledger* (Jackson, MS), December 18, 1990.

13 Pearl Barnett, interview by David Sansing, June 16, 1972, David Sansing Collection, Series 10, Folder 12, Archives and Special Collections, J. D. Williams Library, University of Mississippi.

14 Ross Barnett, interview by David Sansing, June 16, 1972, David Sansing Collection, Series 10, Folder 12, Archives and Special Collections, J. D. Williams Library, University of Mississippi.

15 "Barnett Issues Two Pardons, 32 Commutations of Sentence," *Hattiesburg (MS) American*, January 22, 1964.

16 Ross Barnett, quoted in "Barnett Chides Attorneys on Way Criticism Voiced," *Clarion-Ledger* (Jackson, MS), February 5, 1961.

17 "Affairs of State," *Clarion-Ledger* (Jackson, MS), February 15, 1965.

18 "Respect for Law Urged as Crime Rate Mounts," editorial, *Clarion-Ledger* (Jackson, MS), June 9, 1963.

19 "Perils of False Compassion," *Hattiesburg (MS) American*, January 18, 1967.

20 Paul B. Johnson Jr., Excerpts from Address of Governor Paul B. Johnson Jr. to the Mississippi Legislature, January 5, 1966, RG 27, Series 2808: Mississippi Crime Commission Documents, Box 12453, Folder 1, Item 3, Records of the Office of the Governor, MDAH.

21 "Johnson Gives Pardons to 16," *Clarion-Ledger* (Jackson, MS), January 16, 1968.

22 C. E. Breazeale and Columbus B. Hopper, "Discharges from the Penitentiary," September 29, 1967, RG 27, Series 2808: Mississippi Crime Commission Documents, Box 12453, Folder 2, MDAH.

23 "Voice of the People: Dope Pushers Merit No Clemency," *Clarion-Ledger* (Jackson, MS), December 27, 1971.

24 John Bell Williams, quoted in "JBW Gives Gift to 12 Imprisoned Drug Users," *Enterprise-Journal* (McComb, MS), December 22, 1971.

25 "Grand Jury Takes Broadside at JBW; Scores Former Governor for Abuse of Powers of Executive Clemency," *Hattiesburg (MS) American*, January 28, 1972.

26 "Board, Not Governor, Should Issue Pardons," *Clarion-Ledger* (Jackson, MS), December 29, 1972.

27 "Obviously Wrong," *Delta Democrat-Times* (Greenville, MS), January 30, 1972.

28 "Mansion Servants, Few Others Receive Pardons," *Clarion-Ledger* (Jackson, MS), January 25, 1972.

29 "Mississippi Notebook," *Clarion-Ledger* (Jackson, MS), January 21, 1972.

30 Quoted in "Jones Criticizes Waller," *Greenwood (MS) Commonwealth*, March 19, 1975.

31 "Davis Hands House 34 Bills, Including Segregation Moves," *Times* (Shreveport, LA), May 18, 1960.

32 Brückmann, "Citizens' Councils, Conservatism and White Supremacy," 12.

33 Wilbert Rideau, "The Editor's Pen: What's Going On?," *Lifer*, November–December 1973, 6–7, National Museum of African American History and Culture, https://edan.si.edu/slideshow/viewer/?damspath =/Public_Sets/NMAAHC/NMAAHC_Slideshows/2016_139_2_1.

34 "The Effect of Dunn," *Angolite*, April 1982, 19.

35 Before the Supreme Court's decision striking down the death penalty in 1972, only seven states had statutes for life without the possibility of parole. By 1990, thirty-three states had established such statutes for a wide range of crimes. See Nellis, *Life Goes On*, 3.

36 Burk Foster, "The Meaning of Life," *Angolite*, July/August 1995, 20.

37 "Lafayette DA Joins Criticism of Parole Board," *Shreveport (LA) Journal*, February 26, 1976.

38 Jessica Pishko, "Prosecutors Are Banding Together to Prevent Criminal Justice Reform," *Nation*, October 18, 2017, https://www.thenation.com /article/archive/prosecutors-are-banding-together-to-prevent-criminal -justice-reform/; see also Pfaff, *Locked In*.

39 Harry Connick Sr., Remarks before the Governor's Parole, Probation, and Rehabilitation Commission, James L. Stovall Papers, Louisiana and Lower Mississippi Valley Collections, LSU Libraries, Louisiana State University, Baton Rouge, Mss. 4467 (hereafter Stovall Papers), Series II: Prisons, 1975–1981, Subseries 1: Governor's Pardon, Parole, and Rehabilitation Commission, 1976–1981, Box 3.

40 Louisiana District Attorneys' Association, Position Statement on the Recommendations of the Governor's Commission on Pardon, Parole and Rehabilitation, Stovall Papers, Series II: Prisons, 1975–1981, Subseries 1: Governor's Pardon, Parole, and Rehabilitation Commission, 1976–1981, Box 3.

41 "Wilbert Rideau: Is Pardon Right?," editorial, *Daily World* (Opelousas, LA), December 20, 1984.

42 Governor's Pardon, Parole, and Rehabilitation Commission, *Staff Analysis of Executive Clemency in Louisiana*, 127. In 1982, when Louisiana housed eleven thousand prisoners, only 694 paroles were granted. By contrast, Georgia, with a prison population of over fifteen thousand, released 5,316 parolees that year; Virginia issued 5,165 out of a prison population of ten thousand; Tennessee's nine thousand prisoners were reduced by 3,614 due to parole. See "The Crowded Cage," *Angolite*, November–December 1983, 44.

   Louisiana and Pennsylvania are the only states that mandate a sentence of life without the possibility of parole for second-degree murder. Richard A. Webster, "Thousands Are Serving Life Sentences in Louisiana; A New Case Could Give Them the Chance to Appeal," *Washington Post*, June 18, 2020, https://www.washingtonpost.com /national/thousands-are-serving-life-sentences-in-louisiana-a-new -case-could-give-them-the-chance-to-appeal/2020/06/17/facd58f2 -afff-11ea-8758-bfd1d045525a_story.html.

43 Bennett, "We All Pay."

44 Harry Connick Sr., quoted in Woody Baird, "Bureau for Repeat Offenders," *Morning Call* (Allentown, PA), October 30, 1977.

45 "Habitual Offenders May Lose Reduced Sentence," *St. Mary and Franklin (LA) Banner-Tribune*, June 27, 1975.

46 Harry Connick Sr., quoted in "N.O. Prosecution Loopholes Closing," *Shreveport (LA) Journal*, January 19, 1976.

47 "Rationale for Alternative Proposed Legislation on Parole Release and Decision Making," November 29 1978, Stovall Papers, Series II: Prisons, 1975–1981, Subseries 1: Governor's Pardon, Parole, and Rehabilitation Commission, 1976–1981, Box 3.

48 Johnnie A. Jones, quoted in Rideau, "Lifers of Angola," *Angolite*, April/ May, 1974, 14.

49   Governor's Pardon, Parole, and Rehabilitation Commission, *Staff Analysis of Executive Clemency in Louisiana*, 137. Edwards was himself convicted of bribery and extortion during his last term in office and served more than eight years of a ten-year sentence in a federal prison.

50   William H. Brown, editorial, *Angolite*, December 1973, 1.

51   Jackson, "On the Pardon Board," *Lifer*, January–March, 1974, 6.

52   "Finch Claims Pill Use 'Rediculous'" [*sic*], *Clarksdale (MS) Press Register*, February 26, 1980.

53   "Attorney General Says Clemency Act Routine," *Greenwood (MS) Commonwealth*, January 29 1980.

54   Pelot-Hobbs, "Scaling Up or Scaling Back?," 428.

55   In New York, for example, the passage of mandatory sentencing laws during the administration of Governor Nelson D. Rockefeller (1959–73) was not accompanied by a legislative commitment to funding prison expansion, and voters rejected bond issues to finance prison construction. Significantly, the bond issue garnered more support from the New York City metropolitan area than from rural counties; see Jacobs, "The Politics of Prison Expansion," 218–19. On the history of "prison overcrowding" and its relationship to "get tough" policies, see Rosen, "'It's at the State and Local Level That Problems Exist.'"

56   Guetzkow and Schoon, "If You Build It, They Will Fill It," 402.

57   Bleich, "The Politics of Prison Crowding," 1146, 1172; Holt v. Sarver, 309 F. Supp. 362 (E. E. Ark. 1970); Kessel, "Unconstitutional Prison Overcrowding"; Chung, "Prison Overcrowding."

58   Powell, "A Dilemma," 16.

59   "Senate Okays Prison Bill," *Clarion-Ledger* (Jackson, MS), March 31, 1976; "Only One Senator Votes against Bill," *Yazoo (MS) Herald*, March 31, 1977. On court orders to improve prison conditions, see "Timetable Set Up at Prison," *Clarksdale (MS) Press Register*, June 9, 1976.

60   "Ault Tightens Rules for Christmas Furloughs," *Hattiesburg (MS) American*, January 21, 1977.

61   "Penal System Locked to Deadlines," *Delta Democrat-Times* (Greenville, MS), January 2, 1977.

62   "The Crowded Cage," 36.

63   Though Guetzkow and Schoon, "If You Build It, They Will Fill It," 402, 406, criticize scholars who "lump tough on crime with prison construction as if they were one in the same," they assume that corrections professionals will tend to advocate for greater prison capacity. Bleich, "The Politics of Prison Crowding," 1155, also assumes that prison officials as a constituency have an interest in prisons' perpetual growth.

64   William D. Leeke, quoted in Wayne King, "Prison Officials Call for Reform," *New York Times*, January 25, 1976.

65   Anne Q. Hoy, "Circuit Judges Discuss Justice from Their Side," *Clarion-Ledger* (Jackson, MS), November 23, 1980; "Winter Defends Early Release of Inmates," *Greenwood (MS) Commonwealth*, July 24, 1981.

66   Ron Welch, quoted in Stephen Gettinger, "Mississippi Has Come a Long Way, But It Had a Long Way to Come," *Corrections*, June 1979, 7.

67   L. C. Dorsey to William C. Hammack, August 21, 1980, RG 27, Series 70, Subject Files of William Winter, Box 2171, Folder 2, Correspondence Re: Penitentiary (Parchman), 1979–1980, Records of the Office of the Governor, MDAH. Dorsey, who had a PhD in social work, was a former colleague of Fannie Lou Hammer. Dorsey's thirty-six-page self-published book, *Cold Steel* (1983) was an exposé of conditions inside Parchman.

68   Darwin M. Maples to Governor William Winter, July 1, 1981, RG 27, Series 70, Subject Files of William Winter, Box 2171, Folder Correspondence Re: Penitentiary (Parchman), 1980–1981, Records of the Office of the Governor, MDAH, emphasis added; Theodore Smith to Governor William Winter, April 15, 1981, RG 27, Series 70, Subject Files of William Winter, Box 2171, Folder Correspondence Re: Penitentiary, 1981, Records of the Office of the Governor, MDAH.

69   Jo Ann Klein, "Winter Begins Inmate Pre-release Program," *Clarion-Ledger* (Jackson, MS), July 16, 1980.

70   William Winter, "Notes for Governor Winter's Speech to SCCA, 1982," Series 70, Subject Files of William Winter, Box 2154, Corrections Folder, MDAH.

71   "Governor Defends Prisoner Program," *Clarksdale (MS) Press Register*, July 28, 1981.

72   "A Resolution Memorializing the Governor to Give Thoughtful and Careful Consideration to the Background and Nature of the Crime Committed Prior to Releasing Convicted Felons from the Mississippi State Penitentiary at Parchman," Mississippi Senate Resolution 1, 1982.

73   James Saggus, "Prison Task Force Favors Veto Law Repeal," *Clarksdale (MS) Press Register*, January 5, 1982, 1.

74   "Legislation 'Soft on Crime'?," *Hattiesburg American*, January 23, 1982, 3.

75   Governor William Winter to William H. Morris, December 28, 1982, RG 27, Series 70, Subject Files of William Winter, Box 217, Folder Correspondence from the Governor's Office at the Mansion, Corrections, 1981–1982, Records of the Office of the Governor, MDAH.

76   Governor William Winter to Wayne B. Fancher, November 22, 1982, RG 27, Subject Files of William Winter, Series 70, Box 217, Folder Correspondence from the Governor's Office at the Mansion, Corrections, 1981–1982, Records of the Office of the Governor, MDAH.

77   Mississippi Board of Corrections, Statements of Policy, RG 27, Series 70, Box 217, Subject Files of William Winter, Folder Corrections, Records of the Office of the Governor, MDAH.

78 Brown, Keiser, and Humphries, *Guide to Executive Clemency*; M. Kay
     Harris with Becky Siebens, "Reducing Prison Overcrowding: An Over-
     view of Options," draft submitted to the National Institute of Correc-
     tions, July 1981, "For Governors" page, RG 27, Series 70, Subject Files of
     William Winter, Box 2154, Correspondence from Governor's Office at
     the Mansion, 1981–1982, Folder, Records of the Office of the Gover-
     nor, MDAH. Harris was a founding member of the Inside-Out Prison
     Exchange Program; Bonnie L. Cook, "M. Kay Harris, 71, Cofounded
     the Noted Inside-Out Prison Exchange Program" (obituary), *Phila-
     delphia Inquirer*, December 4, 2018, https://www.inquirer.com/philly
     /obituaries/m-kay-harris-71-cofounded-the-noted-inside-out-prison
     -exchange-program-20181204.html.
79 "The Edge of Madness," *Angolite*, July 1986, 34.
80 Roy Reed, "Louisiana's Jails Are Being Packed," *New York Times*, Sep-
     tember 16, 1975.
81 Pelot-Hobbs, "Louisiana's Turn to Mass Incarceration."
82 Pelot-Hobbs, "Louisiana's Turn to Mass Incarceration."
83 Pelot-Hobbs, "Scaling Up or Scaling Back?," 434.
84 Pelot-Hobbs, "Louisiana's Turn to Mass Incarceration."
85 Edwin Edwards, quoted in "Group to Study Angola Decentralization,"
     Town Talk (Alexandria, LA), April 2, 1975.
86 Pelot-Hobbs, "Louisiana's Turn to Mass Incarceration"; "Pardon Board
     and Gold Seals," *Angolite*, February 1974, 10.
87 Recommendations of Governor's Pardon, Parole, and Rehabilitation
     Commission, December 16, 1981, Stovall Papers, Series II: Prisons,
     1975–1981, Subseries 1: Governor's Pardon, Parole, and Rehabilitation
     Commission, 1976–1981, Box 3.
88 Lloyd Hoyle, quoted in "Overcrowding Cited: Potential Crisis Re-
     ported at Angola," *Shreveport (LA) Times*, March 29, 1975.
89 C. Murray Henderson, quoted in Flanagan and Rideau, "Lifers of
     Angola," *Angolite*, January, 1974, 4–5. Warden Henderson was right, as
     he himself *did* end up committing a crime, the attempted murder of his
     wife; Butler, *Weep for the Living*.
90 "To End the Games," *Angolite*, November–December 1981, n.p.
91 Ross Maggio, quoted in "Warden, Taken Captive, Foils Inmates' Escape
     Bid," *New York Times*, November 1, 1982; "The Crowded Cage," 51.
92 "Resolution on Double Bunk Beds," n.d., Stovall Papers, Series II:
     Prisons, 1975–1981, Subseries 2: Prison Reform, Box 3, p. 1. Rev. James
     Stovall was a white Protestant who, like other religious leaders in the
     South, was committed to civil rights and improving social conditions
     for vulnerable citizens. A US Navy chaplain during World War II,
     Stovall became the co-organizer of the Louisiana Coalition against
     Racism and Nazism in 1989, which was founded in response to the

election of David Duke to the Louisiana State Legislature; "Biographi-
cal/Historical Note," in *James L. Stovall Papers (Mss 4467): Inventory*, 4,
https://www.lib.lsu.edu/sites/default/files/sc/findaid/4467.pdf.

93 Edwin Edwards, quoted in "Edwards May Request Forgotten Men
Study," *Daily Review* (Morgan City, LA), February 23, 1984.

94 Matthew Braniff, quoted in "Purse-Snatcher Gets 40 Years," *Town Talk*
(Alexandria, LA), May 27, 1984.

95 Edwin Edwards, quoted in "Edwards Pledges Prison Changes," *Daily
World* (Opelousas, LA), May 21, 1984.

96 "The Crisis Reports," *Angolite*, March–April 1985, 26.

97 Tonry, "Federal Sentencing Reform since 1984," 99; Murakawa, *The
First Civil Right*, 91.

98 McCay, "It's Time to Rehabilitate the Sentencing Process," 223.

99 Murakawa, *The First Civil Right*, 110.

100 Tonry, "Federal Sentencing Reform since 1984," 106.

101 Murakawa, "The Racial Antecedents to Federal Sentencing Guidelines,"
475, demonstrates that the roots of the Federal Sentencing Reform Act
lie in conservative, white supremacist attacks on judges after the 1954
decision in *Brown v. Board of Education*, denouncing them as "activist,
tyrannical, elitist, out of touch with American values, and sympathetic
to subversive groups."

102 The phrase "the equality of the graveyard over the equality of the
vineyard" was originally used in Caminker, "A Norm-Based Remedial Model," 1185, and it was subsequently used by Albie Sachs, chief
justice of the South African Constitutional Court in the landmark
opinion requiring the recognition of same-sex marriages in South
Africa; Minister of Home Affairs v. Fourie and Another, [2005] ZACC
19, 2005.

103 Prisoners' rights activists also criticized indeterminate sentencing as arbitrary and discriminatory, charging that the rhetoric of rehabilitation
was "hypocritical legitimization"; Kohler-Hausmann, *Getting Tough*,
223. See also Berger, *Captive Nation*; and Mitford, *Kind and Usual
Punishment*, chap. 12. Murakawa, *The First Civil Right*, chap. 3, explains
how prisoners' calls for fair parole practices turned into mandatory
sentencing guidelines.

104 Kohler-Hasumann, *Getting Tough*.

105 "More People Arming Themselves to Protect against the Rising Tide of
Danger, Violent Crime," *Sun Herald* (Gulfport, MS), August 1, 1994.

106 "The Crowded Cage," 36; throughout this piece the authors track the
contemporary panic about crime in relation to actual crime statistics,
hold the news media to account for fanning this fear with disproportionate and distorted news coverage of crime, and make parallels to
earlier hysterias that led to disastrous results, such as the lynching of

Leo Frank in Atlanta in 1913 and noting, "If journalistic irresponsibility was a crime, many television news directors would be serving life sentences as habitual offenders." See also Macek, *Urban Nightmares.*

107 Bleich, "The Politics of Prison Crowding," 1146.

108 Foster, ""Pardons and Politics: How It All Went Wrong," *Angolite,* January–February 1988, 36.

109 Jack Wardlaw, quoted in Foster, "Pardons and Politics," 38.

110 James Stovall, quoted in Foster, "Pardons and Politics," 40.

111 Maginnis, *The Last Hayride,* 208.

112 Edwin Edwards, quoted in "Edwin Edwards Gives Campaign a Personal Touch," *Town Talk* (Alexandria, LA), October 2, 1983.

113 "Treen Hits Pardons: Chiefs Give Edwards Nod," *Shreveport (LA) Times,* October 7, 1983.

114 Rideau, *In the Place of Justice,* 171.

115 Caton Brooks, quoted in Rideau, "Lifers of Angola," 15.

3. THE HOUSE OF THE DYING

1 "Rideau's Attorneys Plan to Appeal Case," *Shreveport (LA) Times,* December 5, 1964.

2 "Rideau Trial Set to Start for 3rd Time," *Shreveport (LA) Journal,* January 5, 1970.

3 Frank Salter, quoted in "Rideau's Attorneys Plan to Appeal Case," *Shreveport (LA) Times,* December 5, 1964.

4 "Rideau Convicted," *Town Talk* (Alexandria, LA), January 8, 1970.

5 "Decision Pleases State Officials," *Crowley (LA) Post-Herald,* June 30, 1972.

6 Gilson, "The Inside Scoop," 71.

7 Butler and Henderson, *Angola, Louisiana State Penitentiary,* 135; Thomas, "Conversations with Literary Ex-Cons: Billy Sinclair."

8 George Colt, "The Most Rehabilitated Prisoner in America," *Life,* March 1993, 69–76.

9 Colt, "The Most Rehabilitated Prisoner in America," 76; Rideau, *In the Place of Justice,* 86–87.

10 Buddy Roemer, quoted in "Roemer Rejects Rideau Clemency," *Crowley (LA) Post-Signal,* January 10, 1992, 2.

11 Wilbert Rideau, quoted in David C. Anderson, "The Redemption of Wilbert Rideau: The Man Changed, But Then Society Altered the Rules," *New York Times,* March 13, 1985.

12 Wilbert Rideau, quoted in untitled article (clipping), *Shreveport (LA) Sun,* December 15, 1988, James L. Stovall Papers, Louisiana and Lower Mississippi Valley Collections, LSU Libraries, Louisiana State Uni-

versity, Baton Rouge, Mss. 4467 (hereafter Stovall Papers), Series II: Prisons, 1975–1981, Subseries 4, Box 3, Wilbert Rideau, 1978–1989.

13 Bornstein and Nemeth, "Jurors' Perception of Violence," 84. Rosen, "The 'Especially Heinous' Aggravating Circumstance in Capital Cases," 945, argues that the definition and application of "the especially heinous aggravating circumstance" as a standard in capital cases, "rather than channeling discretion, has broadened it; instead of limiting the opportunity for arbitrary, capricious, and discriminatory factors to enter the capital sentencing process, has expanded it; rather than providing a meaningful basis for distinguishing those few cases deserving the death penalty from those cases in which death should not be imposed, has allowed death to be imposed at the complete discretion of the sentence."

14 Rick Bryant, quoted in Colt, "The Most Rehabilitated Prisoner in America," 74.

15 Dora McCain, quoted in William K. Stevens, "Vivid Portrayals of Prison Life Bring Recognition to Two Inmates," *New York Times*, March 9, 1980.

16 Newton, "Prison, Where Is Thy Victory?" 22; Berger, *Captive Nation*, 98. Mitford, *Kind and Usual Punishment*, 90, notes complaints by prisoners regarding rehabilitation and that the indeterminate sentence was a "potent psychological instrument of manipulation and control" as well as arbitrary and racist in its application. See also Kamerling, *Capital and Convict*.

17 Quigley, "Louisiana Angola Penitentiary," 196; "Elayn Hunt: She Pushes for Penal Reform," *Shreveport (LA) Journal*, January 4, 1974. On other reforms, see Pelot-Hobbs, "Scaling Up or Scaling Back?"; and Foster, "Angola in the Seventies," in Foster, Rideau, and Dennis, *The Wall is Strong*, 45–60.

18 John Hill, "Mistrust Delays Pardon Decisions," *Shreveport (LA) Times*, August 23, 1998.

19 Burk Foster, "The Meaning of Life: The Evolution and Impact of Natural Life Sentences in Louisiana," *Angolite,* July/August 1995, 20.

20 "Life: No Rhyme, No Reason," *Angolite*, September–October 1982, 41.

21 "Rationale for Alternative Proposed Legislation on Parole Release Decision-Making," Stovall Papers, Series II: Prisons, 1975–1981, Subseries 1: Governor's Pardon, Parole, and Rehabilitation Commission, 1976–1981, Box 3.

22 David C. Treen, quoted in "Treen to Be Tough on Pardons," *Shreveport (LA) Times*, March 9, 1980.

23 While this number demonstrates Treen's reluctance to grant clemency relative to earlier governors, it is startling to compare it with the total number of clemencies at twenty-one, issued by Governor Bobby Jindal

(2008–16). Of these, one was, per southern tradition, for Jindal's personal butler. Elizabeth Crisp and David Mitchell, "See the List: Jindal Grants Clemency to Personal Butler—A Convicted Killer—Plus 20 Other People," *Advocate* (Baton Rouge, LA), January 13, 2016, https://www.theadvocate.com/baton_rouge/news/politics/see-the-list-jindal -grants-clemency-to-personal-butlera-convicted-killer/article_fac55ac5 -4692-5dc5-bff7-8ca12b75947f.html.

24 David C. Treen, quoted in Foster, "'Pardons and Politics, *Angolite*, January/February 1988, 40.

25 Foster, "When Mercy Seasons Justice," 5.

26 Wilbert Rideau, "Angola's History," in Rideau and Wikberg, *Life Sentences*, 38.

27 "The Forgotten Men," *Angolite*, January 1980, 30; Tommy Mason, "The Lifers Association," *Angolite*, September 1982, 48.

28 Wickberg, quoted in "The Forgotten Men," January 1980, 33, emphasis in the original.

29 Wikberg, *A Graphic and Illustrative History*.

30 "The Forgotten Men," *Angolite*, May 1980, 45.

31 Michael Glover, "Opening the 10-6 Floodgate," *Angolite*, July– August 1990, 60. It is worth pointing out that many defendants took plea deals, foregoing a trial by jury, with the understanding that they would be released after ten years and six months. Legal scholars have argued that plea deals were frowned on until the 1970s as corrupt and immoral because they threatened defendants' rights to a trial. Now the criminal justice system depends on plea deals to function, and 94 percent of state criminal cases are resolved through plea deals. See Caldwell, "Coercive Plea Bargaining"; and Hessick, *Punishment without Trial*.

32 "The Forgotten Men," May 1980, 26.

33 Joseph White, quoted in "The Forgotten Men," May 1980, 27.

34 Herman Smith, quoted in "The Forgotten Men," May 1980, 28–29.

35 Kennedy, "'Reflections from Exile,'" 40.

36 Bill Brown, "Education is in," *Angolite*, April 1975, 4.

37 Wilbert Rideau and Billy W. Sinclair, "Getting It Together," *Angolite*, March–April 1979, 2–3.

38 Burk Foster, "Louisiana Penal Crisis: The Quest for Alternatives," *Angolite*, July–August 1988, 48.

39 "News Briefs," *Angolite*, January 1989, n.p.

40 Wilbert Rideau and Ron Wikberg, "The Omen," *Angolite*, May– June 1989, 19. Buddy Roemer used the slogan "Roemer Revolution" in his campaign against Edwards, and in 1991 he switched his party affiliation from Democrat to Republican just in time for the next gubernatorial election, whose candidates included both Edwards and David Duke.

41   Ron Wikberg, "Clemency and Politics," *Angolite*, July–August 1989, 22.

42   "The Crisis Reports," *Angolite*, March–April 1985, 23–27.

43   Ron Wikberg and Wilbert Rideau, "Suicide: The End of the Rope," *Angolite*, May–June 1988, 14.

44   "Angola in State of Emergency," *Shreveport (LA) Journal*, June 22, 1989.

45   Associated Press, "Angola Emergency: Prison Editor Rideau Feels Politics May Be behind Federal Judge's Order," *Town Talk* (Alexandria, LA), June 26, 1989.

46   Wilbert Rideau and Ron Wikberg, "The Omen, II," *Angolite*, July 1989, 10.

47   Linda Ashton, "Gov. Roemer Faulted in Angola Prison Strife," *Shreveport (LA) Times*, July 24, 1989.

48   C. Paul Phelps, quoted in Douglas Dennis, "Suicide in Prison: The Hanging Game," *Angolite*, March–April 1993, 40.

49   Rideau and Wikberg, "The Omen, II," 11.

50   Rideau, *In the Place of Justice*, 210, 199.

51   Francis "Corky" Clifton, quoted in Ashton, "Gov. Roemer Faulted in Angola Prison Strife."

52   John Hill, "Prisoners Blame Hopelessness," *Shreveport (LA) Times*, June 25, 1989.

53   Rideau and Wikberg, "The Omen," 19.

54   Wallace McDonald, quoted in Kennedy, "'Reflections from Exile,'" 37.

55   Buddy Roemer, quoted in Hill, "Prisoners Blame Hopelessness."

56   John Ortego, quoted in Rideau and Wikberg, "The Omen," 20.

57   Hilton Butler, quoted in Robert Morgan, "Money Solution at Angola, Says Head of Budget Panel," *Town Talk* (Alexandria, LA), September 12, 1989; Rideau and Wikberg, "The Omen," 21.

58   Hilton Butler, quoted in Rideau and Wikberg, "The Omen," 21.

59   Shihadeh, Nordyke, and Reed, *Fact Sheet*, 1.

60   Wilbert Rideau, "Conversations with the Dead," in Rideau and Wikberg, *Life Sentences*, 67–68.

61   Gottschalk, *Caught*, 177; Families against Mandatory Minimums, "The Older You Get: Why Incarcerating the Elderly Makes Us Less Safe," n.d., accessed December 12, 2022, https://famm.org/wp-content /uploads/Aging-out-of-crime-FINAL.pdf.

62   Bob Downing, quoted in "House of the Dying," *Angolite*, March–April 1989, 32.

63   Wikberg and Foster, "The Long-Termers," 12.

64   Rideau, *In the Place of Justice*, 194.

65   James Poindexter, quoted in Rideau, "Conversations with the Dead," 63.

66   Peggi Gresham, quoted in Rideau, "Conversations with the Dead," 64.

67   Rideau, "Conversations with the Dead," 64.

68   Pelot-Hobbs, "Organized Inside and Out," 206.

69 Henderson, "What I Learned about Voting Rights." *Counsel substitute* is the term given to incarcerated people who are trained to represent fellow inmates. This legal representation is crucial, as Louisiana prisoners have no right to legal counsel once their conviction is final; Schwartzapfel, "For $12 of Commissary, He Got Ten Years off His Sentence."

70 Lane Nelson, "LCIW Lifers," *Angolite*, March–April 1995, 40.

71 Pelot-Hobbs, "Organizing Inside and Out," 208, 211.

72 Foster, "Louisiana Penal Crisis," 48.

73 Chase, *We Are Not Slaves*, 90–93, discusses the use of African American men incarcerated in Texas prisons as "houseboys," domestic servants to top prison administrators and wardens well into the 1970s. In 2017, a journalist noted that prisoners work in state government buildings in Alabama, Arkansas, Georgia, Louisiana, Missouri, Nebraska, and Oklahoma; Calacal, "At Least Seven States."

74 Paul B. Johnson Jr., quoted in Billy Skelton, "Prisoners Serve Quietly, Effectively at Mansion," *Clarion-Ledger* (Jackson, MS), August 4, 1967.

75 Paul B. Johnson Jr. and Carroll Waller, interview by David Sansing, February 4, 1975, David Sansing Collection, Series 10, Folder 10, Archives and Special Collections, J. D. Williams Library, University of Mississippi.

76 "Going Too Far?," *Monroe (LA) News-Star*, April 17, 1968.

77 Skelton, "Prisoners Serve Quietly, Effectively."

78 Butler and Henderson, *Angola, Louisiana State Penitentiary*, 51.

79 John West, quoted in "Former Governors Talk about Trusties Working at Mansion," *Index-Journal* (Greenwood, SC), January 14, 2001.

80 Maginnis, *The Last Hayride*, 129.

81 Frank Gholar, quoted in Kathy Eyre, "Governor's Mansion Gives Murderers Freedom," *Hattiesburg (MS) American*, April 17, 1988.

82 Eyre, "Governor's Mansion Gives Murderers Freedom."

83 Wilbert Rideau, interview with the author, February 1, 2012.

84 Martin, *With Edwards in the Governor's Mansion*, 201, 200, 204.

85 Martin, *With Edwards in the Governor's Mansion*, 220–23, 225, emphasis in the original.

86 Martin, *With Edwards in the Governor's Mansion*, 208.

87 Martin, *With Edwards in the Governor's Mansion*, 225, 324, 333.

88 "Pharmaceutical Society Asks Investigation into Pardon," *Crowley (LA) Post-Signal*, February 17, 1980.

89 Angelo Deenes, letter to the editor, *Morning Advocate* (Baton Rouge, LA), January 25, 1980. Courts have recently decided, on the basis of expert testimony from cognitive psychologists, that even late adolescents are constitutionally different from adults in their levels of culpability because of differences in brain development and therefore should be sentenced differently. See Graham v. Florida 560 U.S. 48 (2010) (categorical ban on LWOP for juveniles convicted of non-homicide crimes);

Miller v. Alabama 567 U.S. 460 (2012) (prohibited mandatory LWOP for juveniles but stopped short of total ban); Montgomery v. Louisiana (577 U.S. ___ (2016) (Miller applies retroactively to defendants sentenced to LWOP before 2012). See also Marshall, "*Miller v. Alabama* and the Problem of Prediction."

90   Edwin Edwards, quoted in "Edwards Explains Pardon," *Morning Advocate* (Baton Rouge, LA), January 18, 1980.

91   Edwin Edwards, quoted in "Edwards Says Pardons Right," *Daily Advertiser* (Lafayette, LA), March 5, 1980.

92   For a convincing analysis of how civil rights liberals' attacks on racial violence and calls for race-neutral carceral machinery contributed to the rise of mass incarceration, see Murakawa, *The First Civil Right*.

93   Rideau, "The Dynamics of Parole: Myths, Politics, Realities," in Rideau and Wickberg, *Life Sentences*, 134.

94   Brad Lott, quoted in "No More Parole for Some Crimes," *Sun Herald* (Gulfport, MS), August 21, 1994.

95   "Senate Votes $52.9 Million for 4,316 New Prison Beds," *Sun Herald* (Gulfport, MS), August 17, 1994, C2.

96   "Special Session Looks at Crime," *Sun Herald* (Gulfport, MS), August 14, 1994, C3.

97   Kirk Fordice, State of the State Address, January 5, 1994, quoted in "Mississippi Can Do Anything Now," *Sun Herald* (Gulfport, MS), January 13, 1994.

98   Mike Moore, quoted in "The Wheels of Justice Jam," *Sun Herald* (Gulfport, MS), May 3, 1994.

99   Foster, "When Mercy Seasons Justice," 5.

100 "Inside Angola," *Angolite*, January–February 1994, 9.

101 Douglas Dennis, "Victim Boards," *Angolite*, July–August 1996, 9; "Clemency Clarification," *Angolite*, September–October 1997, 41; Ben Daughtery, "Truth in Clemency," *Angolite*, July–August 1998, 68.

102 "News Briefs: Sentencing Reform Needed," *Angolite*, March–April 1993, 5.

103 "Inside Angola," *Angolite*, January–February 1994, 9. Further, new legislation placed limitations on prisoners' ability to request clemency in the first place. In 1997 only offenders who had served fifteen years of their sentences could apply for clemency, and if the petition was denied, the prisoner would have to wait another six years before he could apply again; just a generation earlier, nearly all people serving lengthy sentences would be *released* in just over ten years. LA R.S. 15:572.4 (D), Acts 1997, No. 822 § 1.

104 James V. Miller to Governor Haley Barbour, July 21, 2008, Series 2810: Legal Files, 1993–2011, Box 32375, Folder Michael Graham Clemency, Records of the Office of the Governor, MDAH.

105   Email, Kathy Rayborn to Governor Haley Barbour, August 5, 2008, Series 2810: Legal Files, 1993–2011, Box 32375, Folder Michael Graham Clemency, MDAH.

106   "Pardons: Bryant on the Right Track," editorial, *Clarion-Ledger* (Jackson, MS), January 17, 2012; Jessica Bakeman, "No Mansion Pardons from Me, Bryant Says," *Clarion-Ledger* (Jackson, MS), January 15, 2012.

107   Michael Watson, quoted in Bakeman, "No Mansion Pardons."

108   Haley Barbour, quoted in Anita Lee, "Barbour: 'I Believe in Second Chances,'" *Sun Herald* (Gulfport, MS), January 14, 2012.

109   "The Mississippi Pardons," *New York Times*, October 15, 2010. For a detailed discussion of the case of the Scott sisters, see Bailey, "Please Don't Forget about Me," chap. 1. By contrast, the same judge that sentenced the Scott sisters to two consecutive life sentences each sentenced Edgar Ray Killen, the man convicted in 2005 of manslaughter for the 1964 killings of civil rights workers James Cheney, Andrew Goodman, and Michael Schwerner to a sentence of sixty years. See Emily Wagster Pettus, "Killen's Kin Accused of Threat," *Sun Herald* (Gulfport, MS), August 17, 2005; and Sid Salter, "February Court Term to Begin; Jury Set to Hear Heavy Docket," *Scott County (MS) Times*, February 16, 1994.

110   Schaefer, "The Tragic Case of the Scott Sisters," *Jackson (MI) Free Press*, November 3, 2010, https://www.jacksonfreepress.com/news/2010/nov/03/the-tragic-case-of-the-scott-sisters/.

111   Jamie Scott was not a candidate for conditional medical release, a provision that requires that an inmate have a condition that is incapacitating and totally terminal in nature. Thus, "Jamie Scott appears to be caught in a deadly Catch-22: In order to be released from prison, she must convince the MDOC that her illness is terminal . . . ; but the only sure way for her to prove this is to die in prison"; Ridgeway and Casella, "For Jamie Scott." Rather than allow Scott to leave the prison for dialysis, prison authorities brought in dialysis machines.

112   Krissah Thompson, "'Conditioned on' Kidney Donation, Sisters' Prison Release Prompts Ethics Debate," *Washington Post*, December 30, 2015, https://www.washingtonpost.com/wp-dyn/content/article/2010/12/30/AR2010123002930.html?wprss=rss_nation, accessed December 8, 2021. In 2007, in an effort to make more human organs available for transplant, the South Carolina legislature considered a bill that would cut 180 days from a prison sentence in exchange for the donation of a kidney. Thompson, "From Researching the Past to Reimagining the Future," 60; Burkle, "The Mississippi Decision." While some critiqued the South Carolina law as coercive, others worried that family members would not want their ailing loved one to receive a "prison kidney"; Stone, "Give a Kidney to Shorten Your Prison Sentence?" As Pollock,

"On the Suspended Sentences of the Scott Sisters," 259–60, argues, "the transplant bargains are . . . of a piece with the nature of criminal justice in the United States. Insofar as prison extracts a 'debt to society' from the prisoner, the prisoner's body itself is always part of the payment. Extraction from the body in these cases points to an ever-demanding structure of debt peonage."

113   Thompson, "'Conditioned on' kidney donation"; Associated Press, "Barbour: No Pardon for Sisters Showing No Remorse," *Deseret News* (Salt Lake City, UT), January 13, 2012, https://www.deseret.com/2012 /1/13/20244392/barbour-no-pardon-for-sisters-showing-no-remorse.

114   Haley Barbour, quoted in "Habitual Offenders, Husbands Top List of Murderers Pardoned," *Sun Herald* (Gulfport, MS), January 12, 2012.

115   Michael Schapiro, quoted in Thompson, "'Conditioned on' Kidney Donation."

116   Chokwe Lumumba, quoted in Thomas-Tisdale, "State Leaders Demanding Full Pardon."

117   Bob Herbert, "For Two Sisters, the End of an Ordeal," *New York Times*, December 31, 2010.

118   Goldberg and Frader, "Prisoners as Living Organ Donors," 15.

119   Dittmer, *Local People*, 80.

120   Monte Piliawsky to Mississippi State Parole Board and Governor Haley Barbour, April 7, 2006, in Steven A. Drizin, Bobby Owens, Barry Bradford, Agnieszka Mazur, Mona Ghadiri, and Callie McCune, Exhibits to Memorandum in Support of Application for Clemency of Clyde Kennard, Pardon Docket No. 06-0005, before the Honorable Haley Barbour, Governor, State of Mississippi, n.d. [June 4, 2006], accessed December 16, 2020, https://www.law.northwestern .edu/legalclinic/wrongfulconvictions/exonerations/documents /msKennardExhibits.pdf.

121   Medgar Evers, quoted in Minchin and Salmond, "'The Saddest Story,'" 193, 215.

122   Dittmer, *Local People*, 83; Minchin and Salmond, "'The Saddest Story,'" 217.

123   Clyde Kennard, quoted in Steven A. Drizin, Bobby Owens, Barry Bradford, Agnieszka Mazur, Mona Ghadiri, and Callie McCune, Memorandum in Support of Application for Clemency of Clyde Kennard, Pardon Docket No. 06-0005, before the Honorable Haley Barbour, Governor, State of Mississippi, n.d. [June 4, 2006], accessed December 16, 2020, https://www.law.northwestern.edu/legalclinic /wrongfulconvictions/exonerations/documents/msKennardPetition .pdf, 13.

124   Julian Bond, quoted in Drizin et al., Memorandum in Support of Application for Clemency, 26.

125 Haley Barbour, quoted in "What Will Be Political Fallout over Kennard?" *Enterprise-Journal* (McComb, MS), May 15, 2006. Novak, *Comparative Executive Clemency*, 96, notes a number of posthumous pardons granted in recent decades, such as Alabama's posthumous pardon of the Scottsboro boys, nine African American teenagers falsely accused and convicted of raping two white women on a train in 1931. The governors of at least ten other states, as well as the president of the United States have granted posthumous pardons; Drizin et al., Memorandum in Support of Application for Clemency, 32.

126 Jamie Scott, quoted in Pollock, "On the Suspended Sentences of the Scott Sisters," 256. A circuit court judge finally declared Kennard innocent of "bogus charges" after concerned citizens—including former governor William Winter (1980–84), several members of the US Congress, and one of the white doctors who treated Kennard—sent a petition in federal court. White supremacist leaders from central Mississippi tried to block Kennard's exoneration. See Minchin and Salmond, "'The Saddest Story,'" 230, 232.

127 "EWE Sets Up Panel for 'Forgotten Men,'" *Shreveport (LA) Times*, April 26, 1984; Kondkar, *Incarceration in Louisiana*.

128 Lea Skene, "Report: Number of People Serving Life in Louisiana Dwarfs Entire State Prison Population in 1970," *Advocate* (Baton Rouge, LA), February 21, 2020.

129 Rideau, "Conversations with the Dead," 59.

130 Pelot-Hobbs, "Organized Inside and Out," 213.

131 Arthur Carter, Visiting Room Project, video, 2021, https://www.visitingroomproject.org/archive/arthur_carter.

132 Danny Sermon, Visiting Room Project, video, 2021, https://www.visitingroomproject.org/archive/danny_sermon.

133 Darren James, Visiting Room Project, video, 2021, https://www.visitingroomproject.org/archive/darren_james.

134 Aaron Brent, Visiting Room Project, video, 2021, https://www.visitingroomproject.org/archive/aaron_brent.

135 Ron Hicks, Visiting Room Project, video, 2021, https://www.visitingroomproject.org/archive/ron_hicks.

136 Joe White, quoted in National Public Radio, "Tossing Away the Keys."

137 In an analysis of Pennsylvania, Seeds, "Governors and Prisoners," 82, argues that the decline of clemency has been accompanied by the "deterioration of a social relationship, a discarded line of conversation that once existed between governors and prisoners."

138 Randy Weeks, "Relationships Can Affect Decision to 'Pardon' Others," *Greenwood (MS) Commonwealth*, February 10, 2012.

139 "Mansion Trusties Are Archaic," *Picayune (MS) Item*, January 21, 2012; CBS News, "New Miss. Gov Boots Inmate Workers from Mansion."

140   Murakawa, *The First Civil Right*, 106. Legal scholars have examined the waning use of executive clemency. At the beginning of the twentieth century, US presidents granted between one hundred and two hundred pardons every year. By contrast, President George W. Bush granted two hundred pardons or commutations and President Barack Obama granted 212 during their eight-year terms; Rosenzweig, "Reflections on the Atrophying Pardon Power," 603. See also Love, "The Twilight of the Pardon Power"; and Kobil, "How to Grant Clemency in Unforgiving Times."

4. SOUTHERN HOSPITALITY

1   Louisiana Board of Pardons and Parole, "Holds Pardon Hearing for Ryan Adams," November 16, 2020, audio hearing from board records custodian.

2   Louisiana Board of Pardons and Parole, "Holds Pardon Hearing for Ryan Adams."

3   The knowledge about Adams's child and the illicit use of Butler Park for sexual liaisons was communicated to me by a person formerly incarcerated at Angola who wishes to remain anonymous.

4   Louisiana Board of Pardons and Parole, "Holds Pardon Hearing for Ryan Adams."

5   Hopper, *Sex in Prison*, 50.

6   Lipman, "Mississippi's Prison Experience," 693.

7   Hopper, *Sex in Prison*, 64.

8   Martin, *Break Down the Walls*, 205.

9   Hopper, *Sex in Prison*, 65.

10   Douglass, *My Bondage and My Freedom*, 40.

11   Hopper, *Sex in Prison*, 79–80.

12   Oshinsky, *Worse Than Slavery*, 153. On the politicization of rape allegations, see Hodes, *White Women, Black Men*; Edwards, *Gendered Strife and Confusion*; and Gilmore, "Murder, Memory, and the Flight of the Incubus." Wells, *Southern Horrors*, notes "the thread-bare lie that Negro men rape white women."

13   Hopper, *Sex in Prison*, 80, notes that "it is quite likely that enforced racial integration of the camps would be followed immediately by the termination of the conjugal visiting privilege." See also Oshinsky, *Worse Than Slavery*, 153.

14   "Prison Farm Scandal," *Jackson (MS) Daily News*, January 9, 1919, 4.

15   Hopper, *Sex in Prison*, 95.

16   Hopper, *Sex in Prison*, 73, 74, 68, 82.

17   Hopper, "Conjugal Visiting at the Mississippi State Penitentiary," 41.

18 Hopper, "The Evolution of Conjugal Visiting in Mississippi," 103.

19 Hopper, *Sex in Prison*, 59.

20 Hopper, "The Evolution of Conjugal Visiting in Mississippi," 105; Hopper, *Sex in Prison*, 79.

21 Flip, "50+ or 50–?," *Inside World*, March 1960, 6; "Furloughs or Conjugality?," *Inside World*, June 1960, 17.

22 Hopper, *Sex in Prison*, 101, 57–58.

23 Hopper, *Sex in Prison*, 75, 139, 143. Thompson, "Blinded by a 'Barbaric' South," warns against exaggerating southern exceptionalism with regard to prisons, but whatever the similarities between prisons in the South and elsewhere, it is indisputable that southern prisons formed after emancipation were efforts to fashion a site of exploited planation labor that resembled slavery.

24 Balogh, "Conjugal Visitations in Prisons: A Sociological Perspective," 54.

25 Hopper, "The Evolution of Conjugal Visiting in Mississippi," 105; Hopper, "The Conjugal Visit at Mississippi State Penitentiary," 343. Other reforms introduced that year included a vocational education program, a diagnostic center, and the end of prison stripes; see Hopper, *Sex in Prison*, 30–32.

26 Hopper, "The Conjugal Visit at Mississippi State Penitentiary," 343.

27 H. L. "Buck" Roberts, quoted in Bill Rose, "Parchman Opens Up for Historic Tour," *Delta Democrat-Times* (Greenville, MS), February 6, 1972, 12.

28 Nicholas Horrock, "US Prisons: Rehabilitation or Revenge?" *Democrat and Chronicle* (Rochester, NY), January 19, 1971.

29 Hopper, "The Conjugal Visit at Mississippi State Penitentiary," 343.

30 Tom Graf, quoted in Philip D. Hearn, "Women's Conjugal Visiting Plan Snags," *Delta Democrat-Times* (Greenville, MS), October 31, 1972.

31 John A. Collier, quoted in "Visiting Privileges for Married Women," *Clarion-Ledger* (Jackson, MS), April 29, 1972.

32 "Conjugal Visits Approved for Women!," *Inside World*, May 24, 1972, 1.

33 Roy Reed, "Pressure Mounts for Prison Reform in Mississippi," *New York Times*, September 18, 1972; Jody Correro, "State Penitentiary Hopping with Activity," *Greenwood (MS) Commonwealth*, August 26, 1972; "Going That Extra Mile," *Clarksdale (MS) Press Register*, September 20, 1972; "Pullman Car 'Champaign' [*sic*] Makes Final Trip on Rubber Tires," *Inside World*, Fall 1972, 24–27.

34 Wilkerson, *The Warmth of Other Suns*, 190.

35 Ed Williams, "Conjugal Visiting; Parchman Likes Plan," *Delta Democrat-Times* (Greenville, MS), September 13, 1970.

36 Hensley, Rutland, and Gray-Ray, "Inmate Attitudes," 138.

37 Jean McBride, quoted in Robert Cross, "A Prison's Family Plan," *Chicago Tribune*, October 2, 1985, https://www.chicagotribune.com/news/ct-xpm-1985-10-02-8503060926-story.html.

38 Bill Habig, "A Trusty Speaks," *Inside World*, April 1971, 8. Despite prisoners' awareness of practices at other prisons, Habig apparently did not know that by 1971 conjugal visits were also available in other states.

39 Lux, "From Rehabilitation to Punishment," 10; Flamm, *Law and Order*, chap. 1.

40 May, *Homeward Bound*.

41 Flamm, *Law and Order*, 14.

42 American Correctional Association Committee on Riots, *A Statement*, 5; Sullivan, *The Prison Reform Movement*, 46, 50.

43 Rotman, "The Failure of Reform," 169.

44 "Michel Foucault, on the Role of Prisons," interview by Roger Pol-Droit, trans. Leonard Mayhew, *New York Times*, August 5, 1975.

45 Mitford, *Kind and Usual Punishment*, 105–6, emphasis in the original.

46 American Correctional Association Committee on Riots, *A Statement*, 5.

47 Hopper, *Sex in Prison*, 3.

48 Fishman, *Sex in Prison*, 5, 17–18. Fishman pointed out that the American Prison Association had never formally addressed the subject.

49 Karpman, "Sex Life in Prison," 485, 476.

50 Karpman, "Criminality, Insanity, and the Law," 605.

51 "Medicine: Criminal or Insane?" *Time*, May 23, 1960, http://content.time.com/time/subscriber/article/0,33009,827632,00.html.

52 On concerns about sexual abuse among inmates in Progressive Era reform schools, see Rothman, *Conscience and Convenience*, 276–77. On prison administrators and reformers' efforts to curtail sexual immorality, which they defined as sexual activity of any kind, including masturbation, see Kunzel, *Criminal Intimacy*, chap. 1.

53 Kunzel, *Criminal Intimacy*, 5.

54 Stack, "From Sodomists to Citizens," 175.

55 On the racialized and gendered criminalization and surveillance of female sexuality in the context of Progressive Era reform schools, see Hicks, *Talk with You Like a Woman*.

56 Kunzel, *Criminal Intimacy*, 49–50.

57 Havelock Ellis, quoted in Kunzel, *Criminal Intimacy*, 54.

58 Canaday, *The Straight State*.

59 Kunzel, "Sex Panic," 230.

60 Chauncey, "The Postwar Sex Crime Panic," 161.

61 Kunzel, "Sex Panic."

62 May, *Homeward Bound*.

63 Chauncey, "The Postwar Sex Crime Panic," 162.

64 Clemmer, *The Prison Community*; Kunzel, *Criminal Intimacy*, 88.

65 Kunzel, *Criminal Intimacy*, 102.

66 Lindner, "Sex in Penal Institutions," 202.

67 Karpman, "Sex Life in Prison," 483–84. On fears about the "contagion" of homosexuality spreading in Texas prisons, see Chase, *We Are Not Slaves*, chap. 1.

68 Clinton T. Duffy, as told to Al Hirshberg, "A Frank Discussion of the Prison Problem Nobody Talks About," *Los Angeles Times Magazine*, October 21, 1962, 10.

69 Clinton T. Duffy with Al Hirshberg, "Sex and Crime," *Honolulu Star-Bulletin*, June 16, 1965; Duffy and Hirshberg, "A Frank Discussion," 8, emphasis in the original.

70 Duffy and Hirshberg, "Sex and Crime."

71 Martin, *Break Down the Walls*, 171.

72 Lester Kinsolving, "A Problem in Prisons," *Signal* (Santa Clarita, CA), September 19, 1969.

73 Rich Aregood, "DA Probe Cites 'Sex Epidemic' in Jails, Blasts Sheriff's Office," *Philadelphia Daily News*, September 11, 1968.

74 "Prominent City Attorney, Negotiator Alan Davis Dies," *Philadelphia Inquirer*, May 10, 2007, https://www.inquirer.com/philly/news/homepage/20070510_Prominent_city_attorney__negotiator_Alan_Davis_dies.html.

75 Dave Racher and Bill Fidati, "No Protection, Jail-Sex Victim Freed," *Philadelphia Daily News*, September 27, 1968.

76 Davis, *Report on Sexual Assaults*, 17, 66; see also 98–99.

77 Carroll, "Humanitarian Reform and Biracial Sexual Assault."

78 Kunzel, *Criminal Intimacy*, 169–70.

79 Carroll, "Humanitarian Reform and Biracial Sexual Assault," 422.

80 Murakawa, *The First Civil Right*, chap. 3.

81 Weiss and Friar, *Terror in the Prisons*.

82 Paul W. Valentine, "Homosexuality: A Seething Prison Problem," *Democrat and Chronicle* (Rochester, NY), March 2, 1969.

83 Kunzel, *Criminal Intimacy*, 153.

84 Seeking redress for suffering this sexual violence became one of prisoners' legal battles.

85 Kunzel, *Criminal Intimacy*, 188–89.

86 Raymond Pace Alexander, "Conjugal Visits in Correctional Institutions," brief delivered before the Common Pleas Court, June 1969, Raymond Pace Alexander Papers, Virginia Commonwealth University, Box 78, Folder 36, 6–7.

87 Florida State University, School of Social Welfare, *Fourth Annual Southern Conference on Corrections*, n.p. [3–4].

88 Bill Harpole, quoted in "South's Prisons Ranked Lowest in America Today," *Delta Democrat-Times* (Greenville, MS), February 26, 1959.

89 Dean Donal E. J. MacNamara, quoted in "Police Women's Role Is Praised," *Tallahassee Democrat,* February 19, 1959; and "Sex Responsi-

ble for Most Trouble in Penitentiaries," *Daily World* (Opelousas, LA), February 20, 1959.

90 Silver, *Mississippi: The Closed Society.*

91 Oshinsky, *Worse Than Slavery*, 235.

92 Lipman, "Mississippi's Prison Experience," 696.

93 Fred Jones, quoted in Larry Still, "Freedom Riders Get Solitary, Convicts Get Sex Privileges," *Jet*, December 14, 1961, 53.

94 Still, "Freedom Riders Get Solitary," 51.

95 Richard Lott, "Squawk from High Five," *Inside World*, March 1963, 14.

96 Lipman, "Mississippi's Prison Experience."

97 Oshinsky, *Worse Than Slavery*, 247.

98 Oshinsky, *Worse Than Slavery*, 241.

99 Hopper, "The Impact of Litigation," 58.

100 Gowell, "'The Most Eloquent Dissents,'" 45.

101 Lipman, "Mississippi's Prison Experience," 749.

102 Bill Zeman, quoted in Still, "Freedom Riders Get Solitary," 51.

103 Leon Jackson and Dorothy A. Rice, "The Mississippi Criminal: A Psychological Profile," The Experimental Publication System, quoted in Bailey, "'Please Don't Forget about Me,'" 171.

104 Flip, "50+ or 50−?," 6.

105 Bill Rose, "Parchman Opens for Historic Tour," *Delta Democrat-Times* (Greenville, MS), February 6, 1972.

106 Jack Reed, quoted in Linda Thorsby, "Parchman Goes Positive," *Clarion-Ledger* (Jackson, MS), July 2, 1974; see also "Parchman to Begin Public Relations Program," *Conservative* (Carrollton, MS), December 26, 1974; John Emmerich, "Reed Contends Parchman Not All Bad," *Greenwood (MS) Commonwealth*, October 12, 1974.

107 William Waller, quoted in Ronni Patriquin, "Waller Emphasizes Good after Tour of Parchman," *Clarion-Ledger* (Jackson, MS), May 28, 1974.

108 Reed, "Pressure Mounts"; Roy Reed, "Parchman Still Has a Long Way to Go," *Atlanta Constitution*, September 21, 1972.

109 Columbus B. Hopper, "A Professor Looks at Homosexuality in Prisons," *Enterprise-Journal* (McComb, MS), March 6, 1973; Hopper, *Sex in Prison*, 144.

110 Goffman, "On the Characteristics of the Total Institution," 16.

111 "South Is Ideal Place to Begin Prison Reform," *Hattiesburg (MS) American*, October 4, 1972.

112 Harry Woodward Jr., quoted in "Parchman Said Best Place in U.S. for Prisoner to Do Time," reprinted from *Daily Journal* (Tupelo, MS), *Inside World*, July 1971, 6. These observations and my discussions of them differ from the findings of Robert Chase, who has demonstrated that criminologists concerned about the "contagion" of homosexuality believed that the dormitory housing characteristic of agricultural prisons

of the South "hastened the southern prison's production of homo-sexuality" and thus needed to be replaced with single-cell housing. Separating prisoners in individualized space, prison reformer Austin MacCormick believed, would halt the contagion of sexual perversion. See Chase, *We Are Not Slaves*, 33, 49. Chase also points out that placing prisoners in individual cells only enhanced the power of building tenders (or prison trusties) over other prisoners because they could use the new spatial formation to their advantage (103). In the case of Parchman and Angola, however, my research suggests a different inter-pretation of these open spaces; my emphasis is on the "openness" of the prison to the outside world, and I am not aware of discussions about replacing dormitory housing with cells in these facilities.

113 Douglas E. Kneeland, "Parchman Has Taken Long Strides toward 20th Century Approach," *Delta Democrat-Times* (Greenville, MS), February 19, 1968.

114 Charles D. Hale, letter to the editor, *Los Angeles Times*, April 21, 1969.

115 Graf quoted in Reed, "Parchman Still Has a Long Way to Go"; George John Beto, quoted in Bill Rose, "Beto: Keep Prison Farm," *Delta Democrat-Times* (Greenville, MS), December 20, 1972, 14.

116 George John Beto, quoted in Rose, "Beto: Keep Prison Farm," 14.

117 "Federal Bureau of Prisons Launches Anti-Gay Offensive," *Magnus*, Summer 1977, https://archive.org/stream/Magnus2Summer1977 /Magnus%20%232%20Summer%201977_djvu.txt

118 Berger and Losier, *Rethinking the American Prison Movement*, 102; the phrase "up for grabs" is quoted from Bernstein, *America Is the Prison*, 5.

5. "IT'S SOMETHING WE MUST DO"

1 Canton, *Raymond Pace Alexander*.

2 Raymond Pace Alexander, "Conjugal Visits in Correctional Institu-tions," brief delivered before the Common Pleas Court, June 1969. Raymond Pace Alexander Papers, Virginia Commonwealth University (hereafter Alexander Papers), Box 78, Folder 36, pp. 4, 1.

3 Raymond Pace Alexander, quoted in Nicholas C. Chriss, "Mississip-pi's Parchman Is a Pioneer in Conjugal Visits," *Delta Democrat-Times* (Greenville, MS), May 8, 1969.

4 Raymond Pace Alexander, quoted in Joyce Brothers, "Conjugal Visits in Jail," *Record* (Hackensack, NJ), November 5, 1972, B4.

5 Mrs. Earl Powell to Raymond Pace Alexander, March 31, 1969, Alexander Papers, Box 78, Folder 36; Jan Keebler to Raymond Pace Alexander, n.d., Alexander Papers, Box 78, Folder 36; Estelle Andovich to Raymond Pace Alexander, March 8, 1969, Alexander Papers, Box 78, Folder 36.

6   Johns, "Alternatives to Conjugal Visiting," 49.

7   McGirr, *Suburban Warriors*, 157.

8   Allen, *The Decline of the Rehabilitative Ideal*.

9   McGirr, *Suburban Warriors*, 265.

10   Raymond K. Procunier, statement by Raymond K. Procunier, director, California Department of Corrections, before the House of Representatives Committee on the Judiciary, Subcommittee No. 3, Corrections: Hearings, 92nd Cong., 1st Sess., 1971, pt. 2, 123.

11   Conrad, "We Should Never Have Promised a Hospital," 4, 5.

12   Janssen, "From the Inside Out."

13   Cummins, *The Rise and Fall*, 11–12.

14   Prieur, "In the System," 41, 47.

15   Ed Salzman, "Our Prisons Open Doors for Return to Society," *Oakland (CA) Tribune*, August 8, 1965, 1, 3.

16   Karl Menninger, quoted in Mitford, *Kind and Usual Punishment*, 107–8.

17   Lamott, *Chronicles of San Quentin*, 168; Cummins, *The Rise and Fall of California's Radical Prison Movement*, ch. 1.

18   Davis, *Are Prisons Obsolete?*, 40.

19   Michel Foucault, quoted in Davis, *Are Prisons Obsolete?*, 40.

20   John Irwin, quoted in Sullivan, *The Prison Reform Movement*, 72–74. See also Hollander, "The Adjustment Center," 152–59.

21   Bernard Diamond, quoted in Mitford, *Kind and Usual Punishment*, 108.

22   Cummins, *The Rise and Fall*, 15.

23   Janssen, "From the Inside Out," 119; Cummins, *The Rise and Fall*.

24   Clinton T. Duffy and Dean Jennings, "San Quentin Is My Home 5: World without Women," *Saturday Evening Post*, April 22, 1950, 146.

25   Burstein, *Conjugal Visits in Prison*, 32.

26   Findings from Holt and Miller, cited in Burstein, *Conjugal Visits in Prison*, 33.

27   Clinton T. Duffy with Al Hirshberg, "Alone in the Nation: Conjugal Visits Work Out for Prisons in Mississippi," *Atlanta Constitution*, May 2, 1966.

28   Benjamin A. Katz to Raymond Pace Alexander, March 11, 1969, Alexander Papers, Box 78, Folder 36.

29   Clinton T. Duffy, as told to Al Hirshberg, "A Frank Discussion of the Prison Problem Nobody Talks About," *Los Angeles Times Magazine*, October 21, 1962, 8.

30   California Legislature, Interim Committee on Criminal Procedure, *Report of the Assembly Interim Committee on Criminal Procedure* [Sacramento]: Assembly of the State of California, 1965, 41.

31   Ronald Reagan, quoted in "G.O.P. Testimony on Violence," *New York Times*, August 1, 1968.

32   Cannon, *Governor Reagan*, 218–19.

33   Spencer M. Williams, "Spencer M. Williams: The Human Relations Agency: Perspectives and Programs Concerning Health, Welfare, and Corrections, 1966–1970," interview by Julie Shearer, 1982, Oral History Center, Bancroft Library, University of California–Berkeley, 1986, 21.

34   Allen F. Breed and Raymond K. Procunier, "The Art of Corrections Management, California 1967–1974," interview by Gabrielle Morris, 1982, Oral History Center, Bancroft Library, University of California–Berkeley, 1984, 12.

35   Cannon, *Governor Reagan*; See also Gartner, Doob, and Zimring, "Past as Prologue?"

36   "Conjugal Visitation Rights and the Appropriate Standard of Judicial Review for Prison Regulations," *Michigan Law Review* 73, no. 2 (1974): 419n140.

37   Ed Salzman, "Convicts Break with Tradition," *Oakland (CA) Tribune*, August 9, 1965.

38   "2-day Family Visits Tested for Convicts," *San Francisco Examiner*, July 25, 1968.

39   Lloyd, "A Family Visiting Programme," 147.

40   Lloyd, "A Family Visiting Programme," 148–49. Comfort, "'Papa's House,'" 471, argues that by relocating domestic activities to prison visiting rooms, prisoners' significant others "partake in the paradoxical 'institutionalization' of their own family life and thus extend the reach and intensity of the transformative effects of the carceral apparatus."

41   Lawrence E. Wilson, quoted in Hayner, "Attitudes toward Conjugal Visits for Prisoners," 48, emphasis in the original.

42   Phil Guthrie, quoted in "Conjugal Visit Plan Is Tried Out at Tehachapi Prison," *Fresno Bee*, July 26, 1968.

43   Comfort, "'Papa's House,'" 487.

44   Simpson, "Conjugal Visiting," 22.

45   California Department of Corrections, *Pattern of Change*, n.p.

46   Burstein, *Conjugal Visits in Prison*, 55, 57, 67, 57. Frazier, "The Tower," discusses the gun tower as an immediately recognizable symbol of carceral power.

47   Holt and Miller, *Explorations in Inmate-Family Relationships*, vi, v, 64.

48   E. A. Peterson, quoted in Burstein, *Conjugal Visits in Prison*, appendix A, "Interview with Administrative Staff at Soledad Correctional Facility," July 24, 1975, 110.

49   "Shotgun Blasts Wound Rioting Florida Inmates," *Longview (WA) Daily News*, February 13, 1971, 16; James A. Bax, commissioner of the Community Services Administration of HEW, testimony before the House of Representatives Select Committee on Crime, "American Prisons in Turmoil," 92nd Cong., 1st Sess., 1971, pt. I., 354.

50 Hopper, *Sex in Prison*, 126–27; Sykes, *The Society of Captives*, 70–81.

51 Billy Sinclair, "Effect of Deprivation of Sex on Prison Life and the Convict," *Angolite*, March 1973, 3. The fact that a number of prison publications reprinted excerpts from Columbus Hopper's study of conjugal visits at Parchman demonstrate how engaged incarcerated people were with the issue and how aware they were of currents in penological thinking. See, for example, the *Eye Opener* (Oklahoma State Penitentiary), May 1971, 3, 18–19; and *La Roca* (Arizona State Prison), September 1979, 23–25.

52 Thomas, *Seven Long Times*, 140–41.

53 Gil Leano to Judge Raymond Pace Alexander, May 5, 1969, Alexander Papers, Box 78, Folder 36. While Leano was incarcerated he launched a federal suit alleging that he was denied the right to counsel in his trial on a narcotics charge; see Gil Munoz Leano, Petitioner-appellant, v. United States of America, Respondent-appellee, 494 F.2d 361 (9th Cir. 1974), https://law.justia.com/cases/federal/appellate-courts/F2/494/361 /112671/.

54 Holloway, "Sex at Parchman," 144, emphasis in the original.

55 Holloway, "Prison Abolition or Destruction," 758, emphasis in the original.

56 Holloway, "Sex at Parchman," 151, emphasis in the original.

57 Hopper, "The Conjugal Visit at Mississippi State Penitentiary," 342.

58 Eigenberg, "If You Drop the Soap," 57–58.

59 Rideau, "The Sexual Jungle," in Rideau and Wikberg, *Life Sentences*, 74, 103, 104.

60 Thomas, *Seven Long Times*, 140.

61 Hopper, *Sex in Prison*, 147.

62 "Inmate Dances Proposed," *Angolite*, December 25, 1953, 2, emphasis in the original; "'Dance' Idea Draws Fire," *Angolite*, February 6, 1954, 2.

63 "Inmates May Get Touch of Family Life," *Times* (Shreveport, LA), September 18, 1968.

64 "Angola Conjugal Visits Bill Due in Legislature," *Daily World* (Opelousas, LA), April 10, 1970.

65 Francis Bickford, quoted in Mikel Miller, "Move for Conjugal Visits Hits Snag in LA House," *Town Talk* (Alexandria, LA), May 19, 1970.

66 Francis Bickford, quoted in "Monthly Conjugal Visits for Prison Inmates Refused," *Shreveport (LA) Journal*, June 15, 1970.

67 Archie Davis, quoted in Mikel Miller, "House Bars Conjugal Visits at Angola," *Town Talk* (Alexandria, LA), June 15, 1970.

68 "Inside Angola: Visiting," *Angolite*, March–April 1981, 63.

69 Berger and Losier, *Rethinking the American Prison Movement*, 74, 73.

70 Robert Gruenberg, "Penology Must Change with Convicts," *Press and Sun-Bulletin* (Binghamton, NY), September 19, 1971.

71   American Correctional Association, quoted in Gruenberg, "Penology Must Change with Convicts."

72   Cummins, *The Rise and Fall*, 239–45.

73   Sommer, *The End of Imprisonment*, 65–66.

74   Pears, Cochran, Siennick, and Bales, "Prison Visitation and Recidivism"; Lee, "Far from Home and All Alone"; Duwe and Clark, "Blessed Be the Social Tie That Binds.".

75   Thomas O. Murton, testimony in Corrections Federal and State Parole Systems, Hearings before Subcommitte No. 3 of the Committee on the Judiciary, House of Representatives, 92nd Cong., 2nd Sess., Appendix 2, March 2, 1971, 193, https://www.google.com/books/edition /Hearings_Reports_and_Prints_of_the_House/seo1AAAAIAAJ?hl =en&gbpv=0.

76   Louis Randall, Hearings before Subcommittee No. 3 of the Committee on the Judiciary, House of Representatives, 92nd Cong., Second Sess., pt. 6, January 29, 1972, 28.

77   Norval Morris and James Jacobs, "Proposals for Prison Reform," submitted as an appendix to "Prison Construction Plans and Policy," hearings before the House of Representatives Committee on the Judiciary, Subcommittee on Courts, Civil Liberties, and the Administration of Justice, 94th Cong., 1st Sess., July 28 and 30, 1975, 7.

78   Martin Dykman, "Prison Authorities Ponder Home Visits," *Tampa Bay Times*, January 15, 1971.

79   Robert Sheldon, "Rehabilitation Programs in Prison," quoted in Goetting, "Conjugal Association in Prison," 63.

80   David J. Rothman, "Decarcerating Prisoners and Patients," *Civil Liberties Review*, Fall 1973, 8–30.

81   Schafer, "Prison Visiting," 26.

82   Sol Chaneles, "The Open Prison," *Psychology Today*, March 1975, 123.

83   Sommer, *Final Report*.

84   *Newsweek*, September 27, 1971, quoted in Edwards, "Foreword," 156–57.

85   Thompson, *Blood in the Water*, 558–59.

86   Jorgensen, "Prison Riots as Agents of Prison Reform."

87   Donald Peterson, "He Would Refuse Convict Demands," letter to the editor, *Post-Standard* (Syracuse, NY), October 2, 1971.

88   Goetting, "Conjugal Association in Prison," 58.

89   Robert D. McFadden, "Conjugal Visits for Inmates to Be Allowed at Wallkill," *New York Times*, September 9, 1975.

90   "A Plan for Conjugal Visits Stirs Protests in Wallkill," *New York Times*, February 14, 1976.

91   Paula Bernstein, "Prisons and Sex," *New York Daily News*, May 31, 1978.

92   Freddie Ferraro, quoted in Bernstein, "Prisons and Sex."

93   Bernstein, "Prisons and Sex."

94 "Ridicule of Wives Feared over Visits," *Democrat and Chronicle* (Rochester, NY), June 20, 1977.

95 Bernstein, "Prisons and Sex."

96 Sutor, "The Other Side of the Fence."

97 Robert L. Jackson, "Sensitive Treatment: New Prison Techniques Urged for Radical Inmates," *Spokesman-Review* (Spokane, WA), December 16, 1971.

98 Sue Manning, "Relieving Prison Tension; Conjugal Visits Are Urged," *Semi-weekly Spokesman Review* (Spokane, WA), July 10, 1979, 2.

99 "Calm Prison Awaits Visits," *Spokane (WA) Chronicle*, March 25, 1981.

100 "Conjugal Visits Begin," *Spokane (WA) Chronicle*, April 16, 1981.

101 Paul Chapin, "Prison Opens Door for Family Visits," *Spokesman-Review* (Spokane, WA), April 19, 1981.

102 Kent, "The Legal and Sociological Dimensions," 54; "Texas Prison Reforms Proposed," *Kilgore (TX) News*, December 1, 1974.

103 "Prisoner Visitations Study Gains Support," *Albuquerque Journal*, February 28, 1979; Betty Childers, "Judge Explains Stand Favoring Conjugal Visits," *Albuquerque Journal*, May 13, 1979; "New Mexico Inmates Stage Sitdown Strike," *Winona (MN) Daily News*, April 22, 1980.

104 Don Frederick, "King Has Open Mind on Conjugal Visits," *El Paso (TX) Times*, April 18, 1980; "Inmates Need Contact," editorial, *Santa Fe New Mexican*, April 12, 1980.

105 Goetting, "Conjugal Association in Prison," 149.

106 Burstein, *Conjugal Visits in Prison*, 100.

107 Derral Byers, quoted in Burstein, *Conjugal Visits in Prison*, 113–14.

108 Flanagan and Caulfield, "Public Opinion and Prison Policy," 39.

109 Jean McBride, quoted in Robert Cross, "A Prison's Family Plan," *Chicago Tribune*, October 2, 1985.

110 "Dear Anne Landers," *Petaluma (CA) Argus-Courier*, March 26, 1984.

111 Bennett, "Correctional Administrators' Attitudes," 111.

112 Turner, "Sex in Prison," 24; Boudin, Stutz, and Littman, "Prison Visitation Policies," 172.

113 Ruffin v. Commonwealth, 62 Va. 790 (1871). See also "Beyond the Ken of the Courts." For a legal history of felons' loss of citizenship rights, see Holloway, *Living in Infamy*. This state of civil death echoes Orlando Patterson's concept of social death, which scholars of the carceral state have also applied to incarceration; see Patterson, *Slavery and Social Death*; and Price, *Prison and Social Death*.

114 Bernstein, "The Evolving Right of Due Process," 880.

115 The primary law under which prisoners were found to have standing was Section 1983 of the US Code, passed in 1871 to protect former slaves from abuses of their civil rights. See Carroll, *Lawful Order*, 4.

116 Reiter, *Mass Incarceration*, 12.

117 Jacobs, "The Prisoners' Rights Movement," 439.

118 "Guideline for Jailhouse Lawyers," November 1972, Jessica Mitford Papers, Harry Ransom Center, University of Texas at Austin, Series III, Box 36, Folder 5, p. 5. On prison litigation, see Hillyer, "'Going Up on the Way Down.'"

119 Esposito, "Conjugal Visitation," 314.

120 Polakoff v. Henderson, 370 F. Supp. 690 (N.D. Ga. 1973).

121 Esposito, "Conjugal Visitation," 317.

122 Lyons v. Gilligan, 382 F. Supp. 198 (N.D. Ohio 1974).

123 McGinnis v. Stevens, 543 P. 2d 1221 (Alaska 1975).

124 Singer, "Privacy, Autonomy, and Dignity in the Prison," 669.

125 In Turner v. Safely, 482 U.S. 78 (8th Cir., 1987), the court upheld the right of prisoners to marry but denied their right to have sex. In Gerber v. Hickman, 291 F.3d 617 (9th Cir. 2002), the US Court of Appeals held that "the right to procreate . . . is fundamentally inconsistent with incarceration." See also Roth, "No New Babies."

126 "Conjugal Visitation Rights and the Appropriate Standard of Judicial Review."

127 United States Ex Rel. Wolfish v. Levi (S.D.N.Y. 1977).

128 Jacobs, "The Prisoners' Rights Movement," 433.

129 Alan Sieroty, quoted in "Rights of Prisoners," *Daily Times-Advocate* (Escondido, CA), February 16, 1968.

130 "Rights' Bill for Prisoners Goes to Legislature," *Fresno (CA) Bee*, February 17, 1968; "Inmates: Anti-Crime Sentiment Imperils Rights Bill," *Los Angeles Times*, May 1, 1994.

131 Dan Morain, "State Politicians Take Aim at Inmates' Bill of Rights," *Los Angeles Times*, May 1, 1994.

132 Dennis Carpenter, quoted in "'Rights' Bill for Inmates Gains," *Independent* (Long Beach, CA), September 11, 1975.

133 Schlanger, "Inmate Litigation," 1567, referring to Congress's characterization of these lawsuits as "stylized anecdotes and gerrymandered statistics," pointed out that opponents of prison litigation did not present a balanced or truthful view of the docket.

134 R. E. Commerce to Chuck Robb, August 7, 1984, Governor Charles S. Robb Papers, Library of Virginia, Richmond, Box 21, Letters Received/Sent: Cabinet (Secretary of Public Safety)—State Agencies (Department of Fire Programs).

135 Lyons v. Gilligan.

136 Stewart D'Alessio, quoted in Josh Sanburn, "Mississippi Ending Conjugal Visits for Prisoners," *Time*, January 13, 2014, https://nation.time.com/2014/01/13/mississippi-ending-conjugal-visits-for-prisoners/.

6. "DADDY IS IN PRISON"

1   Dorothy A. Bush, "Stop Prison Marriages," letter to the editor,
    San Bernadino County (CA) Sun, April 23, 1993.

2   Haney, "Riding the Punishment Wave," 58.

3   Lynch, *Sunbelt Justice*, 126.

4   Finn, "No-Frills Prisons and Jails," 35.

5   Simon, *Governing through Crime*, 110.

6   The "mean season," a phrase coined by Francis Cullen, refers to the
    period when politicians wooed the public by devising "creative strate-
    gies to make offenders suffer"; see Cullen, "Assessing the Penal Harm
    Movement," 340.

7   Thuma, *All Our Trials*; Gottschalk, *The Prison and the Gallows*, 86.

8   Dick Zimmer, "Legislation to End Prison Perks Wins Endorse-
    ments," press release, January 31, 1995, https://web.archive.org/web
    /20210904020800/http://www.strengthtech.com/correct/laws
    /federal/luxurypr.htm#jan31.

9   Dick Zimmer, "Close the Door on Federal 'Glamour Slammers,'"
    press release, February 9, 1995, https://web.archive.org/web
    /20210904020800/http://www.strengthtech.com/correct/laws
    /federal/luxurypr.htm#feb9; Bronstein, Wolfgang, and McGettigan,
    "Crime and Punishment, 12–1. Politicians argued that opportunities to
    lift weights would allow prisoners to leave prison as "super criminals";
    see Tepperman, "Prison Weights for No Man," 2.

10 Haney, "Counting Casualties."

11 Ernest B. Furgurson, "Parchman and Prison Reform," *Baltimore Sun*,
    March 7, 1971.

12 Balogh, "Conjugal Visitations in Prisons," 55, 57.

13 Balogh, "Conjugal Visitations in Prisons," 55–56.

14 Holloway, *Sex at Parchman*, 146–50, emphasis in the original.

15 Ed Mead and Alvin Gilchrist, "On Our Courtroom 'Victory,'" *Red
    Dragon*, no. 6, July/August 1981.

16 Alvin Gilchrist, "To Northwest Prisoners," *Red Dragon*, no. 1, January/
    February 1980.

17 Mark LaRue, "Conjugal Visitation," *Red Dragon*, no. 6, July/
    August 1981.

18 Ed Mead, "Editorial Comment," *Red Dragon*, no. 10, April/June 1982.

19 Tom Kennedy, letter to the editor, *United Families and Friends of Pris-
    oners*, October 1977, 8.

20 Ed Mead, "Union Organizing on the Inside," *Red Dragon*, no. 4,
    August/September 1980.

21 Angela Y. Davis, quoted in Jeannine Yeomans, "Brutality Assailed:
    Angela Davis Urges Goal of Abolishing U.S. Prisons," *Spokesman-
    Review* (Spokane, WA), December 28, 1971.

22 Mead and Gilchrist, "On Our Courtroom 'Victory.'"

23 Theres Coupez, "Prisoners and Prisons," *Red Dragon*, no. 7, September/October 1981.

24 LaRue, "Conjugal Visitation," 9, emphasis in the original.

25 Pat Stanley, "Governor Urges Tougher Laws after Memorial," *Napa Valley (CA) Register*, December 10, 1993.

26 Campbell, "The Emergence of Penal Extremism," 380.

27 William Hamilton, "In California, Governor Hopefuls Are Running 'for Hangman,'" *Miami Herald*, January 16, 1994.

28 Clear, *Harm in American Penology*, 4.

29 Ray Cummings, quoted in Jennifer Foote, "Lifer Asks High Court for a Night of Love," *San Francisco Examiner*, April 14, 1981.

30 California Administrative Code, Title 15, § 3177.

31 *In re Cummings on Habeas Corpus*, Cr. No. 21978, February 18, 1982.

32 Philip Hager, "Convicted Slayer Sues over Conjugal Visits," *Los Angeles Times*, May 27, 1981.

33 "Prisoners' Conjugal Visits," *Hanford (CA) Sentinel*, September 21, 1981.

34 Sylvia Riddle, letter to the editor, *Spokesman-Review* (Spokane, WA), March 5, 1993.

35 Lidia Wasowicz, "California's Crisis in Prison Reform: New Inmate Rights Jeopardize Security," *Rutland (VT) Daily Herald*, June 28, 1981.

36 Don Novey, quoted in Wasowicz, "California's Crisis in Prison Reform." See also Haney, "Riding the Punishment Wave," 46–49.

37 Kohler-Hausmann, *Getting Tough*, 254.

38 Pete Wilson, quoted in "Wilson Signs Inmate Visits Measure," *Press Democrat* (Santa Rosa, CA), July 9, 1996.

39 Helen Wilson, letter to the editor, *Clarion-Ledger* (Jackson, MS), October 6, 1994.

40 Donald A. Gregor, letter to the editor, *San Bernadino County (CA) Sun*, April 1, 1996.

41 Orrin Hatch, quoted in Schlanger, "Inmate Litigation," 11.

42 Congressional Record, Senate Proceedings and Debates of the 104th Cong., 2nd Sess., April 19, 1996. 142 Cong. Rec. S3703-01 (1996).

43 Lenz, "'Luxuries' in Prison," 501.

44 John J. Philips, letter to the editor, *Clarion-Ledger* (Jackson, MS), October 6, 1994. See also Jones, "Cruel and Unusual Punishment."

45 "MS Bans Appliances," *Prison Legal News*, January 15, 1995, https://www.prisonlegalnews.org/news/1995/jan/15/ms-bans-appliances/.

46 These forty-eight new air-conditioning units covered 40 percent of the prison population. Courts have found that extremely hot or cold temperatures violate the US Constitution. See Mina Corpuz, "After 121 Scalding Mississippi Summers, Parchman Prison Is Getting Air Conditioning," *Mississippi Today*, July 19, 2022, https://mississippitoday.org/2022/07/19/parchman-mississippi-prisons-air-conditioning/.

47 Donald A. Gregor, letter to the editor, *San Bernadino County (CA) Sun*, April 1, 1996.

48 Wasowicz, "California's Crisis in Prison Reform."

49 Tweksbury and Mustaine, "Insiders' Views of Prison Amenities," 175; White, "The Concept of Less Eligibility."

50 Robert James Bidinotto, "Must Our Prisons Be Resorts?," *Readers' Digest*, November 1994, 67, 69.

51 Jon Marc Taylor, "Must Society Be Misled?," *Prison Life*, July–August 1995, 36, 43; Karl C. Johnson, "Doin' Time," *Prison Life*, July–August 1995, 38; Kenneth Z. Taylor, "The Real Deal on Prison Life," *Prison Life*, July–August 1995, 41.

52 John DiIulio, quoted in Bidinotto, "Must Our Prisons Be Resorts?," 71; Equal Justice Initiative, "The Superpredator Myth."

53 Wozniak, "American Public Opinion"; Finn, "No-Frills Prisons and Jails," 36; Lenz, "'Luxuries' in Prison," 500–502. Some scholars have found that public faith in rehabilitation persisted and punitive beliefs are not hegemonic; see Listwan, Jonson, Cullen, and Latessa, "Cracks in the Penal Harm Movement."

54 Finn, "No-Frills Prisons and Jails," 35.

55 Mack McInnis, quoted in "Jails Debate Takes 'Tough on Crime' Theme," *Enterprise-Journal* (McComb, MS), August 21, 1994.

56 "Opinion: 'Zebra' Stripes Not Worth Costs," *Enterprise-Journal* (McComb, MS), January 6, 1995.

57 Finn, "No-Frills Prisons and Jails," 35; Colin Dayan, "Inside Joe Arpaio's Tent City," *Boston Review*, August 29, 2017, http://bostonreview.net /politics/colin-dayan-inside-joe-arpaios-tent-city; Haney, "Riding the Punishment Wave," 32; "Art, Music Banned in Massachusetts Prisons," *Prison Life*, July–August 1995, 18.

58 Bennett Malone, quoted in Gina Holland, "Conjugal Visits Face Legislative Scrutiny," *Clarion-Ledger* (Jackson, MS), January 19, 1997.

59 Kelly Rudiger, quoted in Rich Harris, "Bill Makes Prison Conjugal Visits a Privilege, Not a Right," *Hanford (CA) Sentinel*, July 9, 1996.

60 Fred Goldman, quoted in Daryl Kelley, "Crime Victims, Witnesses and Prosecutors Gather for 3-Strikes Forum," *Los Angeles Times*, July 10, 1996.

61 Wilson, *Genetics, Crime, and Justice*, 21, suggests that three-strikes laws were also motivated by the desire to prevent felons from procreating. See also Oleson, "The New Eugenics."

62 Sid Salter, "Good Ole Boys: Who Runs the Prisons?" *Winona (MN) Times*, April 30, 1987.

63 Bill Steiger, quoted in Amy Gutman, "Officials Approve Distribution of Condoms to Prison Inmates," *Greenwood (MS) Commonwealth*, July 14, 1987.

64 A. Wunder, "The Extinction of Inmate Privileges," 5.

65 John Garamendi, quoted in Rocky Jaramillo Rushing, "Candidates Battle over Who Will Be Toughest on Prison Inmates," *Times-Advocate* (Escondido, CA), February 6, 1994.

66 As Franke, "Becoming a Citizen," 257, argues, while entering into a marriage contract—as formerly enslaved people did after the Civil War—could confer rights and responsibilities that had been denied under slavery, "the process of becoming husbands and wives was not a benign one whereby the state lent its imprimatur to autonomous, self-defining couples, but rather was coercive in nature: Previously acceptable behavior was punished and the regulatory force of the state was invoked so as to mold the newly freed slaves into citizens." Common-law marriage was recognized in nearly every state in the union by the mid-nineteenth century, but progressive reformers posited that the supposed looseness of such contracts would lead to a disintegration of the social and moral order. Further, it was believed that formal marriage would domesticate "the wanton licentiousness and civiliz[e] uncontrollable desire" (295).

  According to Edwards, *Gendered Strife and Confusion*, 45–46, at the time of emancipation "African Americans retained their own definition of marriage. Many refused to marry legally and even those who did had far different domestic relations than those of wealthier whites." Prisoners at Soledad State Prison were found to have printed counterfeit marriage certificates in order to participate in the institution's conjugal visiting program; Tom Watson, "Inmate Printers Give Soledad Cons 'License' for Connubial Delights," *Californian*, February 11, 1981.

67 Eddie Lucas, quoted in Dennis Camire, "State Prison's Conjugal Visit Policy Object of Crackdown," *Clarion-Ledger* (Jackson, MS), November 2, 1980.

68 Rushing, "Candidates Battle."

69 "A Victory for the CCPOA and Its Allies," *Peacekeeper*, December 1994, quoted in Page, *The Toughest Beat*, 98.

70 Dan Morain, "State Politicians Take Aim at Inmates' Bill of Rights," *Los Angeles Times*, May 1, 1994; Ken Chavez, "Crime Retains Top Billing in Flurry of Capitol Activity," *Sacramento (CA) Bee*, January 19, 1994.

71 Abigail Goldman, "Wedding Bells Often Heard behind Prison Bars," *Los Angeles Times*, July 4, 1996.

72 Kathleen Brown, quoted in William Endicott, "California Focus," *Press Democrat* (Santa Rosa, CA), January 1, 1994; Rushing, "Candidates Battle."

73 Anita Hartman, quoted in "Advocates Offer Testimony for Bill," *Santa Maria (CA) Times*, June 5, 1996.

74 Raymond Shipley, quoted in Eugene Alexander Dey, "Civil Death," *Bohemian*, November 29, 2006, https://bohemian.com/civil-death-1/.

75 Pete Wilson, quoted in Gail Harrington Wisely, "Injunction Saves California Family Visits," *Prison Legal News*, September 15, 1995, 12.

76 Pro-Family Advocates v. Gomez, 46Cal.App.4th, July 1, 1996.

77 Martha Riley, quoted in "Inmates Strike for Conjugal Visits," *Napa Valley (CA) Register*, March 1, 1995.

78 Kathleen Burdan, quoted in Andy Furillo and Janine DeFao, "Inmates Rampage at Folsom," *Sacramento (CA) Bee*, September 28, 1996.

79 Paul Wright, "WA Prisoners under Attack," *Prison Legal News*, March 15, 1995, https://www.prisonlegalnews.org/news/1995/mar/15/wa-prisoners-under-attack/; Paul Wright, "WA Passes Record Anti-prisoner/Defendant Legislation," *Prison Legal News*, August 15, 1995, https://www.prisonlegalnews.org/news/1995/aug/15/wa-passes-record-anti-prisonerdefendant-legislation/.

80 Jim Brunner, "Ida Ballasiotes, Lawmaker and Anti-crime Activist, Dies at 78," *Seattle Times*, November 24, 2014, https://www.seattletimes.com/seattle-news/ida-ballasiotes-lawmaker-and-anti-crime-activist-dies-at-78/.

81 Dan Tennenbaum and Davis Oldham, "Harsher Prison Measures Opposed: 'Family Values' Stop Here," *Prison Legal News*, May 15, 1995, https://www.prisonlegalnews.org/news/1995/may/15/harsher-prison-measures-opposed-family-values-stop-here/.

82 Wright, "WA Prisoners under Attack."

83 Norm Maleng, quoted in David Ammons, "Officials Battle Critics over Prison Reform," *Spokesman-Review* (Spokane, WA), March 1, 1995.

84 Tennenbaum and Oldham, "Harsher Prison Measures Opposed.".

85 Ammons, "Officials Battle Critics."

86 Chase Riveland, quoted in Jim Brunner, "A Different Definition of Justice," *Spokesman-Review* (Spokane, WA), May 28, 1995.

87 Brunner, "A Different Definition of Justice."

88 Wright, "WA Passes Record Anti-prisoner/Defendant Legislation."

89 Emma Childers, quoted in Scott Armstrong, "California Moves to Restrict Quality of Life for Inmates," *Christian Science Monitor*, May 10, 1994, https://www.csmonitor.com/1994/0510/10031.html.

90 "Don't Punish Families," editorial, *North County Times* (Oceanside, CA), July 13, 1996.

91 Sussman, "Media on Prisons," 263.

92 George H. Cullins, letter to the editor, *North Country Times* (Oceanside, CA), January 7, 1996.

93 Jaan Laaman, "Attica: Looking Back 25 Years," *Prison Legal News*, October 15, 1996, https://www.prisonlegalnews.org/news/1996/oct/15/attica-looking-back-25-years/.

94 Sundiata Acoli, "The Meaning of Attica," *Walkin' Steel*, Spring 1997, 1.

95 Lynda V. Mapes, "Rep. Mike Padden Pushes Tough Plan to Reduce Crime," *Spokesman-Review* (Spokane, WA), January 13, 1994.

96 Eric Martin, letter to the editor, *Prison Life*, July–August 1995, 11.

97 Hopper, "The Evolution of Conjugal Visiting in Mississippi," 108.

98 Hopper, quoted in Carmen McCollum, "Conjugal Visits Survive Get-Tough Prison Legislation, *Clarion-Ledger* (Jackson, MS), September 11, 1994.

99 Hallie Gail Bridges, quoted in Carmen McCollum, "Conjugal Visits Survive Get-Tough Prison Legislation."

100 Josh Sanburn, "Mississippi Ending Conjugal Visits for Prisoners," *Time*, January 13, 2014, https://nation.time.com/2014/01/13/mississippi -ending-conjugal-visits-for-prisoners/.

101 Wiggum, "Defining Family in American Prisons," 374.

102 David Lohr, "No More Conjugal Visits for Mississippi Prison Inmates," *HuffPost*, January 14, 2014, https://www.huffpost.com/entry /mississippi-conjugal-visits_n_4597550.

103 Harvey, *The Shadow System*, 110, 112.

104 Victoria Phillips, quoted in Sylvia A. Harvey, "2.7 Million Kids Have Parents in Prison. They're Losing Their Right to Visit," *Nation*, December 2, 2015, https://www.thenation.com/article/archive/2-7m-kids -have-parents-in-prison-theyre-losing-their-right-to-visit/.

105 "Research Finds That Conjugal Visits Correlate with Fewer Sexual Assaults," *Prison Legal News*, May 19, 2014, https://www.prisonlegalnews .org/news/2014/may/19/research-finds-conjugal-visits-correlate-fewer -sexual-assaults/.

106 Jarvis DeBerry, "Mississippi Will End Conjugal Visits, Make Its Notorious Prisons Even Worse," NOLA.com, January 8, 2014, https://www.nola .com/opinions/article_5c35b7bf-61fd-5f47-839e-7ac6b583874c.html.

107 Chris Epps, quoted in McElreath et al., "The End of the Mississippi Experiment," 759–60.

108 Harvey, *The Shadow System*, 114–15.

109 C. J. Page, quoted in "Ban on Conjugal Visits Draws Protest," WLBT, January 17, 2014, https://www.wlbt.com/story/24483797/dozen/.

110 Colleen Jenkins, "Mississippi Move to End Conjugal Visits in Prisons Draws Protest," Reuters, January 16, 2014, https://www.reuters.com /article/us-usa-mississippi-conjugal/mississippi-move-to-end-conjugal -visits-in-prisons-draws-protest-idUSBREA0F11Y20140116.

111 Naeem Anderson, quoted in Harvey, *The Shadow System*, 118.

112 Jimmie E. Gates, "Chris Epps Sentenced to Almost 20 Years," *Clarion-Ledger* (Jackson, MS), May 24, 2017, https://www.clarionledger.com /story/news/2017/05/24/chris-epps-sentencing/341916001/.

113 The states that allow conjugal or extended family visits as of 2020 are California, Connecticut, New York, and Washington.

114 Dayan, *The Law Is a White Dog*, 70.

115 Bazzeta v. McGinnis, 286 F. 2df. 311 (6th Cir. 2002).

116 Heather Ann Thompson, "Conjugal Visits: Costly and Perpetuate Single Parenting?" interview with Michel Martin, *Tell Me More*, Janu-

ary 27, 2014, National Public Radio, https://www.npr.org/2014/01/27/267029376/conjugal-visits-costly-and-perpetuate-single-parenting.

117 Susan V. Koski, quoted in Palash Goosh, "Midnight Special: Conjugal Visitation Rights for U.S. Prisoners Vanishing, While 'Repressed' States Like Iran and Saudi Arabia Permit Them," *International Business Times*, January 14, 2014, https://www.ibtimes.com/midnight-special-conjugal-visitation-rights-us-prisoners-vanishing-while-repressed-states-iran-saudi.

118 Elie Mystal, "Conjugal Visits Are Almost a Thing of the Past," Above the Law, January 13, 2014, https://abovethelaw.com/2014/01/conjugal-visits-are-almost-a-thing-of-the-past/.

7. "TO RUB ELBOWS WITH FREEDOM"

1 Rothman, *The Discovery of the Asylum*, 70, 73, xix.

2 National Institute of Law Enforcement and Criminal Justice, *National Evaluation Program, Phase I Report*, 13–14.

3 Rothman, *Conscience and Convenience*, 32; Kamerling, *Capital and Convict*.

4 Cohn, *God Shakes Creation*, 148, 155.

5 Colvin, *Penitentiaries, Reformatories, and Chain Gangs*, 265.

6 Gill, "Mobility versus Liberty?," chap. 3, points out that though mobility is often equated with freedom, there are plenty of examples wherein (coerced) mobility is employed as a punitive force. One only has to think of the slave trade, deportation, involuntary transfer of prisoners, and other forms of removal to consider mobility as a form of discipline rather than a demonstration of freedom. In the context of electronic monitoring, Gill argues, the technology of surveillance is a kind of confinement without imprisonment, a burden that depends on the illusion of the mobility of the monitored.

7 Cohn, *God Shakes Creation*, 155.

8 Thompson, "Blinded by a 'Barbaric' South," 75–76, points out the problem with this ideology of southern exceptionalism: "Because liberal support for prison reform was so intimately tied to the desire to save southern prisons from a criminal justice system still locked in the inhumane practices of the antebellum era, once Americans came to believe that the South finally had modernized, they had little desire to intervene any further on behalf of inmate rights anywhere."

9 Barragan, "Christmas and Resistance to Slavery in the Americas"; Bigham and May, "The Time o' All Times?," 269.

10 Loguen, *The Rev. J. W. Loguen*, 262. See also Craft and Craft, *Running a Thousand Miles for Freedom*, 31.

11   Nissenbaum, *The Battle for Christmas*, 273.

12   Douglass, *My Bondage and My Freedom*, 255.

13   "Alabama One of Only Eight States Giving Convicts Christmas Freedom," *Dothan (AL) Eagle*, December 23, 1937; Daniel "Puddin' Foot" Clenny, quoted in "550 Step Out of Prison for Yule Freedom," *Montgomery (AL) Advertiser*, December 17, 1937.

14   "600 Convicts Given Christmas Paroles," *Troy (AL) Messenger*, December 17, 1938.

15   "State Convicts Get Christmas Holidays," *Chambers County (AL) News*, December 10, 1936.

16   David Bibbs Graves, "Text of Gov. Graves's Address to the 1939 Alabama State Legislature," *Montgomery (AL) Advertiser*, January 11, 1939.

17   "Convict Christmas Leave," *Miami News*, December 26, 1936.

18   "Alabama One of Only Eight States"; Richard Blystone, "Many Prisons Releasing Inmates for Christmas," *Arizona Daily Star*, December 24, 1969.

19   In Alabama, Christmas leaves were referred to as paroles; in Mississippi they were referred to as furloughs.

20   "World Views Alabama Parole Experiment," *South Alabamian*, January 19, 1938.

21   "Alabama Convict to Explain Christmas Paroles on Radio," *Anniston (AL) Star*, February 2, 1938; "E. M. Duskin Flies to New York to Broadcast on Yule Paroles," *Montgomery (AL) Advertiser*, February 2, 1938, 1. State leaders were upset at the negative attention Alabama was getting due to Scottsboro case; see "An Unfortunate Broadcast about Alabama's Prison System," *Birmingham (AL) News*, February 9, 1938.

22   J. E. Duskin, quoted in Tom F. Smith, "Penitentiary Opens Gates to Let Prisoner Broadcast," *Miami Herald*, February 3, 1938, 15.

23   "An Unfortunate Broadcast"; "Unusual Parole," *News-Journal* (Mansfield, OH), February 4, 1938; "Alabama's Nose Poked Again; Mr. Duskin Forgets Paroles," *Montgomery (AL) Advertiser*, February 5, 1938.

24   Alice Fogleman, letter to the editor, *Montgomery (AL) Advertiser*, February 6, 1938; Judge Walter B. Jones, "Off the Bench," *Montgomery (AL) Advertiser*, February 14. 1938.

25   "600 Convicts Going Back," *Prattville (AL) Progress*, January 5, 1939; "Parole Record Given Setback," *Selma (AL) Times-Journal*, January 6, 1939; "Alabama 'Christmas Parole' Unusually Unsuccessful in 1938," *Cullman (AL) Tribune*, January 19, 1939; "15 Lost Sheep Fail to Worry Prison Chiefs," *Montgomery (AL) Advertiser*, January 11, 1938.

26   David Bibbs Graves, quoted in "23 Convicts Who Got Yule Paroles Violate Pledges," *Birmingham (AL) News*, January 3, 1939.

27   "The Alabama Press," *Birmingham (AL) News*, July 27, 1939.

28   Prison Industries Reorganization Administration, *The Prison Problem in Alabama*, 43; Jones, "Off the Bench."

29 "End to Christmas Paroles Foreseen for Prisoners with Good Rec-
    ords," *Dothan (AL) Eagle*, July 18, 1939; "Parole Board Adopts Rules of
    Procedure," *Montgomery (AL) Advertiser*, October 28, 1939; "'Ain't No
    Santa' for Convicts," *Birmingham (AL) News*, December 6, 1939.

30 "No Christmas Paroles in '39, Board Decides," *Montgomery (AL) Adver-
    tiser*, December 7, 1939; "Convicts Agree to No Christmas Paroles," *Our
    Mountain Home* (Talladega, AL), December 13, 1939.

31 Wood, "Cole Blease's Pardoning Pen," 148, 157; "End of Alabama's Yule
    Paroles Saluted in Publisher's Column," *Montgomery (AL) Advertiser*,
    December 17, 1939.

32 "Most Alabama Parolees Keep Faith with Governor," *Clarion-Ledger*
    (Jackson, MS), January 6, 1937.

33 Sources say that in Mississippi the practice began as early as 1918,
    followed by Louisiana in 1922. See Markley, "Furlough Programs and
    Conjugal Visiting," 21.

34 Taylor, *Down on Parchman Farm*, 92, 94, 119.

35 Oshinsky, *Worse Than Slavery*, 227–28.

36 RG 27, Series 938: Pardon and Suspension Files, 1948–1952, Box 1792,
    Folder Tom Ambrose, Records of the Office of the Governor, Missis-
    sippi Department of Archives and History (hereafter MDAH).

37 Dunbar, *Delta Time*, 150.

38 Mary Anne Sistrunk, "Inside World: Life in the Mississippi State
    Penitentiary at Parchman," *Clarion-Ledger* (Jackson, MS), July 30,
    1950.

39 Frank Smith, "Cotton Kingdom," *Delta Democrat-Times* (Greenville,
    MS), August 15, 1946.

40 "Progress Platform for Mississippi," *Clarion-Ledger* (Jackson, MS),
    July 29, 1947; "Needed at Parchman—A New Policy," *Enterprise-Journal*
    (McComb, MS), July 2, 1953.

41 "Parchman Prisoners Get Deserved Break," *Clarion-Ledger* (Jackson,
    MS), December 20, 1956.

42 Bill Harpole to Governor Coleman, January 28, 1957, RG 27, Series 974:
    Penitentiary Correspondence, 1956–1960, Box 1941, Records of the
    Office of the Governor, MDAH.

43 "Parchman Cons to Get 10-Day Christmas Leave," *Monroe (LA) News-
    Star*, November 29, 1957.

44 "Pen Inmates No Longer Repay Furlough Time," *Enterprise-Journal*
    (McComb, MS), June 7, 1957.

45 Mr. and Mrs. Howard Weeks to Governor Coleman, December 3, 1959,
    RG 27, Series 974: Penitentiary Correspondence, 1956–1960, Box 1941,
    Records of the Office of the Governor, MDAH.

46 "Prison Polices Are Getting Fine Results," *Clarion Ledger* (Jackson,
    MS), April 18, 1957.

47   "Many Wish Them Merry Christmas," *Clarion-Ledger* (Jackson, MS), December 2, 1957.

48   Cliff Sessions, "200 Parchman Trusties Getting Ten Day Christmas Leaves Now," *Delta Democrat-Times* (Greenville, MS), December 3, 1958.

49   "Trusted Prisoners Prove Worthy of Limited Liberty at Christmas," *Clarion-Ledger* (Jackson, MS), December 6, 1945.

50   "They Earned Their Christmas," *Clarion-Ledger* (Jackson, MS), December 20, 1956.

51   O. P. Ferguson, quoted in Robert George, "Front Unit," *Inside World*, October 1959, 16.

52   Fred McGinnis, "Cow Lot," *Inside World*, January 1960, 19. See also Bobby "Petal" Merritt, "Nine Reports," *Inside World*, January 1963, 18; John Keith, "Report from Ten," *Inside World*, January 1963, 25; and "Camp Seven, 'Haps,'" *Inside World*, February 1963, 19.

53   Ozie Lee Townshend, "Camp One News," *Inside World*, December 1963, 19; John Keith, "Camp Ten Reports," *Inside World*, December 1963, 21.

54   "23 Convicts Who Got Yule Paroles Violate Pledges," *Birmingham (AL) News*, January 3, 1939; "16 of 554 Tardy on Yule Paroles," *Montgomery (AL) Advertiser*, January 5, 1938; "Convict Probe Being Pushed," *Birmingham (AL) News*, April 9, 1939.

55   "Alabama Sends 550 Home 'on Honor' to Enjoy Christmas Vacation," *Clarion-Ledger* (Jackson, MS), December 17, 1937; "Blame Weather in Failure of Parolees to Get Back," *Huntsville (AL) Times*, January 3, 1937; "Convicts Start Return to Prison as Paroles End," *Dothan (AL) Eagle*, January 2, 1938.

56   The most famous was Kenny Wagner, a white man who was a legendary circus performer as well as a moonshiner, thief, killer, "barker, roustabout, and trickster." See Oshinsky, *Worse Than Slavery*, 166–67. See also Turner, "Badmen, Black and White," 204, 212; Frank Smith, "Cotton's Kingdom," *Delta Democrat-Times* (Greenville, MS), August 15, 1946; "Bad Day for Bad Kennie," *Newsweek*, February 13, 1956, 31; "Kennie Wagner Visits Governor's Office during Xmas Furlough," *Clarion-Ledger* (Jackson, MS), December 7, 1946; and "Return of Kennie Wagner," *Clarion-Ledger* (Jackson, MS), May 22, 1949.

57   "Christmas Leave Program Is Big Boost," *Clarion-Ledger* (Jackson, MS), December 10, 1957, 10.

58   The incident that triggered the debate was the escape of Dale "Cowboy" Morris, a white man who had previously deserted from the US Marines and was convicted of killing an elderly storekeeper. For press coverage, see "Cowboy Morris Escapes Prison; Fails to Return," *Greenwood (MS) Commonwealth*, March 22, 1961; "Trustee Has Been Missing Eleven Days," *Hope (AR) Star*, March 22, 1961; "Believe Woman Led 'Cowboy' Astray," *Monroe (LA) News-Star*, March 23, 1961; and Cliff

Sessions, "Critics Slap Con Treatment," *Jackson (MS) Daily News*, March 26, 1961.

59   "Change of Attitude Needed," *Delta Democrat-Times* (Greenville, MS), March 28, 1961, emphasis added.

60   Kimble Berry, quoted in Mark Feinberg, "Convict Fights Extradition Tries; on Christmas Leave, Prison Says," *Boston Globe*, January 1, 1962; Mark Feinberg, "Lynn Convict's Prison Charges Jolt Mississippi; 2 Probes Due," *Boston Globe*, January 2, 1962. See also Final Report of Joint Senate/House Subcommittee Concerning the Operation of the State Penitentiary, RG 47, Series 2376: Joint Committee Files and Reports, Box 7152, Folder The Kimble Berry Affair, Records of the Legislature, MDAH.

61   "Burnely Raps Leave Policy at Parchman," *Delta Democrat-Times* (Greenville, MS), January 17, 1964.

62   Final Report of the Joint Senate/House Subcommittee Concerning the Operation of the State Penitentiary, p. 8, RG 47, Box 7152, Folder The Kimble Berry Affair, Records of the Legislature, MDAH.

63   Charles M. Hills, "Affairs of State," *Clarion-Ledger* (Jackson, MS), February 7, 1962.

64   Elliott Chaze, "The Chilling Story of a Rape-Slayer's Prison Leave Here," *Hattiesburg (MS) American*, March 9, 1966.

65   Howard McDonnell, quoted in James Bonney, "Demand Revision of Prison Leave Program," *Hattiesburg (MS) American*, March 10, 1966. McDonnell was an outspoken critic of the use of whipping at Parchman and urged Governor Ross Barnett to ensure its elimination, since the practice was "contrary to every principle of science, Christianity, and humanity."

66   James Bonney, "Miss. Solons Ask Revision of Furlough Plan at Prison," *Town Talk* (Alexandria, LA), March 10, 1966; Elliott Chaze, "Limits Needed in Concern for Prisoners' Morale," *Hattiesburg (MS) American*, March 12, 1966.

67   Richard Blystone, "Many Prisons Releasing Inmates for Christmas," *Arizona Daily Star*, December 24, 1969, 18.

68   Mississippi State Penitentiary, *Annual Report*, 1975, RG 49, Department of the Penitentiary Collection, MDAH.

69   James Saggus, "Lawmakers Agree Parchman to Swing into Spotlight," *Greenwood (MS) Commonwealth*, February 8, 1964; Steve Cannizaro, "Number of Inmates on Festive Leave Down," *Clarion-Ledger* (Jackson, MS), December 13, 1977.

70   Editorial, *Angolite*, May 23, 1953, 1, emphasis in the original.

71   Blue, *Doing Time in the Great Depression*, 167.

72   Robert Roberts and James Alexander, "Sports," *Inside World*, June 1959, 22.

73 "The Cover," *Inside World*, June 1959, 26.

74 "Camp 5," *Inside World*, August, 1965, 18.

75 Gnagy, *Texas Jailhouse Music*, describes the popularity of incarcerated musicians in Texas in the 1930s who communicated their talents on a free-world radio station as well as in person at state fairs and fiddle contests. Blue, *Doing Time in the Depression*, 137–38, argues that Texas prison's radio show, *Thirty Minutes behind the Walls*, served as a form of public punishment whose entertainment value "masked the violence that remained an intrinsic part of incarceration" and reinforced racial and class hierarchies. At the same time, the music incarcerated musicians played "sustained affective pleasure and dignity for prisoners and listeners alike."

76 Wendell Cannon, quoted in James R. Reid, "Prisoners Are Offered An Outlet for Talents—Opportunity for Future," *Memphis (TN) Press-Scimitar*, October 21, 1960.

77 Harry Marsh, "Parchman Adds Unlikely Mixture of Chapel, Rock and Roll Music," *Delta Democrat-Times* (Greenville, MS), November 27, 1960.

78 D. R. Duke, "The Insiders News," *Inside World*, June 1963, 14; Gerald A. Lewis, "The Confiners News," *Inside World*, June 1963, 15; "Your New 'Big Boss' Mr. Fred Jones," *Inside World*, May 1960, 27.

79 Cliff Sessions, "Rock 'n' Roll Takes Place of Screams," *Jackson (MS) Daily News*, June 10, 1960.

80 Reid, "Prisoners Are Offered an Outlet for Talents."

81 Marsh, "Parchman Adds Unlikely Mixture."

82 "The Boss Says," *Inside World*, July 1960, 6.

83 Mississippi State Penitentiary, *Annual Report*, 1976, RG 49, Department of the Penitentiary Collection, MDAH.

84 Moore, "I'm Gonna Stay Right Here until They Tear This Barrelhouse Down," 440.

85 John "Flash" Gordon, in Bob, "Parchman from the Inside," *That's All Rite Mama* (blog), March 7, 2009, http://thatsallritemama.blogspot.com/2009/03/mississippi-state-penitentiary-bands.html.

86 Hemsworth, "Carceral Acoustemologies," 162, analyzes how sound is used by prison authorities as a tool of control and by incarcerated people as a means of reclaiming dignity and ameliorate pain: "The outspreading capacity of sound, which extends touch beyond bodily extremities, reconstitutes prison experience by allowing people to access different spatial and temporal contexts without requiring much movement. Sound stitches people and place together, allowing for sociality to emerge in conditions that might otherwise prohibit it."

87 "Cops and Robbers," editorial, *Angolite*, October 17, 1953, 4, emphasis in the original.

88 "These Pardon Ads," *Angolite*, May 29, 1954, 5.

89   "Are YOU Afraid of Ex-Convicts?," editorial, *Inside World*, March 1960, 3.

90   "Outcasts," *Inside World*, February, 1965, 23, emphasis in the original.

91   "Are YOU Afraid of Ex-Convicts?," 3.

92   "Tell or Not Tell?," editorial, *Angolite*, July 3, 1954, 4.

93   Cohn, *God Shakes Creation*, 143–44. Cohn's view has much in common with those expressed by the Southern Agrarians, whose manifesto, *I'll Take My Stand*, was a romantic and reactionary defense of the Old South. These thinkers opposed the dislocating effects of urbanism, industrialism, and capitalism on southern society. See Twelve Southerners, *I'll Take My Stand*.

94   Cummins, *The Rise and Fall*, 19.

95   John Irwin, quoted in Cummins, *The Rise and Fall*, 19.

96   Reed Cozart, "The Challenge at Angola," 3.

97   Fairclough, *Race and Democracy*, 193; James V. Bennett, "To What Extent Can Open Institutions Take the Place of the Traditional Prison?," Twelfth Annual International Penal and Penitentiary Congress, The Hague, 1950. Reprinted in Bennett, *Of Prisons and Justice*, 151; Bennett, *I Chose Prison*, chap. 8.

98   Significantly, when his work at Angola ended in 1955, Cozart became a pardon attorney for the US Department of Justice. In describing his career at congressional hearings, he remarked, "Maybe I am ready to graduate now—probation, parole, and now pardon." Statement of Reed Cozart, Hearings before the Subcommittee of the Committee on Appropriations, House of Representatives, 84th Cong., 2nd Sess., January 10, 1956, 31, https://www.google.com/books/edition/Hearings /n17WAAAAMAAJ?hl=en&gbpv=0.

99   Reed Cozart, as told to Edward W. Stagg, "Our Prisons Need Not Fail," *Saturday Evening Post*, October 8, 1955, 17, 18, 22.

100   Carpenter, *Federal Correctional Institution,* 1; Frederic Sondern Jr., "Prison without a Wall," *Reader's Digest*, September 1949, 71.

101   Bennett, "To What Extent?," 151.

102   Reed Cozart, "Rehabilitation of Criminal Offenders: The Protection of Society," address delivered before the midwinter meeting of the National Association of County and Prosecuting Attorneys, New Orleans, February 23, 1956, in *Vital Speeches of the Day*, May 1, 1956, 444–448; Cozart in Stagg, "Our Prisons Need Not Fail," 18.

103   Cozart, "The Challenge at Angola," 5.

104   Cozart, "The Challenge at Angola," 25.

105   Perkinson, "Angola and the Agony of Prison Reform," 15; Cozart, "Reforms in Louisiana," *Prison Journal* 34, no. 1 (1954): 23.

106   Cozart, "What Happened to America's Worst Prison?," *Federal Probation* 19, no. 4 (1955): 34. While in Texas, dormitory living was replaced

by single-cells as a measure to "contain" the so-called contagion of homosexuality, Angola kept its dormitory housing and even constructed new dormitories under Cozart's direction. Angola reserved single-cell living for those in maximum security, those on death row, those in extended lockdown, and those in solitary confinement. Chase, *We Are Not Slaves*, 47–49; Johnston, "Recent Trends in Correctional Architecture," *British Journal of Criminology* 1, no. 4 (1961): 331.

107 Bennett, "To What Extent?" 147.

108 Davis, *It Happened by Design*, 89, 24.

109 Cozart, "Should Prisons Be Merely Dungeons?," *Federal Probation* 19, no. 4 (1955): 204–8.

110 Johnson and Rhodes, "Institutionalization," 219–36.

111 Hopper, *Sex in Prison*, 143–44.

112 Cozart in Stagg, "Our Prisons Need Not Fail," 122.

113 Davis, *It Happened by Design*, 24.

114 "Effusions," *Angolite*, May 29, 1954, 5.

115 Editorial, *Angolite*, May 22, 1954, 4.

116 "Reformers Unpopular," editorial, *Angolite*, May 29, 1954, 4. The *Angolite* was a censored magazine until 1975.

117 "Angola Turns the Corner," editorial, *Angolite*, March 27, 1954, 4.

118 "Bad Prison Goes Straight," *Life*, December 12, 1955, 58.

119 "A New Angola, A New Idea," *Angolite*, September 25, 1954, 7. The comparison with a boudoir is made more than once in the *Angolite*. While the term *boudoir* connotes a feminine and therefore perhaps illicit space, the context suggests that the author uses the metaphor as a proxy for a space that is private, luxurious, desirable, and hints at freedom.

120 "Reformers Unpopular," editorial, *Angolite*, May 29, 1954, 4; "Angola Turns the Corner," *Angolite*, March 27, 1954, 4.

121 "Penal Press News: Experiments Indicate Open Prisons May Be Answer," *Inside World*, January 1965, 17.

122 "What's Ahead for Mississippi State Penitentiary?" *Inside World*, August 1965, 5–6.

123 "So This Is Christmas," editorial, *Angolite*, December 25, 1953, 10. During the Christmas season of 1954, a writer for the *Angolite* called the furloughs granted in Mississippi "a good and healthy practice . . . calculated to increase morale"; "300 Furloughs for Christmas," *Angolite*, December 15, 1954, 4.

124 Associated Press, "Texas Prison Helps Convict Stay Free," *Inside World*, April 1965, 25.

125 Tom Runyon, "That Other Wall," *Inside World*, September 1959, 22.

126 "Christmas Leave Program Is Big Boost," *Clarion-Ledger* (Jackson, MS), December 10, 1957; "Penal Program Gets Nationwide Interest," *Clarion-Ledger* (Jackson, MS), April 19, 1960.

127 David Brown, "Parchman Prisoners' Day from 'Can to Can't'; Like
     Baseball," *Delta Democrat-Times* (Greenville, MS), April 10, 1958.

128 Bill Harpole, quoted in "Prison Policies Are Getting Fine Results,"
     Clarion-Ledger (Jackson, MS), April 18, 1957.

129 Zemans and Cavan, "Marital Relationships of Prisoners," 56.

130 Nagel, *The New Red Barn*, 41, 47.

131 "Dateline . . . Angola," *Angolite*, July 24, 1954, 3.

132 President's Commission on Law Enforcement and Administration of
     Justice, *The Challenge of Crime*, 176.

133 Garrett Heyns, M.D., to B. J. Rhay and Ernest C. Timpani, Washington
     State Penitentiary, "Open Letter," *Inside World*, June 1960, 18, emphasis
     in the original.

134 See, for example, McCarthy, "The Development, Function and
     Future."

8. CONQUERING PRISON WALLS

1   John Kendall, "State Parole Program: For Convict or Public?," *Los An-
    geles Times,* December 19, 1971; Richard West, "Convict on Three-Day
    Pass Held in Shooting," *Los Angeles Times*, December 4, 1971.

2   Dial Torgerson, "Chief Tells How Murder Case Was Unraveled," *Los
    Angeles Times*, December 2, 1969; "Four Slave Auction Figures to Be
    Tried," *Oroville (CA) Mercury Register*, April 27, 1976. Davis's task force
    to combat gang violence, which targeted African American and Latinx
    teenagers, was originally called Total Resources against South Bureau
    Hoodlums (TRASH), but was soon renamed Community Resources
    against Street Hoodlums (CRASH); Felker-Kantor, *Policing Los Angeles*,
    104–7.

3   Edward M. Davis, quoted in "State Parole Program: For Convict or
    Public?," *Los Angeles Times*, December 19, 1971.

4   Ronald Reagan, quoted in "Reagan Criticizes Davis' Letter, Backs
    Parole, Furlough Policies," *Los Angeles Times*, October 29, 1971.

5   Milton Burdman, quoted in "State Parole Program." Burdman, "Realism
    in Community-Based Correctional Services," 71, condemns the prison
    as "an inefficient, ineffective, and obsolete social instrument—the total
    institution" and asserts that 70 percent of all offenders can be placed
    immediately in community-based correctional activities." A sociologist
    by training, Burdman was a vocal critic of prisons and opposed fixed
    sentences. In 1967 he served on the President's Commission on Law
    Enforcement and Administration of Justice.

6   "The California Plan—How One State Is Salvaging Its Convicts," *US
    News and World Report*, August 24, 1970, 46.

7 Edward M. Davis, "America at the Crossroads," quoted in Felker-Kantor, *Policing Los Angeles,* 49.

8 A federal commission studying furloughs in 1976 observed, "Although most furlough programs are relatively restricted, law enforcement agencies and prosecutors tend to view them negatively." See National Institute of Law Enforcement and Criminal Justice, *National Evaluation Program, Phase I Report,* 2.

9 John N. Mitchell, "New Doors, Not Old Walls," *LEAA Newsletter* 2, no. 2 (January–February 1972): 13, 2.

10 The Prison Rehabilitation Act of 1965 authorized furloughs, a system of work release, and the use of community residential treatment centers for adult prisoners. See Carpenter, "The Federal Work Release Program," 690.

11 President's Commission on Law Enforcement and Administration of Justice, *The Challenge of Crime in a Free Society,* 176, 177, vii.

12 Carpenter, "The Federal Work Release Program," 692–93.

13 Carpenter, "The Federal Work Release Program," 700.

14 For a critique of community corrections, see O'Brien, "'A Prison in Your Community.'"

15 O'Brien, "'A Prison in Your Community,'" 93–94, demonstrates that the community-based treatment initiatives that emerged under the auspices of community corrections "matured to become part of the broader infrastructures of punishment and confinement that characterized mass incarceration" and eventually "replicated prisons' technologies for surveillance, control, confinement, and management."

16 Nelson, "Community-Based Correctional Treatment," 90–91.

17 President's Commission on Law Enforcement and Administration of Justice, *The Challenge of Crime in a Free Society,* 12, 165, 172.

18 Wodahl and Garland, "The Evolution of Community Corrections," 92.

19 Gerhard O. W. Mueller, quoted in "Pushing Prisons Aside," *Architectural Forum,* March 1973, 29.

20 Stojkovic, "The President's Crime Commission Recommendations," 39.

21 President's Commission on Law Enforcement and Administration of Justice, *The Challenge of Crime in a Free Society,* 163.

22 Ada Louise Huxtable, "New Prison Designs Emphasize Human Elements," *New York Times,* September 21, 1971.

23 Gilbert, "Observations about Recent Correctional Architecture," 10.

24 Sommer, *Tight Spaces,* 2–3.

25 Sommer, *The End of Imprisonment,* 16.

26 Sommer, *Tight Spaces,* 145, 11.

27 "Pushing Prisons Aside," 30.

28 Gilbert, "Observations about Recent Correctional Architecture," 8.

29 William G. Nagel, quoted in Balchen, "Prisons: The Changing Outside View of the Inside," 16. For an analysis of the federal government's

effort to shape human behavior through architectural and environmental design during the Cold War, see Knoblauch, *The Architecture of Good Behavior*.

30 Murakawa, *The First Civil Right*, 97.

31 National Advisory Commission on Criminal Justice Standards and Goals, *Executive Summary*, 47.

32 Markley, "Furlough Programs and Conjugal Visiting," 19–20.

33 Nagel, "A Moratorium on Correctional Construction," 72.

34 Markley, "Furlough Programs and Conjugal Visiting," 22.

35 Johns, "Alternatives to Conjugal Visiting," 48.

36 Nelson, "Community-Based Correctional Treatment," 86; National Institute of Law Enforcement and Criminal Justice, *National Evaluation Program*, 9.

37 McCarthy, "The Development, Function and Future," 18.

38 National Institute of Law Enforcement and Criminal Justice, *National Evaluation Program*, 32, 72–77.

39 McCarthy, "The Development, Function and Future," 26.

40 Michael S. Serrill, "Prison Furloughs in America," *Corrections*, July–August 1975, 2–3.

41 Hogarty, "The Sargent Governorship," 116–17.

42 Ray Richard, "Walpole Prison: A Status Report," *Boston Globe*, April 16, 1973. In 1966 the Massachusetts Legislature passed the Comprehensive Mental Health and Retardation Act, whose guiding principle was "community-based" mental health centers analogous to community-based correctional institutions. One of Goldmark's objectives was to move as many people as possible out of huge state hospitals and into smaller community facilities; Hogarty, "The Sargent Governorship," 117, 129. For an analysis of the broader movement to deinstitutionalize people in mental hospitals and the relationship of this process to the growth of prisons, see Parsons, *From Asylum to Prison*.

43 Richard, "Walpole Prison."

44 Bissonette et al., *When the Prisoners Ran Walpole*, 24.

45 Bissonette et al., *When the Prisoners Ran Walpole*, 29.

46 Bissonette et al., *When the Prisoners Ran Walpole*.

47 Heymann et al., *Massachusetts Department of Correction*, app. G, 337.

48 Robert M. Moore, quoted in John Hough, "A Chronology of Recent Events in Massachusetts State Prisons," Corrections, Part V: Prisons, Prison Reform, and Prisoners' Rights: Massachusetts, Hearings before the House of Representatives Committee on the Judiciary, Subcommittee No. 3, 92nd Cong., 1st Sess., December 18, 1971, app. H, 358.

49 Francis Sargent, quoted in Heymann et al., *Massachusetts Department of Correction*, pt. 1, 16.

50 Corrections, Part V: Prisons, Prison Reform, and Prisoners' Rights, 101.

51 Citizens' Committee on Corrections, *Corrections '71*, 6, 37, 33–34.

52 Peter Goldmark, quoted in Heymann et al., *Massachusetts Department of Correction*, pt. 1, 7.

53 Heymann et al., *Massachusetts Department of Correction*, pt. 2, 10.

54 Heymann et al., *Massachusetts Department of Correction*, pt. 1, 32.

55 "Atlanta Native John O. Boone, Massachusetts' First Black Commissioner of Corrections Dies at Age 93," *Atlanta Daily World*, December 3, 2012, https://atlantadailyworld.com/2012/12/03/atlanta-native-john-o -boone-massachusetts-first-black-commissioner-of-corrections-dies-at -age-93; Bissonette et al., *When the Prisoners Ran Walpole*, 49; Hearings before the Subcommittee to Investigate Juvenile Delinquency of the Committee on the Judiciary, US Senate, 91st Cong., 1st Sess., pt. 20, 1969–70, 5692.

56 Heymann et al., *Massachusetts Department of Correction*, pt. 2, 3.

57 Heymann et al., *Massachusetts Department of Correction*, pt. 2, 4.

58 Hearings before the Subcommittee to Investigate Juvenile Delinquency, 5692.

59 Statement of James O. Chase, Youth Guidance Council, Crime in the National Capital, Hearings before the Committee on the District of Columbia, US Senate, 91st Cong., 2nd Sess., pt. 8, January/February 1970, 2208.

60 Testimony of John O. Boone, Law Enforcement Assistance Administration, Hearings before the Subcommittee on Crime of the Committee of the Judiciary, House of Representatives, 94th Cong., 2nd Sess., pt. 1, March/April 1976, 184.

61 John O. Boone, quoted in Reich, *Public Management in a Democratic Society*, 115.

62 Berger and Losier, *Rethinking the American Prison Movement*, 115.

63 Peter C. Goldmark Jr., quoted in Heymann et al., *Massachusetts Department of Correction*, pt. 2, 5.

64 F. B. Taylor Jr., "Norfolk Guard Says Inmates Shifted for No Reason," *Boston Globe*, November 14, 1971. Corrections hearings state that guards handed Commissioner John J. Fitzpatrick a list of inmates, demanded authorization to lock them up, and threatened to call in sick if he refused. Fitzpatrick denied the threat but explained that the inmates in question were a threat to the safety of the institution. Corrections, Hearings before Subcommittee No. 3 of the Committee on the Judiciary, House of Representatives, 92nd Cong., 1st Sess., pt. 4, November 23, 1971, App. H, 363.

65 Statement of Max D. Stern, Corrections, Hearings before Subcommittee No. 3 of the Committee on the Judiciary, House of Representatives, 92nd Cong., 1st Sess., pt. 5, December 18, 1971, 122.

66 Conrad and Ujlaki, *Three Thousand Years and Life.*

67 Bissonette et al., *When the Prisoners Ran Walpole*, 92–94, 97–100.

68 Berger and Losier, *Rethinking the American Prison Movement*, 114, 116.

69 James B. Witkin, notes, Phyllis M. Ryan Papers, Northeastern University Archives and Special Collections (hereafter Ryan Papers), Ad Hoc Committee Papers 1971–1973, M094, Box 1, Folder 9.

70 Berger and Losier, *Rethinking the American Prison Movement*, 115.

71 Testimony of Jerome G. Miller, Corrections, Part V: Prisons, Prison Reform, and Prisoners' Rights, 16–18.

72 Gerald A. Clark, "An Inmate's Story," *Boston Globe*, November 29, 1971, 12.

73 Gerard Letellier, quoted in James F. Donohue, "Inmates at Walpole Prison Studying Public Relations," *Cumberland News,* September 6, 1972.

74 Charles McDonald, quoted in "Maximum Security Cons Move to Boost Public Image," *Brigham Young University Daily Universe*, September 7, 1972.

75 William Cockerham, "Prisoners' Dance to Coll's Idea," *Hartford (CT) Courant*, July 11, 1972.

76 Paul Durant, quoted in Bruce Kimball, "Elderly Brighten a Day at Walpole," *Boston Globe*, July 10, 1972.

77 Heymann et al., *Massachusetts Department of Correction*, pt. 2, 30.

78 Reddebrek, "1973: Prisoners Take Control of Walpole Prison"; Rev. Edward Rodman and others to Concerned Citizens, April 25, 1973, Ryan Papers, Ad Hoc Committee Papers, 1971–1973, M094, Box 1, Folder 8.

79 Bissonette et al., *When the Prisoners Ran Walpole*, 131.

80 Heymann et al., *Massachusetts Department of Correction*, pt. 2, 27.

81 Robert Healy, "The Real Issue at Walpole," *Boston Globe*, March 26, 1973; Joseph Rosenbloom, "Guards Urge Sargent: Restore Order at Walpole," *Boston Globe*, March 9, 1973.

82 Reddebrek, "1973: Prisoners Take Control of Walpole Prison."

83 Ray Richard, "A Look at the Prison Boone Ran," *Boston Globe*, July 2, 1972; "Atlantan Boone Takes Helm as Mass. Prison Head," *Atlanta Voice*, January 1, 1972; "Lorton Suit Brings Atty. Gen. Miller under Fire," *Winchester (VA) Evening Star*, January 5, 1973.

    Delbert C. Jackson, Boone's successor at Lorton, was a staunch advocate of placing prisoners in community-based settings and granted weekend holiday furloughs. He headed Lorton for eight stormy years that were faced with escapes, strikes, litigation, walkouts by guards, and a takeover by prisoners. In a 1975 interview, Jackson avowed, "As a penologist and a human being, I could not for a moment understand, much less tolerate, warehousing of fellow human beings"; Delbert C.

Jackson, quoted in Paul W. Valentine, "Delbert Jackson, D.C. Chief of Corrections, Dies at 52," *Washington Post*, March 11, 1982, https://www.washingtonpost.com/archive/local/1982/03/11/delbert-jackson-dc-chief-of-corrections-dies-at-52/91d7b0a2-8cf8-4b67-b997-02edc5d3b74c/?noredirect=on&utm_term=.f18017f28761. See also "Washington Article Spotlights Tech Graduate D. C. Jackson," *Beckley (WV) Post-Herald*, May 12, 1972.

84   "Lorton Suit Brings Atty. Gen. Miller under Fire."

85   "Inmate Furlough Program Halted, Police Pressure Seen as Partial Cause," *Corrections Digest*, vol. 2, 1971, 11–12.

86   Heymann et al., *Massachusetts Department of Correction*, pt. 2, 26.

87   Massachusetts Department of Correction, Division of Planning and Research, *Interim Report on Furloughs,* 1973, 1.

88   O'Malley and LeClair, *An Evaluation of the Massachusetts Furlough Experience*, 1.

89   Farrington, *The Massachusetts Furlough Experience*, 1.

90   Bissonette et al., *When the Prisoners Ran Walpole*, 207.

91   Rev. Rodman and others to Concerned Citizens.

92   Juan Matthews, quoted in Serrill, "Prison Furloughs in America," 55.

93   Leo Nolin, "Conversation with Leo Nolin," *Question Mark*, June–July 1977, 10.

94   "Norfolk Lifers," *Question Mark*, June–July 1977, 19, 21.

95   Jerry Taylor, "In Bay State Prisons, the Heat Is on Furloughs," *Boston Globe*, April 8, 1973.

96   Ralph Hamm, quoted in Bissonette et al., *When the Prisoners Ran Walpole*, 151.

97   Conrad and Ujlaki, *Three Thousand Years and Life*.

98   Arnold King, interview with the author, June 10, 2021.

99   "Mass. Furlough System under Legislative Attack," *Black Panther*, June 29, 1974, 9.

100   "Mixed Feelings," *Voice of Prison*, Christmas 1971, 2. Washington State Penitentiary Records, Washington State Penitentiary Collection, Penrose Library, Whitman College, Box 3, Folder 6.

101   Tom Henshaw, "Hannon Announces for Atty. Gen," *Quincy (MA) Sun*, January 31, 1974.

102   "Mass. Furlough System under Legislative Attack"; Jeff McLaughlin, "Inmates, Prison Officials Express Despair, Anger, Fear over Anti-furlough Vote," *Boston Globe*, May 17, 1974.

103   Jonathan L. Healy, quoted in "Mass. House Votes to Curb Prison Furloughs," *Boston Globe*, May 17, 1974; Michael Kenney, "Compromise Sought on Prison Furloughs," *Boston Globe*, May 9, 1974.

104   Serrill, "Prison Furloughs in America," 4.

105   "Commissioner Boone," Editorial, *Lowell (MA) Sun*, June 19, 1973.

106   Tom Wicker, "No More Jive Talk on Reform," *New York Times*, May 27,
       1973. It can be misleading to cite "escape rates" uncritically, as the num-
       bers don't reveal what practitioners counted as an escape. In Massachu-
       setts, evaluations of the furlough program defined *escape* as "failure of
       return within two hours of the allotted furlough time whether or not
       there were extenuating circumstances," but researchers did not create
       a separate category for those who fled and never returned. On a more
       granular level, some studies delineated various abuses of the furlough
       privilege, which included returning intoxicated, being arrested, or
       being late within two hours. Massachusetts Department of Correction,
       Division of Research, Correction/Parole Information System Unit,
       Descriptions of Furloughs Granted, 13.
107   John F. Cullen, "Subilosky Captured in New Hampshire Trailer
       Park," *Boston Globe*, May 4, 1973; "Escapee Subilosky Sought in Bank
       Holdup," *Boston Globe*, May 1, 1973.
108   "Subilosky's Story," *Boston Globe*, May 4, 1973.
109   "Walpole Guards Accused of Rigging Furlough Issue," *North Adams
       (MA) Transcript*, April 3, 1973.
110   Seymour Linscott, "Walpole Talk Resumes; Probe Subilosky Leave,"
       Boston Globe, March 27, 1973.
111   Francis Sargent, quoted in "Sargent Calls Furloughs Best Prison Re-
       form," *Boston Globe*, April 4, 1973.
112   Francis Sargent, quoted in "Boone Out, State Police Head in Charge of
       Walpole," *North Adams (MA) Transcript*, June 22, 1973.
113   Jonathan Fuerbringer, "Boone's Reforms Will Be Implemented," *Boston
       Globe*, June 23, 1973.
114   Stephen Wermiel, "Sargent Pressured to Act, Boone Says," *Boston Globe*,
       June 23, 1973.
115   John O. Boone, quoted in Bissonette et al., *When the Prisoners Ran
       Walpole*, 199.
116   John Buckley, quoted in Kenneth D. Campbell, "Harrington Asks Unity
       at a 'Delicate' Time," *Boston Globe*, June 22, 1973.
117   "Black Prison Official Scapegoated," *Black Panther*, June 30, 1973, 7.
118   Public letter to Governor Sargent, August 21, 1973, Ryan Papers, NPRA,
       M094, Box 4, Folder 44.
119   Robert Dellelo, quoted in Bissonette et al., *When the Prisoners Ran
       Walpole*, 163.
120   Frank Hall, quoted in Pauline Dishmon, "Prison Furlough Program Is
       Most Visible Sign of Reform Mandated By Law," *Winchester (MA) Star*,
       November 21, 1974.
121   Frank Hall, quoted in Serrill, "Prison Furloughs in America," 53.
122   Ad Hoc Press Release, undated, Ryan Papers, Ad Hoc Committee,
       M094, Box 1, Folder 8.

123 Kerry Gruson, "Reforms in the Prisons Hang in the Balance," *Boston Phoenix*, July 17, 1973.

124 "Great Debate Being Waged on Way State Prison Is Run," *Newton (MA) Graphic*, April 5, 1973.

125 Devlin v. Commissioner of Correction, 364 Mass. 435 (1973) 305 N.E.2d 847.

126 Andrea J. Goodman, "Urban Youths Scared Straight by Prisoners' Straight Talk," *Boston Sunday Globe*, July 22, 1990.

127 Lorraine Loviglio, "Furloughs Like a Rebirth to Lifers," *Boston Globe*, July 14, 1974.

128 King, "George Is Ready."

129 "Prison Boxer to Be Released for Fight," *News-Messenger* (Fremont, OH), January 22, 1974.

130 Richard Cote, quoted in Lorraine Loviglio, "Furloughs Like a Rebirth to Lifers," *Boston Globe*, July 14, 1974. Lifers elsewhere were equally determined to prove that they were not vicious animals. At the Washington State Penitentiary, the Lifers' Club held "rap sessions" with community members to disabuse them of stereotypes; the penitentiary also had a program called Take a Lifer to Dinner, which allowed prison employees to take a prisoner serving a life sentence to their home on a Sunday. Lifers were singled out for this privilege because Washington's 1971 law authorizing furloughs for up to thirty days excluded lifers from eligibility. See Murray, *Unusual Punishment*, 43–44; "Lifer's Club and Self-Government," *Voice of Prison*, Christmas 1971, 10; "From a Woman's Point of View," *Voice of Prison*, Christmas 1971, 11; "Lifers are Hosts at Happy Prison," *Lifer* (Louisiana State Penitentiary), November–December 1973, 17; "Membership Exclusive in 'Lifers with Hope," *Longview (WA) Daily News*, August 12, 1971.

131 Loviglio, "Furloughs Like a Rebirth to Lifers."

132 Stephen Wermiel, "Quinn Ignores Facts in Opinion on Lifers," *Boston Globe*, September 20, 1973.

133 Cannon, *First Degree Murder*, 11; Farrington, "The Massachusetts Furlough Experience," 7, 11, 12, 11.

134 Wermiel, "Quinn Ignores Facts"; Jerry Taylor, "First-Degree Lifers Still Furloughed, despite Quinn Ruling," *Boston Globe*, September 1, 1973; Stephen Wermiel, "Furloughs Ended for First-Degree Murder Inmates," *Boston Globe*, September 13, 1973.

135 James McAlister, quoted in McLaughlin, "Inmates, Prison Officials Express Despair."

136 Joseph Harvey, "Furloughs for Lifers Unanimously OK'd by Mass. High Court," *Boston Globe*, December 21, 1973.

137 Devlin v. Commissioner of Correction.

138 "Life Sentence Commuted," *Boston Globe*, July 31, 1975.

1   Farrington and Wittenberg, *The Concord Achievement Rehabilitation Volunteer Experience*, 2.

2   Anderson, *Crime and the Politics of Hysteria*, 97–101.

3   William Horton, Work Evaluation, CARVE Program, in Massachusetts General Court, House of Representatives Post Audit and Oversight Bureau (hereafter Massachusetts General Court), *Department of Correction: Furlough Program*, 78–80.

4   Anderson, *Crime and the Politics of Hysteria*, 112–13. To be clear, the Massachusetts DOC defined a furlough "escape" as failure to return to a correctional facility within two hours of the designated time of return. Eight people that year failed to return entirely, but an additional three were late. Lorant, *1986 Annual Statistical Report*, 4–5.

5   Jeffrey M. Elliott, "The 'Willie' Horton Nobody Knows: The Man and the Symbol," *The Nation*, August 23, 1993, 201–5.

6   "The Campaign Ad that Reshaped Criminal Justice," *The Takeaway* (podcast), NYC Studios, May 18, 2015, https://www.wnycstudios.org/podcasts/takeaway/segments/crime-reshaped-criminal-justice.

7   Anderson, *Crime and the Politics of Hysteria*, 214; Newburn and Jones, "Symbolic Politics and Penal Populism"; Sasson, "William Horton's Long Shadow"; Mendelberg, *The Race Card*, chaps. 5–6; Schwartzapfel and Keller, "Willie Horton Revisited."

8   Anderson, *Crime and the Politics of Hysteria*, 215.

9   Willie Horton, "A Few Words with Willie Horton," interview by Jeffrey M. Elliot, *Playboy*, December 1989, 170.

10 Anderson, *Crime and the Politics of Hysteria*, 59–60.

11 Anderson, *Crime and the Politics of Hysteria*, 132.

12 Alexander Cockburn, "A Disgusting Award for a Disgusting Paper," *Nation*, May 7, 1988, 632–33.

13 Angela Miller, quoted in Anderson, *Crime and the Politics of Hysteria*, 153.

14 Cliff Barnes, quoted in Anderson, *Crime and the Politics of Hysteria*, 153.

15 Anderson, *Crime and the Politics of Hysteria*, 153.

16 McCarthy, "The Development, Function and Future," 16–17.

17 "Inmate Owes Celebrity Tag to Campaign," *Clarion-Ledger* (Jackson, MS), October 11, 1988, 3.

18 Schwartzapfel and Keller, "Willie Horton Revisited"; Lisa Kashinsky, "Horton Case Linked Newspaper and President," *Eagle-Tribune* (North Andover, MA), December 6, 2018, https://www.eagletribune.com/news/merrimack_valley/horton-case-linked-newspaper-and-president/article_9d153aa5-bc8e-573d-9521-a9dd65f4db1f.html.

19 Mike Royko, "Democrats Must Learn to Fight Dirty Too," *Hattiesburg (MS) American*, October 22, 1988, emphasis in the original.

20 Witcover, *No Way to Pick a President*, 93.

21 Phyllis Schlafly to Walter Huss, September 1988, Walter Huss Papers, University of Oregon Special Collections, Box 27, Dukakis Folder; Poster for "Justice on Furlough," Walter Huss Papers, University of Oregon Special Collections, Box 27, Dukakis Folder. My thanks to Seth Cotlar for sharing this source with me.

22 George H. W. Bush, quoted in Sidney Blumenthal, "Willie Horton: The Making of a Campaign Issue," *Washington Post*, October 28, 1988, https://www.washingtonpost.com/archive/lifestyle/1988/10/28/willie -horton-the-making-of-an-election-issue/4395a870-0f0e-4c5a-9eff -9ff1c009d59f/.

23 Roger Ailes, quoted in Blumenthal, "Willie Horton."

24 Such characterizations would be even more seductive when affirmed by the mass media in television shows such as *Cops,* which first aired in 1989. Running thirty-three years, *Cops* portrays a world that appears to be "filled with people of a variety of racial and ethnic backgrounds who are indeed aliens, freaks of nature, subhuman primitive beasts whose words make no sense and whose actions are bizarre." The typical person whom the police encounter is "cut loose from community and cultural cohesion . . . [and] so horribly out of control that he or she reacts only to brute force"; Rapping, *Law and Justice as Seen on* TV, 63–64.

25 Martin Tolchin, "Study Says 53,000 Got Prison Furloughs in '87, and Few Did Harm," *New York Times*, October 12, 1988.

26 Ron Wikberg, "Politics and Furloughs," *Angolite*, January– February 1989, 11.

27 New York Historical Society, "Presidential Ad: 'Revolving Door' George H. W. Bush (R) v. Michael Dukakis (D) [1988-FEAR/ANGER]," 00:29, June 8, 2020, https://www.youtube.com/watch?v=rZToNflF1z8

28 Massachusetts Department of Correction, *Position Paper*, 1, 11.

29 LeClair, *The Effect of Community Reintegration on Rates of Recidivism.*

30 Massachusetts Department of Correction, *Position Paper*, 8–9; Massachusetts General Court, *Department of Correction*, S2–S3.

31 Williams, *1981 Yearly Statistical Report,* 12. State Library of Massachusetts.

32 Williams, *1981 Yearly Statistical Report*, 5.

33 Lorant and Sherwood, *1987 Annual Statistical Report.* 1.

34 "Dukakis Undecided on Jackson Ability," *Los Angeles Times*, June 23, 1988; Anderson, *Crime and the Politics of Hysteria*, 160.

35 Anderson, *Crime and the Politics of Hysteria*, 155.

36 Bonnie V. Winston, "House Investigates Furlough of Inmate Later Charged in Rape," *Boston Globe*, May 27, 1987.

37 Cliff Barnes, testimony, in Massachusetts General Court, *Department of Correction*, S-1.

38 Massachusetts General Court, *Department of Correction*, 10–11, 13.

39 Feely and Simon, "The New Penology," 452.

40 Jean Dietz, "Convicts Earn Parole by Helping Retarded in State Hospitals," *Boston Globe*, February 14, 1972.

41 Farrington and Wittenberg, *The Concord Achievement Rehabilitation Volunteer Experience*, 2.

42 David E. Johnson, quoted in Bob Kerr, "Outside Prison Walls, David Johnson Is Carving a Life," *Burlington (VT) Free Press*, September 23, 1981.

43 Massachusetts General Court, *Department of Correction*, 37–38, emphasis added.

44 Robert Cerasoli, chairman's report, in Massachusetts General Court, *Department of Correction*, 15. This comment about nurses is an allusion to Richard Speck, who killed eight nursing students in their apartment in Chicago in July 1966. Speck, who was white, became the stereotype of mass murderers.

45 Anderson, *Crime and the Politics of Hysteria*, 169.

46 Kennedy, "Monstrous Offenders," 848; Newburn and Jones, "Symbolic Politics and Penal Populism"; Tonry, "Symbol, Substance and Severity."

47 Rentschler, *Second Wounds*, 1, 8.

48 Massachusetts General Court, *Department of Correction*, 35–36.

49 Marie Gottschalk uses the phrase "death in slow motion" to describe life without parole; see Gottschalk, "Days without End," *Prison Legal News*, January 15, 2012, https://www.prisonlegalnews.org/news/2012/jan/15/days-without-end-life-sentences-and-penal-reform/.

50 Robert Bidinotto, "Getting Away with Murder," *Reader's Digest*, July 1988, 60.

51 Cliff and Angela Barnes, testimony, Massachusetts General Court, *Department of Correction*, 35.

52 Rentschler, *Second Wounds*, 8–9. On the victims' rights movement, see, for example, Gaucher, "Punitive Justice and the Victims' Movement"; and Wright, "'Victims' Rights' as a Stalkinghorse for State Repression."

53 Rentschler, *Second Wounds*, 36.

54 Brant et al., "Public Records, FIPA and CORI," 58.

55 Globe Newspaper Co. v. Fenton, 819 F. Supp. 89 (D. Mass. 1993).

56 Ernest Windsor, quoted in "Publishers Parley Eyes Criminal Records," *North Adams (MA) Transcript*, December 4, 1987.

57 In 1978, the original law was amended to allow certain types of employers to request a former prisoner's private information. In the early 1980s, it was amended further to allow jurisdictions to notify the families of victims when a prisoner was being released or transferred to a lower security institution. See Sally Jacobs, "Privacy Law for Criminals Is Reexamined," *Boston Globe*, March 7, 1988.

58 "Publishers Parley Eyes Criminal Records."

59 Massachusetts General Court, *Department of Correction*, 38.

60 Bidinotto, "The Law Criminals Love," *Reader's Digest*, October 1989, 57, 62.

61 Vivianne Rugierro, quoted in Jacobs, "Privacy Law for Criminals Is Reexamined."

62 Dolovich, "Exclusion and Control in the Carceral State," 283.

63 Gilbert, "Free Liberty to Search and View." As Renfro, *Stranger Danger*, 13, points out, Megan's Law corresponded with dramatic rises in incarceration rates for sex crimes and the number of people who were required to register as sex offenders.

64 Rentschler, *Second Wounds*, 43.

65 Massachusetts General Court, *Department of Correction*, 9.

66 Robert Cerasoli, chairman's report, in Massachusetts General Court, *Department of Correction*, 9.

67 John Houston, quoted in "Vote Delayed on Furlough Ban," *North Adams (MA) Transcript*, May 29, 1987.

68 Richard Voke, quoted in Sally Jacobs, "Furloughed Prisoners Straddle Different Worlds," *Boston Globe*, December 13, 1987.

69 Peter B. Sleeper, "Keep Killers behind Bars, Victim's Sister Asks," *Boston Globe*, October 23, 1987.

70 Massachusetts General Court, *Department of Correction*, 34.

71 Minority report, in Massachusetts General Court, *Department of Correction*, sec. C.

72 Schwartzapfel and Keller, "Willie Horton Revisited."

73 Omar Haamid Abdur-Rahim, quoted in Jacobs, "Furloughed Prisoners Straddle Two Worlds."

74 Lerman and Weaver, *Arresting Citizenship*, 111.

75 Evers v. Davoren, SJC, Suffolk, s.s., No. J74-118CI (1974); Dane v. Board of Registrars of Voters of Concord, 371 NE 2d 1358 (1978); Ramos v. Board of Registrars of Voters of Norfolk, 374 Mass. 176 (1978). For an overview of prisoners' franchise in Massachusetts, see the Emancipation Initiative, "Timeline of Massachusetts Incarcerated Voting Rights." https://emancipationinitiative.org/ballots-over-bars/returning-the-right-to-vote/. See also Herwick, "How Massachusetts Prisoners (Recently) Lost the Right to Vote."

76 John Blodgett, letter to the editor, *Boston Globe*, November 9, 1987.

77 Rep. Joseph Hermann, quoted in Sally Jacobs, "Mass. Lawmaker Seeks to Deny Ballot to Serious Offenders," *Boston Globe*, January 30, 1988, 21. The effort to disfranchise felons incarcerated in Massachusetts began in 1997, when Norfolk prisoners sought to create a political action committee; Zachary R. Dowdy, "Prisoners Forming Mass. PAC," *Boston Globe*, August 2, 1997.

78   "Dukakis' Bullish Budget," editorial, *Boston Globe*, January 25, 1985;
      Kenneth J. Cooper, "Dukakis' New Image—Crime Fighter," *Boston
      Globe*, March 31, 1985; "How the Governor's $8.6 Billion Budget Would
      Be Divided," *Boston Globe*, January 24, 1985.

79   "Horton Law Bars a Convict from His Mother's Funeral," *Berkshire
      Eagle* (Pittsfield, MA), February 22, 1990.

80   Sally Jacobs, "Furlough Reversal Saddens Families," *Boston Globe*,
      March 23, 1988.

81   Julian Stone, quoted in Jacobs, "Furloughed Prisoners Straddle Two
      Worlds."

82   Maureen Donovan, quoted in "Horton Law Bars a Convict from His
      Mother's Funeral."

83   John Bolgett, quoted in Sally Jacobs, "Lawmakers Get Top Billing at
      Prison but Many Inmates Take a Furlough," *Boston Globe*, February 6,
      1988.

84   Bonnie Gibson, quoted in Jacobs, "Mass. Lawmaker Seeks to Deny
      Ballot to Serious Offenders."

85   Kris Dodson, quoted in Jacobs, "Furlough Reversal Saddens Families."

86   Pamela Reynolds, "Furlough Programs Still Reeling from 1988 Cam-
      paign," *Boston Globe*, February 16, 1989. Louisiana governor Buddy
      Roemer (1988–92) suspended all furloughs after a trusty working in the
      governor's mansion was indicted for shooting and killing his girlfriend
      while on furlough; "Inmate Indicted," *Crowley (LA) Post-Signal*, Septem-
      ber 22, 1988. See also "States Reviewing Furlough Policies," *Telegram
      and Gazette* (Worcester, MA), March 19, 1989.

87   Edward C. Morris, quoted in Reynolds, "Furlough Programs Still
      Reeling."

88   "Prudent Move," editorial, *Clarion-Ledger* (Jackson, MS), January 25,
      1989; Beverly Pettigrew, "Some Inmates to Come Home for Holidays,"
      Clarion-Ledger (Jackson, MS), November 20, 1988; Jeff Copeskey, "Allain
      Commutes Sentences of Trusties Working at Mansion," *Clarion-Ledger*
      (Jackson, MS), January 16, 1988.

89   Charles Jackson, quoted in Pettigrew, "Some Inmates to Come
      Home."

90   Marilyn Corley, letter to the editor, *Clarion-Ledger* (Jackson, MS),
      October 31, 1988.

91   Tenaglia, *1990 Annual Statistical Report*, 1.

92   Robert Cerasoli, chairman's report, in Massachusetts General Court,
      Department of Correction, 8, 18, emphasis added.

93   Joseph W. Casper, quoted in Steven Marantz, "Casper Enters Race for
      At-Large Council Seat," *Boston Globe*, June 27, 1989; Joseph W. Casper,
      letter to the editor, *Boston Globe*, June 5, 1989.

94   Dolovich, "Exclusion and Control in the Carceral State," 275.

95 Simon, "Megan's Law," 1114. See also Austin, "The Saga of Pennsylvania's 'Willie Horton.'"

96 Jack Anderson and Dale Van Atta, "Dukakis Pardon of Robber Backfired," *Washington Post*, October 24, 1988.

97 Jamieson, *Dirty Politics*, 16.

98 Massachusetts General Court, *Department of Correction*, 12.

99 "House Panel Seeks to Limit Murderer Pardons, Commutation," *North Adams (MA) Transcript*, April 6, 1988.

100 Bidinotto, "Getting Away with Murder," 63.

101 Robert Cerasoli, chairman's report, in Massachusetts General Court, *Department of Correction*, 7.

102 On the Goetz case and its relationship to the growth of aggressive policing, see Hillyer, "The Guardian Angels."

103 In 1987, just as the Willie Horton scandal was gaining attention and Dukakis was contemplating his run for the presidency, the governor commuted the life sentences of three Black radical activists who had been convicted of felony murder in connection with the killing in 1973 of Hakim Jamal, a Muslim leader who once had close ties to Malcolm X, because the men had been incarcerated longer than the person who actually fired the fatal shots. Joan Vennochi, "Dukakis Seeks Release of 3 in '73 Murder," *Boston Globe*, January 1, 1987. Prisoners at Norfolk reported that attorney Robert Quinn, who represented the defendants, interpreted their convictions as a "sign of the times" in that they were likely influenced by Boston's busing crisis, which heightened racial tensions in 1973; "Commuted," *The Question Mark*, May 1987, 6.

104 Chris Black, "Horton Case Keeping the Jail Cells Shut," *Boston Globe*, July 8, 1990.

105 Horton, "A Few Words from Willie Horton," 222.

106 Wolfe, "I Beg Your Pardon," 446–47.

107 Notterman, *Willie Horton's Shadow*, 2. As clemency declined, the proportion of lifers soared.

108 Governor Charlie Baker. "Executive Clemency Guidelines," February 21, 2020, https://www.mass.gov/doc/executive-clemency-guidelines-2212020/download, 3.

109 King, "Arnie King's Public Hearing Notes."

110 Richard Audet, "N.H. Youth Gets Life Sentence for Murder of John Labanara," *Boston Globe*, June 22, 1972.

111 King, "Arnie King's Public Hearing Notes."

112 King, "Arnie King's Public Hearing Notes."

113 Gottschalk, "No Way Out?," 256.

114 Deval Patrick, quoted in Shelley Murphy, "Plea to Cut Killer's Life Term Is Denied," *Boston Globe*, December 17, 2008, http://archive

.boston.com/news/local/massachusetts/articles/2008/12/17/plea_to
_cut_killers_life_term_is_denied/.

115 King, "Restoring Hope."

116 King, "A Place for Me." Remarkably, King was finally released in 2020 after forty-nine years in prison. Citing racism in the jury selection process (prosecutors rejected every prospective Black juror during a moment of heightened racial conflict in Boston), Superior Court justice Janet L. Sanders vacated his conviction of first-degree murder and re-sentenced King to twenty years in prison, which he had already served. See Becker, "Suffolk DA Agrees to Reduce Murder Charges." King never received clemency.

117 Dolovich, "Exclusion and Control in the Carceral State," 98.

118 Marjorie O'Neill Clapprood, quoted in Black, "Horton Case Keeping the Jail Cells Shut."

119 Haas and Fillion, *Life without Parole*, vi.

EPILOGUE

1 Kerry Myers, "Long Time Coming," *Angolite*, September–October 2000, 25–26.

2 Wilbert Rideau, quoted in Myers, "Long Time Coming," 25.

3 Myers, "Long Time Coming," 23.

4 "Longtermers: A Study," editorial, *Angolite*, March–April 1977, 28.

5 Lane Nelson, "The Longtermers: Forever and Ever," *Angolite*, January 1, 2010, 20–21.

6 "Angola Longtermers Incarcerated 40 or More Years," *Angolite*, January 1, 2010, 22.

7 Many studies of those serving extremely long sentences have found this to be true. See, for example, the introduction in Herbert, *Too Easy to Keep*, 1–7.

8 "Longtermers: A Study," 42.

9 Lisa Guenther, *Solitary Confinement*, 48.

10 Many opponents of LWOP sentences have pointed out that, in success-fully leveraging the prospect of LWOP as a viable alternative to the death penalty, death penalty abolitionists have encouraged—perhaps unwittingly—tougher sanctions across the board, even for those "who would not have received the death penalty under the sentencing struc-ture beforehand"—that is, for noncapital crimes; Ogletree and Sarat, "Introduction," 6. See also McCann, "'A Fate Worse Than Death.'"

11 Nellis, "No End in Sight," 4.

12 Gross, "Death by Incarceration." The authors of an Abolitionist Law Center report explain that they use the term *death by incarceration*

because it is preferred by people serving life sentences (the term focuses on the ultimate fact of the sentence, which, barring extraordinary relief, is death), and because it "invokes the social death experienced by the incarcerated"; Cozzens and Grote, *A Way Out*, 11. In the case of juveniles, LWOP has been characterized as cruel and unusual punishment because it "deprives the convict of the most basic liberties without giving hope of restoration." Graham v. Florida, 560 U.S. 48 (2010). Further, courts have recognized that there is a global consensus against such sentences. See Carter, López, and Songster, "Redeeming Justice," 371.

13 Kempis Songster, in Carter, López, and Songster, "Redeeming Justice," 334.

14 "Longtermers: A Study," 34.

15 Lane Nelson, "The Immovable Object: A History of Penal Reform in Angola, Part 2," *Angolite*, November/December, 2009, 29.

16 "Getting It Together," *Angolite*, March–April 2000, 1.

17 "New Clemency Rules," *Angolite*, January–February 2000, 5.

18 Strange, *Discretionary Justice*, 180.

19 Strange, *Discretionary Justice*, chap. 7.

20 Langan et al., *Historical Statistics on Prisoners*, 7–8; West, Sabol, and Greenman, *Bulletin: Prisoners in 2009*, 16.

21 Notterman, *Taking Stock of Clemency*, 7, 2.

22 "Carey Commutes Sentences of Six," *New York Times*, December 24, 1977.

23 Notterman, *The Demise of Clemency*, 4.

24 Kaplan and Mayhew, "The Governor's Clemency Power," 1295–98.

25 Senate Joint Resolution 41, Senate Journal (Oregon Laws 1973), quoted in Amicus Curae Criminal Justice Criminal Reform Clinic at Lewis & Clark Law School, Douglas R. Marteeny et al. v. Katherine Brown, Marion County Circuit Court, filed May 2, 2022, 11.

26 Kaplan and Mayhew, "The Governor's Clemency Power," 1308, 1318–20.

27 Dick Thornburgh, quoted in Notterman, *The Demise of Clemency*, 6.

28 Notterman, *The Demise of Clemency*, 5.

29 Pennsylvania Board of Pardons, "Commutation of Life Sentences."

30 Notterman, *The Demise of Clemency*, 8. The McFadden case sank the political ambitions of Lieutenant Governor Mark S. Singel, who was the Pardon Board's chair and in the majority to recommend commutation. Singel was the Democratic nominee for governor, and his opponent, Republican US congressman Tom Ridge, ran a series of advertisements attacking Singel as soft on crime; see Mark S. Singel, "I Pardoned a Convict Who Killed Again," *America*, August 7, 2017, 34–37.

31 A group of Pennsylvania lifers filed a lawsuit in 1997 challenging the amendment, arguing that diminishing the likelihood of clemency "retroactively increased their punishment by effectively destroying what

had been a tangible likelihood that many of them would one day win commutation of their sentences through the exercise of the governor's executive power. Rather than the Board of Pardons being a gatekeeper, the changes turned it into a roadblock"; see Regina Austin, "The Saga of Reginald McFadden—'Pennsylvania's Willie Horton' and the Commutation of Life Sentences in the Commonwealth, Part 1," *Journal of Crime and Criminology* 61 (2002): 81. Notably, the Pennsylvania Department of Corrections opposed this amendment, fearing prisoner uprising if commutation were so foreclosed; see Seeds, "Governors and Prisoners," 98.

32 Notterman, *The Demise of Clemency*, 4; Pennsylvania Board of Pardons, "Commutation of Life Sentences."

33 Carter, López, and Songster, "Redeeming Justice," 356.

34 Carter, López, and Songster, "Redeeming Justice," 318.

35 The case noted that "the remote possibility" of clemency does not "mitigate the harshness" of an LWOP sentence. Graham v. Florida, 560 U.S. 48 (2010).

36 Guenther, *Solitary Confinement*, xxiii.

37 Antonio, "Making and Unmaking Mass Incarceration."

38 Carter, López, and Songster, "Redeeming Justice," 327.

39 Myers, "Long Time Coming," 23.

40 Seeds, "Governors and Prisoners," 86, argues that in Pennsylvania, "one casualty of the retrenchment of commutation over the past four decades has been this social relation that put the values of the governor and the governor's advisors in conversation with those of some of society's most vulnerable, its long-term prisoners. Lost with this in Pennsylvania was a channel that allowed governors and prisoners each to see dignity in the other."

41 Daryl Waters, Visiting Room Project, video, 2021, https://www.visitingroomproject.org/archive/daryl_waters.

42 Clinton "Nkechi" Walker, quoted in Rosado and Mullett, "Organizing across Prison Walls."

43 Graham v. Florida.

44 Lockwood and Lewis, "The Long Journey."

45 Wright, "Election Year Demagoguery," *Prison Legal News*, January 1992, 3.

46 See Huling, "Building a Prison Economy"; Gilmore, *Golden Gulag*; Story, *Prison Land*, esp. chap. 3; and Bonds, "Building Prisons, Building Poverty."

47 Porter, Voorheis, and Sabol, "Correctional Facility and Inmate Locations; Huling, *Prisons as a Growth Industry*.

48 Rabuy and Kopf, "Separation by Bars and Miles."

49 Boudin, Stutz, and Littman, "Prison Visitation Policies," 161; Monroe Correctional Complex, "Visitor's Guidelines."

50 Boudin, Stutz, and Littman, "Prison Visitation Policies," 172.

51 Sakoda and Simes, "Solitary Confinement and the U.S. Prison Boom."

52 Arizona opened the first supermax prison in 1986, and California opened the second in 1989; Reiter, "The Path to Pelican Bay," 305. The federal penitentiary at Marion, Illinois, is also considered the country's first supermax prison in the sense that it established a twenty-three-hour lockdown in 1983 after an eruption of violence. The entire prison remained in permanent lockdown for decades; Richards, "USP Marion: The First Federal Supermax," 6–22. See also Kurki and Morris, "The Purposes, Practices, and Problems of Supermax Prisons."

53 Guenther, *Solitary Confinement*, 165.

54 Keramet Reiter tracks how the construction of the Pelican Bay supermax prison in California related directly to the revolutionary activity of George Jackson and others, as well as the need to house increasing numbers of prisoners and manage prison violence. See Reiter, *23/7*; and Reiter, "Reclaiming the Power to Punish," 496.

55 Guenther, *Solitary Confinement*, 161.

56 Riveland, *Supermax Prisons*. White, "The Concept of Less Eligibility," 739–40, argues that violence in prison is itself an enactment of the concept of "less eligibility": As conditions of life for the poor have deteriorated due to the decline of manufacturing, organized labor, and welfare, there is "a greater premium on the punitive functions of violence in prison" because without such violence, prison "might become a refuge from the deprivations and uncertainties of a law-abiding life, sought after by the poor."

57 Guenther, *Solitary Confinement*, 165.

58 Extended solitary confinement has been defined as torture by the United Nations and the American Psychology Association. It has been found by researchers to shorten lives and causes permanent damage to people's brains and personalities; Herring, "The Research is Clear."

And solitary confinement can make people more dangerous. A particularly tragic case is that of Evan Ebel, who, after being released directly from eight years of solitary confinement, murdered Colorado Department of Corrections director Tom Clements. Ebel had suffered from behavioral problems as a child, and his father, Jack Ebel, observed that solitary confinement had damaged him even more. Jack Ebel testified, "We are creating mental illness. We are exacerbating mental illness." Tom Clements had pushed for reforms during his tenure at the Department of Corrections and was particularly concerned about overreliance on solitary confinement, which he felt was particularly inappropriate for those deemed "dangerous." Jack Ebel, quoted in John Dannenberg, "Systemic Changes Follow Murder of Colorado Prison Director," *Prison Legal News*, July 19, 2014, https://www.prisonlegalnews

.org/news/2014/jul/10/systemic-changes-follow-murder-colorado
-prison-director/.

59 Reiter, "The Supermax Prison"; White, "The Concept of Less Eligibility," 740, also argues that violence within prison is part of the institution's purpose as a mechanism of social control.

60 Kerry Myers, "The Real Deal," *Angolite*, November/Decem-
ber 2000–January/February 2001, 36.

61 Darwin Willie, Visiting Room Project, video, 2021, https://www
.visitingroomproject.org/archive/darwin_willie.

62 Q, quoted in Guenther, *Solitary Confinement*, 218.

63 Carter, López, and Songster, "Redeeming Justice," 318. The authors
point out that at the same time that R2R was conceptualizing redemption as a human right, the European Court of Human Rights was
articulating a comparable argument: that it was incompatible with
human dignity to forcibly deprive someone of their freedom without
any chance to regain it (321, 345–82).

64 Carter, López, and Songster, "Redeeming Justice," 330–31n32, 330, 318.

65 In 2016, Hundley was the first juvenile lifer in Louisiana to get released
as a result of *Montgomery v. Louisiana*, the landmark Supreme Court
decision that made retroactive an earlier prohibition on mandatory
life sentences to those who committed the crime before the age of
eighteen. Hundley was fifteen when he committed his crime. See Louisiana Parole Project, "Our Staff: Andrew Hundley."

66 Oliver Laughland, "Inside the Division: How a Small Team of
US Prosecutors Fight Decades of Shocking Injustice," *Guardian*,
May 6, 2022, https://www.theguardian.com/us-news/2022/may/06
/prosecutors-new-orleans-mass-incarceration; Oliver Laughland, "An
Extraordinary Story of Forgiveness: From Life without Parole to Finding Grace," *Guardian*, August 8, 2022, https://www.theguardian.com
/us-news/2022/aug/08/life-without-parole-prison-angola-louisiana
-visiting-room.

67 Jason Williams, quoted in Misick, "This Louisiana Prisoner Thought
He'd Only Have to Serve a Decade."

68 Chavez, "Aging Louisiana Prisoners."

69 Joint Post-Conviction Plea Agreement, State of Louisiana v. Louis
Mitchell, docket no. 195–533, 195–491, "G."

70 Louis Mitchell, quoted in Chavez, "Aging Louisiana Prisoners"; Major,
"Louisiana's 10/6 Lifers." See also John Corley, "Forgotten No More,"
Angolite, September–October 2021, 10–12.

71 Jason Williams, quoted in Chavez, "Aging Louisiana Prisoners."

72 The Louisiana Parole Project is pushing for relief for all 10/6 lifers; see Jessica Schulberg, "Louisiana Passes a Bill That Could
Free Some '10/6 Lifers,'" *HuffPost*, May 30, 2022, https://www

.huffpost.com/entry/louisiana-lawmakers-pass-bill-ten-six-lifers_n
_62900f1fe4b0edd2d0215901.

73 Right to Redemption, "Mission Statement," in Carter, López, and
Songster, "Redeeming Justice," 325.

74 Rosado, "Felix Rosado on Dispelling the Myths."

75 Rosado, "Doin' Death."

76 Rosado and Mullett, "Organizing across Prison Walls." There are other
movements to end DBI that foreground the issue of redemption. For
example, there is a movement in New York State—where the prison population went down by half between 2008 and 2021 but the proportion of
incarcerated people over fifty doubled—to advance bills that would render anyone over fifty-five who has served at least fifteen years eligible for
parole; the Fair and Timely Parole Act would change the standard for
supervised release by compelling the New York State Board of Parole to
assess petitioners based on their current character and not the nature of
their crimes. See Walters, "Parole Justice Now."

In New York City, Tahanie Aboushi ran for Manhattan district
attorney in 2021 on a platform that would create a review board to
evaluate cases of elderly prisoners, abolish mandatory minimums, and
limit sentences to twenty years, with parole eligibility after ten years.
See Aboushi, "End Death by Incarceration."

77 Graterford, a maximum-security prison known earlier as the Eastern
Correctional Institution, was the birthplace of the Inside-Out Prison
Exchange Program and the home to the Inside-Out Think Tank until
the facility closed in 2018 and was replaced by State Correctional
Institution–Phoenix.

78 Lyons and Rosado, "There's Urgency Here."

79 Rosado and Mullett, "Organizing across Prison Walls"; Davis and
Roswell, *Turning Teaching Inside Out*.

80 Nellis, "A New Lease on Life."

81 Kempis Songster, in Carter, López, and Songster, "Redeeming Justice,"
333.

BIBLIOGRAPHY

ARCHIVES

James L. Stovall Papers, Louisiana and Lower Mississippi Valley Collections. LSU Libraries, Louisiana State University, Baton Rouge.
Library of Virginia, Richmond.
Mississippi Department of Archives and History, Jackson.
Phyllis M. Ryan Papers, Northeastern University Archives and Special Collections, Boston.
Raymond Pace Alexander Papers, University of Pennsylvania Archives and Records Center, Philadelphia.
Raymond Pace Alexander Papers, Virginia Commonwealth University, Richmond.
Ronald Reagan Governor's Papers, California State Archives, Sacramento.
State Library of Massachusetts, Boston.
Washington State Penitentiary Collection, Penrose Library, Whitman College, Walla Walla.

OTHER SOURCES

Aboushi, Tahanie. "End Death by Incarceration." Web page, n.d. Accessed June 13, 2023. https://web.archive.org/web /20211020043604/https://www.tahanieforda.com/end-death-by -incarceration.
Airstrup, Joseph A. *The Southern Strategy Revisited: Republican Top-Down Advancement in the South.* Lexington: University Press of Kentucky, 1996.
Alexander, Michelle. *The New Jim Crow: Mass Incarceration in the Age of Colorblindness.* New York: New Press, 2010.
Allen, Francis A. *The Decline of the Rehabilitative Ideal: Penal Policy and Social Purpose.* New Haven, CT: Yale University Press, 1981.

American Correctional Association Committee on Riots. *A Statement concerning Causes, Preventative Measures, and Methods of Controlling Prison Riots and Disturbances.* New York: American Prison Association, 1953.

Anderson, David C. *Crime and the Politics of Hysteria: How the Willie Horton Story Changed American Justice.* New York: Times Books, 1995.

Antonio. "Making and Unmaking Mass Incarceration." Presented at the Making and Unmaking Mass Incarceration Conference, December, 2019. Unpublished manuscript. In the possession of the author.

Armstrong, Andrea C. "Slavery Revisited in Penal Plantation Labor." *Seattle University Law Review* 35, no. 3 (2012): 869–910.

Arsenault, Raymond. *Freedom Riders: 1961 and the Struggle for Racial Justice.* New York: Oxford University Press, 2006.

Atkinson, Craig, dir. *Do Not Resist.* Pompton Plains, NJ: Passion River, 2016. DVD.

Austin, Regina. "The Saga of Pennsylvania's 'Willie Horton' and the Commutation of Life Sentences in the Commonwealth." Faculty Scholarship at Penn Carey Law No. 2155. University of Pennsylvania Carey Law School, February 26, 2020. https://scholarship.law .upenn.edu/cgi/viewcontent.cgi?article=3157&context=faculty _scholarship.

Ayers, Edward. *Vengeance and Justice: Crime and Punishment in the 19th-Century South.* New York: Oxford University Press, 1984.

Bailey, Telisha Dionne. "Please Don't Forget about Me: African American Women, Mississippi, and the History of Crime and Punishment in Parchman Prison, 1890–1980." PhD diss., University of Mississippi, 2015.

Baker, Tom, and Jonathan Simon, eds. *Embracing Risk: The Changing Culture of Insurance and Responsibility.* Chicago: University of Chicago Press, 2002.

Balchen, Bess. "Prisons: The Changing Outside View of the Inside." In *Correctional Environments*, edited by Frederic D. Moyer and Edith E. Flynn, 11–22. Urbana, IL: National Clearinghouse for Criminal Justice Planning and Architecture, 1973.

Balough, J. K. "Conjugal Visitations in Prisons: A Sociological Perspective." *Federal Probation* 28, no. 3 (1964): 52–58.

Barkow, Rachel. "The Ascent of the Administrative State and the Demise of Mercy." *Harvard Law Review* 121, no. 4 (2008): 1332–36.

Barkow, Rachel. *Prisoners of Politics: Breaking the Cycle of Mass Incarceration.* Cambridge, MA: Belknap Press of Harvard University Press, 2019.

Barragan, Yesenia. "Christmas and Resistance to Slavery in the Americas." *Black Perspectives* (blog), African American Intellectual History

Society, December 23, 2016. https://www.aaihs.org/christmas-and
-resistance-to-slavery-in-the-americas/.

Becker, Deborah. "Suffolk DA Agrees to Reduce Murder Charges
against Arnold King." WBUR, October 29, 2020. https://www.wbur
.org/news/2020/10/29/arnold-king-sentence-reduction.

Beckett, Katherine, and Steven Herbert. *Banished: The New Social Control In Urban America*. New York: Oxford University Press, 2011.

Bennett, J. V. (James Van Benschoten). *Of Prisons and Justice: A Selection
of the Writings of James V. Bennett*. United States Senate, Committee
on the Judiciary, Subcommittee on National Penitentiaries. Washington, DC: U.S. Government Printing Office, 1964.

Bennett, James V. *I Chose Prison*. New York: Alfred A. Knopf, 1970.

Bennett, Laura. "We All Pay: Mississippi's Harmful Habitual Laws."
FWD.us, n.d. Accessed May 20, 2023. https://www.fwd.us/news/we
-all-pay-mississippis-harmful-habitual-laws/.

Bennett, Lawrence. "Correctional Administrators' Attitudes toward Private Family Visiting." *Prison Journal* 69, no. 1 (1989): 110–14.

Berger, Dan. *Captive Nation: Black Prison Organizing in the Civil Rights
Era*. Chapel Hill: University of North Carolina Press, 2014.

Berger, Dan, and Toussaint Losier. *Rethinking the American Prison
Movement*. New York: Routledge, 2018.

Bergeron, Monica L. "Second Place Isn't Good Enough: Achieving
True Reform through Expanded Parole Eligibility." *Louisiana Law
Review* 80, no. 1 (2019): 110–65.

Bernstein, Lee. *America Is the Prison: Arts and Politics in Prison in the
1970s*. Chapel Hill: University of North Carolina Press, 2010.

Bernstein, Stewart M. "The Evolving Right of Due Process at Prison
Disciplinary Hearings." *Fordham Law Review* 42, no. 4 (1974):
878–90.

"Beyond the Ken of the Courts: A Critique of Judicial Refusal to Review the Complaints of Convicts." *Yale Law Journal* 72, no. 3 (1963):
506–58.

Bigham, Shauna, and Robert E. May. "The Time o' All Times? Masters,
Slaves, and Christmas in the Old South." *Journal of the Early Republic* 18, no. 2 (1998): 263–88.

Bissonette, Jamie, with Ralph Hamm, Robert Dellelo, and Edward Rodman. *When the Prisoners Ran Walpole: A True Story in the Movement
for Prison Abolition*. Cambridge, MA: South End Press, 2008.

Blackmon, Douglas A. *Slavery by Another Name: The Re-enslavement
of Black Americans from the Civil War to World War II*. New York:
Anchor Books, 2008.

Bleich, Jeff. "The Politics of Prison Crowding." *California Law Review*
77, no. 5 (1989): 1125–80.

Blue, Ethan. *Doing Time in the Depression*. New York: New York University Press, 2012.

Bob. "Parchman from the Inside." *That's All Rite Mama* (blog), March 7, 2009. http://thatsallritemama.blogspot.com/2009/03/mississippi-state-penitentiary-bands.html.

Bonds, Anne. "Building Prisons, Building Poverty." In *Beyond Walls and Cages: Prisons, Borders, and Global Crisis*, edited by Jenna M. Loyd, Matt Mitchelson, and Andrew Burridge, 129–42. Athens: University of Georgia Press, 2012.

Bornstein, Brian H., and Robert J. Nemeth. "Jurors' Perception of Violence: A Framework for Inquiry." *Aggression and Violent Behavior* 4, no. 1 (1999): 77–92.

Bortz, Carl. "From the Editor, My Turn: Public Trust." *La Roca* 15, no. 2 (1988): 15.

Boudin, Chesa, Trever Stutz, and Aaron Littman. "Prison Visitation Policies: A Fifty-State Survey." *Yale Law and Policy Review* 32, no. 1 (2013): 149–90.

Brant, Jonathan, James H. Barron, Daniel P. Jaffe, John Graceffa, and Judith Karp Wallis. "Public Records, FIPA and CORI: How Massachusetts Balances Privacy and the Rights to Know." *Suffolk University Law Review* 15, no. 23 (1981): 23–78.

Bronstein, Alvin, Marvin Wolfgang, and Joseph McGettigan. "Crime and Punishment: The Criminal Justice System in the 1990s; Keynote Dialogue of the 14th Annual Edward V. Sparer Public Interest Law Conference." *Hybrid: The University of Pennsylvania Journal of Law and Social Change* 3, no. 1 (1996): 1–18.

Brown, Michelle. *The Culture of Punishment: Prison, Society, and Spectacle*. New York: New York University Press, 2009.

Brown, Raymond C., George M. Keiser, and Kermit Humphries. *Guide to Executive Clemency among the American States*. Washington, DC: U.S. Department of Justice, National Institute of Justice, March 1988.

Brückmann, Rebecca. "Citizens' Councils, Conservatism and White Supremacy in Louisiana, 1964–1972." *European Journal of American Studies* 14, no. 1 (2019): 1–25.

Burdman, Milton. "Realism in Community-Based Correctional Services." *Annals of the American Academy of Political and Social Science* 381, no. 1 (1969): 71–80.

Burkle, Christopher M. "The Mississippi Decision Exchanging Parole for Kidney Donation: Is This the Beginning of Change for Altruistic-Based Human Organ Donation in the United States?" *Mayo Clinic Proceedings*, 86, no. 5 (2011): 414–18.

Burstein, Jules Quentin. *Conjugal Visits in Prison: Psychological and Social Consequences*. Lexington, MA: D. C. Heath, 1977.

Butler, Anne. *Weep for the Living.* Mount Pleasant, SC: Arcadia, 2005.

Butler, Anne, and C. Murray Henderson. *Angola, Louisiana State Penitentiary: A Half-Century of Rage and Reform.* Lafayette: University of Louisiana at Lafayette Press, 1990.

Cacho, Lisa Marie. *Social Death: Racialized Rightlessness and the Criminalization of the Unprotected.* New York: New York University Press, 2012.

Calacal, Celisa. "At Least Seven States Have Prison Inmates Working in Governors' Mansions and Capitol Buildings." TruthDig, June 25, 2017. https://www.truthdig.com/articles/at-least-seven-states -have-prison-inmates-working-in-governors-mansions-and-capitol -buildings/.

Caldwell, H. Mitchell. "Coercive Plea Bargaining: The Unrecognized Scourge of the Justice System." *Catholic University Law Review* 61, no. 1 (2011): 63–96.

California Department of Corrections. *Pattern of Change.* Sacramento: California Department of Corrections, 1972.

Caminker, Evan H. "A Norm-Based Remedial Model for Underinclusive Statutes." *Yale Law Journal* 95, no. 6 (1986): 1185–209.

Camp, Jordan T. *Incarcerating the Crisis: Freedom Struggles and the Rise of the Neoliberal State.* Berkeley: University of California Press, 2016.

Campbell, Michael C. "The Emergence of Penal Extremism in California: A Dynamic View of Institutional Structures and Political Processes." *Law and Society Review* 48, no. 2 (2014): 377–409.

Canaday, Margot. *The Straight State: Sexuality and Citizenship in Twentieth-Century America.* Princeton, NJ: Princeton University Press, 2011.

Cannon, Lou. *Governor Reagan: His Rise to Power.* New York: Public Affairs, 2003.

Cannon, Tom. *First Degree Murder: The Post-Conviction Experience in Massachusetts.* Boston: Massachusetts Department of Correction, January 1974.

Canton, David. *Raymond Pace Alexander: A New Negro Lawyer Fights for Civil Rights in Philadelphia.* Jackson: University Press of Mississippi, 2013.

Carleton, Mark T. *Politics and Punishment: The History of the Louisiana State Penal System.* Baton Rouge: Louisiana State University Press, 1971.

Carpenter, Lawrence A. *Federal Correctional Institution, Seagoville, Texas.* Washington, DC: Federal Bureau of Prisons, 1953.

Carpenter, Lawrence A. "The Federal Work Release Program." *Nebraska Law Review* 45, no. 4 (1966): 690–701.

Carroll, Leo. "Humanitarian Reform and Biracial Sexual Assault in a Maximum Security Prison." *Urban* Life 5, no. 4 (1977): 417–37.

Carroll, Leo. *Lawful Order: A Case Study of Correctional Crisis and Reform.* New York: Garland, 1998.

Carter, Dan T. *From George Wallace to Newt Gingrich: Race in the Conservative Counterrevolution, 1963–1994.* Baton Rouge: Louisiana State University Press, 1999.

Carter, Terrell, Rachel López, and Kempis Songster. "Redeeming Justice." *Northwestern University Law Review* 116, no. 2 (2021): 315–82.

CBS News. "New Miss. Gov. Boots Inmate Workers from Mansion." January 20, 2012. https://www.cbsnews.com/news/new-miss-gov-boots-inmate-workers-from-mansion/.

Chard, Daniel S. "Rallying for Repression: Police Terror, 'Law-and-Order' Politics, and the Decline of Maine's Prisoners' Rights Movement." *The Sixties: A Journal of History, Politics and Culture* 5, no. 1 (2012): 47–73.

Chase, Robert T., ed. *Caging Borders and Carceral States: Incarcerations, Immigrant Detentions, and Resistance.* Chapel Hill: University of North Carolina Press, 2019.

Chase, Robert T. *We Are Not Slaves: State Violence, Coerced Labor, and Prisoners' Rights in Postwar America.* Chapel Hill: University of North Carolina Press, 2020.

Chauncey, George, Jr. "The Postwar Sex Crime Panic." In *True Stories from the American Past*, edited by William Graebner, 160–78. New York: McGraw-Hill, 1997.

Chavez, Roby. "Aging Louisiana Prisoners Were Promised a Chance at Parole after 10 Years. Some Are Finally Free." *PBS Newshour*, November 26, 2021. https://www.pbs.org/newshour/nation/aging-louisiana-prisoners-were-promised-a-chance-at-parole-after-10-years-some-are-finally-free.

Chung, Susanna Y. "Prison Overcrowding: Standards in Determining Eighth Amendment Violations." *Fordham Law Review* 68, no. 6 (2000): 2351–400.

Citizens' Committee on Corrections, *Corrections '71: A Citizens' Report*, Boston: Citizens' Committee on Corrections, November 1971. State Library of Massachusetts. https://archives.lib.state.ma.us/bitstream/handle/2452/41125/ocm32998407.pdf?sequence=1.

Clear, Todd R. *Harm in American Penology: Offenders, Victims, and Their Communities.* Albany: State University of New York Press, 1994.

Clemmer, Donald. *The Prison Community.* New York: Holt, Rinehart, and Wilson, 1958.

Cohn, David. *God Shakes Creation.* New York: Harper and Brothers, 1935.

Colson, Charles W. *Life Sentence.* Lincoln, VA: Chosen Books, 1979.

Colvin, Mark. *Penitentiaries, Reformatories, and Chain Gangs: Social Theory and the History of Punishment in Nineteenth-Century America.* New York: St. Martin's, 1997.

Comfort, Megan. "'Papa's House': The Prison as Domestic and Social Satellite." *Ethnography* 3, no. 4 (2002): 467–99.

"Conjugal Visitation Rights and the Appropriate Standard of Judicial Review for Prison Regulations," *Michigan Law Review* 73, no. 2 (1974): 398–423.

Conrad, John P. "We Should Never Have Promised a Hospital." *Federal Probation* 39 (1975): 3–39.

Conrad, Randall, and Steven Ujlaki, dirs. *Three Thousand Years and Life.* Odeon Films, 1973. YouTube, November 18, 2008. https://www.youtube.com/watch?v=nI0P8NxXdG0

Cozart, Reed. "The Challenge at Angola: Progress and Future Plans." *Prison World* 3, no. 1 (March–April 1954): 3–5.

Cozart, Reed. "Reforms in Louisiana." *Prison Journal* 34, no. 1 (1954): 22–24.

Cozart, Reed. "Should Prisons Be Merely Dungeons?" *Architectural Record* 119 (April 1956): 203–8.

Cozart, Reed. "What Has Happened to America's Worst Prison?" *Federal Probation* 19, no. 4 (1955): 32–38.

Cozzens, Quinn, and Bret Grote. *A Way Out: Abolishing Death by Incarceration in Pennsylvania; Report on Life-without-Parole Sentences.* Pittsburgh: Abolitionist Law Center, n.d. [August 27, 2019]. Accessed June 13, 2023. https://abolitionistlawcenter.org/wp-content/uploads/2018/09/ALC_AWayOut_27August_Full1.pdf.

Craft, William, and Ellen Craft. *Running a Thousand Miles for Freedom, or The Escape of William and Ellen Craft from Slavery.* London: William Tweedie, 1860.

Cullen, Francis. "Assessing the Penal Harm Movement." *Journal of Research in Crime and Delinquency* 32, no. 3 (1995): 338–58.

Cummins, Eric. *The Rise and Fall of California's Radical Prison Movement.* Stanford, CA: Stanford University Press, 1994.

Davis, Alan J. *Report on Sexual Assaults in the Philadelphia Prison System and Sheriff's Vans.* Philadelphia: Philadelphia District Attorney's Office, 1968.

Davis, Angela Y. *Are Prisons Obsolete?* New York: Seven Stories, 2003.

Davis, Arthur Q. *It Happened by Design: The Life and Work of Arthur Q. Davis.* Jackson: University Press of Mississippi, 2009.

Davis, Mike. *City of Quartz: Excavating the Future in Los Angeles.* New York: Vintage Books, 1992.

Davis, Simone Weil, and Barbara Sherr Roswell. "Introduction—Radical Reciprocity: Civic Engagement from Inside Out." In

Turning Teaching Inside Out: A Pedagogy of Transformation for Community-Based Education, edited by Simone Weil Davis and Barbara Sherr Roswell, 1–9. New York: Palgrave Macmillan, 2013.

Davis, Simone Weil, and Barbara Sherr Roswell, eds. *Turning Teaching Inside Out: A Pedagogy of Transformation for Community-Based Education*. New York: Palgrave Macmillan, 2013.

Dayan, Colin. *The Law Is a White Dog: How Legal Rituals Make and Unmake Persons*. Princeton, NJ: Princeton University Press, 2011.

Dayan, Colin. *The Story of Cruel and Unusual*. Cambridge, MA: MIT Press, 2007.

DelSesto, Matthew. "Norfolk's 'Model Prison Community': Howard Belding Gill and the Social Process of Prison Reform." *Prison Journal* 101, no. 2 (2021): 127–46.

Dittmer, John. *Local People: The Struggle for Civil Rights in Mississippi*. Urbana: University of Illinois Press, 1995.

Dolovich, Sharon. "Exclusion and Control in the Carceral State." *Berkeley Journal of Criminal Law* 16, no. 2 (2011): 259–339.

Dolovich, Sharon. "Foreword: Incarceration, American-Style." In "Symposium: Confronting the Costs of Incarceration," special section, *Harvard Law and Policy Review* 3, no. 2 (2009): 237–59.

Dorsey, L. C. *Cold Steel*. Self-published, 1983.

Douglass, Frederick. *My Bondage and My Freedom*. New York: Penguin, 2003.

Dubber, Markus Dirk. *Victims in the War on Crime: The Use and Abuse of Victims' Rights*. New York: New York University Press, 2002.

Dunbar, Tony. *Delta Time: A Journey through Mississippi*. New York: Pantheon Books, 1990.

Duwe, Grant, and Valerie Clark. "Blessed Be the Social Tie That Binds: The Effects of Prison Visitation on Offender Recidivism." *Criminal Justice Policy Review* 24, no. 3 (2013): 271–96.

Edwards, George. "Foreword: Penitentiaries Produce No Penitents." *Journal of Criminal Law and Criminology* 63, no. 2 (1972): 154–61.

Edwards, Laura F. *Gendered Strife and Confusion: The Political Culture of Reconstruction*. Urbana: University of Illinois Press, 1997.

Eigenberg, Helen. "If You Drop the Soap in the Shower You Are On Your Own: Images of Male Rape in Selected Prison Movies." *Sexuality and Culture* 7, no. 4 (2003): 56–89.

Emancipation Initiative. "Timeline of Massachusetts Incarcerated Voting Rights." Web page, n.d. Accessed June 12, 2023. https://emancipation initiative.org/ballots-over-bars/returning-the-right-to-vote/.

Equal Justice Initiative. "The Superpredator Myth, 25 Years Later." April 7, 2014. https://eji.org/news/superpredator-myth-20-years-later/.

Esposito, Shaun C. "Conjugal Visitation in American Prisons Today." *Journal of Family Law* 19, no. 2 (1980): 313–30.

Fairclough, Adam. *Race and Democracy: The Civil Rights Struggle in Louisiana, 1915–1972*. Athens: University of Georgia Press, 1999.

Farrington, Faye. *The Massachusetts Furlough Experience*. Boston: Massachusetts Department of Correction, April 1974. State Library of Massachusetts. https://archives.lib.state.ma.us/handle/2452/264062.

Farrington, Faye, and Shari Wittenberg. *The Concord Achievement Rehabilitation Volunteer Experience: An Evaluation*. Boston: Massachusetts Department of Correction, August 1977. https://www.ncjrs.gov/pdffiles1/Digitization/44699NCJRS.pdf.

Feely, Malcolm M., and Jonathan Simon. "The New Penology: Notes on the Emerging Strategy of Corrections and Its Implications." *Criminology* 30, no. 4 (1992): 449–74.

Felber, Garrett. *Those Who Know Don't Say: The Nation of Islam, the Black Freedom Movement, and the Carceral State*. Chapel Hill: University of North Carolina Press, 2020.

Felker-Kantor, Max. *Policing Los Angeles: Race, Resistance, and the Rise of the LAPD*. Chapel Hill: University of North Carolina Press, 2018.

Fields, Barbara J. *Slavery and Freedom on the Middle Ground*. New Haven, CT: Yale University Press, 1987.

Finn, Peter. "No-Frills Prisons and Jails: A Movement in Flux." *Federal Probation* 60, no. 3 (1996): 35–44.

Fishman, Joseph F. *Sex in Prison: Revealing Sex Conditions in American Prisons*. New York: National Library Press, 1934.

Flamm, Michael W. *Law and Order: Street Crime, Civil Unrest, and the Crisis of Liberalism in the 1960s*. New York: Columbia University Press, 2005.

Flanagan, Timothy J., and Susan L. Caulfield. "Public Opinion and Prison Policy." *Prison Journal* 64, no. 2 (1984): 31–46.

Fleetwood, Nicole R. *Marking Time: Art in the Age of Mass Incarceration*. Cambridge, MA: Harvard University Press, 2020.

Florida State University, School of Social Welfare. *Fourth Annual Southern Conference on Corrections*. Program, February 8–9, 1959. https://web.archive.org/web/20200604020450/http://fsu.digital.flvc.org/islandora/object/fsu%3A438

Forman, James, Jr. *Locking Up Our Own: Crime and Punishment in Black America*. New York: Farrar, Straus and Giroux, 2017.

Foster, Burk. "'Pardon Me, Governor!' The Politics of Executive Clemency in Louisiana, 1985." Paper presented to the Academy of Criminal Justice Sciences, April 1985.

Foster, Burk. "When Mercy Seasons Justice: Executive Clemency for First Degree Murderers in Louisiana." Paper presented at the Southwestern Social Science Association Annual Meeting, Dallas, March 24, 1995.

Foster, Burk, Wilbert Rideau, and Douglas Dennis. *The Wall Is Strong: Corrections in Louisiana*. Lafayette: University of Louisiana at Lafayette Press, 2014.

Foucault, Michel. *Discipline and Punish: The Birth of the Prison*. Translated by Alan Sheridan. New York: Vintage Books, 1995.

Frampton, Mary Louise, Ian Haney López, and Jonathan Simon, eds. *After the War on Crime: Race, Democracy, and a New Reconstruction*. New York: New York University Press, 2008.

Franke, Katherine M. "Becoming a Citizen: Reconstruction Era Regulation of African American Marriages." *Yale Journal of Law and the Humanities* 11, no. 2 (1999): 251–310.

Frazier, Jordan. "The Tower: Prison Architecture and the Verticality of Carcerality." Master's thesis, Eastern Kentucky University, 2017.

Garland, David. *The Culture of Control: Crime and Social Order in Contemporary Society*. Chicago: University of Chicago Press, 2001.

Gartner, Rosemary, Anthony N. Doob, and Franklin E. Zimring. "Past as Prologue? Decarceration in California, Then and Now." *Criminology and Public Policy* 10, no. 2 (2011): 291–325.

Garton, Stephen. "Managing Mercy: African Americans, Parole and Paternalism in the Georgia Prison System, 1919–1945." *Journal of Social History* 36, no. 3 (2003): 675–99.

Gaucher, Bob. "Punitive Justice and the Victims' Movement." *Journal of Prisoners on Prisons* 9, no. 2 (1998): 2–16.

Giardini, Giovanni I., and Richard G. Farrow. "The Paroling of Capital Offenders." *Annals of the American Academy of Political and Social Science* 284, no. 1 (1952): 85–94.

Gilbert, Alfred. "Observations about Recent Correctional Architecture." In Alfred Gilbert, Robert Sommer, and Kenneth Ricci, *New Environments for the Incarcerated*, 7–14. Washington, DC: US Department of Justice, 1972.

Gilbert, James G. "Free Liberty to Search and View: A Look at Public Access to Criminal Offender Record Information in the Commonwealth." *Boston Bar Journal* 41, no. 5 (1997): 12–23.

Gill, Nick. "Mobility versus Liberty? The Punitive Uses of Movement within and outside Carceral Environments." In *Carceral Spaces: Mobility and Agency in Imprisonment and Migrant Detention*, edited by Nick Gill and Dominque Moran, 19–35. Farnham, UK: Ashgate, 2013.

Gilmore, Glenda Elizabeth. "Murder, Memory, and the Flight of the Incubus." In *Democracy Betrayed: The Wilmington Race Riot of 1898 and Its Legacy*, edited by David Cecelski and Tim Tyson, 73–93. Chapel Hill: University of North Carolina Press, 1998.

Gilmore, Ruth Wilson. *Golden Gulag: Prisons, Surplus, Crisis, and Opposition in Globalizing California*. Berkeley: University of California Press, 2007.

Gilmore, Ruth Wilson. "Ruth Wilson Gilmore on Abolition, the Climate Crisis and What Must Be Done." Interview by Kelly Hayes. Truthout, April 14, 2022. https://truthout.org/audio/ruth-wilson -gilmore-on-abolition-the-climate-crisis-and-what-must-be-done/.

Gilmore, Ruth Wilson, and Craig Gilmore. "Restating the Obvious." In *Indefensible Space: The Architecture of the National Insecurity State*, edited by Michael Sorkin, 141–62. New York: Routledge, 2008.

Gilson, Dave. "The Inside Scoop: An Interview with Wilbert Rideau." *Mother Jones* 35, no. 3 (May–June 2010): 70–71.

Gnagy, Caroline. *Texas Jailhouse Music: A Prison Band History*, Charleston, SC: History Press, 2016.

Goetting, Ann. "Conjugal Association in Prison: Issues and Perspectives." *Crime and Delinquency* 28, no. 1 (1982): 52–71.

Goffman, Erving. "On the Characteristics of the Total Institution: The Inmate World." In *The Prison: Studies in Institutional Organisation and Change*, edited by Donald R. Cressey, 15–67. New York: Holt, Reinhart and Winston, 1961.

Goldberg, Aviva M., and Joel Frader. "Prisoners as Living Organ Donors: The Case of the Scott Sisters." *American Journal of Bioethics*, 11, no. 10 (2011): 15–16.

Gottschalk, Marie. *Caught: The Prison State and the Lockdown of American Politics.* Princeton, NJ: Princeton University Press, 2015.

Gottschalk, Marie. "No Way Out? Life Sentences and the Politics of Penal Reform." In *Life without Parole: America's New Death Penalty?*, edited by Charles J. Ogletree Jr. and Austin Sarat, 227–81. New York: New York University Press, 2012.

Gottschalk, Marie. *The Prison and the Gallows: The Politics of Mass Incarceration in America.* Cambridge: Cambridge University Press, 2006.

Governor's Pardon, Parole, and Rehabilitation Commission [of Louisiana]. *Staff Analysis of Executive Clemency in Louisiana.* February 2, 1978. National Criminal Justice Reference Service. https://www. ncjrs.gov/pdffiles1/Digitization/52493NCJRS.pdf.

Gowell, Aleyah. "'The Most Eloquent Dissents': Writ Writing at Parchman Penitentiary." BA honors thesis, College of William and Mary, 2020.

Grasso, Anthony. "The Unity of Individualism and Determinism in the Rehabilitative Ideal." *Nonsite*, February 11, 2018. https://nonsite.org /the-unity-of-individualism-and-determinism-in-the-rehabilitative -ideal/#foot_2-10684.

Griffith, Aaron. *God's Law and Order: The Politics of Punishment in Evangelical America.* Cambridge, MA: Harvard University Press, 2020.

Gross, Richard. "Death by Incarceration: Cruel and Unusual." PEN America, September 9, 2019. https://pen.org/death-by -incarceration-cruel-and-unusual/.

Guenther, Lisa. *Solitary Confinement: Social Death and Its Afterlives.* Minneapolis: University of Minnesota Press, 2013.

Guetzkow, Joshua, and Eric Schoon. "If You Build It, They Will Fill It: The Consequences of Prison Overcrowding Litigation." *Law and Society Review* 49, no. 2 (2015): 401–32.

Haas, Gordon, and Lloyd Fillion. *Life without Parole: A Reconsideration.* 2nd ed. Boston: Criminal Justice Policy Coalition, n.d. [2015]. Accessed May 14, 2021. https://www.cjpc.org/uploads/1 /0/4/9/104972649/life-without-parole-a-reconsideration.pdf.

Haley, Sarah. "Care Cage: Black Women, Political Symbolism, and 1970s Prison Crisis." *Souls: A Critical Journal of Black Politics, Culture, and Society* 20, no. 1 (2018): 58–85.

Halperin, David M., and Trevor Hoppe, eds. *The War on Sex.* Durham, NC: Duke University Press, 2017.

Hamilton, Alexander. *Federalist 74: The Command of the Military and Naval Forces, and the Pardoning Power of the Executive.* In Alexander Hamilton, John Jay, and James Madison, *The Federalist: A Commentary on the Constitution of the United States,* 552–55. Philadelphia: Lippincott, 1864.

Haney, Craig. "Counting Casualties in the War on Prisoners." *University of San Francisco Law Review* 43, no. 1 (2008): 87–138.

Haney, Craig. "Riding the Punishment Wave: On the Origins of Our Devolving Standards of Decency." *Hastings Women's Law Journal* 9, no. 1 (1998): 27–78.

Harcourt, Bernard E. *Profiling, Policing, and Punishing in an Actuarial Age.* Chicago: University of Chicago Press, 2007.

Hartnett, Stephen John, Eleanor Novek, and Jennifer K. Wood. *Working for Justice: A Handbook of Prison Education and Activism.* Urbana: University of Illinois Press, 2013.

Harvey, Sylvia A. *The Shadow System: Mass Incarceration and the American Family.* New York: Bold Type Books, 2020.

Hayner, Norman S. "Attitudes toward Conjugal Visits for Prisoners." *Federal Probation* 36, no. 1 (1972): 43–49.

Hemsworth, Katie. "Carceral Acoustemologies: Sonic Enactments of Space and Power in Prisons." PhD diss., Queen's University (Kingston, ON), 2015.

Henderson, Norris. "What I Learned about Voting Rights in the Fields of Angola." Marshall Project, March 12, 2020. https://www .themarshallproject.org/2020/03/12/what-i-learned-about-voting -rights-in-the-fields-of-angola.

Hensley, Christopher, Sandra Rutland, and Phyllis Gray-Ray. "Inmate Attitudes toward the Conjugal Visitation Program in Mississippi Prisons: An Exploratory Study." *American Journal of Criminal Justice* 25, no. 1 (2000): 137–45.

Hensley, Christopher, Cindy Struckman-Johnson, and Helen M. Eigenberg. "The History of Prison Sex Research." *Prison Journal* 80, no. 4 (2000): 360–67.

Herbert, Steven. *Too Easy to Keep: Life-Sentenced Prisoners and the Future of Mass Incarceration*. Berkeley: University of California Press, 2019.

Herivel, Tara, and Paul Wright, eds. *Prison Nation: The Warehousing of America's Poor*. New York: Routledge, 2003.

Herring, Tiana. "The Research Is Clear: Solitary Confinement Causes Long-Lasting Harm." Prison Policy Initiative, December 8, 2020. https://www.prisonpolicy.org/blog/2020/12/08/solitary _symposium/.

Herwick, Edgar B., III. "How Massachusetts Prisoners (Recently) Lost the Right to Vote." WGBH, May 29, 2019. https://www.wgbh.org /news/local-news/2019/05/29/how-massachusetts-prisoners-lost -the-right-to-vote.

Hessick, Carissa Byrne. *Punishment without Trial: Why Plea Bargaining Is a Bad Deal*. New York: Abrams, 2021.

Heymann, Philip B., Alan Konefsky, Richard Peers, and Donald Simon. *Massachusetts Department of Correction*. Cambridge. MA: Kennedy School of Government, 1977.

Hicks, Cheryl. *Talk with You Like a Woman: African American Women, Justice, and Reform in New York, 1890–1935*. Chapel Hill: University of North Carolina Press, 2010.

Hill, Rickey. "The Bogalusa Movement: Self-Defense and Black Power in the Civil Rights Struggle." *Black Scholar* 41, no. 3 (2011): 43–54.

Hillyer, Reiko. "'Going Up on the Way Down': The Virginia State Penitentiary, *Landman v. Royster*, and the Rise and Fall of Prison Litigation." *Journal of Civil and Human Rights* 5, no. 1 (2019): 1–42.

Hillyer, Reiko. "The Guardian Angels: Law and Order and Citizen Policing in New York City." *Journal of Urban History* 43 (2017): 886–914.

Hinton, Elizabeth. *From the War on Poverty to the War on Crime*. Cambridge, MA: Harvard University Press, 2017.

Hodes, Martha. *White Women, Black Men: Illicit Sex in the Nineteenth-Century South*. New Haven, CT: Yale University Press, 1997.

Hogarty, Richard A. "The Sargent Governorship: Leader and Legacy." *New England Journal of Public Policy* 15, no. 1 (1999): 113–39.

Holloway, Louis X. "Prison Abolition or Destruction Is a Must." *Mississippi Law Journal* 45, no. 3 (1974): 757–62.

Holloway, Louis X. "Sex at Parchman: Conjugal Visiting at the Mississippi State Penitentiary." *New England Law Review* 10, no. 1 (1974): 143–55.

Holloway, Pippa. *Living in Infamy: Felon Disfranchisement and the History of American Citizenship*. New York: Oxford University Press, 2013.

Holt, Norman, and Donald Miller. *Explorations in Inmate-Family Relationships.* Sacramento: California Department of Corrections, 1972.

Hoppe, Trevor. *Punishing Disease: HIV and the Criminalization of Sick-
ness.* Berkeley: University of California Press, 2018.

Hopper, Columbus B. "The Conjugal Visit at Mississippi State Penitentiary." *Journal of Criminal Law and Criminology* 53, no. 2 (1962):
340–43.

Hopper, Columbus B. "Conjugal Visiting at the Mississippi State Penitentiary." *Federal Probation* 29, no. 2 (1965): 39–46.

Hopper, Columbus B. "The Evolution of Conjugal Visiting in Mississippi." *Prison Journal* 69, no. 1 (1989): 103–9.

Hopper, Columbus B. "The Impact of Litigation on Mississippi's Prison
System." *Prison Journal* 65, no. 1 (1985): 54–63.

Hopper, Columbus B. *Sex in Prison: The Mississippi Experiment with
Conjugal Visiting.* Baton Rouge: Louisiana State University Press,
1969.

Huling, Tracy. "Building a Prison Economy in Rural America." In *Invisible Punishment: The Collateral Consequences of Mass Imprisonment,*
edited by Marc Mauer and Meda Chesney-Lind, 197–213. New
York: New Press, 2002.

Huling, Tracy L. *Prisons as a Growth Industry in Rural America: An
Exploratory Discussion of the Effects on Young African American
Men in the Inner Cities.* Washington, DC: Prison Policy Initiative,
April 15–16, 1999. https://static.prisonpolicy.org/scans/prisons_as
_rural_growth.shtml.

Jackson, Henry Theodore. "Prison Labor." *Journal of Criminal Law and
Criminology* 18, no. 2 (1927): 218–68.

Jacobs, James B. "The Politics of Prison Expansion." *New York University Review of Law and Social Change* 12, no. 1 (1983–84): 209–42.

Jacobs, James B. "The Prisoners' Rights Movement and Its Impacts,
1960–1980." In *Crime and Justice: An Annual Review of Research,* vol.
2, edited by Norval Morris and Michael Tonry, 429–70. Chicago:
University of Chicago Press, 1980.

Jamieson, Kathleen Hall. *Dirty Politics: Deception, Distraction, and
Democracy.* New York: Oxford University Press, 1992.

Janssen, Volker. "From the Inside Out: Therapeutic Penology and
Political Liberalism in Postwar California." *Osiris* 22, no. 1 (2007):
116–34.

Janssen, Volker. "When the 'Jungle' Met the Forest: Public Work, Civil
Defense and Prison Camps in Postwar California." *Journal of American History* 96, no. 3 (2009): 702–26.

Johns, Donald R. "Alternatives to Conjugal Visiting." *Federal Probation*
35, no. 1 (1971): 48–52.

Johnson, Carla Ann Hage. "Entitled to Clemency: Mercy in the Criminal Law." *Law and Philosophy* 10, no. 1 (1991): 109–18.

Johnson, Miriam McNown, and Rita Rhodes. "Institutionalization: A Theory of Human Behavior and the Social Environment." *Advances in Social Work* 8, no. 1 (2007): 219–36.

Johnston, Normal. "Recent Trends in Correctional Architecture." *British Journal of Criminology* 1, no. 4 (1961): 317–38.

Jones, Alexi. "Cruel and Unusual Punishment: When States Don't Provide Air Conditioning in Prison." Blog post, Prison Policy Initiative, June 18, 2019. https://www.prisonpolicy.org/blog/2019/06/18/air-conditioning/.

Jones, Michelle. "Biographical Mediation and the Formerly Incarcerated: How Dissembling and Disclosure Counter the Extended Consequences of Criminal Convictions." *Biography* 42, no. 3 (2019): 486–513.

Jorgenson, Robert R. "Prison Riots as Agents of Prison Reform: A Sociological Study of Violence and Change." Master's thesis, University of Nebraska at Omaha, 1974. https://digitalcommons.unomaha.edu/studentwork/2180.

Kamerling, Henry. *Capital and Convict: Race, Region, and Punishment in Post–Civil War America.* Charlottesville: University of Virginia Press, 2017.

Kaplan, Aliza B., and Venetia Mayhew. "The Governor's Clemency Power: An Underused Tool to Mitigate the Impact of Measure 11 in Oregon." *Lewis & Clark Law Review* 23, no. 4 (2020): 1285–330.

Karpman, Benjamin. "Criminality, Insanity, and the Law." *Journal of Criminal Law and Criminology* 39, no. 5 (1949): 584–605.

Karpman, Benjamin. "Sex Life in Prison." *Journal of Criminal Law and Criminology* 38, no. 5 (1948): 475–86.

Karpowitz, Daniel. *College in Prison: Reading in an Age of Mass Incarceration.* New Brunswick, NJ: Rutgers University Press, 2017.

Kennedy, Joseph E. "Monstrous Offenders and the Search for Solidarity through Modern Punishment." *Hastings Law Journal* 51, no. 5 (2000): 829–908.

Kennedy, Liam. "'Longtermer Blues': Penal Politics, Reform, and Carceral Experience at Angola." *Punishment and Society* 15, no. 3 (2013): 304–22.

Kennedy, Liam. "'Reflections from Exile': Exploring Prisoner Writings at the Louisiana State Penitentiary." PhD diss., University of Toronto, 2015.

Kent, Norman Elliott. "The Legal and Sociological Dimensions of Conjugal Visitation in Prisons." *New England Journal on Prison Law* 2, no. 1 (1975): 47–66.

Kessel, Alan J. "Unconstitutional Prison Overcrowding." *Annual Survey of American Law* 4 (1986): 737–52.

Kilgore, James. *Understanding E-carceration: Electronic Monitoring, the Surveillance State, and the Future of Mass Incarceration.* New York: New Press, 2022.

King, Arnie. "Arnie King's Public Hearing Notes." Transcript of clemency hearing and board opinion. Through Barbed Wire, n.d. Accessed June 12, 2023. https://web.archive.org/web /20230330011039/http://www.arnoldking.org/post-hearing.html.

King, Arnie. "George Is Ready." Boston Institute for Nonprofit Journalism, April 10, 2017. https://binjonline.com/2017/04/10/george-is -ready/.

King, Arnie. "A Place for Me." Through Barbed Wire, n.d. Accessed June 12, 2023. https://web.archive.org/web/20160128003100 /http://www.arnoldking.org/a_place_for_me.html.

King, Arnie. "Restoring Hope." Through Barbed Wire, n.d. Accessed June 12, 2023. https://web.archive.org/web/20160128003744 /http://www.arnoldking.org/restoring_hope.html.

Knoblauch, Joy. *The Architecture of Good Behavior: Psychology and Modern Institutional Design in Postwar America.* Pittsburgh: University of Pittsburgh Press, 2020.

Kobil, Daniel T. "How to Grant Clemency in Unforgiving Times." *Capital University Law Review* 31, no. 2 (2003): 219–42.

Kobil, Daniel T. "The Quality of Mercy Strained: Wresting the Pardoning Power from the King." *Texas Law Review* 69, no. 3 (1991): 569–642.

Kohler-Hausmann, Julilly. *Getting Tough: Welfare and Imprisonment in 1970s America.* Princeton, NJ: Princeton University Press, 2018.

Kondkar, Marcus M. *Incarceration in Louisiana: Sentencing Patterns in America's Prison Capital: A Report for Vital Projects Fund.* New York: Vital Projects Fund, October 14, 2016.

Kunzel, Regina. *Criminal Intimacy: Prison and the Uneven History of Modern American Sexuality.* Chicago: University of Chicago Press, 2008.

Kunzel, Regina. "Sex Panic, Psychiatry, and the Expansion of the Carceral State." In *The War on Sex*, edited by David M. Halperin and Trevor Hoppe, 229–46. Durham, NC: Duke University Press, 2017.

Kurki, Leena, and Norval Morris. "The Purposes, Practices, and Problems of Supermax Prisons." *Crime and Justice* 28 (2001): 385–424.

Lamott, Kenneth Church. *Chronicles of San Quentin: The Biography of a Prison.* Philadelphia: D. McKay, 1961.

Lancaster, Roger N. *Sex Panic and the Punitive State.* Berkeley: University of California Press, 2011.

Langan, Patrick A., Jolut V. Fundis, Lawrence A. Greenfeld, and Victoria W. Schneider, *Historical Statistics on Prisoners in State and Federal Institutions, Yearend 1925–1986*. Washington, DC: US Department of Justice, Bureau of Justice Statistics, 1988. https://www.ojp.gov/pdffiles1/Digitization/111098NCJRS.pdf.

Lassiter, Matthew. *The Silent Majority: Suburban Politics in the Sunbelt South*. Princeton, NJ: Princeton University Press, 2006.

Lee, Logan M. "Far from Home and All Alone: The Impact of Prison Visitation on Recidivism." *American Law and Economics Review* 21, no. 2 (2019): 431–81.

Lenz, Nygel. "'Luxuries' in Prison: The Relationship between Amenity Funding and Public Support." *Crime and Delinquency* 48, no. 4 (2002): 499–525.

Lerman, Amy E., and Vesla M. Weaver. *Arresting Citizenship: The Democratic Consequences of American Crime Control*. Chicago: University of Chicago Press, 2014.

Lichtenstein, Alex. "Flocatex and the Fiscal Limits of Mass Incarceration: Toward a New Political Economy of the Postwar Carceral State." *Journal of American History* 102, no. 1 (2015): 113–25.

Lindner, Robert. "Sex in Penal Institutions." In *Sex Habits of American Men: A Symposium on the Kinsey Report*, edited by Albert Deutsch, 201–15. New York: Prentice Hall, 1948.

Lipman, David M. "Mississippi's Prison Experience." *Mississippi Law Journal* 45, no. 3 (1974): 685–756.

Listwan, Shelley Johnson, Cheryl Lero Jonson, Francis T. Cullen, and Edward J. Latessa, "Cracks in the Penal Harm Movement: Evidence from the field." *Criminology and Public Policy* 7, no. 3 (2008): 423–65.

Lloyd, G. P. "A Family Visiting Programme for Offenders in Custody." *Medical and Biological Illustration* 19, no 3 (1969): 146–49.

Lockwood, Beatrix, and Nicole Lewis. "The Long Journey to Visit a Family Member in Prison." Marshall Project, December 18, 2019. https://www.themarshallproject.org/2019/12/18/the-long-journey-to-visit-a-family-member-in-prison.

Loguen, J. W. *The Rev. J. W. Loguen, as a Slave and as a Freeman: A Narrative of Real Life*. Syracuse, NY: J. G. K. Truair, 1859.

Lorant, Lisa. *1986 Annual Statistical Report of the Furlough Program*. Boston: Massachusetts Department of Correction, August 1987. https://www.mass.gov/doc/316furloughpdf/download.

Lorant, Lisa, and John Sherwood. *1987 Annual Statistical Report of the Furlough Program*. Boston: Massachusetts Department of Correction, December 1988. https://www.mass.gov/doc/334furloughpdf/download.

Louisiana Parole Project. "Our Staff: Andrew Hundley." Web page, n.d. Accessed June 13, 2023. https://www.paroleproject.org/our-staff/.

Love, Margaret Colgate. "Fear of Forgiving: Rule and Discretion in the Theory and Practice of Pardoning." *Federal Sentencing Reporter* 13, nos. 3–4 (2000): 125–33.

Love, Margaret Colgate. "The Twilight of the Pardon Power." *Journal of Criminal Law and Criminology* 100, no. 3 (2010): 1169–212.

Lux, Erin. "From Rehabilitation to Punishment: American Corrections after 1945." Master's thesis, University of Ottawa, 2012. https://www .researchgate.net/publication/274370895_From_Rehabilitation_to _Punishment_American_Corrections_After_1945.

Lynch, Mona P. *Sunbelt Justice: Arizona and the Transformation of American Punishment.* Stanford, CA: Stanford Law Books, 2010.

Lyons, J. Michael, and Felix Rosado. "'There's Urgency Here': A Pedagogy of Discomfort in a Prison Basement." *Beyond Mass Incarceration: New Horizons of Liberation and Freedom* 5, no. 2 (2019). https://public.imaginingamerica.org/blog/article/theres -urgency-here-a-pedagogy-of-discomfort-in-a-prison-basement/.

Macek, Steve. *Urban Nightmares: The Media, The Right, and the Moral Panic over the City.* Minneapolis: University of Minnesota Press, 2006.

Maginnis, John. *The Last Hayride.* Baton Rouge, LA: Gris Gris, 1984.

Major, Derek. "Louisiana's 10/6 Lifers Were Promised Parole after 10 Years, but Many Ended Up Serving Life." Black Enterprise, November 29, 2021. https://www.blackenterprise.com/louisianas-10 -6-lifers-were-promised-parole-after-10-years-but-many-ended-up -serving-life/.

Malcolm X with Alex Haley. *The Autobiography of Malcolm X.* New York: Random House, 1992.

Marcum, Catherine D., and Tammy L. Castle. *Sex in Prison: Myths and Realities.* Boulder, CO: Lynne Rienner, 2013.

Markley, Carson W. "Furlough Programs and Conjugal Visiting in Adult Correctional Institutions." *Federal Probation* 37, no. 1 (1973): 19–26.

Marshall, Mary. "*Miller v. Alabama* and the Problem of Prediction." *Columbia Law Review* 119, no. 6 (2019): 1633–70.

Martin, Forest C. *With Edwards in the Governor's Mansion: From Angola to Free Man.* Gretna, LA: Pelican, 2012.

Martin, John Bartlow. *Break Down the Walls.* New York: Ballantine Books, 1954.

Massachusetts Department of Correction. *Position Paper: The Massachusetts Furlough Program.* Boston: Massachusetts Department of Correction, May 1987.

Massachusetts Department of Correction, Division of Planning and Research. *Interim Report on Furloughs.* Boston: Massachusetts De-

partment of Correction, April 12, 1973. https://www.mass.gov/doc
/65furloughpdf/download.

Massachusetts Department of Correction, Division of Research,
Correction/Parole Information System Unit. *Descriptions of
Furloughs Granted November 6, 1972 thru December 31, 1973.*
Boston: Massachusetts Department of Correction, Sep-
tember 1974. https://www.mass.gov/doc/97afurloughpdf
/download.

Massachusetts General Court, House of Representatives Post Audit
and Oversight Bureau. *Department of Correction: Furlough Program.*
(Boston: The Committee, 1988).

Mauer, Marc, and Meda Chesney-Lind, eds. *Invisible Punishment: The
Collateral Consequences of Mass Imprisonment.* New York: New
Press, 2002.

Mauer, Marc, and Ashley Nellis. *The Meaning of Life: The Case for Abolishing Life Sentences.* New York: New Press, 2018.

Maurutto, Paula, and Kelly Hannah-Moffat. "Assembling Risk and the
Restructuring of Penal Control." *British Journal of Criminology* 46,
no. 3 (2006): 438–54.

May, Elaine Tyler. *Homeward Bound: Families in the Cold War Era.*
New York: Basic Books, 1988.

McCann, Bryan J. "'A Fate Worse Than Death': Reform, Abolition,
and Life without Parole in Anti–Death Penalty Discourse." In
Working for Justice: A Handbook of Prison Education and Activism,
ed. Stephen John Hartnett, Eleanor Novek, and Jennifer K. Wood,
187–202. Urbana: University of Illinois Press, 2013.

McCarthy, Belinda Rodgers. "The Development, Function and Future
of Home Furlough Programs." *American Journal of Criminal Justice*
4 (1977): 16–29.

McCay, Robert. "It's Time to Rehabilitate the Sentencing Process."
Judicature 60, no. 5 (1976–77): 223–28.

McClennan, Rebecca. *The Crisis of Imprisonment: Protest, Politics, and
the Making of an American Penal State, 1776–1941.* Cambridge:
Cambridge University Press, 2008.

McDowell, Deborah E., Claudrena N. Harold, and Juan Battle, eds. *The
Punitive Turn: New Approaches to Race and Incarceration.* Charlottesville: University of Virginia Press, 2013.

McElreath, David H., D. Adrian Doss, Carl J. Jensen III, Michael P.
Wigginton, Steve Mallory, Terry Lyons, Lori Williamson, and
Don W. Jones. "The End of the Mississippi Experiment with Con-
jugal Visitation." *Prison Journal* 96, no. 5 (2016): 752–64.

McGirr, Lisa. *Suburban Warriors: The Origins of the New American
Right.* Princeton, NJ: Princeton University Press, 2001.

Mendelberg, Tali. *The Race Card: Campaign Strategy, Implicit Messages, and the Norm of Equality.* Princeton, NJ: Princeton University Press, 2001.

Miller, Vivien M. L. *Crime, Sexual Violence, and Clemency: Florida's Pardon Board and the Penal System in the Progressive Era.* Gainesville: University Press of Florida, 2000.

Minchin, Timothy J., and John A. Salmond, "'The Saddest Story of the Whole Movement': The Clyde Kennard Case and the Search for Racial Reconciliation in Mississippi, 1955–2007." *Journal of Mississippi History* 81, no. 3 (Fall 2009): 191–234.

Misick, Bobbi-Jeanne. "This Louisiana Prisoner Thought He'd Only Have to Serve a Decade. 57 Years Later, He's Free." wwno, October 25, 2021. https://www.wwno.org/news/2021-10-25/this -louisiana-prisoner-thought-hed-only-have-to-serve-a-decade-57 -years-later-hes-free.

Mitford, Jessica. *Kind and Usual Punishment: The Prison Business.* New York: Vintage, 1971.

Mogul, Joey L., Andrea J. Ritchie, and Kay Whitlock. *Queer (In)justice: The Criminalization of LGBT People in the United States.* Boston: Beacon, 2011.

Monroe Correctional Complex, "Visitor's Guidelines." Washington State Department of Corrections, n.d. Accessed June 13, 2023. https://web.archive.org/web/20151010134317/http://www.doc .wa.gov/facilities/prison/mcc/docs/mccvisitguidelines.pdf.

Moore, Taylor DeWayne. "I'm Gonna Stay Right Here until They Tear This Barrelhouse Down: Black Power and the Origins of Blues Tourism in Greenville, Mississippi." PhD diss., University of Mississippi, 2018.

Moran, Dominque. *Carceral Geography: Spaces and Practices of Incarceration.* New York: Routledge, 2016.

Moran, Dominique. "Linking the Carceral and the Punitive State: A Review of Research on Prison Architecture, Design, Technology and the Lived Experience of Carceral Space." *Annales de géographie* 702–3, nos. 2–3 (2015): 163–84.

Morison, Samuel T. "The Politics of Grace: On the Moral Justification of Executive Clemency." *Buffalo Criminal Law Review* 9, no. 1 (2005): 1–138.

Morris, James McGrath. *Jailhouse Journalism: The Fourth Estate behind Bars.* New Brunswick, NJ: Transaction, 2002.

Morris, Norval, and David J. Rothman, eds. *The Oxford History of the Prison: The Practice of Punishment in Western Society.* New York: Oxford University Press, 1998.

Muhammad, Khalil Gibran. *The Condemnation of Blackness: Race, Crime, and the Making of Modern Urban America.* Cambridge, MA: Harvard University Press, 2010.

Murakawa, Naomi. *The First Civil Right: How Liberals Built Prison America.* New York: Oxford University Press, 2014.

Murakawa, Naomi. "The Origins of the Carceral Crisis: Racial Order as 'Law and Order' in Postwar American Politics." In *Race and American Political Development*, edited by Joseph E. Lowndes, Julie Novkov, and Dorian T. Warren, 234–55. New York: Routledge, 2008.

Murakawa, Naomi. "The Racial Antecedents to Federal Sentencing Guidelines: How Congress Judged the Judges from Brown to Booker." *Roger Williams University Law Review* 11, no. 2 (2006): 473–94.

Murray, Christopher. *Unusual Punishment: Inside the Walla Walla Prison, 1970–1985.* Pullman: Washington State University Press, 2016.

Myers, Martha A. *Race, Labor and Punishment in the New South.* Columbus: Ohio State University Press, 1998.

Nagel, William G. "A Moratorium on Correctional Construction." *Prison Journal* 52, no. 2 (1972): 66–72.

Nagel, William G. *The New Red Barn: A Critical Look at the Modern American Prison.* Philadelphia: American Foundation, 1973.

National Advisory Commission on Criminal Justice Standards and Goals, *Executive Summary: Reports of the National Advisory Commission on Criminal Justice Standards and Goals.* Washington, DC: US Department of Justice, Law Enforcement Assistance Administration, 1974.

National Institute of Law Enforcement and Criminal Justice. *National Evaluation Program, Phase I Report: Summary; Furlough Programs for Inmates.* Washington, DC: US Department of Justice, 1976.

National Public Radio. "Tossing Away the Keys." *Weekend All Things Considered*, April 29, 1990. https://storycorps.org/stories/tossing-away-the-keys/.

Nellis, Ashley. *Life Goes On: The Historic Rise in Life Sentences in America.* Washington, DC: Sentencing Project, 2013. https://www.sentencingproject.org/app/uploads/2022/08/Life-Goes-On.pdf.

Nellis, Ashley. "A New Lease on Life." Sentencing Project, June 30, 2021. https://www.sentencingproject.org/publications/a-new-lease-on-life/.

Nellis, Ashley. *No End in Sight: America's Enduring Reliance on Life Imprisonment.* Washington, DC: Sentencing Project, 2021. https://www.sentencingproject.org/wp-content/uploads/2021/02/No-End-in-Sight-Americas-Enduring-Reliance-on-Life-Imprisonment.pdf.

Nellis, Ashley. *Still Life: America's Increasing Use of Life and Long-Term Sentences*. Washington, DC: Sentencing Project, May 2017.

Nelson, Elmer K., Jr. "Community-Based Correctional Treatment: Rationale and Problems." *Annals of the American Academy of Political and Social Science* 374 (1967): 82–91.

Newburn, Tim, and Trevor Jones. "Symbolic Politics and Penal Populism: The Long Shadow of Willie Horton." *Crime Media Culture* 1, no. 1 (2005): 72–87.

Newton, Huey. "Prison, Where Is Thy Victory?" In *The Genius of Huey Newton*, 10–13. San Francisco: Ministry of Information, Black Panther Party, 1970.

Nissenbaum, Steven. *The Battle for Christmas: A Cultural History of America's Most Cherished Holiday*. New York: Alfred A. Knopf, 1996.

Notterman, Ben. *The Demise of Clemency for Lifers in Pennsylvania*. Edited by Courtney M. Oliva. New York: State Clemency Project, New York University Center on the Administration of Criminal Law, n.d. Accessed June 13, 2023. https://www.law.nyu.edu/sites/default/files/CACL%20Clemency%20PA_Accessible.pdf.

Notterman, Ben. *Taking Stock of Clemency in the Empire State: A Century in Review*. Edited by Courtney M. Oliva. New York: State Clemency Project, New York University Center on the Administration of Criminal Law, n.d. Accessed June 13, 2023. https://www.law.nyu.edu/sites/default/files/CACL%20NY%20Clemency%20_3_4_A_Accessible.pdf.

Notterman, Ben. *Willie Horton's Shadow: Clemency in Massachusetts*. Edited by Courtney M. Oliva. New York: State Clemency Project, New York University Center on the Administration of Criminal Law, n.d. [June 3, 2019]. Accessed June 12, 2023. https://www.law.nyu.edu/sites/default/files/CACL%20Clemency%20MA_Accessible.pdf.

Novak, Andrew. *Comparative Executive Clemency: The Constitutional Pardon Power and the Prerogative of Mercy in Global Perspective*. New York: Routledge, 2016.

O'Brien, Cyrus J. "'A Prison in Your Community': Halfway Houses and the Melding of Treatment and Control." *Journal of American History* 108, no. 1 (2021): 93–117.

Ogletree, Charles J., Jr., and Austin Sarat. "Introduction: Lives on the Line; from Capital Punishment to Life without Parole." In *Life without Parole: America's New Death Penalty?*, edited by Charles J. Ogletree Jr. and Austin Sarat, 1–24. New York: New York University Press, 2012.

Ogletree, Charles J., Jr., and Austin Sarat, eds. *Life without Parole: America's New Death Penalty?* New York: New York University Press, 2012.

Oleson, James C. "The New Eugenics: Black Hyper-incarceration and Human Abatement." *Social Sciences* 5, no. 66 (2016): 1–20.

O'Malley, Joanne, and Daniel P. LeClair. *An Evaluation of the Massachusetts Furlough Experience, November 1972–August 1973.* Boston: Massachusetts Department of Correction, 1974. State Library of Massachusetts. https://archives.lib.state.ma.us/handle/2452/264063.

O'Malley, Pat. "Globalising Risk? Distinguishing Styles of Neoliberal Criminal Justice in Australia and the USA." In *Criminal Justice and Political Cultures: National and International Dimensions of Crime Control*, edited by Tim Newburn and Richard Sparks, 30–48. Cullompton, UK: Willan, 2004.

Oshinsky, David M. *Worse Than Slavery: Parchman Farm and the Ordeal of Jim Crow Justice.* New York: Free Press Paperbacks, 1994.

Page, Joshua. *The Toughest Beat: Politics, Punishment, and the Prison Officers Union in California.* New York: Oxford University Press, 2011.

Parsons, Anne. *From Asylum to Prison: Deinstitutionalization and the Rise of Mass Incarceration after 1945.* Chapel Hill: University of North Carolina Press, 2018.

Patterson, Orlando. *Slavery and Social Death.* Cambridge, MA: Harvard University Press, 1982.

Pears, Daniel P., Joshua C. Cochran, Sonja E. Siennick, and William D. Bales. "Prison Visitation and Recidivism." *Justice Quarterly* 29, no. 6 (2021): 888–918.

Pelot-Hobbs, Lydia. "Louisiana's Turn to Mass Incarceration: The Building of a Carceral State." Association of American Geographers, February 1, 2018. https://www.aag.org/louisianas-turn-to-mass-incarceration-the-building-of-a-carceral-state/.

Pelot-Hobbs, Lydia. "Organized Inside and Out: The Angola Special Civics Project and the Crisis of Mass Incarceration." *Souls: A Critical Journal of Black Politics, Culture and Society* 15, no. 3 (2013): 199–217.

Pelot-Hobbs, Lydia. "Scaling Up or Scaling Back? The Pitfalls and Possibilities of Leveraging Federal Interventions for Abolition." *Critical Criminology* 26, no. 3 (2018): 423–41.

Pennsylvania Board of Pardons. "Commutation of Life Sentences (1971–Present)." Web page, n.d. Accessed June 13, 2023. https://www.bop.pa.gov/Statistics/Pages/Commutation-of-Life-Sentences.aspx.

Perkinson, Robert. "Angola and the Agony of Prison Reform." *Radical Philosophy Review* 3, no. 1 (2000): 8–19.

Perkinson, Robert. *Texas Tough: The Rise of America's Prison Empire.* New York: Metropolitan Books, 2010.

Pfaff, John F. *Locked In: The True Causes of Mass Incarceration and How to Achieve Real Reform.* New York: Basic Books, 2017.

Phelps, Michelle S. "Rehabilitation in the Punitive Era: The Gap between Rhetoric and Reality in U.S. Prison Programs." *Law and Society Review* 45, no. 1 (2022): 33–68.

Pollock, Anne. "On the Suspended Sentences of the Scott Sisters: Mass Incarceration, Kidney Donation, and the Biopolitics of Race in the United States." *Science, Technology, and Human Values* 40, no. 2 (2015): 250–71.

Pompa, Lori. "One Brick at a Time: The Power and Possibility of Dialogue across the Prison Wall." *Prison Journal* 93, no. 2 (June 2013): 127–34.

Porter, Sonya R., John L. Voorheis, and William Sabol. "Correctional Facility and Inmate Locations: Urban and Rural Status Patterns." CARRA Working Paper Series, Working Paper 2017-08, US Census Bureau, Washington, DC, July 2017. https://www.census.gov /content/dam/Census/library/working-papers/2017/adrm/carra -wp-2017-08.pdf.

Powell, Bob. "A Dilemma: Overpopulation in Southern Prisons." *Southern Changes* 1, no. 1 (1978): 16–17.

Pratt, John, and Jordan Anderson, eds. *Criminal Justice, Risk and the Revolt against Uncertainty.* New York: Palgrave Macmillan, 2020.

President's Commission on Law Enforcement and Administration of Justice. *The Challenge of Crime in a Free Society.* Washington, DC: GPO, 1967.

Price, Joshua M. *Prison and Social Death.* New Brunswick, NJ: Rutgers University Press, 2015.

Prieur, Nina Billone. "In the System: Art, Prison, and the Performance of Social Welfare." PhD diss., University of California–Berkeley, 2010.

Prison Industries Reorganization Administration. *The Prison Problem in Alabama.* Washington, DC: Prison Industries Reorganization Administration, 1939.

Purnell, Derecka. *Becoming Abolitionists: Police, Protests, and the Pursuit of Freedom.* New York: Astra House, 2021.

Quigley, William. "Louisiana Angola Penitentiary: Past Time to Close." *Loyola Journal of Public Interest Law* 19, no. 2 (2018): 163–222.

Rabuy, Bernadette, and Daniel Kopf. "Separation by Bars and Miles: Visitation in State Prisons." Prison Policy Initiative, October 20, 2015. https://www.prisonpolicy.org/reports/prisonvisits.html.

Rapaport, Elizabeth. "Retribution and Redemption in the Operation of Executive Clemency." *Chicago-Kent Law Review* 74, no. 4 (1999): 1501–35.

Rapping, Elayne. *Law and Justice as Seen on TV.* New York: New York University Press, 2003.

Reddebrek. "1973: Prisoners Take Control of Walpole Prison." Libcom, January 22, 2017. https://libcom.org/history/1973-prisoners-take -control-walpole-prison.

Reich, Robert B. *Public Management in a Democratic Society*. Englewood Cliffs, NJ: Prentice Hall, 1990.

Reiter, Keramet. "The Path to Pelican Bay." In *Caging Borders and Carceral States: Incarcerations, Immigrant Detentions, and Resistance*, edited by Robert T. Chase, 303–40. Chapel Hill: University of North Carolina Press, 2019.

Reiter, Keramet. "Reclaiming the Power to Punish: Legislating and Administrating the California Supermax, 1982–1989." *Law and Society Review* 50, no. 2(2016): 484–518.

Reiter, Keramet. "The Supermax Prison: A Blunt Means of Control, or a Subtle Form of Violence?" *Radical Philosophy Review* 17, no. 2 (2014): 457–75.

Reiter, Keramet. *23/7: Pelican Bay Prison and the Rise of Long-Term Solitary Confinement*. New Haven, CT: Yale University Press, 2016.

Reiter, Keramet A. *Mass Incarceration*. New York: Oxford University Press, 2017.

Renfro, Paul M. *Stranger Danger: Family Values, Childhood, and the American Carceral State*. New York: Oxford University Press, 2020.

Rentschler, Carrie A. *Second Wounds: Victims' Rights and the Media in the U.S.* Durham, NC: Duke University Press, 2011.

Rhodes, Lorna A. *Total Confinement: Madness and Reason in the Maximum Security Prison*. Berkeley: University of California Press, 2004.

Richards, Stephen C. "USP Marion: The First Federal Supermax." *Prison Journal* 88, no. 1 (2008): 16–22.

Rideau, Wilbert. *In the Place of Justice: A Story of Punishment and Deliverance*. New York: Alfred A. Knopf, 2010.

Rideau, Wilbert, and Ron Wikberg. *Life Sentences: Rage and Survival behind Bars*. New York: Times Books, 1992.

Ridgeway, James, and Jean Casella. "For Jamie Scott, An $11 Robbery in Mississippi May Carry a Death Sentence." Solitary Watch, n.d. Accessed June 1, 2023. https://solitarywatch.org/about/for-jamie -scott-an-11-robbery-in-mississippi-may-carry-a-death-sentence/.

Riveland, Chase. *Supermax Prisons: Overview and General Considerations*. Washington, DC: US Department of Justice, National Institute of Corrections, January 1999. https://www.prisonpolicy .org/scans/NIC_014937.pdf.

Rodríguez, Dylan. "Abolition as Praxis of Human Being: A Foreword." *Harvard Law Review* 132 (2019): 1575–612.

Rosado, Felix. "Doin' Death." Minutes before Six, August 8, 2019. https://minutesbeforesix.com/wp/doin-death/.

Rosado, Felix. "Felix Rosado on Dispelling the Myths about Incarcerated People." Lifelines: Voices against the Other Death Penalty, June 8, 2014. https://lifelines-project.org/2016/02/14/phill-rosado -interview-1/.

Rosado, Felix, and Layne Mullett. "Organizing across Prison Walls Is How We'll Bring Them Down." Critical Resistance, December 14, 2018. https://criticalresistance.org/resources/organizing-across -prison-walls-is-how-well-bring-them-down/.

Rosen, Charlotte. "Carceral Crisis: The Challenge of Prison Overcrowding and the Rise of Mass Incarceration, 1970–2000." PhD diss., Northwestern University, 2023.

Rosen, Charlotte. "'It's at the State and Local Level That Problems Exist': The Armed Career Criminal Act and the Puzzle of Federal Crime Control in the Reagan Era." *Journal of Policy History* 35, no. 2 (2023): 161–94.

Rosen, Richard A. "The 'Especially Heinous' Aggravating Circumstance in Capital Cases—The Standardless Standard." *North Carolina Law Review* 64, no. 5 (1986): 941–92.

Rosenzweig, Paul. "Reflections on the Atrophying Pardon Power." *Journal of Law and Criminology* 102, no. 3 (2012): 593–611.

Roth, Rachel. "No New Babies: Gender Inequality and Reproductive Control in the Criminal Justice and Prison Systems." *American University Journal of Gender, Social Policy, and the Law* 12, no. 3 (2004): 391–426.

Rothman, David J. *Conscience and Convenience: The Asylum and Its Alternatives in Progressive America.* New York: Aldine de Gruyter, 1980.

Rothman, David J. *The Discovery of the Asylum: Social Order and Disorder in the New Republic.* New York: Routledge, 2002.

Rotman, Edgardo. "The Failure of Reform." In *The Oxford History of the Prison: The Practice of Punishment in Western Society*, edited by Norval Morris and David J. Rothman, 151–77. New York: Oxford University Press, 1998.

Ruckman, P. S., Jr. "Executive Clemency in the United States: Origins, Development, and Analysis." *Presidential Studies Quarterly* 27, no. 2 (1997): 251–71.

Sabo, Don, Terry A. Kupers, and Willie London, eds. *Prison Masculinities.* Philadelphia: Temple University Press, 2001.

Sansing, David G., and Carroll Waller. *A History of the Mississippi Governor's Mansion.* Jackson: University Press of Mississippi, 1977.

Sasson, Theodore. "William Horton's Long Shadow: 'Punitiveness' and 'Managerialism' in the Penal Politics of Massachusetts, 1988–99." In *Crime, Risk and Insecurity*, edited by Timothy J. Hope and Richard J. Sparks, 238–51. New York: Routledge, 2000.

Schafer, N. E. "Prison Visiting: Is It Time to Review the Rules?" *Federal Probation* 53, no. 4 (1989): 25–30.

Scheingold, Stuart. *The Politics of Street Crime*. Madison: University of Wisconsin Press, 1991.

Schenwar, Maya, and Victoria Law. *Prison by Any Other Name: The Harmful Consequences of Popular Reforms*. New York: New Press, 2020.

Schlanger, Margo. "Inmate Litigation." *Harvard Law Review* 116, no. 6 (2003): 1557–706.

Schwartzapfel, Beth. "For $12 of Commissary, He Got Ten Years off His Sentence." Marshall Project, August 13, 2015. https://www .themarshallproject.org/2015/08/13/for-12-of-commissary-he-got -10-years-off-his-sentence.

Schwartzapfel, Beth, and Bill Keller. "Willie Horton Revisited." Marshall Project, May 13, 2015. https://www.themarshallproject.org /2015/05/13/willie-horton-revisited.

Seeds, Christopher. *Death by Prison: The Emergence of Life without Parole and Perpetual Confinement*. Berkeley: University of California Press, 2022.

Seeds, Christopher. "Governors and Prisoners: The Death of Clemency and the Making of Life Sentences without Release in Pennsylvania." *Social Justice* 46, no. 4 (2019): 81–106.

Seeds, Christopher. "Hope and the Life Sentence." *British Journal of Criminology* 62, no. 1 (2022): 234–50.

Seeds, Christopher. "Life Sentences and Perpetual Confinement." *Annual Review of Criminology* 4 (2021): 287–309.

Seigel, Micol. *Violence Work: State Power and the Limits of Police*. Durham, NC: Duke University Press, 2018.

Shakur, Assata. *Assata Shakur: An Autobiography*. Westport, CT: Lawrence Hill, 1987.

Sherry, Michael S. *The Punitive Turn in American Life: How the United States Learned to Fight Crime Like a War*. Chapel Hill: University of North Carolina Press.

Shihadeh, Edward S., Keith Nordyke, and Anthony Reed. *Fact Sheet: Recidivism in the State of Louisiana: An Analysis of 3- and 5-Year Recidivism Rates among Long-Serving Offenders*. Baton Rouge: Crime and Policy Evaluation Research Group, Louisiana State University, October 2014. https://www.lsu.edu/hss/sociology/research /CAPER/CAPER_Fact_Sheets/FS13.pdf.

Silver, James. *Mississippi: The Closed Society*. New York: Harcourt, Brace and World, 1966.

Simes, Jessica T., and Ryan T. Sakoda. "Solitary Confinement and the U.S. Prison Boom." *Criminal Justice Policy Review* 54 (2019): 66–102.

Simon, Jonathan. *Governing through Crime: How the War on Crime Transformed American Democracy and Created a Culture of Fear.* New York: Oxford University Press, 2007.

Simon, Jonathan. "The 'Hard Back' of Mass Incarceration: Fear, Structural Racism, and the Overpunishment of Violent Crime." In *The Punitive Turn: New Approaches to Race and Incarceration*, edited by Deborah E. McDowell, Claudrena N. Harold, and Juan Battle, 192–210. Charlottesville: University of Virginia Press, 2013.

Simon, Jonathan. "Megan's Law: Crime and Democracy in Late Modern America." *Law and Social Inquiry* 25, no. 4 (2000): 1111–1150.

Simon, Jonathan. *Poor Discipline: Parole and the Social Control of the Underclass, 1890–1990.* Chicago: University of Chicago Press, 1993.

Simon, Jonathan. "A Radical Need for Criminology." *Social Justice* 40, nos. 1–2 (2014): 9–23.

Simon, Jonathan. "Wake of the Flood: Crime, Disaster, and the American Risk Imaginary after Katrina." *Issues in Legal Scholarship* 6, no. 3 (2007): 1–19.

Simpson, Carolyn. "Conjugal Visiting in United States Prisons." *Columbia Human Rights Law Review* 10, no. 2 (1978–79): 963–1033.

Sinclair, Billy Wayne, and Jodie Sinclair. *A Life in the Balance: The Billy Wayne Sinclair Story.* New York: Arcade, 2000.

Singer, Richard G. "Privacy, Autonomy, and Dignity in the Prison: A Preliminary Inquiry Concerning Constitutional Aspects of the Degradation Process in Our Prisons." *Buffalo Law Review* 21, no. 3 (1972): 669–716.

Smith, Neil. *The New Urban Frontier: Gentrification and the Revanchist City.* New York: Routledge, 1996.

Sommer, Robert. *The End of Imprisonment.* New York: Oxford University Press, 1976.

Sommer, Robert. *Final Report: Research Priorities in Correctional Architecture.* Pt. 2, *Proposals for the Physical and Social Organization of Prisons.* Washington, DC: National Criminal Justice Reference Service, 1976. https://www.ncjrs.gov/pdffiles1/Digitization /31711NCJRS.pdf.

Sommer, Robert. *Tight Spaces: Hard Architecture and How to Humanize It.* Englewood Cliffs, NJ: Prentice-Hall, 1974.

Sorkin, Michael, ed. *Indefensible Space: The Architecture of the National Security State.* New York: Routledge, 2008.

Stack, Brian. "From Sodomists to Citizens: Same-Sex Sexuality and the Progressive Era Washington State Reformatory." *Journal of the History of Sexuality* 28, no. 2 (2019): 173–204.

Stanley, Eric A., and Nat Smith, eds. *Captive Genders: Trans Embodiment and the Prison Industrial Complex.* Oakland, CA: AK Press, 2011.

Stevenson, Bryan. *Just Mercy: A Story of Justice and Redemption.* New York: Spiegel and Grau, 2015.

Stojkovic, Stan. "The President's Crime Commission Recommendations for Corrections: The Twilight of the Idols." In *The 1967 President's Crime Commission Report: Its Impact 25 Years Later,* edited by John A. Conley. Highland Heights: Anderson, 1994.

Stone, Gigi. "Give a Kidney to Shorten Your Prison Sentence?" ABC News, March 9, 2007. https://abcnews.go.com/US/LegalCenter/story?id=2940289&page=1.

Story, Brett. *Prison Land: Mapping Carceral Power in Neoliberal America.* Minneapolis: University of Minnesota Press, 2019.

Strain, Christopher B. "'We Walked Like Men': The Deacons for Self Defense and Justice." *Louisiana History: The Journal of the Louisiana Historical Association* 38, no. 1 (1997): 43–62.

Strange, Carolyn. *Discretionary Justice: Pardon and Parole in New York from the Revolution to the Depression.* New York: New York University Press, 2016.

Sullivan, Larry E. *The Prison Reform Movement: Forlorn Hope.* Boston: Twayne, 1990.

Sussman, Peter Y. "Media on Prisons: Censorship and Stereotypes." In *Invisible Punishment: The Collateral Consequences of Mass Imprisonment,* edited by Marc Mauer and Meda Chesney-Lind, 258–78. New York: New Press, 2002.

Sutor, Grey. "The Other Side of the Fence: Self-Government, Carceral Repression, and the Radical Prisoners' Movement at Washington State Penitentiary." Bachelor's thesis, Lewis & Clark College, 2020.

Sykes, Gresham. *The Society of Captives.* Princeton, NJ: Princeton University Press, 1958, 2007.

Tait, David. "Pardons in Perspective: The Role of Forgiveness in Criminal Justice." *Federal Sentencing Reporter* 13, nos. 3–4 (2000): 134–38.

Taylor, Keeyanga-Yamahtta. *From #BlackLivesMatter to Black Liberation.* Chicago: Haymarket Books, 2016.

Taylor, William Banks. *Down on Parchman Farm: The Great Prison in the Mississippi Delta.* Columbus: Ohio State University Press, 1999.

Tenaglia, Robert J., Jr. *1990 Annual Statistical Report of the Furlough Program.* Boston: Massachusetts Department of Correction, July 1991. https://www.mass.gov/doc/362furloughpdf/download.

Tepperman, Alexander. "Prison Weights for No Man: Interpreting a Modern Moral Panic." *Critical Issues in Justice and Politics* 7, no. 1 (2014): 1–16.

Tewksbury, Richard, and Elizabeth Ehrhardt Mustaine. "Insiders' Views of Prison Amenities: Beliefs and Perceptions of Correctional Staff Members." *Criminal Justice Review* 30, no. 2 (2005): 174–88.

Thomas, Cullen. "Conversations with Literary Ex-Cons: Billy Sinclair." The Rumpus, May 3, 2017. https://therumpus.net/2017/05 /conversations-with-literary-ex-cons-billy-sinclair/.

Thomas, Piri. *Seven Long Times*. New York: Praeger, 1974.

Thomas-Tisdale, Alice. "State Leaders Demanding Full Pardon for Scott Sisters." *Free the Scott Sisters* (blog), January 22, 2012. https:// freethescottsisters.blogspot.com/2012/.

Thompson, Heather Ann. "Blinded by a 'Barbaric' South: Prison Horrors, Inmate Abuse, and the Ironic History of American Penal Reform." In *The Myth of Southern Exceptionalism*, edited by Matthew D. Lassiter and Joseph Crespino, 74–95. New York: Oxford University Press, 2010.

Thompson, Heather Ann. *Blood in the Water: The Attica Prison Uprising of 1971 and Its Legacy*. New York: Penguin Random House, 2017.

Thompson, Heather Ann. "From Researching the Past to Reimagining the Future: Locating Carceral Crisis and the Key to Its End, in the Long Twentieth Century." In *The Punitive Turn: New Approaches to Race and Incarceration,* edited by Deborah E. McDowell, Claudrena N. Harold, and Juan Battle, 45–72. Charlottesville: University of Virginia Press, 2013.

Thompson, Heather Ann. "Rethinking Working-Class Struggle through the Lens of the Carceral State: Toward a Labor History of Inmates and Guards." *Labor: Studies in Working-Class History of the Americas* 8, no. 3 (2011): 15–45.

Thompson, Heather Ann. "Why Mass Incarceration Matters: Rethinking Crisis, Decline, and Transformation in Postwar American History." *Journal of American History* 97, no. 3 (2010): 703–34.

Thuma, Emily. *All Our Trials: Prisons, Policing, and the Feminist Fight to End Violence*. Urbana: University of Illinois Press, 2019.

Tonry, Michael. "Federal Sentencing Reform since 1984: The Awful as the Enemy of the Good." *Crime and Justice: A Review of Research* 44 (2015): 99–164.

Tonry, Michael. *Sentencing Fragments: Penal Reform in America, 1975–2025*. New York: Oxford University Press, 2016.

Tonry, Michael. "Symbol, Substance and Severity in Western Penal Policies." *Punishment and Society* 34, no. 4 (2001): 517–36.

Turner, Frederick William, III. "Badmen, Black and White: The Continuity of American Folk Traditions." PhD diss., University of Pennsylvania, 1965.

Turner, Jennifer. *Prison Boundary: Between Society and Carceral Space.* New York: Palgrave Macmillan, 2016.

Turner, Ronald G. "Sex in Prison." *Tennessee Bar Journal* 36, no. 8 (2000): 12–30.

Twelve Southerners [Donald Davidson, John Gould Fletcher, Henry Blue Kline, Lyle H. Lanier, Andrew Lytle, Herman Clarence Nixon, Frank Lawrence Owsley, John Crowe Ransom, Allen Tate, John Donald Wade, Robert Penn Warren, and Stark Young]. *I'll Take My Stand: The South and the Agrarian Tradition.* New York: Harper, 1930.

Vick, Tony. "Look at Me!" In *Turning Teaching Inside Out: A Pedagogy of Transformation for Community-Based Education*, edited by Simone Weil Davis and Barbara Sherr Roswell, 65–66. New York: Palgrave Macmillan, 2013.

Wacquant, Loïc. "Deadly Symbiosis: When Ghetto and Prison Meet and Mesh." *Punishment and Society* 3, no. 1 (2001): 95–133.

Walters, Jonah. "Parole Justice Now: Confronting Death by Incarceration in New York." *Nonprofit Quarterly*, March 22, 2022. https://nonprofitquarterly.org/parole-justice-now-confronting-death-by-incarceration-in-new-york/.

Wang, Jackie. *Carceral Capitalism.* South Pasadena, CA: Semiotext(e), 2018.

Ward, Jesmyn. *Sing, Unburied, Sing.* New York: Scribner, 2017.

Weaver, Vesla M. "Frontlash: Race and the Development of Punitive Crime Policy." *Studies in American Political Development* 21, no. 2 (2007): 230–65.

Weiss, Carl, and David James Friar. *Terror in the Prisons: Homosexual Rape and Why Society Condones It.* Indianapolis: Bobbs-Merrill, 1974.

Wells, Ida B. *Southern Horrors: Lynch Law in All Its Phases.* Pamphlet, 1892. Project Gutenberg. https://www.gutenberg.org/files/14975/14975-h/14975-h.htm.

West, Heather C., William J. Sabol, and Sarah J. Greenman. *Bulletin: Prisoners in 2009.* Washington, DC: Bureau of Justice Statistics, 2011. https://bjs.ojp.gov/content/pub/pdf/p09.pdf.

White, Ahmed A. "The Concept of Less Eligibility and the Social Function of Prison Violence in Class Society." *Buffalo Law Review* 56, no. 3 (2008): 737–820.

Whitlock, Kay, and Nancy A. Heitzeg. "'Bipartisan' Criminal Justice Reform: A Misguided Merger." Truthout, February 24, 2015. https://truthout.org/articles/bipartisan-criminal-justice-reform-pushes-privatization-erases-root-causes/.

Wiggum, Kacy Elizabeth. "Defining Family in American Prisons." *Women's Rights Law Reporter* 30, no. 2 (2009): 384–404.

Wikberg, Ronald. *A Graphic and Illustrative History, 1879–1979, Life Sentences in Louisiana.* Mimeographed pamphlet, n.d. In possession of the author.

Wikberg, Ronald, and Burk Foster. "The Long-Termers: Louisiana's Longest Serving Inmates and Why They Have Stayed So Long." *Prison Journal* 70, no. 1 (1990): 9–14.

Wilkerson, Isabel. *The Warmth of Other Suns: The Epic Story of America's Great Migration.* New York: Random House, 2011.

Williams, Lawrence T. *1981 Yearly Statistical Report of the Furlough Program.* Boston: Massachusetts Department of Correction, May 1982. https://www.ojp.gov/ncjrs/virtual-library/abstracts/yearly-statistical-report-furlough-program-1980.

Wilson, Debra. *Genetics, Crime, and Justice.* Northampton, MA: Edward Elgar, 2015.

Witcover, Jules. *No Way to Pick a President: How Money and Hired Guns Have Debased American Elections.* New York: Routledge, 2001.

Wodahl, Eric J., and Brett Garland, "The Evolution of Community Corrections." *Prison Journal* 89, no. 1 (2009): 81–104.

Wolfe, Gavriel B. "I Beg Your Pardon: A Call for Renewal of Executive Clemency and Accountability in Massachusetts." *Boston Third World Law Journal* 27, no. 4 (2007): 417–54.

Wood, Amy Louise. "Cole Blease's Pardoning Pen: State Power and Penal Reform in South Carolina." In *Crime and Punishment in the Jim Crow South,* edited by Amy Louise Wood and Natalie J. Ring, 147–69. Urbana: University of Illinois Press, 2019.

Woodfox, Albert, with Leslie George. *Solitary: Unbroken by Four Decades in Solitary Confinement; My Story of Transformation and Hope.* New York: Grove, 2019.

Wozniak, Kevin H. "American Public Opinion about Prisons." *Criminal Justice Review* 39, no. 3 (2014): 305–24.

Wright, Paul. "'Victims' Rights' as a Stalkinghorse for State Repression." *Journal of Prisoners on Prisons* 9, no. 2 (1998): 17–22.

Wunder, A. (1995). "The Extinction of Inmate Privileges: Survey Summary." *Corrections Compendium* 20, no. 6 (1995): 5–24.

Yates, Mark T., and Richard D. Lakes. "After Pell Grants: The Neoliberal Assault on Prisoners." *Policy Futures in Education* 8, no. 1 (2010): 61–70.

Zemans, Eugene, and Ruth Shonle Cavan. "Marital Relationships of Prisoners." *Journal of Criminal Law, Criminology and Police Science* 49, no. 1 (1958): 50–57.

Zieger, Robert H., ed. *Life and Labor in the New South.* Gainesville: University Press of Florida, 2012.

Zukin, Sharon. *Landscapes of Power: From Detroit to Disney World.* Berkeley: University of California Press, 1993.

INDEX

Page locators in italics indicate figures.

clemency (*continued*)

system, 48; as contract in Louisiana, 42–45; as corrective to human error, 29, 40, 217, 235–36n22; as customary practice, 16, 21, 31–32, 36, 54, 66–68, 78; denial of as violation of law, 69–70; for drug sentences, 51, 78; as entitlement, 21, 30, 32, 67–68; expectation of, 32, 36; as "extraordinary remedy" for injustice, 209; forbidden in four states, 218; forms of, 32; good furlough record, 187; Jim Crow bolstered by, 28; lack of as abuse of constitutional power, 63; law enforcement criticisms of, 50; as "legalistic ritual" in Louisiana, 52–53; Massachusetts activism against, 208–9; in Mississippi, 12, 27–28, 36–42; no supervision after, 33; as only route to freedom, 215–16; and overcrowding, 16, 32, 55–64; as part of legitimate legal system, 69; as paternalistic, 11, 28, 30, 45; personalism, culture of, 30, 78, 84, 93, 217; petitions, 36–42; petitions by segregationists, 46; petitions by those ineligible for parole, 54; petitions required to be publicized, 216; politicization of, 32, 47, 51–52, 54–55; as poor judgment, 52; poverty or ill health as reason for petition, 41; presidential, 234n4, 235n16, 257n140; process of, 32–33; psychological impact on released prisoners, 41, 249n16; reasons for, 30; Rideau's petition for, 66; ritual supplications, 32–33; romanticization of, 35; spearheaded by white citizens, 37; tied to labor extraction, 28, 39–40; as tradition in Mississippi, 27, 32, 36–37; unreviewable by the courts, 29; waiting periods, 43, 253n103; white assumptions of inherent Black criminality as justification for, 37–39; white supremacy reinforced by, 11, 19, 28, 46, 81. *See also* 10/6 rule; early release; governor's mansion, prison labor used at; mercy; pardon; paternalism

Clements, Tom (corrections official), 300n58
Clenny, Daniel "Puddin' Foot" (prisoner), 157
Clifton, Francis "Corky" (prisoner), 72
Clinton, Bill, 137

Clyde Kennard Day, 83
Coalition to Abolish Death by Incarceration, 225
Cohn, David, 154, 166, 281n93
Cold War, 100
Coleman, James P. (governor, Mississippi), 34, 36, 39, 160
College Republican National Committee, 197
Collier, John A. (corrections official), 95, 133
Colorado Board of Pardons, 29
Colvin, Mark, 154
Commercial-Appeal (Memphis, Tennessee), 96
common-law marriages and nonmarried partners, 119, 141–42, 272n66
common sense, 12, 16, 20, 22, 57, 108, 156, 173, 197
community corrections, 14, 155, 176–80, 183, 187, 202, 283n5, 284n15. *See also* reintegration into society
commutation: legislation against, 8; of life without parole sentences, 193; by Mississippi governors, 10; to time served, 45. *See also* clemency, gubernatorial; pardon
compassionate release, 83
Concord Achievement Rehabilitation Volunteer Experience (CARVE), 193, 200–201
conditions in prison, 105–7, 119–22, 126, 230n37; brutality, 9–10, 20, 31, 42, 49, 95, 97, 99, 104, 120, 122, 145, 154–55, 158, 164, 179–80, 184–85, 245n67; exposure of, 20, 49, 145, 155, 179–80, 245n67; misinformation about, 131, 137–39; and sexual violence, 117–18
conjugal visits, 10, *94*; activism by prisoners, 13–14, 116–19, 125–28; California experiment, 14–15, 91, 111–16, 124–25, 142; children of targeted by political rhetoric, 110, 129, 132, 140; common-law marriages and nonmarried partners, 119, 122, 135–36, 141–42; counterfeit marriage licenses, 141, 272n66; criticisms of, 109–10, 119, 131–34; decency arguments against, 96, 99, 104, 105, 109, 116, 131, 141, 147; decline of, 129–49; to deter homosexuality, 15, 90, 98–103, 101, 113–14, 117–19, 121; as disciplinary tools, 90–91, 119–25, 132–33; as emotional

and conjugal visits, 126–27, 135, 142; harsh sentencing as, 204; security as, 18

"environmentalist" view of human behavior, 99–100

Epps, Chris (corrections commissioner), 147–48

Equal Justice Initiative, 2

escapes and attempts, 4–5, 31, 43–44, 71, 170–72, 278n58; and Christmas leaves, 156, 158, 159–61; conjugal visits as dissuasion, 101, 113; definitions, 289n106, 291n4; by enslaved people, 156; media portrayals of, 161–62, 189; rates, 172, 176, 195, 289n106; Subilosky, 189–92; suicidal motivation for, 72–73; Virginia incident, 128. *See also* furloughs; Horton, William "Willie"; Subilosky, Joseph (prisoner)

eugenicist thinking, 132, 140

European Court of Human Rights, 301n63

Evers, Medgar, 49, 81, 83

exceptionalism, Southern, 166–73, 258n23, 275n8

exclusion, 208, 232n63; internalized, 218–19; penal harm movement, 91; perpetual, 12, 19, 156; shift to from reintegrationist approach, 212

expressive punishment, 201

Extended Family Visit Program (Washington State Penitentiary), 124, 144–45

Fair, Michael V. (corrections commissioner), 197, 198–99, 204–5

Fair and Timely Parole Act (New York State), 302n76

fairness, 19, 30, 61, 78, 80, 158–59, 216

FamilyNet, 143

"family values," 141, 145, 148–49

Family Visiting Program (Tehachapi), 114–15

Farber, Rebecca (victim), 174

fearmongering, 55; by media, 14, 23, 78, 100, 106; racialized, 16, 19, 32, 51

Federal Bureau of Prisons, 167

Federal Correctional Institution (Seagoville, Texas), 167, 170, 177

federal courts: *Cooper v. Pate*, 126; hands-off doctrine, 125; *Lyons v. Gilligan*, 126, 128; orders to remedy overcrowding, 56, 58, 59; *United States Ex Rel. Wolfish v. Levi*, 127

Federalist 74, 29

Federal Sentencing Reform Act, 61–62, 79, 247n101

"felony murder" rule, 196, 201, 205, 296n103

Ferguson, Julia (victim), 65

Ferguson, O. P. (prisoner), 161

Ferraro, Freddie (prisoner), 123

fictive kinship, 28, 50

Fields, Barbara J., 22–23

Fields, Emmett (prisoner), 35

Finch, Charles (governor, Mississippi), 55

Fink, Donald (prisoner), 72–73

Fishman, Joseph F., 98

Florida Department of Corrections, 121

Fogleman, Alice (victim), 158

Fordice, Kirk (governor, Mississippi), 79–80

Forgotten Man Committees, 43, 60–61, 68, 223

"forgotten men," 9, 33, 43, 60–61, 68–69, 219, 223–24

Forgotten Men Project, 223–24

Forrest, Susan (reporter), 196–97

Foster, Burk, 43, 53, 67–68, 71, 75

Foster, Mike (governor, Louisiana), 80, 215

Foucault, Michel, 97, 112, 232n63, 232n66

Fournier, Joseph (victim), 196

Fourth Annual Southern Conference on Corrections, 104

Frader, Joel, 83

Francis, Jerry (prisoner), 222

Frank, Gary (corrections official), 89

Frazier, Charles (prisoner), 43

freedom, mobility associated with, 154–55, 275n6

Freedom Riders, 49, 104–5

Freire, Paolo, 3

Friar, David James, 103

Friends Committee on Legislation, 145

Fuqua, Henry L. (Angola general manager; governor), 42–43, 68, 69

furloughs: additional days on sentence to make up for, 160; as alternative to conjugal visits, 113, 131, 180; backlash against, 14, 196; changing eligibility standards, 20; clemency decisions based on, 187; coercive aspects of, 161, 187–88; and community corrections, 14, 155, 176–80; crimes committed during, 8, 174, 189, 196–97, 209; danger to prisoners in method of return, 161; decrease in Massachusetts, 198–99; due to bureaucratic error or sabotage, 189–90; emergency-only, 158, 180, 206; as extension of white supremacy, 154–55; to facilitate reintegration, 175–76, 182–83; failure to return in time, 157–58, 160–61, 189, 278n58, 289n106, 291n4; fairness concerns, 158–59; family ties strengthened by, 172–73, 176; fault lines in debate about, 188–91; in federal prison system, 176, 180; "Horton Law" ban on, 206; increase in 1970s, 180; for lifers, 191–93; Massachusetts, 155, 181–85; and morale of prisoners, 160, 171, 282n123; moral panics about, 155–56; "Norfolk Fourteen," 189; prisoner criticism of, 187–88; and prison expansion, 56, 175, 206; return rates, 172, 176, 189, 191, 192, 195, 198; and risk, 19, 156–58, 175–76, 190, 196, 199–200; and secondary victims, 201–2; struggle over banning, 204–7; and Subilosky escape, 189–92. *See also* Christmas leaves; escapes and attempts; rehabilitation; work and school release
Furman v. Georgia, 52–53, 65, 242n35

Gambles, Clyde T. (prisoner), 143
Garamendi, John (candidate), 141
Gates v. Collier, 105
genetic rhetoric, 47, 140, 271n61
George, Robert (prisoner), 161
George Jackson Brigade, 133
Germany, Jim (prisoner), 157
ghetto, continuum with carcerality, 18
Gholar, Frank (prisoner), 76
Gibson, Bonnie (wife of prisoner), 207
Gideons International, 163
Gilbert, Alfred (architect), 178, 179

Gilchrist, Alvin (prisoner-activist), 133, 134
Gill, Nick, 275n6
Gilmore, Craig, 16–17, 18–19
Gilmore, Ruth Wilson, 15, 16–17, 18–19, 22
Gingrich, Newt, 62, 197
Giordano, Larry (state representative), 199
Gladstone, William, 153
G. Nagel, William, 180
Goebbels, Joseph, 139
Goetz, Bernard (shooter), 209
Goffman, Erving, 107
Goldberg, Aviva, 83
Goldman, Fred, 140
Goldmark, Peter C., Jr. (administrative official), 181, 183–84, 285n42
good conduct, time off sentence for, 12, 43, 51, 54, 58, 70, 114
Good Morning, Angola Style (television program), 5
"good time," 43, 51, 54, 58
Gottschalk, Marie, 9, 293n49
governor's mansion, prison labor used at, 19, 27, 32, 34–37, 45, 47, 86, 237n44; during Barnett's term, 49–52; clemency for laborers as guarantee of safety, 55; as corridor to freedom, 75–79; criticism of, 80–83; flattery by servants, 50; union views of, 36. *See also* clemency, gubernatorial
Governor's Statewide Anti-Crime Council, 206
Graf, Tom (prison psychologist), 95, 107, 108
Graham, Michael (prisoner), 80–81
Graham v. Florida, 218
Graves, David Bibbs (governor, Alabama), 157–58
Gray, Will (prisoner), 44–45
Great Society, 47, 176
Gresham Peggi (warden), 74
Griffin, John Howard, 83
Groeschel, John Lee (prisoner), 174
guards, inmates as, 42, 105
Guenther, Lisa, 23, 218, 221–22

habeas corpus rights, 126
Haber, Roy (activist; attorney), 105

Habig, Bill (prisoner), 96, 259n38
habitual offender laws. *See* three-strikes laws
  (habitual offender laws)
Haley, Sarah, 35
Hall, Ben (prisoner), 213
Hall, Frank (corrections commissioner, Massachusetts), 191
Hamilton, Alexander, 29
Hamm, Ralph (prisoner), 184, 188
Hammond, James Henry (enslaver and politician), 156
Hammond-Martin, Forest C. (prisoner), 76–78
hands-off doctrine, 125
"hands," sugar cane workers referred to, 31
Haney, Craig (psychologist), 129, 140
Hannon, Barr T. (state representative), 188
hardening of carceral state, 13, 18, 21; interrupted by overcrowding, 47–48, 56; pain, as purpose of prison, 138–39, 178–79; as response to civil rights movement, 47
Harpole, Bill (corrections official), 39, 104, 160, 171
Harris,, M. Kay, 59, 246n78
harsh sentencing, 61–62, 191, 204, 217
Hartman, Anita (spouse of prisoner), 143
Harvey, Paul, 17
Harvey, Sylvia E., 13
Hatch, Orrin (Senator), 137–38
Healy, Jonathan L. (state representative), 189
"heinousness" classification, 66, 249n13
Hemsworth, Katie, 280n86
Henderson, C. Murray (warden), 6, 7, 60, 246n89
Henderson, Norris (prisoner, counsel substitute), 8, 74, 222
Henry (prisoner), 23, 226
Herbert, Bob (columnist), 82–83
Hester, Gilbert (prisoner), 182
Hicks, Ned, 8
Hicks, Ron (prisoner), 85–86
holiday suspensions. *See* Christmas leaves
Holloway, Louis X. (prisoner), 117, 132–33
Holt, Norman (social scientist), 116

homosexuality: changing assumptions about, 99–100; conjugal visits as means of preventing, 15, 90, 98–103, 113–14, 117–19, 121; gay rights movement, 133; partners from outside, conjugal visits with, 122; prison architecture blamed, 261–62n112, 281–82n106; rape, 101–2; same-sex partners, 122, 133–34, 140–41; situational, 100–101, 118; state construction of, 100; "true homosexuals," 101
hope, maintenance of, 222–23, 233n81
hopelessness, sense of, 71–73, 85–86
Hopper, Columbus B. (sociologist), 91–94, 99, 107, 118, 127, 146, 168, 178, 257n13, 265n51
Hopper, Lewis B., 46–47
Horton, Myles, 3
Horton, William "Willie," 18; in CARVE program, 193, 200; cast as typical furlough recipient, 199–200; comments by, 195, 209; as creation myth for exclusionist system, 212; furloughs granted to, 195; moral panic about, 155–56; yearlong escape, 196–97
"Horton effect," 156, 195
hospice, prison, 9, 10
House, Robert (prisoner), 160
Houston, John (state senator), 204
Hoyle, Lloyd (warden), 60
Huling, Tracy, 220
Human Relations Club (Angola), 213
human rights framework, 223
Hundley, Andrew (former prisoner), 233, 301n65
Hunt, Elayn (corrections official), 59, 60, 67
Huxtable, Ada Louise, 178

Illinois Central Railroad, 95–96
incarceration: as abnormal, 167–69; alternatives to, 56, 58–59, 177; and broader carcerality, 17–18; constructed as impermeable, 3; continuum with slavery, 166; crime perpetuated by, 175–76; death by (DBI), 214, 218, 219, 223, 225, 297–98n12, 302n76; during early republic, 153; invented to snare freedpeople in South, 30; as part of culture, 92; punitive turn, 15, 78, 231n56; slavery comparisons, 23, 125, 137, 166, 211;

social death, 11–12, 23, 90, 221, 267n113, 298n12. *See also* civil death; life without parole sentences (LWOP)

social scientists, 15, 16, 90, 98–100, 111, 115–16, 121, 148, 177

social welfare, 62, 135; antiwelfare rhetoric, 16, 129; children of conjugal visits targeted, 110, 129, 132, 140, 144; conjugal visits to deter, 114; state move away from, 16, 18, 74–75; "undeserving poor" rhetoric, 130; white conservative views of, 110

Soledad State Prison (California), 111, 115, 124–25, 272n66

solitary confinement, 20, 67, 105, 161, 171; defined as torture, 300n58; extension of into community, 193; as form of torture, 72; Freedom Riders assigned to, 49; removal of blocks from Angola, 168–69; rising use of, 221–22. *See also* isolation, social

Sommer, Robert (environmental psychologist), 120, 122, 178–79

Songster, Kempis "Ghani" (former prisoner), 214–15, 218, 223, 226–27

Sostre, Martin, 18

soul death, 148

Southern Agrarians, 281n93

Southern Coalition of Jails and Prisons, 57

Southern Regional Council, 183

Southern States Correctional Association, 57

Southern States Prison Association, 171

Speck, Richard (mass murderer), 293n44

Spencer, John (prisoner), 193

Stack, Brian, 99

Stanford Prison Experiment, 140

state: conditional freedoms as mechanisms of, 10; homosexuality, construction of, 100; penal harm as planned governmental act, 135; "protection racket" of, 18–19; as set of institutions, 15; shift away from social welfare, 16, 18; supermax prison as site of violence, 222

State Correctional Institution–Graterford (Pennsylvania), 214–15, 223, 302n77

"State Experiments with the Conjugal Visit, A" panel, 104

Stennis, John, 49

Stern, Max D. (NAACP attorney), 184

Stevenson, Bryan, 2

Still, Larry (journalist), 105

Stone, Julian (prisoner), 206

Story, Brett, 232n66

Storyland (children's television show), 5

Stovall, James (clergy), 60, 63, 246–47n92

Strange, Carolyn, 29

Subilosky, Joseph (prisoner), 189–92

subpoenas, 45

suicides, 71–72

supermax prisons, 20, 221–22, 300n52, 300n54

"superpredator" myth, 139, 140, 215

supervision, 41

Supreme Court, 220; *Brown v. Board of Education*, 247n101; *Furman v. Georgia*, 52–53, 65, 242n35; *Graham v. Florida*, 218; *Loving v. Virginia*, 46; *Montgomery v. Louisiana*, 301n65

surveillance, 18

survival, 21, 222; after release, 187; conjugal visits as, 96, 134, 148

Symbionese Liberation Army, 120

10/6 rule, 9, 31–32, 43–44, 223–24, 239n85; generational shift in memory of, 84; Louisiana's ending of, 48, 52–55; and Rideau's petition for clemency, 66

Terror in Prisons (Weiss and Friar), 103

Thirty Minutes behind the Walls (Texas prisons radio show), 280n75

Thomas, Piri (former prisoner), 117

Thompson, Heather Ann, 122, 148, 258n23, 275n8

Thornburgh, Dick (governor, Pennsylvania), 217

three-strikes laws (habitual offender laws), 48, 54, 58, 134–35, 140, 144, 271n61

Till, Emmett, 81

tough-on-crime policies, 12, 32, 53, 56, 68, 80, 135, 174, 244n63. *See also* penal harm

Townshend, Ozie Lee (prisoner), 161

Travasio, Anthony (corrections official), 123